The Writer's World: Paragraphs and Essays

Lynne Gaetz
Lionel Groulx College

Suneeti Phadke
St. Jerome College

PEARSON

Prentice Hall

Upper Saddle River, New Jersey 07458

Library of Congress Cataloging-in-Publication Data

Gaetz, Lynne
  The Writer's World: paragraphs and essays / Lynne Gaetz, Suneeti Phadke.
    p. cm.
  Includes index.
  ISBN 0-13-140946-8
    1. English language—Paragraphs—Problems, exercises, etc. 2. English
language—Rhetoric—Problems, exercises, etc. 3. English language—Grammar—Problems,
exercises, etc. 4. English language—Textbooks for foreign speakers. 5. Report writing—
Problems, exercises, etc. I. Phadke, Suneeti II. Title.

PE1439.G26 2006
808'.042—dc22   2005047633

Editorial Director: Leah Jewell
Executive Editor: Craig Campanella
Acquisitions Assistant: Joan Polk
VP/Director, Production and Manufacturing: Barbara Kittle
Production Editor: Joan E. Foley
Production Assistant: Marlene Gassler
Copyeditor: Kathryn Graehl
Text Permissions Specialist: Jane Scelta
Development Editor in Chief: Rochelle Diogenes
Development Editor: Veronica Tomaiuolo
Manufacturing Manager: Nick Sklitsis
Prepress and Manufacturing Buyer: Benjamin Smith
VP/Director, Marketing: Brandy Dawson
Marketing Manager: Kate Mitchell
Marketing Assistant: Anthony DeCosta
Media Production Manager: Lynn Pearlman

Media Project Manager: Alison Lorber
Director, Image Resource Center: Melinda Reo
Manager, Image Rights and Permissions: Zina Arabia
Manager, Visual Research: Beth Brenzel
Image Permissions Coordinator: Frances Toepfer
Image Researcher: Sheila Norman
Manager, Cover Visual Research & Permissions: Karen
    Sanatar
Director, Creative Design: Leslie Osher
Art Director, Interior Design: Laura Gardner
Cover Design: Anne DeMarinis
Cover Art: (front) Judith Miller Archive/Dorling Kindersley
    Media Library; (rear) Photodisc Green/Getty Images, Inc.;
    Brand X Pictures/Getty Images, Inc.; Royalty Free/
    CORBIS; Stockdisc Classice/Getty Images, Inc.

This book was set in 11/13 Janson by Pine Tree Composition, Inc., and was printed and bound by
Courier Companies, Inc. Covers and insert were printed by Phoenix Color Corp.

For permission to use copyrighted material, grateful acknowledgment is made to the copyright holders on page 613, which
is considered an extension of this copyright page.

PEARSON EDUCATION LTD.
PEARSON EDUCATION SINGAPORE, PTE. LTD
PEARSON EDUCATION, CANADA, LTD
PEARSON EDUCATION–JAPAN
PEARSON EDUCATION AUSTRALIA PTY, LIMITED

PEARSON EDUCATION NORTH ASIA LTD
PEARSON EDUCACIÓN DE MEXICO, S.A. DE C.V.
PEARSON EDUCATION MALAYSIA, PTE. LTD
PEARSON EDUCATION, UPPER SADDLE RIVER, NJ

10 9 8 7 6 5 4 3 2 1

ISBN 0-13-140946-8

Contents

Inside Front Cover
Paragraph and Essay Checklists

Preface   x

PART I — The Writing Process   2

 Exploring   3

The Paragraph and the Essay   3
What Is Exploring?   4
Topic   5
Audience   5
Purpose   7
Exploring Strategies   9
Journal and Portfolio Writing   13

 Developing   16

What Is Developing?   16
Narrow the Topic   18
The Topic Sentence   19
The Supporting Ideas   24
The Paragraph Plan   31
The First Draft   35

 Revising and Editing   38

What Is Revising and Editing?   38
Revise for Unity   39
Revise for Adequate Support   40
Revise for Coherence   43
Revise for Style   45
Edit for Errors   47
Write the Final Draft   49

PART II — Paragraph Patterns   52

 Illustration   53

Explore Topics   53
What Is Illustration?   54
The Illustration Paragraph   54
The Topic Sentence   57
The Supporting Ideas   57
The Paragraph Plan   58
The First Draft   59
Revise and Edit an Illustration Paragraph   60

 Narration   64

Explore Topics   64
What Is Narration?   65
The Narrative Paragraph   65
The Topic Sentence   68
The Supporting Ideas   70
The Paragraph Plan   71
The First Draft   72
Revise and Edit a Narrative Paragraph   72

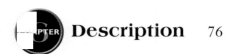

Description   76

Explore Topics   76
What Is Description?   77
The Descriptive Paragraph   77
The Topic Sentence   80
The Supporting Ideas   81
The Paragraph Plan   82
The First Draft   83
Revise and Edit a Descriptive Paragraph   84

Process   88

Explore Topics   88
What Is a Process?   89
The Process Paragraph   89
The Topic Sentence   92
The Supporting Ideas   93
The Paragraph Plan   94
The First Draft   95
Revise and Edit a Process Paragraph   96

Definition   100

Explore Topics   100
What Is Definition?   101
The Definition Paragraph   101
The Topic Sentence   103
The Supporting Ideas   106
The Paragraph Plan   107
The First Draft   108
Revise and Edit a Definition Paragraph   109

Classification   113

Explore Topics   113
What Is Classification?   114
The Classification Paragraph   114
The Topic Sentence   119
The Supporting Ideas   120
The Paragraph Plan   120
The First Draft   121
Revise and Edit a Classification
   Paragraph   121

Comparison and Contrast   126

Explore Topics   126
What Is Comparison and Contrast?   127
The Comparison and Contrast
   Paragraph   127
The Topic Sentence   132
The Supporting Ideas   134
The Paragraph Plan   134
The First Draft   135
Revise and Edit a Comparison and Contrast
   Paragraph   136

Cause and Effect   140

Explore Topics   140
What Is Cause and Effect?   141
The Cause and Effect Paragraph   141
The Topic Sentence   144
The Supporting Ideas   146
The Paragraph Plan   147
The First Draft   148
Revise and Edit a Cause and Effect
   Paragraph   149

Argument   153

Explore Topics   153
What Is Argument?   154
The Argument Paragraph   155
The Topic Sentence   157
The Supporting Ideas   158
The Paragraph Plan   162
The First Draft   163
Revise and Edit an Argument
   Paragraph   164

PART III — The Essay 168

 CHAPTER 13 **Writing the Essay** 169

Explore Topics 169
The Thesis Statement 171
The Supporting Ideas 174
The Essay Plan 178
The Introduction 181
The Conclusion 185
The First Draft 186
Revising and Editing the Essay 187
The Essay Title 189
The Final Draft 191

 CHAPTER 14 **Essay Patterns** 193

The Illustration Essay 194
The Narrative Essay 198
The Descriptive Essay 203

The Process Essay 208
The Definition Essay 213
The Classification Essay 217
The Comparison and Contrast Essay 222
The Cause and Effect Essay 227
The Argument Essay 231

 CHAPTER 15 **Enhancing Your Writing with Research** 237

What Is Research? 237
Research for Academic Writing 237
Evaluate Sources 238
Add a Paraphrase, Summary, or Quotation 240
Cite Sources 246

 PART IV — The Editing Handbook 252

GRAMMAR SECTION 1: Effective Sentences 254

 CHAPTER 16 **Simple Sentences** 254

Identify Subjects 254
Identify Prepositional Phrases 257
Identify Verbs 259
Helping Verbs 261

 CHAPTER 17 **Compound Sentences** 266

Compare Simple and Compound Sentences 266
Combine Sentences Using Coordinating Conjunctions 267
Combine Sentences Using Semicolons 270
Combine Sentences Using Transitional Expressions 272

Complex Sentences   278

What Is a Complex Sentence?   278
Use Subordinating Conjunctions   279
Use Relative Pronouns   285
Use Embedded Questions   287

 Sentence Variety   291

What Is Sentence Variety?   291
Combine Sentences   292
Include a Question, a Quotation,
    or an Exclamation   293
Vary the Opening Words   294
Combine Sentences with a
    Present Participle   296
Combine Sentences with a
    Past Participle   298
Combine Sentences with an Appositive   300

 GRAMMAR SECTION 2: Common Sentence Errors   306

 **Fragments
and Run-Ons**   306

Fragments   306
Run-Ons   312

 **Faulty Parallel
Structure**   320

What Is Parallel Structure?   320
Identify Faulty Parallel Structure   322

 GRAMMAR SECTION 3: Problems with Verbs   330

 **Present and
Past Tenses**   330

What Is Verb Tense?   330
The Simple Present Tense   331
The Simple Past Tense   335
Avoid Double Negatives   341

 Past Participles   345

Past Participles   345
The Present Perfect Tense: *have/has* +
    Past Participle   348
The Past Perfect Tense: *had* +
    Past Participle   350
The Passive Voice: *be* + Past Participle   351

 Other Verb Forms   358

Problems with Progressive Forms
    (-*ing*) Verbs   358
Nonstandard Forms: *gonna, gotta,
    wanna*   360
Problems with Conditional Forms   362
Nonstandard Forms: *would of, could of,
    should of*   363

GRAMMAR SECTION 4: Verb Agreement and Consistency   368

 CHAPTER 25 **Subject-Verb Agreement**   368

Basic Subject-Verb Agreement Rules   368
More Than One Subject   373
Special Subject Forms   374
Verb Before the Subject   377
Interrupting Words and Phrases   378

 CHAPTER 26 **Tense Consistency**   383

Consistent Verb Tense   383

GRAMMAR SECTION 5: More Parts of Speech   389

 CHAPTER 27 **Nouns, Determiners, and Prepositions**   389

Singular and Plural Nouns   389
Count Nouns and Noncount Nouns   394
Determiners   396
Prepositions   399

 CHAPTER 28 **Pronouns**   405

Pronoun Case   405
Relative Pronouns (*who, whom, which, that, whose*)   411
Reflexive Pronouns (*-self/-selves*)   412
Pronoun-Antecedent Agreement   414
Indefinite Pronouns   415
Vague Pronouns   419
Pronoun Shifts   420

GRAMMAR SECTION 6: Modifiers   425

 CHAPTER 29 **Adjectives and Adverbs**   425

Adjectives   425
Adverbs   428
Comparative and Superlative Forms   432

 CHAPTER 30 **Mistakes with Modifiers**   439

Misplaced Modifiers   439
Dangling Modifiers   443

GRAMMAR SECTION 7: Word Use and Spelling   450

 Exact Language   450

Use Specific and Detailed Vocabulary   450
Avoid Wordiness and Redundancy   453
Avoid Clichés   454
Standard English vs. Slang   455

 Spelling and Commonly Confused Words   459

Spelling Rules   459
120 Commonly Misspelled Words   466
Look-Alike and Sound-Alike Words   469

GRAMMAR SECTION 8: Punctuation and Mechanics   477

 Commas   477

What Is a Comma?   477
Commas in a Series   478
Commas After Introductory Words
    or Phrases   479
Commas Around Interrupting Words
    and Phrases   480
Commas in Compound
    Sentences   482
Commas in Complex
    Sentences   483
Commas in Business Letters   484

 The Apostrophe, Quotation Marks, and Titles   490

The Apostrophe   490
Quotation Marks   495
Punctuation of Titles   498

 Capitalization and Other Punctuation Marks   503

Capitalization   503
Other Punctuation Marks   506

GRAMMAR SECTION 9: Editing   512

 Editing Paragraphs and Essays   512

PART V — Reading Strategies and Selections   524

 CHAPTER 37 From Reading to Writing   525

Reading Strategies   525
Reading Selections   530
- Reading 1: **"Aunt Tee,"** by Maya Angelou   530
- Reading 2: **"Dealing with People,"** by Greg McGrew   533
- Reading 3: **"How to Get All-Day Energy,"** by Maria Noel Mandile   536
- Reading 4: **"When the Legal Thing Isn't the Right Thing,"** by Deborah Mead   538
- Reading 5: **"My Head Rolled in Syria,"** by Josh Freed   541
- Reading 6: **"Enough Is Enough,"** by Judy Sheindlin, with Josh Getlin   545
- Reading 7: **"Growing Up in Cyberspace,"** by Brent Staples   548
- Reading 8: **"Nothing But Net,"** by Scott Bekker   552
- Reading 9: **"Fads,"** by David A. Locher   554
- Reading 10: **"The Never-Ending Question: Who Am I?"** by Raúl A. Reyes   557
- Reading 11: **"Dancing with Fear,"** by Bebe Moore Campbell   560
- Reading 12: **"Interview with Jimmy Baca,"** by Elizabeth Farnsworth   562
- Reading 13: **"It's Class, Stupid!"** by Richard Rodriguez   565
- Reading 14: **"The Case for Affirmative Action: An Open Letter to Five Justices,"** by Dave Malcolm   568
- Reading 15: **"Body Over Mind,"** by Mitch Albom   572
- Reading 16: **"Dying to Be Bigger,"** by H.D.   575
- Reading 17: **"Bound Feet,"** by Jung Chang   580
- Reading 18: **"The Old-Time Pueblo World,"** by Leslie Marmon Silko   583
- Reading 19: **"The Diagnosis,"** by Richard Selzer   586
- Reading 20: **"Religious Faith Versus Spirituality,"** by Neil Bissoondath   589

— Appendices

- Appendix 1: Grammar Glossary   593
- Appendix 2: Irregular Verbs   595
- Appendix 3: A Quick Guide to Verb Tenses   597
- Appendix 4: Combining Ideas in Sentences   598
- Appendix 5: Punctuation and Mechanics   599
- Appendix 6: Writing Paragraphs and Essays in Exams   602
- Appendix 7: Spelling, Grammar, and Vocabulary Logs   608

Credits   613

Index   615

Inside Back Cover
Editing Checklist
Revising and Editing Symbols

About the First Edition of *The Writer's World: Paragraphs and Essays*

Preface

Whether your students enroll in the course with varying skill levels, whether they are native or nonnative speakers of English, or whether they learn better through the use of visuals, *The Writer's World* can help students produce writing that is technically correct and rich in content. It is our goal for this preface to give you a deeper understanding of how we arranged the text and the key components found in *The Writer's World: Paragraphs and Essays*.

A Research-Based Approach

From the onset of the development process, we have comprehensively researched the needs and desires of current developmental writing instructors. We met with more than 45 instructors from around the country, asking for their opinions and insights regarding (1) the challenges posed by the course, (2) the needs of today's ever-changing student population, and (3) the ideas and features we were proposing in order to provide them and you with a more effective teaching and learning tool. Prentice Hall also commissioned dozens of detailed manuscript reviews from instructors, asking them to analyze and evaluate each draft of the manuscript. These reviewers identified numerous ways in which we could refine and enhance our key features. Their invaluable feedback was incorporated throughout *The Writer's World*. The text you are seeing is truly the product of a successful partnership between the authors, publisher, and well over 100 developmental writing instructors.

How We Organized *The Writer's World*

The Writer's World is separated into five parts for ease of use and convenience.

Part I: The Writing Process teaches students (1) how to formulate ideas (Exploring), (2) how to expand, organize, and present those ideas in a piece of writing (Developing), and (3) how to polish writing so that they convey their message as clearly

as possible (Revising and Editing). The result is that writing a paragraph or an essay becomes far less daunting because students have specific steps to follow.

Part II: Paragraph Patterns gives students a solid overview of the patterns of development. Using the same easy-to-understand process (Exploring, Developing, and Revising and Editing), each chapter in this section explains how to convey ideas using one or more writing patterns. As they work through the practices and write their own paragraphs and essays, students begin to see how using a writing pattern can help them fulfill their purpose for writing.

Part III: The Essay covers the parts of the essay and explains how students can apply the nine patterns of development to essay writing. This section also discusses the role research plays in writing and explains some ways that students can incorporate research in their essays.

Part IV: The Editing Handbook is a thematic grammar handbook. In each chapter, the examples correspond to a section theme, such as The Workplace or Health Care. As students work through the chapters, they hone their grammar and editing skills while gaining knowledge about a variety of topics. In addition to helping retain interest in the grammar practices, the thematic material provides a spark that ignites new ideas that students can apply to their writing.

Part V: Reading Strategies and Selections offers tips, readings, and follow-up questions. Students learn how to write by observing and dissecting what they read. The readings contain themes that are found in Part IV: The Editing Handbook, thereby providing more fodder for generating writing ideas.

How *The Writer's World* Meets Students' Diverse Needs

We created *The Writer's World* to meet your students' diverse needs. To accomplish this, we asked both the instructors in our focus groups and the reviewers at every stage not only to critique our ideas but to offer their suggestions and recommendations for features that would enhance the learning process of their students. The result has been the integration of many elements that are not found in other textbooks, including our visual program, coverage of nonnative speaker material, and strategies for addressing the varying skill levels students bring to the course.

The Visual Program

A stimulating, full-color book, *The Writer's World* recognizes that today's world is a visual one, and it encourages students to become better communicators by responding to images. Chapter opening visuals in Parts I, II, and III help students to think about the chapter's key concept in a new way. For example, in the Chapter 9 opener, a photograph of a car lot sets the stage for classification. Cars are grouped according to their models and makes, which helps students understand the premise of classification.

Each **At Work** box in Part II features an image from the workplace, along with content on how that particular pattern of development is utilized on the job.

In Part IV, **photos on the part-opening page** give students additional visual cues highlighting the importance of correct grammar and mechanics. These nine photos are carried through each section, and even serve as a visual tabbing guide for Part IV. In addition, **each chapter in Part IV opens with another photo** to help illustrate the theme of the examples and exercises in that chapter and section. These visual aids can also serve as sources for writing prompts.

Finally, each copy of *The Writer's World* includes a free **Visualizing Writing CD-ROM** with 55 audio and animated "mini-lectures" to help students understand key concepts. These lectures, taken from the Prentice Hall library of animations, offer more support to visual and auditory learners, and can be accessed on any computer. The audio portion of the grammar lectures can also be heard on a home or car CD player.

Seamless Coverage for Nonnative Speakers

Instructors in our focus groups noted the growing number of nonnative/ESL speakers enrolling in the developmental writing courses. Although some of these students have special needs relating to the writing process, many of you still have a large portion of native speakers in your course whose more traditional needs must also be satisfied. In order to meet the challenge of this rapidly changing dynamic, we have carefully implemented and integrated content throughout to assist these students. *The Writer's World* does not have separate ESL boxes, ESL chapters, or tacked-on ESL appendices. Instead, information that traditionally poses a challenge to nonnative speakers is woven seamlessly throughout the book. In our extensive experience teaching writing to both native and nonnative speakers of English, we have learned that both groups learn best when they are not distracted by ESL labels. With the seamless approach, nonnative speakers do not feel self-conscious and segregated, and native speakers do not tune out to detailed explanations that may also benefit them. Many of these traditional problem areas receive more coverage than you would find in other textbooks, arming the instructor with the material to effectively meet the needs of nonnative speakers. Moreover, the Annotated Instructor's Edition provides over 75 ESL Teaching Tips designed specifically to help instructors better meet the needs of their nonnative speaking students.

Issue-Focused Thematic Grammar

In our survey of the marketplace, many of you indicated that one of the primary challenges in teaching your course is finding materials that are engaging to students in a contemporary context. This is especially true in grammar instruction. **Students come to the course with varying skill levels**, and many students are simply not interested in grammar. To address this challenge, we have introduced **issue-focused thematic grammar** into *The Writer's World*.

Each section in Part IV revolves around a common theme. These themes include Culture, Psychology, Espionage, College Life, Inventions and Discoveries, Health Care, The Legal World, and The Workplace. Each chapter, within the sections, includes issues related to the theme. The thematic approach enables students to broaden their awareness of important subjects, allowing them to infuse their writing with reflection and insight. Also, we believe (and our reviewers concurred) that it makes grammar more engaging. And the more engaging grammar is, the more likely students will retain key concepts—raising their skill level in these important building blocks of writing.

We also feel that it is important to teach grammar in the context of the writing process. Students should not think that grammar is an isolated exercise. Therefore, each **grammar chapter includes a warm up writing activity**. Students write and edit their paragraphs paying particular attention to the grammar point covered in the chapter. The end of each grammar section also contains paragraph and essay writing topics that are related to the theme of the section and that follow different writing patterns. There are also suggestions for readings found in the reading section that relate to the grammar themes.

What Tools Can Help Students Get the Most from *The Writer's World*?

Overwhelmingly, focus group participants and reviewers asked that both a larger number and a greater diversity of exercises and activities be incorporated into a new text. In response to this feedback, we have developed and tested the following items in *The Writer's World*. These tools form the pedagogical backbone to *The Writer's World* and we are confident they will help your students become better writers.

Hints

In each chapter, **Hint** boxes highlight important writing and grammar points. Hints are useful for all students, but many will be particularly helpful for nonnative speakers. For example, in Chapter 12 there is a hint about being direct and avoiding circular reasoning, and in Chapter 21 there is one about using the past conditional correctly.

The Writer's Desk

Parts I, II, and III include **The Writer's Desk** exercises that help students get used to practicing all stages and steps of the writing process. Students begin with prewriting and then progress to developing, organizing (using paragraph and essay plans), drafting, and finally, revising and editing to create a final draft.

Paragraph Patterns "At Work"

To help students appreciate the relevance of their writing tasks, Chapters 4-12 begin with an authentic writing sample. Titled **Illustration at Work, Narration at Work,** and so on, this feature offers a glimpse of the writing patterns people use in different types of workplace writing.

Reflect On It

Each **Reflect On It** is a chapter review exercise. Questions prompt students to recall and review what they have learned in the chapter.

The Writer's Room

The Writer's Room contains writing activities that correspond to general, college, and workplace topics. Some prompts are brief to allow students to freely form ideas while others are expanded to give students more direction.

There is literally something for every student writer in this end-of-chapter feature. Students who respond well to visual cues will appreciate the photo writing exercises in **The Writer's Room** in Part II: Paragraph Patterns. Students who learn best by hearing through collaboration will appreciate the discussion and group work prompts in **The Writers' Circle** section of selected **The Writer's Rooms**. In Part III: The Essay, students can respond to thought-provoking quotations. To help students see how grammar is not isolated from the writing process, there are also **The Writer's Room** activities at the end of sections 1 to 8 in Part IV: The Editing Handbook.

Acknowledgments

Many people have helped us produce *The Writer's World*. First and foremost, we would like to thank our students for inspiring us and providing us with invaluable feedback. Their words and insights pervade this book.

We also benefited greatly from the insightful comments and suggestions from over 200 instructors across the nation, all of whom are listed in the opening pages of the Annotated Instructor's Edition. Our colleagues' feedback was invaluable and helped shape *The Writer's World* series content, focus, and organization.

We are indebted to the team of dedicated professionals at Prentice Hall who have helped make this project a reality. They have boosted our spirits and have believed in us every step of the way. Special thanks to Veronica Tomaiuolo for her magnificent job in polishing this book and to Craig Campanella for trusting our instincts and enthusiastically propelling us forward. Kate Stewart worked tirelessly to ensure we were always meeting the needs of instructors. We owe a deep debt of gratitude to Yolanda de Rooy, whose encouraging words helped ignite this project. Joan Foley's attention to detail in the production process kept us motivated and on task and made *The Writer's World* a much better resource for both instructors and students. We would also like to thank Laura Gardner for her brilliant design, which helped keep the visual learner in all of us engaged.

Finally, we would like to dedicate this book to our husbands and children who supported us and who patiently put up with our long hours on the computer. Manu, Octavio, and Natalia continually encouraged us. We especially appreciate the help and sacrifices of Diego, Becky, Kiran and Meghana.

Lynne Gaetz and Suneeti Phadke

A Note to Students

Your knowledge, ideas, and opinions are important. The ability to clearly communicate those ideas is invaluable in your personal, academic, and professional life. When your writing is error-free, readers will focus on your message, and you will be able to persuade, inform, entertain, or inspire them. *The Writer's World* includes strategies that will help you improve your written communication. Quite simply, when you become a better writer, you become a better communicator. It is our greatest wish for *The Writer's World* to make you excited about writing, communicating, and learning.

Enjoy!
Lynne Gaetz & Suneeti Phadke
TheWritersWorld@hotmail.com

Lynne Gaetz and family in Mexico

Suneeti Phadke and family in Quebec, Canada

PART I

The Writing Process

An Overview

The writing process is a series of steps that most writers follow to get from thinking about a topic to preparing the final draft. Generally, you should follow the process step by step; however, sometimes you may find that your steps overlap. For example, you might do some editing before you revise, or you might think about your main idea while you are prewriting. The important thing is to make sure that you have done all of the steps before preparing your final draft.

Before you begin the next chapters, review the steps in the writing process.

Exploring

Step 1: Think about your topic.

Step 2: Think about your audience.

Step 3: Think about your purpose.

Step 4: Try exploring strategies.

Developing

Step 1: Narrow your topic.

Step 2: Express your main idea.

Step 3: Develop your supporting ideas.

Step 4: Make a plan or an outline.

Step 5: Write your first draft.

Revising and Editing

Step 1: Revise for unity.

Step 2: Revise for adequate support.

Step 3: Revise for coherence.

Step 4: Revise for style.

Step 5: Edit for technical errors.

Exploring

CHAPTER 1

"Writing is an exploration. You start from nothing and learn as you go."

—E. L. DOCTOROW
American author (b. 1931)

CONTENTS

- The Paragraph and the Essay
- What Is Exploring?
- Topic
- Audience
- Purpose
- Exploring Strategies
- Journal and Portfolio Writing

Before placing clay on a pottery wheel, a potter takes time to consider what to make. Similarly, before developing a draft, a writer needs to explore the topic.

The Paragraph and the Essay

Most of the writing that we do—e-mail messages, work reports, college papers—is made up of paragraphs and essays. A **paragraph** is a series of sentences that are about one central idea. Paragraphs can stand alone or they can be part of a longer work such as an essay, a letter, or a report. An **essay** is a series of paragraphs that are about one central idea. Both the paragraph and the essay are divided into three parts.

Characteristics of a Paragraph

- The **topic sentence** introduces the subject of the paragraph and shows the writer's attitude towards the subject.

- The **body** of the paragraph contains details that support the topic sentence.

- The paragraph ends with a **concluding sentence.**

Characteristics of an Essay

- The **introduction** engages the reader's interest and contains the **thesis statement.**

- The **body** paragraphs each support the main idea of the essay.

- The **conclusion** reemphasizes the thesis and restates the main points of the essay. It brings the essay to a satisfactory close.

Look at the relationship between paragraphs and essays. Both examples are about real-life heroes. However, in the essay, each supporting idea is expanded into paragraph form.

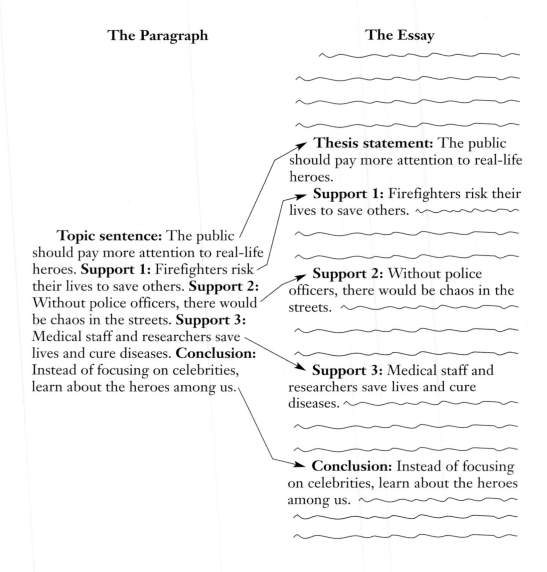

The Paragraph

Topic sentence: The public should pay more attention to real-life heroes. **Support 1:** Firefighters risk their lives to save others. **Support 2:** Without police officers, there would be chaos in the streets. **Support 3:** Medical staff and researchers save lives and cure diseases. **Conclusion:** Instead of focusing on celebrities, learn about the heroes among us.

The Essay

Thesis statement: The public should pay more attention to real-life heroes.

Support 1: Firefighters risk their lives to save others.

Support 2: Without police officers, there would be chaos in the streets.

Support 3: Medical staff and researchers save lives and cure diseases.

Conclusion: Instead of focusing on celebrities, learn about the heroes among us.

All writing begins with ideas. In the next section of this chapter, you will practice ways to explore ideas.

ESSAY LINK

When you plan an essay, you should follow the four exploring steps.

What Is Exploring?

Have you ever been given a writing subject and then stared at the blank page, thinking, "I don't know what to write?" Well, it is not necessary to write a good paragraph or essay immediately. There are certain things that you can do to help you focus on your topic.

Understand Your Assignment

As soon as you are given an assignment, make sure that you understand what your task is. Answer the following questions about the assignment:

- How many words or pages should I write?
- What is the due date for the assignment?
- Are there any special qualities my writing should include?

After you have considered your assignment, follow the four steps in the exploring stage of the writing process.

EXPLORING

STEP 1	➤	**Think about your topic.** Determine what you will write about.
STEP 2	➤	**Think about your audience.** Consider your intended readers and what interests them.
STEP 3	➤	**Think about your purpose.** Ask yourself why you want to write.
STEP 4	➤	**Try exploring strategies.** Experiment with different ways to generate ideas.

Topic

Your **topic** is what you are writing about. When an instructor gives you a topic for your writing, you can give it a personal focus. For example, if the instructor asks you to write about "travel," you can take many approaches to the topic. You might write about the dangers in travel, describe a trip that you have taken, or explain the lessons that travel has taught you. When you are given a topic, find an angle that interests you and make it your own.

When you think about the topic, ask yourself the following questions.

- What about the topic interests me?
- Do I have special knowledge about the topic?
- Does anything about the topic arouse my emotions?

Audience

Your **audience** is your intended reader. In your personal, academic, and professional life, you will often write for a specific audience; therefore, you can keep your readers interested by adapting your tone and vocabulary to suit them. **Tone** is your general attitude or feeling toward a topic. For example, you might write in a tone that is humorous, sarcastic, serious, friendly, or casual.

When you consider your audience, ask yourself the following questions.

- Who will read my assignment—an instructor, other students, or people outside the college?
- Do my readers have a lot of knowledge about my topic?
- Will my readers expect me to write in proper, grammatically correct English?

In academic writing, your audience is generally your instructor or other students, unless your instructor specifically asks you to write for another audience such as the general public, your employer, or a family member.

Instructor as the Audience

When you write for your instructor, use standard English. In other words, try to use correct grammar, sentence structure, and vocabulary. Also, do not leave out information because you assume that your instructor is an expert in the field. Generally, when your instructor reads your work, he or she will expect you to reveal what you have learned or what you have understood about the topic.

PRACTICE I

E-mail messages A and B are about career goals. As you read the messages, consider the differences in both the tone and the vocabulary the writer uses. Then answer the questions that follow. Circle the letter of the correct answer.

1. Who is the audience for E-mail A?
   a. A friend
   b. A family member
   c. A potential employer
   d. An instructor

2. Who is the audience for E-mail B?
   a. A friend
   b. A family member
   c. A potential employer
   d. An instructor

E-mail A

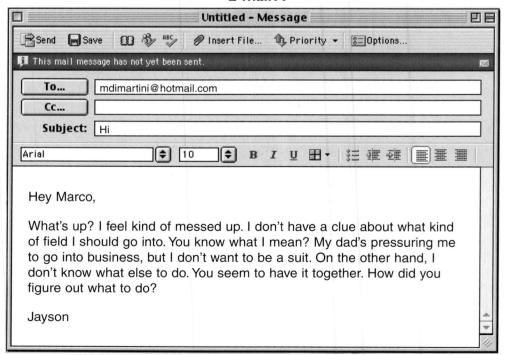

Hey Marco,

What's up? I feel kind of messed up. I don't have a clue about what kind of field I should go into. You know what I mean? My dad's pressuring me to go into business, but I don't want to be a suit. On the other hand, I don't know what else to do. You seem to have it together. How did you figure out what to do?

Jayson

E-mail B

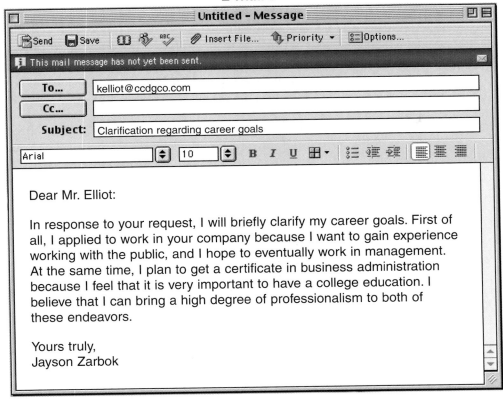

3. In a word or two, describe the tone in each e-mail.

E-mail A: _____   E-mail B: _____

4. **Language clues** are words or phrases that help you determine the audience. What language clues helped you determine the audience of E-mails A and B? The first clue in each e-mail message has been identified for you.

E-mail A: _____   E-mail B: _____

Hey Marco, _____   Dear Mr. Elliot: _____

_____   _____

_____   _____

_____   _____

Purpose

Your **purpose** is your reason for writing. Keeping your purpose in mind will help you focus your writing.

When you consider your purpose, ask yourself the following questions.

- Is my goal to **entertain?** Do I want to tell a story?
- Is my goal to **persuade?** Do I want to convince the reader that my point of view is the correct one?
- Is my goal to **inform?** Do I want to explain something or give information about a topic?

Sometimes you may have more than one purpose. For example, a narrative paragraph or essay about a personal experience can also inform the reader about something interesting. It is possible to write for a combination of reasons.

 General and Specific Purpose

Your **general purpose** is to entertain, to inform, or to persuade. Your **specific purpose** is your more precise reason for writing. For example, imagine that you have to write a piece about music. Your general purpose may be to inform while your specific purpose may be to explain how to become a better musician.

PRACTICE 2

Selections 1 to 3 are about music; however, each has a different purpose, has been written for a different audience, and has been taken from a different source. To complete this practice, read each selection carefully. Then underline any language clues (words or phrases) that help you identify its source, audience, and purpose. Finally, answer the questions that follow each selection.

EXAMPLE:

Slang ➤

Slang, informal tone ➤

    I'm totally <u>psyched</u> about learning the drums. It's taken me a while to get used to keeping up a steady beat, but I think I'm getting it. My drum teacher is <u>cool</u>, and he's <u>pretty patient</u> with me. I try to practice, but it bugs the neighbors when I hit the cymbals.

What is the most likely source of this paragraph?

    a. web site article   b. novel   c. textbook   ⓓ personal letter

What is its purpose? <u> To inform </u>

Who is the audience? <u> Friend or family member </u>

1.   Lomax also found a relationship between polyphony, where two or more melodies are sung simultaneously, and a high degree of female participation in food-getting. In societies in which women's work is responsible for at least half of the food, songs are likely to contain more than one simultaneous melody, with the higher tunes usually sung by women.

    What is the most likely source of this paragraph?

    a. web site article   b. novel   c. textbook   d. personal letter

What is its purpose? _____

Who is the audience? _____

_____

2.　　When dealing with club managers, it is *imperative* that you act professionally. Get all the details of a gig in advance. Doing so will eliminate any confusion or miscommunication that could result in a botched deal. It will also instantly set you apart from the legions of flaky musicians that managers must endure on a daily basis. That's a good thing.

What is the most likely source of this paragraph?

a. web site article　　b. novel　　c. textbook　　d. personal letter

What is its purpose? _____

Who is the audience? _____

_____

3.　　But there was no reason why everyone should not dance. Madame Ratignolle could not, so it was she who gaily consented to play for the others. She played very well, keeping excellent waltz time and infusing an expression into the strains which was indeed inspiring. She was keeping up her music on account of the children, she said, because she and her husband both considered it a means of brightening the home and making it attractive.

What is the most likely source of this paragraph?

a. web site article　　b. novel　　c. textbook　　d. personal letter

What is its purpose? _____

Who is the audience? _____

_____

Exploring Strategies

After you determine your topic, audience, and purpose, try some **exploring strategies**—also known as **prewriting strategies**—to help get your ideas flowing. The four most common strategies are *freewriting, brainstorming, questioning,* and *clustering*. It is not necessary to do all of the strategies explained in this chapter. Find the strategy that works best for you.

Freewriting

Freewriting is writing for a limited period of time without stopping. The point is to record the first thoughts that come to mind. If you have no ideas, you can indicate that fact in a sentence such as "I don't know what to write." As you write, do not be concerned with your grammar or spelling. If you use a computer, let your ideas flow and do not worry about typing mistakes.

When to Use Exploring Strategies

You can use exploring strategies at any stage of the writing process.

• To find a topic

• To narrow a broad topic

• To generate ideas about your topic

• To generate supporting details

TECHNOLOGY LINK

On a computer, try typing without looking at the screen or with the screen turned off. Don't worry about mistakes.

SANDRA'S FREEWRITING

College student Sandra Ahumada did freewriting about work. During her freewriting, she wrote everything that came to mind.

> Work. I've only worked in a restaurant. A lot of reasons to work in a restaurant. Schedules are good for college students. Can work nights or weekends. Serving people so different from studying. You can relax your brain, go on automatic pilot. But you have to remember people's orders so it can be hard. And some customer are rude, rude, RUDE. What else . . . It is hard to juggle a job and college work. But it forces me to organize my time. What types of jobs pay a good salary? Day-care work? In some jobs, you get tips in addition to the salary. The tips can be very good. Like for hairdressers. Taxi drivers.

PRACTICE 3

In Sandra's freewriting, underline each idea that could be expanded into a complete paragraph.

The Writer's Desk **Freewriting**

Choose one of the following topics and do some freewriting. Remember to write without stopping.

The family   Travel   Telling lies

Brainstorming

Brainstorming is like freewriting except that you create a list of ideas, and you can take the time to stop and think when you create your list. As you think about the topic, write down words or phrases that come to mind. Do not be concerned about grammar or spelling; the point is to generate ideas.

WADE'S BRAINSTORMING

College student Wade Vong brainstormed about city life. He made a list of ideas.

- living in a city vs. living in a town
- my favorite cities
- the bad side of city life
- reasons people move to large cities
- Los Angeles full of pollution
- reasons to live in a large city
- my impressions of Las Vegas
- reasons to get out of cities
- the physical differences between rich and poor neighborhoods
- developing the inner city to keep it vibrant

PRACTICE 4

Underline any of Wade's ideas that could be developed into complete paragraphs.

The Writer's Desk **Brainstorming**

Choose one of the following topics and brainstorm. Write down a list of ideas.

Ceremonies   An issue in the news   Good or bad manners

Questioning

Another way to generate ideas about a topic is to ask yourself a series of questions and write responses to them. The questions can help you define and narrow your topic. One common way to do this is to ask yourself *who, what, when, where, why,* and *how* questions.

CLAYTON'S QUESTIONING

College student Clayton Rukavina used a question-and-answer format to generate ideas about binge drinking.

What is binge drinking?	having too much alcohol in a short time
Who binge-drinks?	students who are away from home for the first time, or insecure students
Why do students drink too much?	peer pressure, want to be more relaxed, don't think about consequences
When do students drink too much?	spring break, weekends, to celebrate legal age
How dangerous is binge drinking?	may get alcohol poisoning, may choke, and may drink and drive
Where does it happen?	dorm rooms, house parties, fraternities
Why is it an important topic?	can die from binge drinking or drunk driver can kill somebody else

PRACTICE 5

Underline any of Clayton's ideas that could be developed into complete paragraphs.

The Writer's Desk **Questioning**

Choose one of the following topics and write questions and answers. Try to ask *who, what, when, where, why,* and *how* questions.

Beliefs   Patriotism   Health

Clustering

Clustering is like drawing a word map; ideas are arranged in a visual image. To begin, write your topic in the middle of the page and draw a box or a circle around it. That idea will lead to another, so write the second idea, and draw a line connecting it to your topic. Keep writing, circling, and connecting ideas until you have groups or "clusters" of them on your page.

ADELA'S CLUSTERING

College student Adela Santana used clustering to explore ideas about crime. She identified some main topics. Then she created clusters around each topic.

PRACTICE 6

Look at Adela's clustering. Think of two other topics that she could add to her cluster.

The Writer's Desk **Clustering**

Choose one of the following topics and make a cluster on a separate sheet of paper. Begin by writing the key word in the middle of the space. Then connect related ideas.

Jobs   College   Relationships

Journal and Portfolio Writing

Keeping a Journal

You may write for work or school, but you can also practice writing for pleasure. One way to practice your writing is to keep a journal. A **journal** is a book, a computer file, or a blog (Web log) where you record your thoughts, opinions, ideas, and impressions. Journal writing gives you a chance to practice your writing without worrying about your readers and what they might think about it. It also gives you a source of material when you want to write about a topic of your choice. According to the author Anaïs Nin, "Keeping a diary is a way of making everyday life seem as exciting as fiction."

In your journal, you can write about any topic that appeals to you. Here are some topics for journal writing.

- Anything related to your personal life, such as your feelings about your career goals, personal problems and solutions, opinions about your college courses, reflections about past and future decisions, or feelings about your job
- Your reactions to controversies in the world, in your country, in your state, in your city, or in your college
- Facts that interest you
- Your reflections on the opinions and philosophies of others, including your friends or people that you read about in your courses

Keeping a Portfolio

A **writing portfolio** is a binder or an electronic file folder where you keep samples of all of your writing. The purpose of keeping a portfolio is to have a record of your writing progress. In your portfolio, keep all drafts of your writing assignments. When you work on new assignments, review your previous work in your portfolio. Identify your main problems, and try not to repeat the same errors.

REFLECT ON IT

Think about what you learned in this chapter. If you do not know an answer, review that topic.

1. Before you write, you should think about your topic, audience, and purpose. Explain what each one is.

   a. Topic: _____

   b. Audience: _____

   c. Purpose: _____

2. Briefly define each of the following exploring styles.

   a. Freewriting: _____

   b. Brainstorming: _____

   c. Questioning: _____

   d. Clustering: _____

 The Writer's Room **Topics to Explore**

Writing Activity 1

Choose one of the following topics, or choose your own topic. Then generate ideas about the topic. You may want to try the suggested exploring strategy.

General Topics

1. Try freewriting about a strong childhood memory. Try freewriting about your childhood.
2. Try brainstorming and list any thoughts that come to mind about anger.
3. Try clustering. First, write "Rules" in the middle of the page. Then write clusters of ideas that connect to the general topic.
4. Ask and answer some questions about cosmetic surgery.

College and Work-Related Topics

5. Try freewriting about a comfortable place. Include any emotions or other details that come to mind.
6. Try brainstorming about study or work habits. List any ideas that come to mind.
7. To get ideas, ask and answer questions about gossip.
8. Try clustering. First, write "Cell phones" in the middle of the page. Then write clusters of ideas that relate to the general topic.

Writing Activity 2

Look carefully at the poster. Use questioning as your exploring strategy. Ask and answer *who, what, when, where, why,* and *how* questions.

 EXPLORING CHECKLIST

As you explore your topics, ask yourself the following questions.

- What is my topic? (Consider what you will write about.)

- Who is my audience? (Think about your intended reader.)

- What is my purpose? (Determine your reason for writing.)

- How can I explore? (You might try freewriting, brainstorming, questioning, or clustering.)

CHAPTER 2

Developing

"You can only learn to be a better writer by actually writing."

—DORIS LESSING
British author (b. 1919)

CONTENTS

• What Is Developing?
• Narrow the Topic
• The Topic Sentence
• The Supporting Ideas
• The Paragraph Plan
• The First Draft

After finding an idea, a potter begins to knead and shape the clay. Like a potter, a writer shapes ideas to create a solid paragraph or essay.

ESSAY LINK

When you develop an essay, you follow similar steps. For details about essay writing, see Chapter 13.

What Is Developing?

In Chapter 1, you learned how to narrow topics and how to use exploring strategies to formulate ideas. In this chapter, you will focus on the second stage of the writing process: **developing.** There are five key steps in the developing stage.

DEVELOPING

STEP 1	**Narrow your topic.** Focus on some aspect of the topic that interests you.
STEP 2	**Express your main idea.** Write a topic sentence (for a paragraph) or a thesis statement (for an essay) that expresses the main idea of the piece of writing.
STEP 3	**Develop your supporting ideas.** Find facts, examples, or anecdotes that best support your main idea.
STEP 4	**Make a plan.** Organize your main and supporting ideas, and place your ideas in a plan or an outline.
STEP 5	**Write your first draft.** Communicate your ideas in a single written piece.

Reviewing Paragraph Structure

Before you practice developing your paragraphs, review the paragraph structure. A **paragraph** is a series of related sentences that develop one central idea. Because a paragraph can stand alone or be part of a longer piece of writing, it is the essential writing model. You can apply your paragraph writing skills to longer essays, letters, and reports.

A stand-alone paragraph generally has the following characteristics.

- A **topic sentence** states the topic and introduces the idea the writer will develop.
- **Body sentences** support the topic sentence.
- A **concluding sentence** ends the paragraph.

CATHERINE'S PARAGRAPH

College student Catherine Niatum wrote the following paragraph. Read her paragraph and notice how it is structured.

> **The commercialization of traditional holidays helps our economy.** People spend a lot of money celebrating religious and popular holidays. For example, the clothing industry benefits because people spend money on new outfits. Also, toy stores and other gift shops profit when the public celebrates by giving presents to loved ones. Department stores see their sales increase when customers buy special lights, candles, and other decorations for their homes. Grocery stores and restaurants profit during holiday seasons because people prepare feasts, and companies have staff parties in restaurants and hotels. Finally, the travel industry has a financial windfall during celebrations such as Thanksgiving because people cross the nation to visit their loved ones. The next time anyone complains about the commercialization of holidays, remind the person that holiday spending is very beneficial for our economy.

◄ The topic sentence expresses the idea that Catherine develops in the paragraph.

◄ Catherine supports the paragraph with examples.

◄ The concluding sentence brings the paragraph to a satisfying close.

Hint Paragraph Form

When you write a paragraph, make sure that it has the following form.

- Always indent the first word of a paragraph. Move it about one inch, or five spaces, from the left-hand margin.

- Try to leave a margin of an inch to an inch and a half on each side of your paragraph.

> The legal drinking age is an ineffective deterrent to underage drinking.

Narrow the Topic

A paragraph has one main idea. If your topic is too broad, you might find it difficult to write only one paragraph about it. When you **narrow** your topic, you make it more specific.

To narrow your topic, you can use exploring strategies such as freewriting, brainstorming, and questioning. These strategies are explained in more detail in Chapter 1, "Exploring."

Review the following examples of general and narrowed topics.

ESSAY LINK

An essay contains several paragraphs and can have a broader topic than a paragraph.

General Topic	Narrowed Topic
The job interview	How to dress for a job interview
College	My misconceptions about college life
Rituals	The high school prom

Hint Narrowing the Topic

One way to narrow your topic is to break it down into smaller categories.

Sports

Steroids in sports   Team sports   Dangerous sports

SANDRA'S EXAMPLE OF NARROWING A TOPIC

College student Sandra Ahumada practiced narrowing a topic by thinking of ideas about work.

- types of work: paid work, housework, homework
- jobs I have done in the service industry: server, cashier
- reasons to work in a restaurant
- how to find a job
- bad jobs that I have had
- finding the right career
- dangerous jobs such as firefighter, police officer
- are online job sites useful?

The Writer's Desk Narrow the Topic

Topics 1 to 5 are very broad. Practice narrowing topics by writing three ideas for each one.

EXAMPLE: City life: *living in a city vs. living in a small town*

impressions of Las Vegas

keeping the inner cities vibrant

1. The family: _____
   _____
   _____

2. Telling lies: _____
   _____

3. Travel: _____
   _____
   _____

4. An issue _____
   in the news: _____
   _____

5. Jobs: _____
   _____
   _____

After you have narrowed your topic, you can develop your topic sentence.

The Topic Sentence

After you have narrowed the topic of your paragraph, your next step will be to write a topic sentence. The **topic sentence** has specific characteristics.

- It introduces the topic of the paragraph.
- It states the paragraph's controlling idea.
- It is the most general sentence in the paragraph.
- It is followed by other sentences that provide supporting facts and examples.

The **controlling idea** makes a point about the topic and expresses the writer's opinion, attitude, or feeling. You can express different controlling ideas about the same topic. For example, the following topic sentences are about youth offenders, but each sentence makes a different point about the topic.

narrowed topic   controlling idea
Youth offenders should not receive special treatment from the

correctional system.

controlling idea
Rehabilitation and education are the best ways for the state to handle

narrowed topic
youth offenders.

ESSAY LINK

Just as a topic sentence expresses the main point of a paragraph, the thesis statement expresses the main point of an essay. Both have a controlling idea.

PRACTICE I

Read each topic sentence. Underline the topic once and the controlling idea twice.

EXAMPLE:

Learning to play the guitar requires practice, patience, and perseverance.

1. Music education is essential in public schools.

2. My furnished room has everything a student could need.

3. You can learn to make decisions and think critically with a liberal arts education.

4. Several interesting things happened during the Stanford Prison Experiment.

5. The new youth center has a very impressive design.

6. There should not be a lower legal drinking age in our state.

7. We encountered many problems on our journey to Honduras.

8. Rory was known for his rumpled, unfashionable clothing.

9. IQ tests are not always accurate and valid.

10. The Beatles went through many musical phases.

Identifying the Topic Sentence

Before you write topic sentences, practice finding them in paragraphs by other writers. To find the topic sentence of a paragraph, follow these steps.

- Read the paragraph carefully.
- Look for a sentence that sums up the paragraph's subject. Professional writers may place the topic sentence anywhere in the paragraph.
- After you have chosen a sentence, see if the other sentences in the paragraph provide evidence that supports that sentence.

If you find one sentence that sums up what the paragraph is about and is supported by other sentences in the paragraph, then you have identified the topic sentence.

PRACTICE 2

Underline or highlight the topic sentences in paragraphs A, B, and C.

EXAMPLE:

Researchers say they have found the remains of a rodent the size of a buffalo in South America. Fossils suggest a 1,545-pound rodent that was a plant eater lived 6 million to 8 million years ago in what was then a lush, swampy forest. Marcelo R. Sanchez-Villagra of the University of Tubingen in Germany described the creature as "a weird guinea pig . . . with a long tail for balancing on its hind legs." The fossils were found in a desert area some 250 miles west of Caracas, Venezuela.

—Lee Krystek, "Strange Science," *Unnatural Museum.com*

A.   The idea of controlling music in society has been around for a long time. About 2,400 years ago, the Greek philosopher Plato said that the types of music people listened to should be controlled by the state. During the Middle Ages and the Renaissance, it was the Church that specified how music should be composed and performed. And in later centuries secular rulers held a virtual monopoly over the music that was allowed in their realm. Often, composers had to submit a work to a committee before it was allowed to be published or performed.

—Jeremy Yudkin, *Understanding Music*

B.   Cosmetic surgery is not like fooling around with a bottle of hair dye or getting a set of fake fingernails. The procedures are invasive, the recovery sometimes painful, and mistakes, while not common, can be difficult or impossible to correct. Breast implants may rupture, noses sink inward, and smiles turn unnaturally tight. People who merely wanted fat vacuumed from their thighs have died, while balding men have found themselves sporting new hair in symmetrical rows like tree farms. Stephen Katz, a sociologist at Trent University in Ontario, Canada, says, "To have plastic surgery, you have to think of your body as an object. It's a kind of social madness."

—Patricia Chisholm, "The Body Builders," *MacLean's*

C.   Imagine a society without laws. People would not know what to expect from one another (an area controlled by the law of contracts), nor would they be able to plan for the future with any degree of certainty (administrative law); they wouldn't feel safe knowing that the more powerful or better armed could take what they wanted from the less powerful (criminal law); and they might not be able to exercise basic rights which would otherwise be available to them as citizens of a free nation (constitutional law).

—Frank Schmalleger, *Criminal Justice Today*

Writing an Effective Topic Sentence

When you develop your topic sentence, avoid some common errors by asking yourself these three questions.

TECHNOLOGY LINK

If you write your paragraph on a computer, make your topic sentence bold (ctrl B). Then you and your instructor can easily identify it.

1. **Is my topic sentence a complete sentence that has a controlling idea?** You might state the topic in one word or phrase, but your topic sentence should always reveal a complete thought and have a controlling idea. It should not announce the topic.

Incomplete:	Working in a restaurant.
	(This is a topic but *not* a topic sentence. It does not contain both a subject and a verb, and it does not express a complete thought.)
Announcement:	I will write about part-time jobs.
	(This announces the topic but says nothing relevant about it. Do not use expressions such as *My topic is . . .* or *I will write about. . . .*)
Topic sentence:	Part-time jobs help college students build self-esteem.

2. **Does my topic sentence make a valid and supportable point?**
   Your topic sentence should express a valid point that you can support with your evidence. It should not be a vaguely worded statement, and it should not be a highly questionable generalization.

Vague:	Beauty is becoming more important in our culture.
	(Beauty is more important than what?)
Invalid point:	Beauty is more important than it was in the past.
	(Is this really true? Cultures throughout history have been concerned with notions of beauty.)
Topic sentence:	Fashion magazines do not provide people with enough varied examples of beauty.

ESSAY LINK

If you find that your topic is too broad for a paragraph, you might want to save it so you can try using it for an essay.

3. **Can I support my topic sentence in a single paragraph?**
   Your topic sentence should express an idea that you can support in a paragraph. It should not be too broad or too narrow.

Too broad:	Love is important.
	(It would be difficult to write a paragraph about this topic. There are too many things to say.)
Too narrow:	My girlfriend was born on March 2nd.
	(What more is there to say?)
Topic sentence:	During my first relationship, I learned a lot about being honest.

  Write an Interesting Topic Sentence

Your topic sentence should not express an obvious or well-known fact. Write something that will interest your readers and make them want to continue reading.

Obvious: Money is important in our world.
              (Everybody knows this.)

Better: There are several effective ways to save money.

PRACTICE 3

Choose the word from the list that best describes the problem with each topic sentence. Correct the problem by revising each sentence.

Announces	Incomplete	Narrow
Broad	Invalid	Vague

EXAMPLE:

This paragraph is about television advertisements.

Problem: _Announces_

Revised statement: _Television advertisements should be banned during_
children's programming.

1. How to pack a suitcase.

   Problem: _____

   Revised statement: _____

2. I will write about negative political campaigns.

   Problem: _____

   Revised statement: _____

3. Today's journalists never tell both sides of the story.

   Problem: _____

   Revised statement: _____

4. History teaches us lessons.

   Problem: _____

   Revised statement: _____

5. Deciding to go to college.

   Problem: _____

   Revised statement: _____

6. The subject of this paragraph is school uniforms.

   Problem: _____

   Revised statement: _____

7. Everybody believes in ghosts.

   Problem: _____

   Revised statement: _____

8. The coffee shop walls are painted green.

   Problem: _____

   Revised statement: _____

The Writer's Desk Write Topic Sentences

Narrow each of the topics in this exercise. Then, write a topic sentence that contains a controlling idea. You could look at the Writer's Desk: Narrow the Topic on page 18 for ideas.

EXAMPLE: City life

Narrowed topic: Impressions of Las Vegas
Topic sentence: Las Vegas is a vibrant city of extremes.

1. The family

   Narrowed topic: _____
   Topic sentence: _____

2. Telling lies

   Narrowed topic: _____
   Topic sentence: _____

3. Travel

   Narrowed topic: _____
   Topic sentence: _____

4. An issue in the news

   Narrowed topic: _____
   Topic sentence: _____

5. Jobs

   Narrowed topic: _____
   Topic sentence: _____

ESSAY LINK

When writing an essay, place the thesis statement in the introduction. Then each supporting idea becomes a distinct paragraph with its own topic sentence.

The Supporting Ideas

Once you have written a clear topic sentence, you can focus on the **supporting details**—the facts and examples that provide the reader with interesting information about the subject matter. There are three steps you can take to determine your paragraph's supporting details.

- Generate supporting ideas.
- Choose the best ideas.
- Organize your ideas.

Generating Supporting Ideas

You can try an exploring strategy such as brainstorming or freewriting to generate ideas.

WADE'S SUPPORTING IDEAS

College student Wade Vong narrowed his topic and wrote his topic sentence. Then he listed ideas that could support his topic sentence.

Las Vegas is a vibrant city of extremes.

- crowds of tourists
- peaceful suburbs
- beautiful parks and canyons
- superhot summers
- roads lined with palm trees
- lots of beige and pink buildings with clay-tiled roofs
- variety of great entertainment
- Cirque du Soleil has permanent shows
- close to the Grand Canyon
- fast-paced, glitzy tourist strip
- sea of neon lights

The Writer's Desk List Supporting Ideas

Choose two of your topic sentences from the Writer's Desk on page 24. For each topic sentence, develop a list of supporting ideas.

Choosing the Best Ideas

An effective paragraph has **unity** when all of its sentences directly relate to and support the topic sentence. Create a unified paragraph by selecting three or four ideas that are most compelling and that clearly support your topic sentence. You may notice that several items in your list are similar; therefore, you can group them together. If some ideas do not support the topic sentence, remove them.

WADE'S BEST SUPPORTING IDEAS

Wade highlighted three of his most appealing ideas. Then he grouped together related ideas. Finally, he crossed out some ideas that did not relate to his topic sentence.

Las Vegas is a vibrant city of extremes.

- crowds of tourists
- peaceful suburbs
- beautiful parks and canyons
- ~~super-hot summers~~
- roads lined with palm trees
- lots of beige and pink buildings with clay-tiled roofs   A
- variety of great entertainment
- Cirque du Soleil has permanent shows   C
- ~~close to the Grand Canyon~~
- fast-paced, glitzy tourist strip
- sea of neon lights   B

TECHNOLOGY LINK

On a computer, you can cut (ctrl X) and paste (ctrl V) similar ideas together.

   Identifying the Best Ideas

There are many ways that you can highlight your best ideas. You can circle the best supporting points and then use arrows to link them with secondary ideas. You can also use highlighter pens or asterisks to identify the best supporting points.

PRACTICE 4

College student Sandra Ahumada brainstormed ideas about tipping. Her purpose was to persuade, so she created a topic sentence that expressed her opinion about the issue.

Underline three ideas from her list that you think are most compelling and that most clearly illustrate the point she is making in her topic sentence. Then group together any related ideas under each of the main subheadings. If any ideas do not relate to her topic sentence, remove them.

TOPIC SENTENCE: **Customers should always tip restaurant servers.**

- part of the cost of going to a restaurant
- shows appreciation for the server's work
- servers need tips to have an adequate standard of living
- their salaries below the standard minimum wage
- some customers rude
- servers often don't get benefits such as health care
- you tip hairdressers and taxi drivers
- mistakes aren't always the server's fault
- slow service could be the cook's fault
- sometimes there are not enough servers
- some people in the service industry get good money (cooks, I think)

The Writer's Desk **Choose the Best Ideas**

Choose *one* of the two lists of supporting ideas that you prepared for the previous Writer's Desk on page 25. Identify some compelling ideas that clearly illustrate the point you are trying to make. If any ideas are related, you can group them together. Cross out any ideas that are not useful.

Organizing Your Ideas

To make your ideas easy for your readers to follow, organize your ideas in a logical manner. You can use one of three common organizational methods: (1) time order, (2) emphatic order, or (3) space order.

    Transitional expressions help guide the reader from one idea to another. A complete list of transitional expressions appears on pages 43–44 in Chapter 3.

ESSAY LINK

In an essay, you can use time, space, or emphatic order to organize your ideas.

Time Order

When you organize a paragraph using **time order (chronological order),** you arrange the details according to the sequence in which they have occurred. When you narrate a story, explain how to do something, or describe a historical event, you generally use time order.

first   then   after that

Here are some transitional expressions you can use in time-order paragraphs.

after that	first	last	next
eventually	in the beginning	meanwhile	suddenly
finally	later	months after	then

The next paragraph is structured using time order.

    One morning, I found out the use of a key. I locked my mother up in the pantry where she was obliged to remain three hours, as the servants were in a detached part of the house. She kept pounding on the door while I sat outside on the porch steps and laughed with glee as I felt the jar of the pounding. This most naughty prank of mine convinced my parents that I must be taught as soon as possible. After my teacher, Miss Sullivan, came to me, I sought an early opportunity to lock her in her room. I went upstairs with something which my mother made me understand I was to give to Miss Sullivan. No sooner had I given it to her than I slammed the door, locked it, and hid the key under the wardrobe in the hall. I could not be induced to tell where the key was. My father was obliged to get a ladder and take Miss Sullivan out through the window—much to my delight. Months after, I produced the key.

—Helen Keller, *The Story of My Life*

Emphatic Order

When you organize the supporting details of a paragraph using **emphatic order,** you arrange them in a logical sequence. For example, you can arrange details from least to most important, from least appealing to most appealing, and so on.

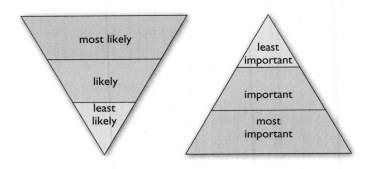

Here are some transitional expressions you can use in emphatic-order paragraphs.

above all	especially	moreover	principally
clearly	in particular	most importantly	the least important
first	last	of course	the most important

The following paragraph uses emphatic order. The writer presents the conditions from bad ones to worst ones.

The conditions experienced by the eager young volunteers of the Union and Confederate armies included massive, terrifying, and bloody battles, apparently unending, with no sign of victory in sight. First, soldiers suffered from the uncertainty of supply, which left troops, especially in the South, without uniforms, tents, and sometimes even food. They also endured long marches over muddy, rutted roads while carrying packs weighing fifty or sixty pounds. Most importantly, disease was rampant in their dirty, verminous, and unsanitary camps, and hospitals were so dreadful that more men left them dead than alive.

— Adapted from John Mack Faragher et al., *Out of Many: A History of the American People*

Using Emphatic Order

When you organize details using emphatic order, use your own values and opinions to determine what is most or least important, upsetting, remarkable, and so on. Another writer might organize the same ideas in a different way.

Space Order

When you organize ideas using **space order,** you help the reader visualize what you are describing in a specific space. For example, you can describe something or someone from top to bottom or bottom to top, from left to right or right to left, or from far to near or near to far.

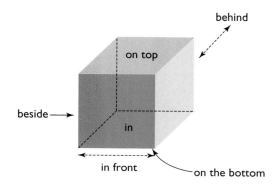

Here are some transitional expressions you can use in space-order paragraphs.

above	beneath	nearby	on top
behind	closer in	on the bottom	toward
below	farther out	on the left	under

In the next paragraph, the writer describes a location beginning at the beach and ending up at the front of the house.

> Their house was even more elaborate than I expected. It was a cheerful red-and-white Georgian Colonial mansion overlooking the bay. The lawn started at the beach and ran toward the front door for a quarter of a mile, jumping over sundials and brick walks and burning gardens—finally, when it reached the house, drifting up the side in bright vines as though from the momentum of its run. The front was broken by a line of French windows.
>
> —F. Scott Fitzgerald, *The Great Gatsby*

PRACTICE 5

Read each paragraph and decide what order the writer used: time, space, or emphatic.

A. That night, I lay awake and anxiously listened to the thunder as it continued to get closer and louder. Then I couldn't hear the thunder any more as it was replaced by another sound. I had never heard that sound before but I knew what it had to be. A split second later, I yelled "Tornado!" My wife jumped about two feet. We couldn't even get out of bed. Suddenly, everything was moving, and all we could do was hold on to each other. The roar, the sound of splintering wood and the screeching sound of tearing sheet metal seemed to last forever. In fact, it lasted about 15 seconds. Finally, silence returned like someone flipping a switch.

—Louis M. Tursi, "The Night Crawler"

Order: _____

B.　Many factors contribute to racist attitudes. First, there are often higher levels of racist incidents in societies that have historically had very little contact with different ethnic groups. According to writer and political analyst Gwynne Dyer, such isolated societies may feel threatened when there is an influx of immigrants. Moreover, racist attitudes become more prevalent when various ethnic communities do not intermingle. If different cultural communities do not work and study together, stereotypes about other groups become entrenched. Most importantly, high levels of poverty contribute to racist reactions; immigrants become easy and available scapegoats when there is competition for limited jobs.

—Eliot Mandel, student

Order: _____

C.　The bomb had demolished a group of houses two hundred meters up the street. A black plume of smoke hung in the sky, and below it a cloud of plaster dust in which a crowd was already forming around the ruin. There was a little pile of plaster lying on the pavement ahead of him, and in the middle of it he could see a bright red streak. When he got up to it, he saw that it was a human hand severed at the wrist.

—George Orwell, *1984*

Order: _____

PRACTICE 6

Read the following topic sentences. Decide what type of order you can use to develop the paragraph details. Choose space, time, or emphatic order. (There may be more than one correct organizational method.)

EXAMPLE:

Learning to play the guitar requires practice, patience, and perseverance.　　　　　　_____Emphatic_____

1. Music education is essential in public schools.　_____

2. My furnished room has everything a student could need.　_____

3. You can learn to make decisions and think critically with a liberal arts education.   _____

4. Several interesting things happened during the Stanford Prison Experiment.   _____

5. The new youth center has a very impressive design.   _____

6. There should not be a lower legal drinking age in our state.   _____

7. We encountered many problems on our journey to Honduras.   _____

8. Rory was known for his rumpled, unfashionable clothing.   _____

9. IQ tests are not always accurate and valid.   _____

10. The Beatles went through many musical phases.   _____

The Paragraph Plan

A **plan,** or **outline,** of a paragraph is a map showing the paragraph's main and supporting ideas. To make a plan, write your topic sentence, and then list supporting points and details. Remember to use emphatic, time, or space order to organize the supporting points. In a more formal outline, you can use letters and numbers to indicate primary and secondary ideas.

WADE'S PARAGRAPH PLAN

Wade completed his paragraph plan. He narrowed his topic, wrote a topic sentence, and thought of several supporting details. Here is his paragraph plan.

ESSAY LINK

Make a plan when you write an essay. In essay plans, each supporting idea becomes a separate paragraph.

TOPIC SENTENCE:	**Las Vegas is a vibrant city of extremes.**
Support 1:	Peaceful suburbs integrate the desert landscape.
Details:	—roads lined with palm trees
	—beige and pink buildings with clay-tiled roofs
	—beautiful parks and canyons
Support 2:	The tourist strip is fast-paced and glitzy.
Details:	—roving crowds of tourists
	—sea of neon lights
	—massive replicas of pyramids, Eiffel Tower
Support 3:	There is a huge variety of entertainment.
Details:	—Cirque du Soleil has permanent shows
	—well-known singers such as Celine Dion perform there
	—hypnotists and magicians in clubs
	—gambling for every taste and budget

Adding Specific Details

When you prepare your paragraph plan, ask yourself if you have enough supporting details. If not, then you could add details to make your points stronger. For example, when Wade first brainstormed a list of supporting details (page 25) he thought of only one detail to support his point about the great variety of entertainment in Las Vegas. In his paragraph plan, however, he decided to add a few more details (Céline Dion, hypnotists, magicians, gambling) to make that point stronger and more complete.

The Writer's Desk **Write a Paragraph Plan**

Look at the topic sentence and the organized list of supporting ideas that you created for the previous Writer's Desk exercises. Now, in the space provided, make a paragraph plan. Remember to include details for each supporting idea.

Topic
sentence: _____

_____

Support 1: _____

Details: _____

_____

_____

Support 2: _____

Details: _____

_____

Support 3: _____

Details: _____

_____

Writing the Concluding Sentence

A stand-alone paragraph may have a **concluding sentence** that brings it to a satisfactory close. There are several ways to write a concluding sentence.

- Restate the topic sentence in a new, refreshing way.
- Make an interesting final observation.
- End with a prediction, suggestion, or quotation.

ESSAY LINK

Essays end with a concluding paragraph. For more information, see pages 185–186.

 Problems with Concluding Sentences

When you write your concluding sentence, do not introduce a contradictory idea or change the focus of the paragraph. For example, in Wade's paragraph about Las Vegas, he should not end with a statement that questions or contradicts his main point.

Weak: Las Vegas can be a bit boring.

(This concluding sentence undermines the main point, which is that Las Vegas is a vibrant city of extremes.)

Better: If you would like to visit a truly unique city, go to Las Vegas.

(This suggestion brings the paragraph to a satisfactory close.)

PRACTICE 7

The topic sentences in paragraphs A and B are underlined. For each paragraph, circle the letter of the most effective concluding sentence, and then explain why the other choice is not as effective.

EXAMPLE:

Picasso painted many different types of people that he saw in the Paris neighborhood of Montmartre. He painted musicians, prostitutes, street vendors, circus performers, and fellow artists, as well as his many lovers. During his blue period, he was drawn to emaciated figures; impoverished mothers and hungry children populated his art.

a. Picasso painted many different types of people.

b. The human body was ultimately the most important and repeated image in his paintings and sculptures.

Why is the other choice not as effective?

Sentence "a" just repeats the topic sentence.

A. Our state should insist that day-care centers provide more flexible hours for families. Today, in many families, both parents work outside the home. These parents do not necessarily work from nine to five. For example, nurses and factory employees work in shifts. For such parents, flexible day care is very important. Also, many parents who are in the service and retail industry work on weekends. For these parents, it is important to have adequate child-care facilities during their work hours.

a. The current opening hours of most day-care centers do not meet the needs of a great number of families.

b. However, maybe day-care owners do not want to open on nights and weekends.

Why is the other choice not as effective?

_____

B. <u>College students should find part-time jobs that require them to exercise different muscles.</u> If a business student spends hours sitting in front of a computer screen, then he should try to find a job that requires physical activity. If an engineering student has to do advanced calculus, then maybe her part-time job should allow her to rest her brain. Students who do a lot of solitary study could try to find jobs that allow them to interact socially.

a. Some college students should not take part-time jobs because they need to concentrate on their studies.

b. Humans need to do a variety of activities to be mentally and physically strong, so college students should keep that in mind when they look for work.

Why is the other choice not as effective?

_____

PRACTICE 8

Read the next paragraph by college student Veena Thomas. Then answer the questions that follow.

After completely immersing myself in college life for nine months, it was easy to forget the existence of normal civilization, so returning home for the summer was an awakening. First, I had my own room, but no roommates for company and conversation. My house was amazingly clean. There were no dust bunnies under the furniture, and there was no dirty ring in the bathtub. The food at dinner was delicious, and it was free! It was always nutritious and beautifully prepared.

1. What is the topic of this paragraph?

_____

2. Underline the topic sentence.

3. List the supporting details.

_____

_____

_____

4. Write two possible concluding sentences for this paragraph.

a. _____

_____

b. _____

_____

The First Draft

After making a paragraph plan, you are ready to write your first draft, which is a very important step in the writing process. Your first draft includes your topic sentence, some supporting details, and a concluding sentence.

As you write your first draft, you might find it difficult sometimes to say what you mean. If you are having trouble, underline that section or put a check mark beside it so that you can come back to revise it later. If possible, put your first draft aside for a few hours before rereading it. Then, when you revise your paragraph, you will read it with a fresh perspective. The next chapter contains information about revising a paragraph.

WADE'S FIRST DRAFT

Here is Wade Vong's first draft. You may notice that his paragraph has errors. He will correct these when he gets to the revising and editing stage of the process.

> **Las Vegas is a vibrant city of extremes.** Peaceful suburbs integrate the desert landscape. Neighborhoods have pink and beige buildings with clay-tiled roofs, many yards contain various species of cactus. White roads are lined with palm trees. There are beautifull parks and canyons. Other parts of the city are extremely fast-paced and glitzy. On the Las Vegas Strip, neon lights illuminate the night sky. Crowds of tourists gaze at massive replicas of the pyramids, the Statue of liberty, and the Eiffel Tower. The strip is also vibrant because of the great entertainment available, including gambling for every taste and budget. The city attract world-class entertainment. Such as Celine Dion. The Cirque du Soleil has permanent shows. Even small clubs have magicians and hypnotists. If you would like to visit a truly unique city, go to Las Vegas.

The Writer's Desk **Write Your First Draft**

In the previous Writer's Desk on page 32, you made a paragraph plan. Now use the plan's information to type or write your first draft paragraph.

REFLECT ON IT

Think about what you have learned in this chapter. If you do not know an answer, review that topic.

1. What is a topic sentence? _____

_____

2. What is time order? _____

_____

3. What is emphatic order? _____

_____

4. What is space order? _____

_____

Are the following sentences true or false? Circle the best answer.

5. A paragraph has more than one main idea.   True   False

6. A paragraph's details support its topic sentence.   True   False

 The Writer's Room **Topics to Develop**

Writing Activity I

In the Writer's Room in Chapter 1, "Exploring," you used various strategies to find ideas about the following topics. Select one of the topics and write a paragraph. Remember to follow the writing process.

General Topics

1. a childhood memory
2. anger
3. rules
4. cosmetic surgery

College and Work-Related Topics

5. a comfortable place
6. study or work habits
7. gossip
8. cell phones

Writing Activity 2

Choose a topic that you feel passionate about and write a paragraph. Your topic could be an activity (painting, basketball) or an interest (music, politics). Your topic sentence should make a point about the topic.

DEVELOPING CHECKLIST

As you develop your paragraph, ask yourself the following questions.

☐ Have I narrowed my topic?

☐ Does my topic sentence make a valid and supportable point about the topic?

☐ Is my topic sentence interesting?

☐ Does my paragraph focus on one main idea?

☐ Do the details support the topic sentence?

☐ Do the supporting details follow a logical order?

☐ Does my paragraph end in a satisfactory way?

See Chapter 2 of the Visualizing Writing CD for additional mini-lectures on **Topic Sentence** and **Organizing the Paragraph.**

CHAPTER 3

Revising and Editing

> **" Life is trying things to see if they work. "**
>
> —RAY BRADBURY
> *American author (b. 1920)*

CONTENTS

- What Is Revising and Editing?
- Revise for Unity
- Revise for Adequate Support
- Revise for Coherence
- Revise for Style
- Edit for Errors
- Write the Final Draft

The revising and editing stage of the writing process is similar to adding the finishing touches to a piece of pottery. Small improvement can make the difference between an ordinary creation and a remarkable one.

What Is Revising and Editing?

After you have written the first draft of your paragraph, the next step in the writing process is to revise and edit your work. When you **revise,** you modify your writing to make it stronger and more convincing. You do this by reading your first draft critically, looking for faulty logic, poor organization, or poor sentence style. Then you reorganize and rewrite it, making any necessary changes. When you **edit,** you proofread your final draft for errors in grammar, spelling, punctuation, and mechanics.

There are five key steps to follow during the revising and editing stage.

REVISING AND EDITING

STEP 1 ➤	**Revise for unity.** Ensure that all parts of your work relate to the main idea.
STEP 2 ➤	**Revise for adequate support.** Determine that your details effectively support the main idea.

STEP 3	➤	**Revise for coherence.** Verify that your ideas flow smoothly and logically.
STEP 4	➤	**Revise for style.** Ensure that your sentences are varied and interesting.
STEP 5	➤	**Edit for technical errors.** Proofread your work and correct errors in grammar, spelling, mechanics, and punctuation.

Revise for Unity

Unity means that all of the sentences in a paragraph support the topic sentence. If a paragraph lacks unity, then some sentences drift from the main idea that a writer has expressed in the topic sentence. To check for unity, ensure that every sentence in the body of the paragraph relates to one main idea.

PARAGRAPH WITHOUT UNITY

In the next paragraph, the writer drifted away from her main idea. Some sentences do not relate to the topic sentence. If the highlighted sentences are removed, then the paragraph has unity.

> **During World War II, the status of women changed profoundly.** The military industry needed "manpower" to fight the war, but it also needed womanpower. From 1940 to 1944, about 17 million women joined the work force. They filled jobs in defense industries, steel mills, shipyards, and aircraft factories. By the end of the war, women had proved that they could be invaluable workers. Today many women work in these industries and it isn't considered unusual. In fact, according to Brigid O'Farrell, women represent over 17 percent of all blue-collar workers in the United States. Now women earn the same salary as men in most jobs. When men returned home in 1945, most women left the factories; however, women developed confidence and earning power, and North America's workplace changed forever.

◄ The writer took a detour here.

PRACTICE I

Paragraphs A and B contain problems with unity. In each paragraph, underline the topic sentence and cross out any sentences that do not support the controlling idea.

A. Car-based cell phones should be banned. One study published by the *New England Journal of Medicine* found that the risk of a collision quadruples if drivers use a cellular phone. The findings indicate that the major problem with cell phones is that they affect the driver's concentration. Jeffrey Blain repairs roads, and he says that sometimes drivers using their phones go through barriers and into road repair sites because they are so distracted. I also hate it when people use their cell phones in movie theaters. At a recent movie, I heard the beeps of various cell phones at least five times during the film. The problem is especially bad in cars, though. Our government should outlaw cell phones in motor vehicles.

ESSAY LINK

When revising and editing your essay, check that the body paragraphs support the thesis statement. Also, ensure that each body paragraph has unity.

B.   Orville and Wilbur Wright had an unlikely dream, but they turned it into reality. When the brothers first tried to make a plane fly, they were unsuccessful. In fact, in 1901, a frustrated Wilbur Wright said that humans wouldn't fly for a thousand years. However, just two years later, on December 17, 1903, Wilbur and Orville Wright flew a plane for 105 feet. The brothers were overjoyed; their hard work and planning had finally paid off. Since that time, air travel has changed a lot. Many different types of planes exist today. Jets fly across our skies and can go from London to New York in a few hours. Eventually the Wright brothers produced nineteen types of aircraft. By sticking with an idea and persevering, the Wright brothers made their dream a reality.

ESSAY LINK

When revising your essay, ensure that you have adequately supported the thesis statement. Also ensure that each body paragraph has sufficient supporting details.

Revise for Adequate Support

A paragraph has **adequate support** when there are enough details and examples to make it strong, convincing, and interesting. The following paragraph attempts to persuade, but it does not have any specific details that make a strong point.

> In European films, the star can be wrinkled or overweight. **Unfortunately, American filmmakers have not figured out that people like to see reflections of themselves on screen.** To get a job, American movie actors must be in perfect shape and have perfect bodies. It is often hard to believe that the beautiful actor is really the waiter or car mechanic that is pictured on screen. The problem is especially acute when the star is older. You can be sure that he or she has had a lot of surgery to look as young as possible. Ordinary audience members have trouble identifying with surgically enhanced actors. Perhaps one day American producers will use regular-looking people in their films.

PRACTICE 2

When the preceding paragraph about film stars is expanded with specific details and examples, the paragraph becomes more convincing. Try adding details on the lines provided. You can do this alone or with a partner.

In European films, the star can be wrinkled or overweight. Unfortunately, American filmmakers have not figured out that people like to see reflections of themselves on screen. To get a job, American movie actors must be in perfect shape and have perfect bodies. For example, _____ and _____ are incredibly good-looking. It is often hard to believe that the beautiful actor is really the waiter or car mechanic that is pictured on screen. In the movie titled _____, the actor _____ looks too perfect to be a _____.

The problem is especially acute when the star is older. You can be sure that he or she has had a lot of surgery to look as young as possible. For instance, _____ looks much younger than the actor's real age. Ordinary audience members have trouble identifying with surgically enhanced actors. Perhaps one day American producers will use regular-looking people in their films.

Avoiding Circular Reasoning

Circular reasoning means that a paragraph restates its main point in various ways but does not provide supporting details. The main idea goes in circles and never progresses. Avoid using circular reasoning by providing a clear, concise topic sentence and by supporting the topic sentence with facts, examples, statistics, or anecdotes.

CELIA'S PARAGRAPH

Celia Raines, a student, wrote the following paragraph about a popular proverb. In the paragraph, she repeats her main point over and over and does not provide any evidence to support her topic sentence.

Circular   Those who make the most noise usually get what they want. People sometimes shout and make a fuss and then others listen to them. Those who are quiet get ignored and their opinions do not get heard. It is important for people to speak up and express their needs. This attitude is expressed in the proverb "The squeaky wheel gets the grease."

In the second version of this paragraph, Celia added a specific example (an anecdote) that helped illustrate her main point.

Not Circular   Those who make the most noise usually get what they want. Those who are quiet get ignored, and their opinions do not get heard. For example, two years ago, the local government started a passenger train service that helped local commuters get into the city. Many citizens loved commuting by train, but those who live near the train tracks complained about the noise. They made petitions, wrote to newspapers, and lobbied the local government to cancel the train service. Those people were so loud and persistent that they got their wish and the train service was canceled. The silent majority disagreed with that lobby group, but as the proverb says, "The squeaky wheel gets the grease."

PRACTICE 3

Paragraphs A and B use circular reasoning. There is no specific evidence to support the topic sentence. List supporting examples for each paragraph. With numbers, indicate where you would place the supporting examples.

EXAMPLE:

American teenagers go through several rites of passage. These rites of passage help the teenager navigate the transition from childhood to adulthood. (1) Some rites of passage are shared with the community. (2) These rites are an important part of every youth's life.

Examples: (1) the first date and the first kiss

the first job

(2) the high school prom

A. Police officers have an important function in our society. They provide many useful and necessary services in the community. If there were no police officers, there would be anarchy in the streets. Law-enforcement officers deserve our respect and appreciation.

Examples: _____

_____

_____

_____

_____

_____

_____

B. When you move out of your family home and live on your own, you should plan your budget carefully. There are many things that you will have to pay for, and a lot of items will be expensive. You will need to pay for services. Even small household items add up. It is expensive to live on your own.

Examples: _____

_____

_____

_____

_____

_____

_____

Revise for Coherence

When you drive along a highway and you suddenly hit a pothole, it is an uncomfortable experience. Readers experience similar discomfort if they encounter potholes in a piece of writing. Make your writing as smooth as possible by ensuring that it has **coherence:** the sentences should flow smoothly and logically.

Transitional Expressions

Transitional expressions are linking words or phrases, and they ensure that ideas are connected smoothly. Here are some common transitional expressions.

> **ESSAY LINK**
>
> To create coherence in an essay, you can place transitional expressions at the beginning of each body paragraph.

Function	Transitional Word or Expression	
Addition	again	in addition
	also	in fact
	besides	last
	finally	moreover
	first (second, third)	next
	for one thing	then
	furthermore	
Concession of a point	certainly	of course
	even so	no doubt
	indeed	to be sure
Comparison and contrast	as well	likewise
	equally	nevertheless
	even so	on the contrary
	however	on the other hand
	in contrast	similarly
	instead	
Effect or result	accordingly	otherwise
	as a result	then
	consequently	therefore
	hence	thus
Example	for example	in particular
	for instance	namely
	in other words	specifically to illustrate
Emphasis	above all	least of all
	clearly	most important
	first	most of all
	especially	of course
	in fact	particularly
	in particular	principally
	indeed	
Reason or purpose	for this purpose	the most important reason
	for this reason	
Space	above	near
	behind	nearby
	below	on one side / on the other side
	beneath	on the bottom
	beside	on the left/right
	beyond	on top

(continued)

Function	Transitional Word or Expression	
Space	closer in farther out inside	outside to the north/east/south/west under
Summary or conclusion	in conclusion in other words in short generally on the whole	therefore thus to conclude to summarize ultimately
Time	after that at that time at the moment currently earlier eventually first (second, etc.) gradually immediately in the beginning in the future in the past	later meanwhile months after now one day presently so far subsequently suddenly then these days

 Hint **Use Transitional Expressions with Complete Sentences**

When you add a transitional expression to a sentence, ensure that your sentence is complete. Your sentence must have a subject and a verb, and it must express a complete thought.

Incomplete: For example, the rules posted on the wall.

Complete: For example, the rules <u>were</u> posted on the wall.

PRACTICE 4

The next paragraph contains eight transitional expressions that appear at the beginning of sentences. Underline each expression, and then, in the chart, indicate its purpose. The first one has been done for you.

For those who love eating out, a new type of dining experience is rearing its ugly head. <u>Indeed</u>, service with a sneer is popping up in Canada and the United States. For instance, in the New York City teahouse Tea and Sympathy, customers must follow a rigid list of rules. Those who plan to wait for friends are sharply told to leave. Moreover, patrons who manage to get a table are kicked out as soon as they finish their tea. Similarly, in Vancouver, the Elbow Room Café posts rules on the wall, including one that asks customers to get their own coffee and water. Also, the owner and staff members ridicule customers. Even so, clients keep coming back, comparing the experience to going to a show. The bad service trend has always been there. However, people in previous decades would have left such eateries without leaving a tip. These days, customers line up to be abused.

Transitional Expression	Function
1. Indeed	Emphasis
2.	
3.	
4.	
5.	
6.	
7.	
8.	

PRACTICE 5

Add appropriate transitional expressions to the following paragraph. Choose from the following list, and use each transitional word once. There may be more than one correct answer for each blank.

furthermore	as a result	in fact
first	on the whole	for example

The most interesting college course I have ever had was Introductory Psychology 101. _____, I found the course material very interesting because the textbook contained true case studies. _____, my instructor was the most stimulating teacher I have ever had. He used humor to engage the students' attention. _____, I enjoyed going to class. _____, my instructor had found a way to make the horrible experience of taking exams interesting. His exams were so original that I looked forward to test periods. _____, he devised tests and exams in the form of mysteries to solve. The solution to each question lay in the problem that we had studied in each chapter of our textbook. _____, Introductory Psychology 101 was the most appealing course I have ever taken.

Revise for Style

When you revise for sentence **style,** you ensure that your paragraph has concise and appropriate language and sentence variety. You can ask yourself the following questions.

ESSAY LINK

You should also revise your essays for style, ensuring that sentences are varied and parallel. Also, ensure that your language is exact.

- Have I used a **variety of sentence patterns?** (To practice using sentence variety, see Chapter 19.)
- Have I used **exact language?** (To learn about slang, wordiness, and overused expressions, see Chapter 31.)
- Are my sentences **parallel in structure?** (To practice revising for parallel structure, see Chapter 21.)

WADE'S REVISION

On page 35 in Chapter 2, you read the first draft of student Wade Vong's paragraph about Las Vegas. Look at his revisions for unity, support, coherence, and style.

Transition ➤

Detail ➤

Combined sentences ➤

Transition ➤

Detail ➤

Transition ➤

Combined sentences ➤

Las Vegas is a vibrant city of extremes. ~~Peaceful~~ *First, peaceful* suburbs integrate the *stunning* desert landscape. ~~Neighborhoods~~ *Some neighborhoods* have pink and beige buildings with clay-tiled roofs, many yards contain various species of cactus. White roads ~~are~~ lined with palm trees. *lead to* ~~There are~~ beautifull parks and canyons. ~~Other~~ *In contrast, other* parts of the city are extremely fast-paced and glitzy. On the Las Vegas Strip, *for instance,* neon lights illuminate the night sky. Crowds *jostling* of tourists gaze at massive replicas of the pyramids, the Statue of liberty, and the Eiffel Tower. The strip is also vibrant because of the great entertainment available, including gambling for every taste and *In addition, the* budget. ~~The~~ city attract world-class entertainment. Such as Céline Dion. The Cirque du Soleil has permanent shows. *, and even* ~~Even~~ small clubs have magicians and hypnotists. If you would like to visit a truly unique city, go to Las Vegas.

 Adding Strong Support

When you revise, look at the strength of your supporting details. Ask yourself the following questions.

- Are my supporting details interesting, and do they grab the reader's attention? Should I use more vivid words?

- Is my concluding sentence appealing? Could I end the paragraph in a more interesting way?

PRACTICE 6

In Chapters 1 and 2, you saw examples of Sandra Ahumada's prewriting and planning. Now look at the first draft of Sandra's paragraph, and revise it for unity, support, and coherence. Also, ask yourself what you could do to enhance her writing style.

> Customers should always tip restaurant servers. Servers need tips to live. Their salary is very low. They depend on tips to pay for food, housing, and other necessities. They do not get benefits such as health care. If you do not like the service, remember that mistakes are not always the server's fault. Poor service could be the cook's fault. Sometimes there are not enough servers. I work as a server in a restaurant. I know how hard it is when customers leave bad tips. Always tip your restaurant server.

Edit for Errors

When you **edit,** you reread your writing and make sure that it is free of errors. You focus on the language, and you look for mistakes in grammar, punctuation, mechanics, and spelling.

There is an editing guide in the rear of this book. It contains some common error codes that your teacher may use. It also provides you with a list of things to check for when you proofread your text.

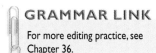

GRAMMAR LINK

For more editing practice, see Chapter 36.

Editing Tips

The following tips will help you proofread your work more effectively.

- Put your writing aside for a day or two before you do the editing. Sometimes, when you have been working closely with a text, you might not see the errors.
- Begin your proofreading at any stage of the writing process. For example, if you are not sure of the spelling of a word while writing the first draft, you could either highlight the word for later verification or immediately look up the word in the dictionary.
- Keep a list of your common errors in a separate grammar log. When you finish a writing assignment, consult your error list, and make sure that you have not repeated any of those errors. After each assignment has been corrected, you could add new errors to your list. For more information about grammar and spelling logs, see Appendix 7.

TECHNOLOGY LINK

Word processors have spelling and grammar checkers. Do not always choose the first suggestion for a correction. Make sure that suggestions are valid before you accept them.

WADE'S EDITED PARAGRAPH

Wade Vong edited his paragraph about Las Vegas. He corrected errors in spelling, capitalization, punctuation, and grammar.

> **Las Vegas is a vibrant city of extremes.** First, peaceful suburbs integrate the stunning desert landscape. Some neighborhoods have pink and beige buildings with clay-tiled roofs, many yards _and_ contain various species of ~~cactus.~~ _cacti_ White roads lined with palm

beautiful

trees lead to ~~beautifull~~ parks and canyons. In contrast, other parts

of the city are extremely fast-paced and glitzy. On the Las Vegas

Strip, for instance, neon lights illuminate the night sky. Crowds of

jostling tourists gaze at massive replicas of the pyramids, the Statue

Liberty

of ~~liberty~~, and the Eiffel Tower. The strip is also vibrant because

of the great entertainment available, including gambling for every

attracts

taste and budget. In addition, the city ~~attract~~ world-class

such

entertainment~~.~~ ~~Such~~ as Céline Dion. The Cirque du Soleil has

permanent shows, and even small clubs have magicians and

hypnotists. If you would like to visit a truly unique city, go to Las

Vegas.

The Writer's Desk   **Revise and Edit**

Choose a paragraph you wrote for Chapter 2, or choose one that you have written for another assignment. Carefully revise and edit the paragraph. You can refer to the Revising and Editing Checklist at the end of this chapter.

Peer Feedback

After you write a paragraph or essay, it is useful to get peer feedback. Ask another person such as a friend, family member, or fellow student to read your work and give you comments and suggestions on its strengths and weaknesses.

   Offer Constructive Criticism

When you peer-edit someone else's writing, try to make your comments useful. Phrase your comments in a positive way. Look at these examples.

Instead of saying . . .	**You could say . . .**
Your sentences are boring.	Maybe you could combine some sentences.
Your supporting ideas are weak.	You could add more details here.

You can use the following peer feedback form to evaluate written work.

Peer Feedback Form

Written by: _____   Feedback by: _____

Date: _____

1. What is the main point of the written work?

    _____

2. What details effectively support the topic sentence?

    _____

3. What, if anything, is unclear or unnecessary?

    _____

4. Give some suggestions about how the work could be improved.

    _____

5. What is an interesting or unique feature of this written work?

    _____

    _____

Write the Final Draft

When you have finished making revisions on the first draft of your paragraph, write the final draft. Include all of the changes that you have made during the revision and editing phases. Before you hand in your final draft, proofread it one last time to ensure that you have caught any errors.

The Writer's Desk   Write Your Final Draft

You have developed, revised, and edited your paragraph. Now write the final draft. Before you offer it to readers, proofread it one last time to ensure that you have found all of your errors.

Hint   **Spelling, Grammar, and Vocabulary Logs**

- **Keep a spelling and grammar log.** You probably repeat, over and over, the same types of grammar and spelling errors. You will find it very useful to record your repeated grammar mistakes in a spelling and grammar log. You can refer to your list of spelling and grammar mistakes when you revise and edit your writing.

- **Keep a vocabulary log.** Expanding your vocabulary will be of enormous benefit to you as a writer. In a vocabulary log, you can make a list of unfamiliar words and their definitions.

  See Appendix 7 for more information about spelling, grammar, and vocabulary logs.

REFLECT ON IT

Think about what you have learned in this chapter. If you do not know an answer, review that topic.

1. What are four things that you should look for when revising?

    _____   _____

    _____   _____

2. Circle the best answer(s). A paragraph is unified if

    a. there are no irrelevant supporting details.

    b. there are many facts and statistics.

    c. all details support the topic sentence.

3. Circle the best answer: Transitional words are _____ that help ideas flow in a logical manner.

    a. links   b. sentences   c. verbs

4. The Editing Handbook in Part IV includes information about grammar, spelling, and punctuation errors. In what chapter would you find information about the following topics? Look in the table of contents to find the chapter number.

    a. Capitalization   _____

    b. Subject-verb agreement   _____

    c. Faulty parallel structure   _____

    d. Commas   _____

    e. Commonly confused words   _____

 The Writer's Room **Paragraph Topics**

Writing Activity 1

Choose a paragraph that you have written for work or another course. Revise and edit that paragraph, and then write a final draft.

Writing Activity 2

Choose any of the following topics, or choose your own topic. Then write a paragraph. Remember to follow the writing process.

General Topics

1. interesting things about yourself
2. how to write a paragraph
3. heroes in the media
4. the meaning of the quotation at the beginning of this chapter
5. bad service

College and Work-Related Topics

6. something you learned in a college course or on campus
7. an unusual work experience
8. reasons to turn down a job
9. telemarketing
10. an interesting job

REVISING AND EDITING CHECKLIST

When you revise and edit, ask yourself the following questions. (For a more detailed editing checklist, refer to the inside back cover of this book.)

Unity

- Is my paragraph unified under a single topic?
- Does each sentence relate to the topic sentence?

Support

- Does my paragraph have an adequate number of supporting details?

Coherence

- Is my paragraph logically organized?
- Do I use transitional words or expressions to help the paragraph flow smoothly?

Style

- Do I use a variety of sentence styles?
- Is my vocabulary concise?
- Are my sentences parallel in structure?

Editing

- Do my sentences contain correct grammar, spelling, punctuation, and mechanics?

See Chapter 3 of the Visualizing Writing CD for an additional mini-lecture on **Revising the Paragraph for Coherence.**

PART II

Paragraph Patterns

What Is a Paragraph Pattern?

A *pattern* or *mode* is a method used to express one of the three purposes: to inform, to persuade, or to entertain. Once you know your purpose, you will be able to choose which writing pattern or patterns can help you to express it.

Patterns can overlap, and it is possible to use more than one pattern in a single piece of writing. For example, imagine you are writing a paragraph about bullying, and your purpose is to inform the reader. You might use *definition* as your predominant pattern but, in the supporting details, you might use *comparison and contrast* to compare a bully and a victim. You might also use *narration* to highlight an incident in which a bully harassed a victim.

Before you work through the next chapters, review the paragraph patterns.

Illustration
To illustrate or prove a point using specific examples

Narration
To narrate or tell a story about a sequence of events that happened

Process
To inform the reader about how to do something, how something works, or how something happened

Description
To describe using vivid details and images that appeal to the reader's senses

Definition
To define or explain what a term or concept means by providing relevant examples

Classification
To classify or sort a topic to help readers understand different qualities about that topic

Comparison and contrast
To present information about similarities (compare) or differences (contrast)

Cause and effect
To explain why an event happened (the cause) or what the consequences of the event were (the effects)

Argument*
To argue or to take a position on an issue and offer reasons for your position

*Argument is included as one of the nine patterns, but it is also a purpose in writing.

Illustration

> *A wisely chosen illustration is essential to fasten the truth upon the ordinary mind.*
>
> —HOWARD CROSBY
> *American preacher and educator (1826—1891)*

CONTENTS

Exploring
- Explore Topics
- What Is Illustration?
- The Illustration Paragraph

Developing
- The Topic Sentence
- The Supporting Ideas
- The Paragraph Plan
- The First Draft

Revising and Editing
- Revise and Edit an Illustration Paragraph

Vendors offer many examples of a product to interest consumers and to make a sale. In illustration writing, you give examples to support your point.

EXPLORING

Explore Topics

In the Warm Up, you will try an exploring strategy to generate ideas about different topics.

The Writer's Desk Warm Up

Think about the following questions, and write the first ideas that come to your mind. Try to think of two to three ideas for each topic.

EXAMPLE: What do students learn during the first week of college?

—how to find their way around campus (where is the computer lab, etc.?)

—the importance of keeping an agenda (they might have a lot of courses!)

—good places to study (library, coffee shop, campus grounds)

1. What are some habits or behaviors that really annoy you?

_____

_____

_____

2. What qualities do people need to work in the service industry?

_____

_____

_____

3. What are some qualities that you look for in a mate?

_____

_____

_____

What Is Illustration?

When you write using **illustration,** you include specific examples to clarify your main point. You illustrate or give examples anytime you want to explain, analyze, narrate, or give an opinion about something. As a writer, you can use many different types of examples to help your reader acquire a deeper and clearer understanding of your subject. You can include personal experience or factual information, such as a statistic.

You give examples every day. When telling a friend why you had a good day or a bad day, you might use examples to make your story more interesting. At college, you might give an oral presentation using examples that will help your audience better understand your point. At work, you might give examples to show clients where or how they might market their products.

ESSAY LINK

You can develop illustration essays with a series of examples or extended examples.

The Illustration Paragraph

There are two ways to write an illustration paragraph.

- **Use a series of examples** to illustrate your main point. For example, if you are writing a paragraph about an innovative teacher that you had, you might list things that the teacher did, such as wear a costume, let students teach parts of the course, and use music to make a point.
- **Use an extended example** to illustrate your main point. The example can be an anecdote or a description of an event. For example, if you are writing about a stressful vacation, you might describe what happened when you lost your wallet.

The following *Illustration at Work* paragraph illustrates using a series of examples.

Illustration at Work

Patti Guzman is a registered nurse at a large hospital. She was invited to speak to nursing students in a local university. In the following excerpt from her speech, she gives examples to explain why a nurse must be in good physical health.

Physically, the job of a nurse is demanding. On a daily basis, we must lift patients and move them. When patients are bedridden for prolonged periods, we must change their positions on their beds. When new patients arrive, we transfer them from stretchers to beds or from beds to wheelchairs. If patients fall, we must be able to help them stand up. If patients have difficulty walking, we must assist them. Patients who have suffered paralysis or stroke need to be lifted and supported when they are bathed and dressed. Keep in mind that some patients may be quite heavy, so the job requires a good level of physical strength.

PRACTICE 1

Read the next paragraph and answer the questions.

Across the country, lawmakers are coming up with inventive ways to punish criminals. Some judges in New Orleans, for example, treat offenders like unruly children. In 2003, one of the judges ordered a shoplifter in Baton Rouge to stand in front of a Dillard's store holding a sign that says "I will not shoplift anymore," and another judge ordered an offender to write "I will not steal other people's property" 2,500 times. In Florida, a hardworking judge orders drunk drivers to put bumper stickers on their cars that read, "How's my driving? The judge wants to know." The stickers feature a toll-free number. A Kentucky judge sometimes instructs **deadbeat dads** to choose between jail or a **vasectomy.** The best creative sentencing is done by a judge from Santa Fe, New Mexico. Judge Frances Gallegos, arguing that traditional anger management courses are ineffective, sentences violent offenders to tai chi, meditation, and Japanese flower-arranging classes.

—Rebecca Bloom, student

deadbeat dad: a father who avoids paying for his child's upkeep

vasectomy: medical procedure to sterilize a male

1. Underline the topic sentence of this paragraph. (The topic sentence expresses the main idea of the paragraph.)

2. What type of illustration paragraph is this? Circle the best answer.
   a. Series of examples   b. Extended example

3. List the examples that the writer gives to illustrate her point.

   _____

   _____

   _____

   _____

   _____

   _____

PRACTICE 2

Read the next paragraph and answer the questions.

> If there is a single trait that most distinguishes entrepreneurs, it is this: they have an uncanny ability to anticipate and supply what large numbers of people want. For example, here's how Akio Morita, the legendary founder of Sony, got his idea for the Sony Walkman. He would go to the beach with his children, and the kids and their friends would listen to high-volume ghetto blasters from morning to evening. Morita asked himself, "Why should I have to listen to this **ghastly** music?" And he wondered, "Why should they have to carry those **cumbersome** machines?" Morita told his engineers to figure out a way to build a small radio and cassette player that would sound like a high-quality car stereo and yet could be attached to a person's head. They obliged, and the Sony Walkman stormed the market.
>
> —Dinesh D'Souza, "Billionaires," *Business 2.0*

ghastly: terrible

cumbersome: large and heavy

1. Underline the topic sentence.

2. What does the writer use to present his supporting details? Circle the best answer.

   a. a series of examples   b. an extended example

3. What example(s) does the writer give to illustrate his point? _____

   _____

4. What are the main events in the narrative? List them.

   _____

   _____

   _____

   _____

   _____

DEVELOPING

The Topic Sentence

The topic sentence of the illustration paragraph is a general statement that expresses both your topic and your controlling idea. To determine your controlling idea, think about what point you want to make.

topic   controlling idea

During my first months as a reporter, <u>I was often surprised at people's behavior.</u>

controlling idea   topic

<u>Our father became anxious</u> **when my sister started dating.**

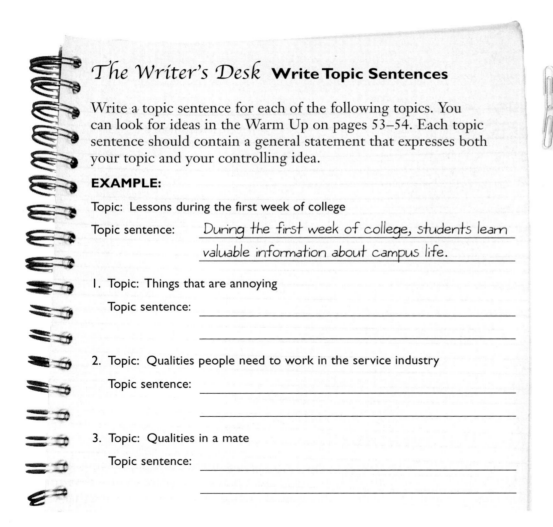

The Writer's Desk   Write Topic Sentences

Write a topic sentence for each of the following topics. You can look for ideas in the Warm Up on pages 53–54. Each topic sentence should contain a general statement that expresses both your topic and your controlling idea.

EXAMPLE:

Topic: Lessons during the first week of college

Topic sentence: *During the first week of college, students learn valuable information about campus life.*

1. Topic: Things that are annoying

    Topic sentence: _____

    _____

2. Topic: Qualities people need to work in the service industry

    Topic sentence: _____

    _____

3. Topic: Qualities in a mate

    Topic sentence: _____

    _____

ESSAY LINK

In an illustration essay, the thesis statement expresses the controlling idea.

The Supporting Ideas

After you have developed an effective topic sentence, generate supporting ideas. In an illustration paragraph, you can give a series of examples or an extended example.

When you use a series of examples, you can arrange your examples in emphatic order. Emphatic order means that you can place your examples from the most to the least important or from the least to the most important. If you use an extended example, you can arrange your ideas using time order.

The Writer's Desk **Generate Supporting Ideas**

Generate some supporting examples under each topic. Make sure your examples support the topic sentences that you wrote for the previous Writer's Desk.

EXAMPLE: Lessons during the first week of college

when the sports complex opens

clubs on campus

where is the library

good instructors

1. Things that annoy you

_____

_____

_____

_____

2. Qualities needed to work in the service industry

_____

_____

_____

_____

3. Qualities you look for in a mate

_____

_____

_____

_____

ESSAY LINK

In an illustration essay, place the thesis statement in the introduction. Then, structure the essay so that each supporting idea becomes a distinct paragraph with its own topic sentence.

The Paragraph Plan

A paragraph plan helps you organize your topic sentence and supporting details before writing a first draft. When you write a paragraph plan, ensure that your examples are valid and relate to the topic sentence. Also include details that will help clarify your supporting examples. Organize your ideas in a logical order.

TOPIC SENTENCE: During the first week of college, students learn valuable information about campus life.

Support 1: They learn how to find their way around campus.

Details: —locations of classrooms and instructors' offices

Support 2: They get information about the personalities of instructors.

    Details: —nice versus strict instructors

Support 3: They find good places to eat.

    Details: —try cafeteria food

              —find out if there are coffee shops or fast-food outlets on campus

Support 4: They discover the availability of computers.

    Details: —computer lab opening hours

              —lab technician availability

The Writer's Desk **Write a Paragraph Plan**

Choose one of the topic sentences that you wrote for the Writer's Desk on page 57. Write a paragraph plan using some of the supporting ideas that you have generated. Include details for each supporting idea.

Topic sentence: _____

_____

Support 1: _____

   Details: _____

_____

Support 2: _____

   Details: _____

_____

Support 3: _____

   Details: _____

_____

Support 4: _____

   Details: _____

_____

The First Draft

After you outline your ideas in a plan, you are ready to write the first draft. Remember to write complete sentences. You might include transitional words or expressions to help your ideas flow smoothly.

Transitional Words and Expressions

Transitional expressions can help you introduce an example or show an additional example. The next transitional words are useful in illustration paragraphs.

To Introduce an Example		To Show an Additional Example	
for example	namely	also	in addition
for instance	specifically	first (second, etc.)	in another case
in other words	to illustrate	furthermore	moreover

The Writer's Desk **Write the First Draft**

In the previous Writer's Desk, you developed a paragraph plan. Now write the first draft of your illustration paragraph. Before you write, carefully review your paragraph plan and make any necessary changes.

REVISING AND EDITING

Revise and Edit an Illustration Paragraph

When you finish writing an illustration paragraph, review your work and revise it to make the example(s) as clear as possible to your readers. Check to make sure that the order of ideas is logical, and remove any irrelevant details. Before you work on your own paragraph, practice revising and editing a student paragraph.

PRACTICE 3

Read the next student paragraph and answer the questions.

> During the first week of college, students learn valuable information about campus life. First, new students learn how to find your way around campus. They discover the location of the classrooms and the instructors' offices. Furthermore, they learn about the personalities of their instructors. Perhaps one instructor is strict, another is easygoing. Students often gossip on campus. In the first week, students also learn about good places to study. For example, many students like to work in the library because it is peaceful. Some also study in the campus coffee shop. On the other hand, the cafeteria may be noisy and is not

a good place to study. Basically, it is important to find out how the campus functions early in the semester.

Revising

1. Highlight the topic sentence in this paragraph.

2. List the examples that illustrate the topic sentence.

   _____

   _____

   _____

3. This paragraph lacks unity, and one sentence is not relevant. Cross it out.

Editing

4. There is a pronoun error in the paragraph: one pronoun does not agree with its antecedent. Identify the incorrect sentence. Then write the correct sentence in the space below. (For more information about pronouns, see Chapter 28.)

   Correction: _____

   _____

5. This paragraph contains a type of run-on sentence called a comma splice. Two complete sentences are incorrectly connected with a comma. Identify the incorrect sentence. Then correct it in the space below. (For more information about run-on sentences, see Chapter 20.)

   Correction: _____

   _____

The Writer's Desk   Revise and Edit Your Paragraph

Revise and edit the paragraph that you wrote for the Writer's Desk on page 60. Ensure that your paragraph has unity, adequate support, and coherence. Also, correct any errors in grammar, spelling, punctuation, and mechanics.

REFLECT ON IT

Think about what you have learned in this chapter. If you do not know an answer, review that topic.

1. In an illustration paragraph, you _____

2. There are two ways to write illustration paragraphs. Explain each of them.

    a. Using a series of examples: _____

    b. Using an extended example: _____

    _____

3. List three transitional expressions that indicate an additional idea.

    _____

    _____

    _____

The Writer's Room **Topics for Illustration Paragraphs**

WRITING LINK

More Illustration Writing Topics
Chapter 21, Writer's Room topic 1 (page 328)
Chapter 24, Writer's Room topic 1 (page 367)
Chapter 28, Writer's Room topic 1 (page 424)

Writing Activity 1

Choose any of the following topics, or choose your own topic. Then write an illustration paragraph.

General Topics

1. ridiculous fads or fashions
2. good or bad habits
3. punishment for crimes
4. activities that relieve stress
5. possible future inventions
6. the consequences of losing your temper

College and Work-Related Topics

7. items that every student needs
8. qualities that can help you succeed
9. comfortable work clothes
10. reasons for working
11. tools or equipment needed for your job
12. qualities of a good boss

READING LINK

More Illustration Readings
"When the Legal Thing Isn't the Right Thing" by Deborah Mead (page 538)
"The Case for Affirmative Action" by Dave Malcolm (page 568)

Writing Activity 2

The image depicts a man who feels like he is walking on a tightrope, and the image expresses anxiety. What things make you feel worried? Write an illustration paragraph about things that make you feel worried or stressed.

ILLUSTRATION PARAGRAPH CHECKLIST

After you write your illustration paragraph, review the checklist on the inside front cover. Also ask yourself the following questions.

Does my topic sentence make a point that can be supported with examples?

Does my paragraph contain sufficient examples that clearly support the topic sentence?

Do I use transitions to smoothly connect my examples?

Have I arranged my examples in a logical order?

See Chapter 4 of the Visualizing Writing CD for an additional mini-lecture on **Illustration.**

ESSAY LINK

In a narrative essay, you can use first- or third-person narration.

person singular) or *we* (first-person plural). For example: "When I was a child, I thought that the world began and ended with me. I didn't know, or care, how other children felt. Thus, when schoolmates ridiculed a shy boy, I gleefully joined in." The *Narration at Work* paragraph on this page is an example of first-person narration.

2.   Use third-person narration.

In third-person narration, you do not refer to your own experiences. Instead, you describe what happened to somebody else. The story is told in the third person using *he, she, it,* or *they*. You might tell a story about your mother's childhood, or you might explain what happened during the last election. In this type of narration, you are simply an observer or storyteller; you are not a participant in the action. For example: "The students gathered to protest against the war. One student threw a chair through the window of the student center. Suddenly, people started pushing and shoving."

 Choose an Interesting Topic

When you write a narrative paragraph, try to choose a topic that will interest the reader. For example, the reader might not be interested if you write about the act of eating your lunch. However, if you write about a time when your best friend argued with a waiter during a meal, you could create an entertaining narrative paragraph.

Think about a topic that you personally find very interesting, and then share it with your readers.

Narration at Work

Joseph Roth, a boiler and pressure vessel inspector, used narrative writing in a memo he wrote to his supervisor.

As you know, I recently inspected the boiler and pressure vessels in the refinery on Highway 11. I had a few problems that I would like to mention. When I first arrived, the manager of the unit was uncooperative and initially tried to stop me from examining the boiler! After much discussion, I was finally permitted into the boiler room where I noticed several defects in the operation and condition of the equipment. Immediately, I saw that the low-water fuel cut-off chamber was filled with sludge and could not possibly function properly. Then I realized that the boiler heating surfaces were covered with scale. Finally, I found stress cracks in the tube ends and in tube seats. This is a sure sign of caustic imbrittlement, making the boiler unsafe to operate and in danger of exploding. I have asked that the boiler be taken out of service immediately. We must follow up to make sure that measures are being taken to replace the boiler.

PRACTICE 1

The author of the next paragraph was born in 1876 and was raised on the Pine Ridge Reservation in South Dakota. At the age of twelve, she was sent to a Quaker missionary school. Read the paragraph and answer the questions.

There were eight in our party of bronzed children who were going East with the missionaries. We had anticipated much pleasure from a ride on the train, but the **throngs** of staring palefaces disturbed and troubled us. Fair women, with tottering babies on each arm, stopped their haste and **scrutinized** the children of absent mothers. Large men, with heavy bundles in their hands, halted nearby, and **riveted** their glassy blue eyes upon us. I sank deep into the corner of my seat, for I resented being watched. Directly in front of me, children who were no larger than I hung themselves upon the backs of their seats, with their bold white faces toward me. Sometimes they took their forefingers out of their mouths and pointed at my moccasined feet. Their mothers, instead of **reproving** such rude curiosity, looked closely at me, and attracted their children's further notice to my blanket. This embarrassed me, and kept me constantly on the verge of tears.

—Sitkala Sa, *Impressions of an Indian Childhood* (1900)

throngs: crowd or group

scrutinized: examined in detail

riveted: concentrated; focused intently

reproving: criticizing severely

1. Underline the topic sentence of this paragraph. (Remember, the topic sentence is not always the first sentence.)

2. What type of narration is this? Circle the best answer.
   a. First person   b. Third person

3. Who or what is the paragraph about? _____

   _____

4. In a few words, explain what happened in this paragraph. _____

   _____

5. When did it happen? _____

6. Where did it happen? _____

7. By combining your answers to questions 3 through 6, write a one-sentence summary of the paragraph. Someone who has never read the paragraph should have a clear idea of the paragraph's content after reading your sentence.

   _____

   _____

   _____

PRACTICE 2

Read the next paragraph and answer the questions.

> The 1960s was a decade of profound social upheaval. The period began with optimism and excitement, as the young and charismatic John F. Kennedy was elected president of the United States. Idealistic civil rights workers, both black and white, sought to increase registration of black voters in the South and end housing discrimination in the North. The Reverend Dr. Martin Luther King attracted nationwide attention as he fought with **unprecedented** success (and immense dignity) to end segregation and racism in America without the use of violence. Soon, however, the idealism and optimism were shattered. President Kennedy was assassinated in 1963. The passage of the Civil Rights Act in 1965 was regarded by many new militant black groups as "too little, too late." Riots broke out in many cities in the summers of 1965–68. In 1968, both Martin Luther King and Robert Kennedy, the president's brother, were gunned down. But the most divisive force in American society in the 1960s was the Vietnam War.
>
> —Jeremy Yudkin, *Understanding Music*

unprecedented: something that never happened before; without precedent

1. Who or what is the paragraph about? _____

2. Underline the topic sentence of this paragraph.

3. What type of narration is this? Circle the best answer.
   a. First person   b. Third person

4. How does the writer support the topic sentence? List the smaller events that make up this narrative.

   _____

   _____

   _____

   _____

   _____

   _____

   _____

5. Do the supporting facts provide adequate support for the topic sentence?

   _____

ESSAY LINK

In a narrative essay, the thesis statement expresses the controlling idea.

DEVELOPING

The Topic Sentence

When you write a narrative paragraph, it is important to express a main point. If you simply describe a list of activities, it is boring for the reader. To make your paragraph interesting, make sure that your topic sentence has a controlling idea.

topic   controlling idea
When somebody broke into my house, <u>I felt totally invaded.</u>

controlling idea   topic
<u>I learned to be responsible</u> **during my first job.**

(**Hint**) **Make a Point**

In a narrative paragraph, the topic sentence should make a point. To help you find the controlling idea, you can ask yourself the following questions.

• What did I learn?   • How did it make me feel?

• How did I change?   • What is important about it?

Example:

Topic: *Moving out of the family home*

Possible controlling idea: *Becoming more independent*

topic   controlling idea
When I moved out of the family home, <u>I became more independent.</u>

PRACTICE 3

Practice writing topic sentences. Complete the following sentences by adding a controlling idea.

1. When I moved out of the family home, I felt (or I will feel) _____

   _____

2. In my first job, I learned _____

   _____

3. When I read _____, I realized _____

   _____

The Writer's Desk **Write Topic Sentences**

Write a topic sentence for each of the following topics. You can look for ideas in the Warm Up on page 64. Each topic sentence should mention the topic and express a controlling idea.

EXAMPLE:

Topic: A family story

Topic sentence: *When my father found his first job in America, there was a humorous misunderstanding.*

1. Topic: A serious decision

   Topic sentence: _____

   _____

2. Topic: A life-changing event

   Topic sentence: _____

   _____

3. Topic: A funny story

   Topic sentence: _____

   _____

The Supporting Ideas

A narrative paragraph should contain specific details so that the reader understands what happened. To come up with the details, ask yourself a series of questions. Your paragraph should provide answers to these questions.

- Who is the paragraph about?
- What happened?
- When did it happen?
- Where did it happen?
- Why did it happen?
- How did it happen?

When you recount a story to a friend, you may go back and add details, saying, "I forgot to mention something." When you write a narrative paragraph, however, your sequence of events should be clearly chronological so that your reader can follow your story.

The Writer's Desk Develop Supporting Ideas

Generate supporting ideas for each topic. List what happened.

EXAMPLE: A family story   1. A serious decision

dad saw an ad   _____

"busboy" job   _____

bowling alley   _____

dad didn't understand ad   _____

man gave him a dishcloth   _____

2. A life-changing event   3. A funny story

_____   _____
_____   _____
_____   _____
_____   _____
_____   _____

The Paragraph Plan

Before you write a narrative paragraph, it is a good idea to make a paragraph plan. Write down main events in the order in which they occurred. To make your narration more complete, include details about each event.

ESSAY LINK

In a narrative essay, you place the thesis statement in the introduction. Each main event is developed in a supporting paragraph.

TOPIC SENTENCE: When my father found his first job in America, there was a humorous misunderstanding.

Support 1:   —In a newspaper, he found an ad for a busboy.
Details: —job was in a bowling alley
　　　　　　—dad didn't speak English

Support 2:   —He went to the bowling alley.
Details: —applied for the job, and got it
　　　　　　—was excited

Support 3:   —On his first day, his boss asked him to put on an apron and told him to pick up some dishes in the bowling alley's restaurant.
Details: —father was disappointed and asked, "Where's the bus?"
　　　　　　—thought that a "busboy" would work on a bus

The Writer's Desk **Write a Paragraph Plan**

Choose one of the topic sentences that you wrote for the Writer's Desk on page 69. Write a paragraph plan using some of the supporting ideas that you have generated. Include details for each supporting idea.

Topic sentence: _____

Support 1: _____

Details: _____

_____

_____

Support 2: _____

Details: _____

_____

_____

Support 3: _____

Details: _____

_____

_____

The First Draft

After you outline your ideas in a plan, you are ready to write the first draft. Remember to write complete sentences. You might include transitional words or expressions to help your ideas flow smoothly.

Transitional Words and Expressions

Transitions can help you show a sequence of events. The next transitional words are useful in narrative paragraphs.

To Show a Sequence of Events			
afterward	finally	in the end	meanwhile
after that	first	last	next
eventually	in the beginning	later	then

The Writer's Desk Write the First Draft

In the previous Writer's Desk, you developed a paragraph plan. Now write the first draft of your narrative paragraph. Before you write, carefully review your paragraph plan and make any necessary changes.

REVISING AND EDITING

Revise and Edit a Narrative Paragraph

When you finish writing a narrative paragraph, carefully review your work and revise it to make the events as clear as possible to your readers. Check that you have organized events chronologically, and remove any irrelevant details. Before you revise and edit your own paragraph, practice revising and editing a student paragraph.

PRACTICE 4

Read the next student paragraph and answer the questions.

When my father found his first job in America, there was a humorous misunderstanding. My father, originally from Mexico City, had just moved to Dallas, Texas, and he did not speak English. One day, he sees an ad for a busboy job. He wanted the job, so he called the number in the ad. Later that day, he went for an interview in a bowling alley. The restaurant manager spoke with my father and offered him the job. That night, my father went home feeling very excited. The next day, when he arrived for work, the manager gave him an apron and asked him to pick up some dishes in the bowling alley restaurant. My father, feeling confused and dissapointed, asked, "Where is the bus?" He thought that a busboy would work on a bus collecting tickets. The owner laught and explained what a busboy's job is. When my father told the family this story, everybody thought it was funny, but they were also proud of his perseverance because today he has a university degree and a good job.

Revising

1. Write down the two parts of the topic sentence.

    topic   +   controlling idea

    _____

2. What type of order do the specific details follow? Circle the best answer.
    a. Space   b. Time
    c. Emphatic   d. No order

3. What are some transitional expressions that the author used?

    _____

4. What type of narration is this?
    a. First person   b. Third person

Editing

5. This paragraph contains a tense inconsistency. The tense shifts for no apparent reason. Identify the incorrect sentence. Then write the correct sentence in the space below. (You can find more information about tense consistency in Chapter 26.)

    Correction: _____

    _____

6. This paragraph contains two misspelled words. Identify and correct them.

Misspelled words	**Corrections**
_____	_____
_____	_____

The Writer's Desk **Revise and Edit Your Paragraph**

Revise and edit the paragraph that you wrote for Writer's Desk: Write the First Draft on page 72. Ensure that your paragraph has unity, adequate support, and coherence. Also correct any errors in grammar, spelling, punctuation, and mechanics.

REFLECT ON IT

Think about what you have learned in this chapter. If you do not know an answer, review that topic.

1. In narrative writing, you _____

2. What are the differences between the two following types of narration?

   First person: _____

   _____

   Third person: _____

   _____

3. What are some questions that you should you ask yourself when you write a narrative paragraph?

   _____

4. What organizational method is commonly used in narrative paragraphs? Circle the best answer.

   a. Space order   b. Time order   c. Emphatic order

 The Writer's Room **Topics for Narrative Paragraphs**

WRITING LINK

More Narrative Writing Topics

Chapter 28, Writer's Room topic 2 (page 424)
Chapter 30, Writer's Room topics 1 and 2 (pages 448–449)

Writing Activity 1

Choose any of the following topics, or choose your own topic. Then write a narrative paragraph.

General Topics

1. a proud moment
2. a risky adventure
3. a move to a new place
4. a surprising coincidence
5. a news event that affected you
6. a memorable family story

College and Work-Related Topics

7. a embarrassing incident at college or work
8. an inspiring teacher or instructor
9. a positive or negative job interview
10. a difficult co-worker
11. your best experience at work
12. your first job

Writing Activity 2

Have you ever lived through an earthquake, a tornado, a flood, a large storm, an extended power outage, or any other event caused by nature? What happened? What did you do? Write a narrative paragraph about a big storm or a natural event that you have lived through.

READING LINK

More Narrative Readings
"My Head Rolled in Syria" by Josh Freed (page 541)
"The Diagnosis" by Richard Selzer (page 586)

NARRATIVE PARAGRAPH CHECKLIST

As you write your narrative paragraph, review the checklist on the inside front cover. Also ask yourself the following questions.

☐ Does my topic sentence clearly express the topic of the narration?

☐ Does my topic sentence contain a controlling idea that is meaningful and interesting?

☐ Does my paragraph answer most of the following questions: *who, what, when, where, why, how?*

☐ Do I use transitional expressions that help clarify the order of events?

☐ Do I include details to make my narration more interesting?

See Chapter 5 of the Visualizing Writing CD for an additional mini-lecture on **Narration.**

CHAPTER 6

Description

CONTENTS

Exploring
- Explore Topics
- What Is Description?
- The Descriptive Paragraph

Developing
- The Topic Sentence
- The Supporting Ideas
- The Paragraph Plan
- The First Draft

Revising and Editing
- Revise and Edit a Descriptive Paragraph

A fine artist uses a variety of colors and brush strokes to make an impression on the viewer. In descriptive writing, you use words to create an image that your readers can visualize.

EXPLORING

Explore Topics

In the Warm Up, you will try an exploring strategy to generate ideas about different topics.

The Writer's Desk Warm Up

Think about the following questions, and write down the first ideas that come to your mind. Try to think of two or three ideas for each topic.

EXAMPLE: What are some useless products or other items that you own?

The plastic apple cutter (makes six perfect pieces). Never use it.
Useless toy called a Furby. As a kid, I used it a couple of times.
The juicer. It sits and collects dust.

1. What were some very emotional moments in your life? (Think about two or three moments when you felt extreme joy, sadness, excitement, anxiety, or other strong emotions.)

_____

_____

_____

2. Describe your food quirks. What are your unusual tastes or eating habits? Which foods do you really love or hate?

_____

_____

_____

3. What are some very busy places?

_____

_____

_____

What Is Description?

Description creates vivid images in the reader's mind by portraying people, places, or moments in detail.

You use description every day. At home, you might describe a new friend to your family, or you might describe an object that you bought. At college, you might describe the structure of a cell or the results of a lab experiment. At work, you may describe a new product to a client, or you could describe the qualities of potential clients to your boss. The *Description at Work* paragraph on the following page shows how one company used description in their brochure.

The Descriptive Paragraph

When you write a descriptive paragraph, focus on three main points.

1. **Create a dominant impression.**
   The dominant impression is the overall atmosphere that you wish to convey. It can be a strong feeling, mood, or image. For example, if you are describing a business meeting, you can emphasize the tension in the room.

ESSAY LINK

In descriptive essays, you should also create a dominant impression, express your attitude toward the subject, and include concrete details.

Description at Work

In this excerpt from an Alba Tours travel brochure, the writer describes the amenities offered at a vacation resort.

With its lavish open-air lobby complete with curving staircase, the gleaming marble columns, and the rich mahogany furniture, Sandals Dunn's River captures the romance of an Italian-style Mediterranean paradise. The centerpiece of this spectacular resort is one of Jamaica's largest swimming pools with its own cascading waterfall and swim-up bar. You can try out the facilities at the open-air fitness center, play some tennis, or shoot a round of golf at the Sandals Golf and Country Club where greens fees and transfers are included. After that, why not take a complimentary tour of the world-famous Dunn's River Falls or just relax in the Oriental hot and cold plunge pools followed by a soothing sauna?

2. **Express your attitude toward the subject.**

   Do you feel positive, negative, or neutral toward the subject? For example, if you feel positive about your best friend, then the details of your paragraph should convey the good feelings you have toward him or her. If you describe a place that you do not like, then your details should express how uncomfortable that place makes you feel. You might make a neutral description of a science lab experiment.

3. **Include concrete details.**

   Details will enable a reader to visualize the person, place, or situation that is being described. You can use active verbs and adjectives so that the reader imagines the scene more clearly. You can also use **imagery,** which is description using the five senses. Review the following examples of imagery.

Sight	At five-foot-nine, and a hundred and seventy-four pounds, I was muscularly inferior to the guys on the same athletic level and quite conscious of the fact.

   —H. D., "Dying to Be Bigger"

Sound	They hooked wrist-thick hanks of laghmien noodles and shoveled them into their mouths, slurping, sucking, inhaling, and chomping off portions. . . .

   —Jeffrey Tayler, "A Cacophony of Noodles"

Smell	For several days the wind blew, full of dust scents and the dryness of sagebrush, carrying eastward our own autumn smell of falling maple leaves, green walnuts, and the warm lemon odor of quince and yellow apples.

   —Josephine Johnson, "September Harvest"

Touch   My heart started racing, perspiration dripped down my face causing my glasses to slide, and I had a hard time breathing.

—Bebe Moore Campbell, "Dancing with Fear"

Taste   I asked for fresh lemonade, and got it—delicious, and cold, and tangy with real fruit.

—Mary Stewart, *My Brother Michael*

PRACTICE 1

Read the next paragraph and answer the questions.

> He had changed since his New Haven years. Now he was a sturdy straw-haired man of thirty with a rather hard mouth and a **supercilious** manner. Two shining arrogant eyes had established dominance over his face and gave him the appearance of always leaning aggressively forward. Not even the **effeminate swank** of his riding clothes could hide the enormous power of that body—he seemed to fill those glistening boots until he strained the top lacing, and you could see a great pack of muscle shifting when his shoulder moved under his thin coat. It was a body capable of enormous leverage—a cruel body.
>
> —F. Scott Fitzgerald, *The Great Gatsby*

supercilious: arrogant

effeminate: having feminine qualities

swank: flashy appearance

1. What is the attitude of the writer toward the subject of the paragraph? Circle the best answer.

   a. Positive   b. Negative   c. Neutral

2. Write at least two examples that support your answer to question 1.

   _____

   _____

3. What is the dominant impression conveyed through this paragraph? Circle the best answer.

   a. Weakness   b. Laziness   c. Femininity   d. Strength

4. Write at least two examples from the text that show the dominant impression.

   _____

   _____

5. What sense is used to describe the character portrayed in this paragraph? Circle the best answer.

   a. Touch   b. Smell   c. Sight   d. Sound   e. Taste

6. Identify an example of imagery, and write it in the following spaces.

   _____

   _____

ESSAY LINK

In a descriptive essay, the thesis statement expresses the controlling idea.

DEVELOPING

When you write a descriptive paragraph, choose a subject that lends itself to description. In other words, find a subject to describe that appeals to the senses. For example, you can describe the sounds, sights, and smells in a bakery.

The Topic Sentence

In the topic sentence of a descriptive paragraph, you should convey a dominant impression about the subject. The dominant impression is the overall impression or feeling that the topic inspires.

topic   controlling idea

When Amory was five, he was already a delightful companion for her.

—F. Scott Fitzgerald, *This Side of Paradise*

topic   controlling idea

Lady Patricia was a perfect example of beauty that is but skin deep.

—Nancy Mitford, *Love in a Cold Climate*

The Writer's Desk **Write Topic Sentences**

Write a topic sentence for each of the following topics. You can look for ideas in the Warm Up on pages 76–77. Each topic sentence should state what you are describing and contain a controlling idea.

EXAMPLE:

Topic: A useless product

Topic sentence: *When I was nine years old, I was desperate to own a Furby.*

1. Topic: An emotional moment

   Topic sentence: _____

   _____

2. Topic: Food quirks (unusual food habits or foods you love or hate)

   Topic sentence: _____

   _____

3. Topic: A busy place

   Topic sentence: _____

   _____

The Supporting Ideas

After you have developed an effective topic sentence, generate supporting details. The details can be placed in space, time, or emphatic order.

 Using Vivid Language

When you write a descriptive paragraph, try to use **vivid language.** Use specific action verbs and adjectives to create a clear picture of what you are describing.

She looked ~~nice.~~ *stunning*   (Use a more vivid, specific adjective.)

The young man ~~left~~ *bolted from* the room.   (Use a more vivid, specific verb.)

PRACTICE 2

Each sentence contains a familiar word in italics. Write down at least two more descriptive ways to say each word. Try to find words that are more specific.

EXAMPLE:

She *laughed* during her gym class.   *giggled, snickered, chuckled*

1. I *ran* to work. _____

2. She *shouted* at her sister. _____

3. She felt *surprised* when she won the award. _____

4. That is a *bad* movie. _____

5. The child was *nice.* _____

List Sensory Details

To create a dominant impression, think about your topic, and make a list of your feelings and impressions. These details can include imagery (images that appeal to sight, sound, hearing, taste, and smell).

> **TOPIC:** An abandoned building
>
> **Details:**
> —damp floors
> —boarded-up windows
> —broken glass
> —graffiti on the walls
> —musty
> —gray bricks
> —chipping paint

 ESSAY LINK

When you plan a descriptive essay, it is useful to list sensory details.

The Writer's Desk **List Sensory Details**

Think about images, impressions, and feelings that the following topics inspire in you. Refer to your topic sentences on page 80, and make a list under each topic.

EXAMPLE: A useless product:

Furby looks like a strange bird

black and white fur

round owl–like eyes

pointy beak that opens

a hard plastic body under the fur

speaks in a low, gurgling voice

not cuddly

1. An emotional moment: _____

_____

_____

_____

_____

_____

_____

2. Food quirks: _____

_____

_____

_____

_____

_____

_____

3. A busy place: _____

_____

_____

_____

_____

_____

_____

The Paragraph Plan

A descriptive paragraph should contain specific details so that the reader can clearly imagine what is being described. When you make a paragraph plan, remember to include concrete details. Also think about the organizational method that you will use.

ESSAY LINK

In a descriptive essay, place the thesis statement in the introduction. Then, develop each supporting idea in a body paragraph.

TOPIC SENTENCE: When I was nine years old, I was desperate to own a Furby.

Support 1: The toy looks like a small owl.
  Details: —large round eyes
  —small yellow beak

Support 2: It learns to speak and repeat words.
  Details: —has a low, gurgling voice
  —does not say many things

Support 3: The hard plastic body is not cuddly.
  Details: —cannot bring it to bed
  —sits on a counter
Support 4: The toy becomes boring quickly.
  Details: —after it says a few words, the novelty wears off
  —cannot really be played with because it is fragile

The Writer's Desk **Write a Paragraph Plan**

Choose one of the topic sentences that you wrote for the Writer's Desk on page 80, and write a detailed paragraph plan. You can include some of the sensory details that you have generated in the previous Writer's Desk on page 82.

Topic sentence: _____

_____

Support 1: _____
  Details: _____

_____

_____

Support 2: _____
  Details: _____

_____

_____

Support 3: _____
  Details: _____

_____

_____

The First Draft

After you outline your ideas in a plan, you are ready to write the first draft. Remember to write complete sentences. You might include transitional words or expressions to help your ideas flow smoothly.

Transitional Words and Expressions

You can use space order to describe a person, place, or thing. The following transitions are useful in descriptive paragraphs.

To Show Place or Position			
above	beyond	in the distance	outside
behind	closer in	nearby	over there
below	farther out	on the left/right	under
beside	in front	on top	underneath

The Writer's Desk Write the First Draft

In the previous Writer's Desk on page 83, you developed a paragraph plan. Now write the first draft of your descriptive paragraph. Before you write, carefully review your paragraph plan and make any necessary changes.

REVISING AND EDITING

Revise and Edit a Descriptive Paragraph

When you finish writing a descriptive paragraph, carefully review your work and revise it to make the description as clear as possible to your readers. Check that you have organized your steps logically, and remove any irrelevant details.

PRACTICE 3

Read the following student paragraph and answer the questions.

When I was nine years old, I was desperate to own a Furby. In 1998, an onslaught of television commercials announced the product, and a Furby craze developed. I begged my mother for the furry little toy. Even though it was expensive and hard to find. I whined so much that my mother bought me one for my birthday. When I opened the package, I was initialy thrilled. It looked like a small owl, with large round eyes and a yellow pointy beak. Black and white fur covered its hard plastic body. Unfortunately, I could not cuddle it and bring it to bed because it was too fragile. The toy was suppose to speak, but the instructions were complicated. I became disappointed because it only repeated a few words in a low gurgling voice, and the toy quickly became boring. After two weeks, I dropped my Furby, and it stopped speaking, so I never played with it again. I have other toys that I stopped using soon after I bought them. Now the Furby is in a box somewhere in my closet, and I feel ridiculous for having wanted such a useless product.

Revising

1. Underline the topic sentence.

2. What is the dominant impression in this paragraph? Circle the best answer.
   a. Anger   b. Disappointment   c. Joy   d. Tension

3. Highlight three vivid verbs in the paragraph.

4. Revise the paragraph for unity. Cross out a sentence that does not belong.

Editing

5. A fragment lacks a subject or verb and is an incomplete sentence. Identify and correct one fragment in the paragraph. (You can find more information about fragments in Chapter 20.)

6. This paragraph contains a misspelled word. Circle it and correct it.

7. This paragraph contains a past participle error. Circle and correct it. (You can find more information about past participles in Chapter 23.)

The Writer's Desk Revise and Edit Your Paragraph

Revise and edit the paragraph that you wrote for the previous Writer's Desk. Ensure that your paragraph has unity, adequate support, and coherence. Also correct any errors in grammar, spelling, punctuation, and mechanics.

REFLECT ON IT

Think about what you have learned in this chapter. If you do not know an answer, review that topic.

1. What are the main features of a descriptive paragraph? _____

_____

_____

2. Define imagery. _____

3. Look at the familiar words below. Write down at least two more descriptive ways to say each word. Try to find words that are more specific.

a. Cute _____ b. Angry _____

c. Sad _____ d. Mean _____

 The Writer's Room **Topics for Descriptive Paragraphs**

Writing Activity 1

Choose any of the following topics, or choose your own topic. Then write a descriptive paragraph.

General Topics

1. a coffee shop
2. an interesting house or building
3. a useless product or item
4. an evening out
5. a scene from nature
6. a silly fashion trend

College and Work-Related Topics

1. a quiet area on campus
2. vn unusual student or co-worker
3. a loud place
4. appropriate work clothing
5. a difficult job
6. an embarrassing moment at work

WRITING LINK

More Descriptive Writing Topics

Chapter 26, Writer's Room topic 1 (page 388)

Chapter 30, Writer's Room topic 2 (page 449)

Chapter 35, Writer's Room topic 4 (page 511)

Writing Activity 2

Visit a public place and take notes about the sights, sounds, and smells. Then, write a paragraph describing that place. Include vivid details.

DESCRIPTIVE PARAGRAPH CHECKLIST

As you write your description paragraph, review the checklist on the inside front cover. Also ask yourself the following questions.

Does my topic sentence clearly show what I will describe?

Does my topic sentence have a controlling idea that makes a point about the topic?

Does my paragraph make a dominant impression?

Does my paragraph contain supporting details that appeal to the reader's senses?

Do I use vivid language?

READING LINK

More Descriptive Readings
"Bound Feet" by Jung Chang (page 580)
"Aunt Tee" by Maya Angelou (page 530)

See Chapter 6 of the Visualizing Writing CD for an additional mini-lecture on **Description.**

CHAPTER 7

Process

> *It is easier to know how to do something than it is to do it.*
> —CHINESE PROVERB

CONTENTS

Exploring
• Explore Topics
• What Is a Process?
• The Process Paragraph

Developing
• The Topic Sentence
• The Supporting Ideas
• The Paragraph Plan
• The First Draft

Revising and Editing
• Revise and Edit a Process Paragraph

A pastry chef begins with basic ingredients and follows a process to end up with a delicious dessert. In process writing, you can describe how to do something.

EXPLORING

Explore Topics

In the Warm Up, you will try an exploring strategy to generate ideas about different topics.

The Writer's Desk Warm Up

Think about the following questions, and write down the first ideas that come to your mind. Try to think of two or three ideas for each topic.

EXAMPLE: Imagine that you have a new opportunity and want to leave your current job. What are some things that you should do before you quit your job?

-give supervisor a lot of notice (needs time to hire someone else)

-ask for a reference letter (I might need it later)

-have a going-away party, and thank co-workers and supervisor

1. When you feel stressed, what do you do to relax?

_____

_____

_____

2. What are some things you should do to succeed in college?

_____

_____

_____

3. What are some events, holidays, or ceremonies that require a great deal of preparation?

_____

_____

_____

What Is a Process?

A **process** is a series of steps done in chronological order. In process writing, you explain how to do something, how an incident took place, or how something works.

You explain processes every day. At home, you may explain to a family member how to use an electronic appliance. You may need to give written instructions to a baby-sitter or caregiver. At college, you may explain how to perform a scientific experiment or how a new product was invented. At work, you may explain how to operate a machine or how to do a particular job. The *Process at Work* paragraph on the following page shows how process writing is used in a workplace situation.

The Process Paragraph

There are two main types of process paragraphs.

ESSAY LINK

Process essays also focus on completing or understanding a process.

- **Complete a process.** This type of paragraph contains directions on how to complete a particular task. For example, a writer might explain how to paint a picture, how to repair a leaky faucet, or how to get a job. The reader should be able to follow the directions and complete the task.
- **Understand a process.** This type of paragraph explains how something works or how something happens. In other words, the goal is to help the reader understand a process rather than do a process. For example, a writer might explain how the heart pumps blood to other organs in the body or how a country elects its political leaders.

Process at Work

In this memo to fellow employees, Mawlid Abdul Aziz, a network administration assistant, uses process writing to explain how to install antivirus software on a computer.

Due to a new security threat circulating on the Internet, the IT department strongly recommends that you update your antivirus software. To do so, double-click on the antivirus icon at the bottom right on your computer screen (system tray). The correct icon should appear at the far left of the row of icons. Then, a window will appear that is called the virus scan console. In this window, there are several items, one of which is labeled "Automatic Update." By double-clicking on that button, another window will appear that contains the button "Run Now." Click on it, and after a minute or two, there will be a message box saying "completed." Please do not hesitate to contact the IT department if you encounter any difficulty with this procedure.

PRACTICE 1

Read the next paragraph and answer the questions.

> Packing for a move does not have to be stressful. Moving is already stressful enough. If you are going to pack up your house, however, you might as well do it properly. Do not spend time and money transporting junk. Take a deep breath and go through it all. Have a garage sale, or give junk to organizations that can put your unwanted items to good use. Now, set aside space for packing, and, if you can, **designate** a table or workbench so you can pack at a comfortable height. "You will also want," says Dan Descheneau of Two Small Men With Big Hearts Moving, "a portable packing kit with marking pens, tape measure, tape, twine, and scissors. Carry it with you around the home as you pack." Other things you will need are boxes, bubble wrap, or newsprint. The best way to pack is room by room. Pack from least to most important items. Begin with seasonal clothing, sports equipment, etc. Things you will need first and during the move should be packed last. This includes telephones, address books, bills, clothes, toiletries, medicine, maps, food, and drink.

> —Joel Ceausu, "How to Pack Up a House," *Montreal Gazette*

designate: to choose

1. a. What is the topic of this paragraph? _____

   _____

   b. What is the controlling idea in the topic sentence? _____

   _____

2. What type of process paragraph is this? Circle the best answer.
   a. Complete a process.   b. Understand a process.

3. Look at the paragraph and number each step. What are the main steps that you should take when you move? List each step.

   _____

   _____

   _____

   _____

   _____

4. This paragraph does not have a concluding sentence. Write a concluding sentence that sums up the main ideas in this paragraph.

   _____

   _____

PRACTICE 2

Scrabble, one of the world's most popular board games, has an interesting history. Read the next paragraph and answer the questions.

Alfred Mosher Butts, a quiet architect from Poughkeepsie, New York, was unemployed when he invented the world's most popular word game. Lexico was played without a board, and players earned points based on the lengths of words that they could build. By carefully analyzing the *New York Times*, Butts discovered that *S* is the most frequently used letter, so he reduced the number of *S*'s in the game, and he gave additional points to letters such as *J*, *Q*, and *Z*. Unable to interest game companies, Butts produced the games himself and sold them to friends. Then in 1938, inspired by crossword puzzles, Butts combined the letters with a playing board and renamed his game Criss-Cross, but game manufacturers continued to reject his idea. Things finally changed for Butts in 1948, when a small entrepreneur, James Brunot, picked up Butts's game and renamed it Scrabble. By 1953, the demand for Scrabble was so great that a large manufacturer licensed and mass-produced the game. According to Mattel Incorporated, Scrabble is now the world's best-selling board game, with over 100 million copies sold in 29 different languages.

—Iannick Di Sanza, student

1. Underline the topic sentence of this paragraph.

2. What type of process paragraph is this? Circle the best answer.

   a. Complete a process   b. Understand a process

3. Look at the paragraph and number the steps that Alfred Butts took to complete his board game.

PRACTICE 3

For each of the following topics, write *C* if it explains how to complete a process, or write *U* if it explains how to understand a process (how something works or how something happens).

1. How to discipline a child   _____

2. The stages in a child's development   _____

3. How a cell phone works   _____

4. Things to remember when you write a song   _____

5. Five ways to keep your motorcycle in top condition   _____

6. The chemical process of a firefly's light   _____

DEVELOPING

ESSAY LINK

In a process essay, the thesis statement expresses the controlling idea.

When you write a process paragraph, choose a process that you can easily cover in a single paragraph. For example, you might be able to explain how to send an e-mail message in a single paragraph; however, you would need much more than a paragraph to explain how to use a particular computer software program.

The Topic Sentence

In a process paragraph, the topic sentence states what process you will be explaining and what readers will be able to do or understand after they have read the paragraph.

topic   controlling idea
To calm your child during a tantrum, <u>follow the next steps</u>.

controlling idea   topic
<u>With inexpensive materials</u>, **you can redecorate a room in your house.**

 Make a Point

Your topic sentence should not simply announce the topic. It should make a point about the topic.

Announces: This is how you do speed dating.

                                 controlling idea   topic
Correct: <u>It is surprisingly easy and efficient</u> **to meet someone using speed dating.**

The Writer's Desk **Write Topic Sentences**

Write a topic sentence for each of the following topics. You can look for ideas in the Warm Up on pages 88–89. Each topic sentence should state the process and should contain a controlling idea.

EXAMPLE:

Topic: How to leave a job

Topic sentence: _If you want to leave your job on a positive note, there are a few things that you should consider._

1. Topic: How to relax

   Topic sentence: _____

   _____

2. Topic: How to succeed in college

   Topic sentence: _____

   _____

3. Topic: How to prepare for a specific event

   Topic sentence: _____

   _____

The Supporting Ideas

A process paragraph contains a series of steps. When you develop supporting ideas for a process paragraph, think about the main steps that are necessary to complete the process. Most process paragraphs use time order.

ESSAY LINK

In an essay, each body paragraph could describe a process. For example, in an essay about how to get rich, one body paragraph could be about buying lottery tickets and another could be about inventing a product.

 Give Steps, Not Examples

When you explain how to complete a process, describe each step. Do not simply list examples of the process.

Topic: How to Get Rich

List of Examples	Steps in the Process
- write a bestseller	- do market research
- win the lottery	- find a specific need
- invent a product	- invent a product to fulfill that need
- inherit money	- heavily promote the product

The Writer's Desk List Main Steps

Think about three or four essential steps for each process. Make a list under each topic.

EXAMPLE: How to leave a job

explain your reason for going

give enough notice

ask for a reference letter

find out about benefits

I. How to relax

_____

_____

_____

_____

2. How to succeed in college

_____

_____

_____

_____

3. How to prepare for an event

_____

_____

_____

_____

ESSAY LINK

In a process essay, place the thesis statement in the introduction. Then use each body paragraph to explain a step in the process.

The Paragraph Plan

A paragraph plan helps you organize your topic sentence and supporting details before writing a first draft. Decide which steps and which details your reader will really need to complete the process or understand it. Write down the steps in chronological order.

> **TOPIC SENTENCE:**   If you want to leave your job on a positive note, there are a few things that you should consider.
>
> **Step 1:**   Give positive reasons for leaving.
> **Details:**   —do not complain about the company
> —say you need a new challenge
> **Step 2:**   Give employers enough notice.
> **Details:**   —the company might need time to hire a replacement
> **Step 3:**   Ask for a reference letter.
> **Details:**   —may need it in the future
> **Step 4:**   Find out about employment benefits.
> **Details:**   —might get unused vacation pay

 Include Necessary Tools or Supplies

When you are writing a plan for a process paragraph, remember to include any special tools or supplies a reader will need to complete the process. For example, if you want to explain how to pack for a move, you should mention that you need boxes, felt-tip markers, newsprint, twine, scissors, and tape.

The Writer's Desk **Write a Paragraph Plan**

Choose one of the topic sentences that you wrote for the Writer's Desk on page 93, and then list the main steps to complete the process. Also add details and examples that will help to explain each step.

Topic sentence: _____

_____

Supporting points:

Step 1: _____

   Details: _____

_____

Step 2: _____

   Details: _____

_____

Step 3: _____

   Details: _____

_____

Step 4: _____

   Details: _____

_____

Step 5: _____

   Details: _____

_____

The First Draft

After you outline your ideas in a plan, you are ready to write the first draft. Remember to write complete sentences. You might include transitional words or expressions to help your ideas flow smoothly.

 Using Commands

In process writing, address the reader directly. For example, instead of writing "You should travel in a group," you could simply write "Travel in a group."

Transitional Words and Expressions

Most process paragraphs explain a process using time (or chronological) order. The following transitions are useful in process paragraphs.

To Begin a Process	To Continue a Process		To End a Process
(at) first	after that	later	eventually
initially	afterward	meanwhile	finally
the first step	also	second	in the end
	furthermore	then	ultimately
	in addition	third	

The Writer's Desk Write the First Draft

In the previous Writer's Desk on page 95, you developed a paragraph plan. Now write the first draft of your process paragraph. Before you write, carefully review your paragraph plan and make any necessary changes.

REVISING AND EDITING

Revise and Edit a Process Paragraph

When you finish writing a process paragraph, carefully review your work and revise it to make the process as clear as possible to your readers. Check to make sure that you have organized your steps chronologically and remove any irrelevant details.

PRACTICE 4

Read the next student paragraph and answer the questions.

If you want to leave your job on a positive note, there are a few things that you should consider. First, give a positive reason for leaving. Instead of complaining about something in the company, you could say that you need a change and want a different challenge. Give as much notice as possible, this will leave a favorable impression. It will also give your boss time to find a replacement. If you think you deserve it, ask for a reference letter. Even if you already have a new job, the reference letter could be useful at a future date. Find out if you are entitled to benefits. You may be eligible for back pay or vacation pay. Business consultant Cho Matsu says "The impression you make when you leave a job could have an impact on your future career".

Revising

1. Underline the topic sentence.

2. The author uses *first* to introduce the first step. Subsequent steps would be more clearly recognizable if the writer had used more transitions. Indicate, with a number, where more transitional expressions could be added, and write possible examples on the lines provided.

_____

_____

_____

3. How does the writer conclude the paragraph?
   a. With a prediction   b. With a suggestion   c. With a quotation

Editing

4. This paragraph contains a type of run-on sentence called a comma splice. Two complete sentences are incorrectly connected with a comma. Identify and correct the comma splice. (For more information about run-on sentences, see Chapter 20.)

5. This paragraph contains two punctuation errors in the direct quotation. Correct the mistakes directly on the paragraph. (For more information about punctuating quotations, see Chapter 34.)

The Writer's Desk   Revise and Edit Your Paragraph

Revise and edit the paragraph that you wrote for the previous Writer's Desk. Ensure that your paragraph has unity, adequate support, and coherence. Also correct any errors in grammar, spelling, punctuation, and mechanics.

REFLECT ON IT

Think about what you have learned in this unit. If you do not know an answer, review that topic.

1. What are the two types of process paragraphs? Briefly explain each type.

   a. _____

   _____

   b. _____

   _____

2. What organizational method is generally used in process writing? Circle the best answer.

   a. Space order   b. Time order   c. Emphatic order

3. Why are transitional words important in process writing?

   _____

   _____

 The Writer's Room **Topics for Process Paragraphs**

WRITING LINK

More Process Writing Topics
Chapter 19, Writer's Room Topic 3 (page 305)
Chapter 26, Writer's Room Topic 2 (page 388)
Chapter 32, Writer's Room Topic 4 (page 476)

Writing Activity I

Choose any of the following topics, or choose your own topic. Then write a process paragraph.

General Topics

1. how to make your home safe
2. how to decorate a room with very little money
3. how to make a friend
4. how to break up with a mate
5. how to train a pet
6. how to build something

College and Work-Related Topics

7. how to choose a college
8. how to stay motivated at college
9. how to prepare for a job interview
10. how to get along with your co-workers
11. how to organize your desk or tools
12. how something was discovered

READING LINK

More Process Reading
"How to Get All-Day Energy" by Maria Noel Mandile (page 536)
"Enough Is Enough" by Judy Sheindlin, with Josh Getlin (page 545)

Writing Activity 2

Pop artist Andy Warhol once said that everyone would be famous for fifteen minutes. Think of some processes related to fame. Some ideas might be how to become famous, how to stay famous, how to lose fame, how to survive fame, or how to meet a celebrity. Then, write a process paragraph.

PROCESS PARAGRAPH CHECKLIST

As you write your process paragraph, review the checklist on the inside front cover. Also ask yourself the following questions.

☐ Does my topic sentence make a point about the process?

☐ Do I include all of the steps in the process?

☐ Do I clearly explain each step so my reader can accomplish the process or understand it?

☐ Do I mention all of the supplies that my reader needs to complete the process?

☐ Do I use transitions to connect all of the steps in the process?

See Chapter 7 of the Visualizing Writing CD for an additional mini-lecture on **Process.**

CHAPTER 8

Definition

" A successful marriage requires falling in love many times, always with the same person. "

—MIGNON MCLAUGHLIN
American journalist (1913–1983)

CONTENTS

Exploring
• Explore Topics
• What Is Definition?
• The Definition
  Paragraph

Developing
• The Topic Sentence
• The Supporting Ideas
• The Paragraph Plan
• The First Draft

Revising and Editing
• Revise and Edit
  a Definition Paragraph

For many people, the definition of happiness is having a loving relationship with someone. In definition writing, you define what a term means.

EXPLORING

Explore Topics

In the Warm Up, you will try an exploring strategy to generate ideas about different topics.

The Writer's Desk **Warm Up**

Think about the following questions, and write down the first ideas that come to your mind. Try to think of two or three ideas for each topic.

EXAMPLE: What is an optimist? Think of some qualities that an
            optimist has.

Always sees the bright side of life

Doesn't dwell on bad things and hopes for the best

Is usually pretty happy, which can be annoying

1. What are some qualities that a leader should have?

_____

_____

_____

2. What is talent? Give examples of talent.

_____

_____

_____

3. What are some characteristics of a workaholic?

_____

_____

_____

What Is Definition?

When you **define,** you explain the meaning of a word. Some terms have concrete meanings, and you can define them in a few words. For example, a pebble is "a small stone." Other words, such as *culture, happiness,* or *evil,* are more abstract and require longer definitions. In fact, it is possible to write a paragraph, an essay, or even an entire book on such concepts.

The simplest way to define a term is to look it up in a dictionary. However, many words have nuances that are not necessarily discussed in dictionaries. For example, suppose that your boss calls your work "unsatisfactory." You might need clarification of that term. Do you have poor work habits? Do you miss deadlines? Is your attitude problematic? What does your boss mean by "unsatisfactory?"

The ability to define difficult concepts is always useful. At home, a friend or loved one may ask you to define *commitment.* If you mention that a movie was *great,* you may need to clarify what you mean by that word. In a political science class, you might define *socialism, capitalism,* or *communism.* At work, you might define your company's *winning strategy.* The *Definition at Work* paragraph on the following page shows definition writing used in a workplace situation.

The Definition Paragraph

When you write a definition paragraph, try to explain what a term means to you. For example, if someone asks you to define *bravery,* you might tell stories to illustrate the meaning of the word. You may also give examples of acts of bravery. You might even explain what bravery is not.

When you write a definition paragraph, remember the following two points.

- **Choose a term that you know something about.** You need to understand a term in order to say something relevant and interesting about it.
- **Give a clear definition.** In your first sentence, write a definition that is understandable to your reader, and support your definition with examples.

 Consider Your Audience

When you write a definition paragraph, consider your audience. You may have to adjust your tone and vocabulary, depending on who reads the paragraph. For example, if you write a definition paragraph about computer viruses for your English class, you will have to use easily understandable terms. If you write the same paragraph for your computer class, you can use more technical terms.

Definition at Work

In the following memo to a parent, reading specialist Amanda Wong defines a common reading disorder.

As we have discussed, your daughter exhibits signs of a reading disorder commonly referred to as dyslexia. Dyslexia is not the result of damage to the brain or nervous system. It is, more accurately, a problem that is often found in visual learners. Such learners associate pictures with words. For example, your daughter would associate the word *tiger* with the animal, but she has no image to associate with words such as *a* or *the*. Therefore, she may become confused when she reads such words. A feeling of disorientation when reading the letters in words can further compound the problem. She may not perceive individual letters in sequence but might interpret them in a variety of orders and directions. Thus, a dyslexic child may see the word *dog* as *god* or *bog*. In our next meeting, I will give you some strategies to help your daughter with her reading.

PRACTICE I

Read the paragraph, and then answer the questions.

innate: built in

"Cool" can be described as a certain **innate** quality that clearly sets something above its surroundings and makes one wish to be associated with it. There must be a certain degree of exclusivity associated with cool things; they should make you feel like you're superior to the general public. Cool things often involve expending some effort to associate with them. For example, the popular 1990s sitcom *Seinfeld* was indisputably an excellent show, but it was not cool because everybody watched it. On the other hand, it was cool to watch *Seinfeld* during its first two seasons when nobody had heard of it, and when it changed time slots every other week. It should be noted that, occasionally, something's coolness is so entrenched that it overcomes the popularity factor and remains on the list. These occasions are rare, however, and usually only apply to the most elite. For example, the Beatles disbanded in 1970, yet a lot of people would say the band is still cool.

—Paul Sabourin, "What Is Cool"

1. Underline the topic sentence.

2. What is the writer defining? _____

   _____

3. List the supporting details. _____

   _____

   _____

   _____

4. Think of another example to add to this paragraph. _____

   _____

DEVELOPING

The Topic Sentence

A clear topic sentence for a definition paragraph introduces the term and provides a definition. There are three basic ways to define a term.

- By synonym
- By category
- By negation

ESSAY LINK

In a definition essay, the thesis statement expresses the controlling idea. In the thesis, you can define the term by synonym, category, or negation.

Definition by Synonym

The easiest way to define a term is to supply a synonym (a word that has a similar meaning). This type of definition is useful if the original term is difficult to understand and the synonym is a more familiar word.

term	+	synonym
A Mickey Mouse course		is an easy course to complete.
I am a procrastinator,		which means I tend to put things off.

Definition by Category

A more effective way to define a term is to give a definition by category (or class). When you define by category, you determine the larger group to which the term belongs. Then you determine what unique characteristics set the term apart from others in that category.

term	+	category	+	detail
A kingfisher is		a type of bird		that is small and brightly colored.
Luddites		are people		who are skeptical about new technology.

ESSAY LINK

You can join two independent ideas with a semicolon. For more information, see Chapter 17.

Definition by Negation

When you define by negation, you explain what a term does not mean. You can then include a sentence explaining what it does mean.

term	+	what it is not	+	what it is
Alcoholism		is not an invented disease;		it is a serious physical dependency.
Hackers		are not playful computer geeks;		they are criminals.

PRACTICE 2

A. Write a one-sentence definition by synonym for each of the following terms. Your definition should include the term and a synonym. If necessary, you can look up the terms in the dictionary; however, define each one using your own words.

EXAMPLE:

To capitulate _means to give up or surrender._

1. Ravenous _____

2. A celebrity _____

3. Malaria _____

B. Write a one-sentence definition by category for the following terms. Make sure that your definition includes the term, a category, and details.

EXAMPLE:

A cockroach _is an insect that lives in the cracks and crevices of buildings._

4. Stilettos _____

_____

5. Paparazzi _____

_____

6. A deadbeat parent _____

_____

C. Write a one-sentence definition by negation for the following terms. Explain what each term is not, followed by what each term is.

EXAMPLE:

A television addict _is not a regular TV viewer but a person who_
watches television excessively.

7. A placebo _____

_____

8. Good parents _____

_____

9. A dog _____

_____

Hint **Be Precise!**

When you write a definition paragraph, it is important to use the precise words to
define the term. Moreover, when you define a term by category, make sure that the
category for your term is correct. For example, look at the following imprecise
definitions of insomnia.

Insomnia is the (inability) to sleep well.

(Insomnia is not an ability or an inability.)

Insomnia is (when) you cannot sleep well.

(*When* refers to a time, but insomnia is not a time.)

Insomnia is the (nights) when you do not get enough sleep.

(Insomnia is not days or nights.)

Insomnia is (where) it is hard to fall asleep.

(*Where* refers to a place, but insomnia is not a place.)

Now look at a better definition of insomnia.

category

Insomnia is a **sleeping disorder** characterized by the inability to sleep well.

PRACTICE 3

Revise each sentence using precise language.

EXAMPLE:

Tuning out is when you ignore something.

Tuning out is the action of ignoring something.

1. A scapegoat is when a person gets blamed for something.

   _____

2. Claustrophobia is the inability to be in a small place.

   _____

3. A bully is the abuse of power over others.

_____

_____

4. Adolescence is where you are between childhood and adulthood.

_____

_____

5. Ego surfing is when you surf the Internet to find references to yourself.

_____

_____

The Writer's Desk **Write Topic Sentences**

Write a topic sentence in which you define each of the following topics. You can look for ideas in the Warm Up on pages 100–101. Remember to use precise language in your definition.

EXAMPLE:

Topic: An optimist

Topic sentence: *An optimist is a person who always looks on the bright side of life.*

1. Topic: A leader

   Topic sentence: _____

   _____

2. Topic: Talent

   Topic sentence: _____

   _____

3. Topic: A workaholic

   Topic sentence: _____

   _____

The Supporting Ideas

After you have developed an effective topic sentence, generate supporting ideas. In a definition paragraph, you can give examples that clarify your definition.

Think about how you will organize your examples. Most definition paragraphs use emphatic order, which means that examples are placed from the most to the least important or from the least to the most important.

The Writer's Desk   **Develop Supporting Ideas**

Choose one of your topic sentences from the Writer's Desk on page 106. List three or four examples that best illustrate the definition.

EXAMPLE: An optimist is a person who always looks at the bright side of life.

> sees things positively
> is healthy
> genetic?
> has a longer life span

Topic sentence: _____

_____

Supports: _____

_____

_____

_____

The Paragraph Plan

A good definition paragraph includes a complete definition of the term and provides adequate examples to support the central definition. When creating a definition paragraph plan, make sure that your examples provide varied evidence, and do not just repeat the definition. Also add details that will help clarify your supporting examples.

ESSAY LINK

In a definition essay, the thesis statement is in the introduction. Each supporting idea is in a distinct body paragraph with its own topic sentence.

TOPIC SENTENCE:	An optimist is a person who always looks on the bright side of life.
Support 1:	He or she sees positive ways out of negative situations.
Details:	—my mother saw her divorce as a new beginning —contrast to father who saw divorce as a terrible ending
Support 2:	An optimist has a healthy mind and body.
Details:	—tend to be healthier, according to psychiatrists —have lower blood pressure
Support 3:	Optimism runs in families.
Details:	—optimistic parents have optimist children (genetic) —parents model positive attitudes to their children

The Writer's Desk **Write a Paragraph Plan**

Create a detailed paragraph plan using one of the topic sentences that you wrote for the Writer's Desk on page 106. Arrange the supporting details in a logical order.

Topic sentence: _____

_____

Support 1: _____

Details: _____

_____

_____

Support 2: _____

Details: _____

_____

Support 3: _____

Details: _____

_____

_____

The First Draft

After you outline your ideas in a plan, you are ready to write the first draft. Remember to write complete sentences. You might include transitional words or expressions to help your ideas flow smoothly.

Transitional Words and Expressions

Transitional expressions can show different levels of importance. The following transitions are useful in definition paragraphs.

To Show the Level of Importance	
clearly	next
first	one quality . . . another quality
most of all	second
most important	undoubtedly

The Writer's Desk **Write the First Draft**

In the previous Writer's Desk, you developed a paragraph plan. Now write the first draft of your definition paragraph. Before you write, carefully review your paragraph plan and make any necessary changes.

REVISING AND EDITING

Revise and Edit a Definition Paragraph

When you finish writing a definition paragraph, carefully review your work and revise it to make the definition as clear as possible to your readers. Check that you have organized your steps logically, and remove any irrelevant details.

PRACTICE 4

Read the next student paragraph and answer the questions.

> An optimist is a person who always looks on the bright side of life. Optimists see positive ways out of negative situations. They see bad events as temporary and controllable. For example, my mother is an optimist. She divorced my father. She saw the divorce as a new beginning. Now she is very happy. My father, on the contrary, is not an optimist. He saw the divorce as a terrible ending. He stayed depressed. According to an August 2002 study in the *Mayo Clinic Proceedings*, optimists have a more lower risk of premature death. They live longer. People may have a genetic predisposition to optimism. It often run's in families. For example, my grandmother, my mother, and I are all optimists.

Revising

1. Underline the topic sentence.

2. What type of definition does the topic sentence contain? Circle the best answer.
   a. Definition by synonym   b. Definition by category
   c. Definition by negation

3. This paragraph lacks sentence variety. Revise the paragraph to give it more sentence variety by combining sentences or changing the first word of some sentences. (For more information about combining sentences and sentence variety, see Chapters 17–19.)

Editing

4. There is one incorrectly written comparison. Circle the error and correct it. (For more information about adverbs and adjectives, see Chapter 29.)

5. There is one apostrophe error. Circle the error and correct it. (For more information about apostrophes, see Chapter 34.)

The Writer's Desk **Revise and Edit Your Paragraph**

Revise and edit the paragraph that you wrote for the previous Writer's Desk.

Ensure that your paragraph has unity, adequate support, and coherence. Also correct any errors in grammar, spelling, punctuation, and mechanics.

REFLECT ON IT

Think about what you have learned in this chapter. If you do not know an answer, review that topic.

1. In definition writing, you _____

   _____

2. Explain each of the following types of definitions. Then give an example of each definition. Use your own ideas.

   a. Explain definition by synonym. _____

   _____

   Give an example of a definition by synonym. _____

   _____

   b. Explain definition by category. _____

   _____

   Give an example of a definition by category. _____

   _____

   c. Explain definition by negation. _____

   _____

   Give an example of a definition by negation. _____

   _____

The Writer's Room **Topics for Definition Paragraphs**

Writing Activity 1

Choose any of the following topics, or choose your own topic. Then write a definition paragraph.

General Topics

1. a miracle
2. fame
3. a spoiled child
4. fashion police
5. bling bling
6. mind games

College and Work-Related Topics

7. integrity
8. a slacker
9. a headhunter
10. an opportunist
11. the glass ceiling
12. an apprentice

WRITING LINK

More Definition Writing Topics
Chapter 19, Writer's Room topic 1 (page 305)
Chapter 24, Writer's Room topic 4 (page 367)
Chapter 35, Writer's Room topic 1 (page 511)

Writing Activity 2

Write a paragraph in which you define censorship. What sorts of things get censored? Think of some interesting examples that support your definition.

READING LINK

More Definition Readings
"The Never-Ending Question: Who Am I?" by Raúl Reyes (page 557)
"Dancing with Fear" by Bebe Moore Campbell (page 560)

EXAMPLE: What are some different types of diets?

Some people don't eat at all. Starvation diets?

Fad diets. Some diet books become bestsellers.

Protein shakes. Aren't there diet pills?

1. List some clothing that you own. You might think about old clothing, comfortable clothing, beautiful clothing, and so on.

_____

_____

_____

2. What are some different types of consumers? To get ideas, you might think about some people you know and the way that they shop.

_____

_____

_____

3. What are some types of jobs that students can get?

_____

_____

_____

What Is Classification?

When you classify, you sort a subject into more understandable categories. Each of the categories must be part of a larger group, yet they must also be distinct. For example, you might write a paragraph about the most common types of pets and sort the subject into cats, dogs, and birds.

Classification occurs in many situations. At home, you could classify the responsibilities of each person in the family, or you could classify your bills. In a biology course, you might write a paper about the different types of cells, or in a commerce course, you may write about the categories in a financial statement. On the job, you might advertise the different types of products or services that your company sells.

ESSAY LINK

Classification essays also require a classification principle and distinct categories.

The Classification Paragraph

To find a topic for a classification paragraph, think of something that can be sorted into different groups. Also determine a reason for classifying the items. When you are planning your ideas for a classification paragraph, remember these two points.

1. **Use a common classification principle.** A **classification principle** is the overall method that you use to sort the subject into categories. To find the classification principle, think about one common characteristic that unites the different categories. For example, if your subject is "the telephone," your classification principle might be any of the following:

   – types of annoying phone calls

   – reasons that people buy cell phones

   – types of long-distance services

   – types of customer reactions to telephone salespeople

2. **Sort the subject into distinct categories.** A classification paragraph should have two or more categories.

Topic: Phone calls

Classification principle: Calls that are annoying

Category 1	**Category 2**	**Category 3**
Telephone surveys	Prank calls	Wrong numbers

The following *Classification at Work* paragraph discusses a topic that has been divided into categories.

Classification at Work

Robert Luzynski, an allergy specialist, wrote the following information in a brochure for his patients.

If you exhibit allergic symptoms to animals, there are three types of treatment that you can follow. The most effective is to avoid contact with known allergens. Thus, avoid bringing pets into the home. If you have a pet, consider using an air cleaner, vacuum two to three times a week, and ensure that the animal is groomed frequently to remove loose fur and dander. The second type of treatment consists of medications. Antihistamines help alleviate the symptoms of allergic reactions, but they do not cure allergies. It is important to read the labels carefully as some antihistamines cause drowsiness. A final method, desensitization, is an extended treatment involving allergy shots. You would be exposed to gradually increasing amounts of specific allergens. The treatment lasts for an extended period of time, and the goal is to reduce your sensitivity to the allergens.

PRACTICE I

Read the next paragraph and answer the questions.

Hackers come in three stripes, according to Drew Williams, a computer security specialist for Maryland-based Axent Technologies.

depredations: acts of destruction

There are the "newbies," or inexperienced hackers, who generally stumble upon a Web site offering free hacking software. They try to break into targets through their Web sites as an after-school hobby. "White hat" hackers are more talented—and serious—but they use their talents to expose weak security. According to Williams, "They hack for a cause." White hat infiltrators might squirm into the computer innards of a bank or government ministry and steal a few nuggets of data, but the white hat hacker will then expose his deed to his victim and offer security suggestions—often for a fee. Then there are the "black hat" hackers whose **depredations** include sabotage of government Web sites; the Pentagon and Department of Justice are among favorite targets. They plunder bank deposits, shut down public services such as telephones and electricity, and steal trade secrets, Williams said.

—Kim Krane, "Computer Crime Tops $100 Million," *APBnews.com*

1. Underline the topic sentence of this paragraph.

2. State the three categories that the author discusses and list some details about each category.

   a. _____

   Details: _____

   b. _____

   Details: _____

   c. _____

   Details: _____

3. Who is the audience for this paragraph?

   _____

4. What is the purpose of this paragraph? Circle the best answer.
   a. To persuade   b. To inform   c. To entertain

Making a Classification Chart

A **classification chart** is a visual representation of the main topic and its categories. Making a classification chart can help you identify the categories more clearly so that you will be able to write more exact topic sentences.

When you classify items, remember to use a single method of classification and a common classification principle to sort the items. For example, if you are classifying movies, you might classify them according to their ratings: General Audience, Parental Guidance, and Restricted. You could also classify movies according to their country of origin: British, American, and French, for example. Remember that one classification principle must unite the group.

Television shows

Situation comedy   Reality show   Talk show

Classification principle: Relaxing TV programs

Categories Should Not Overlap

When sorting a topic into categories, make sure that the categories do not overlap. For example, you would not classify drivers into careful drivers, aggressive drivers, and bad drivers, because aggressive drivers could also be bad drivers. Each category should be distinct.

PRACTICE 2

In the following classification charts, a subject has been broken down into distinct categories. The items in the group should have the same classification principle. Cross out one item in each group that does not belong. Then write down the classification principle that unites the group.

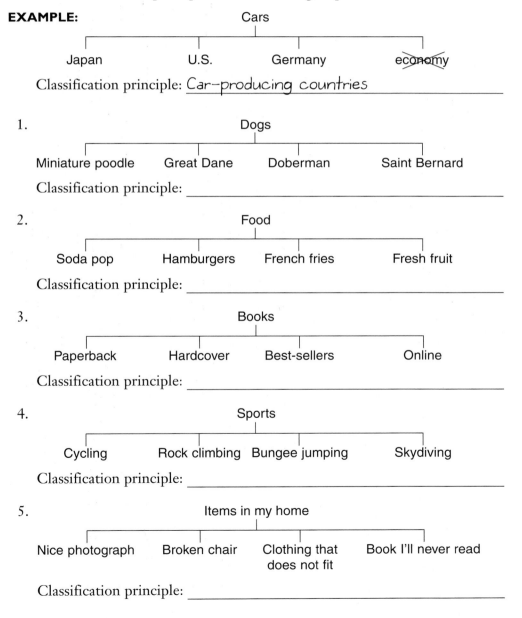

EXAMPLE:

Cars

Japan   U.S.   Germany   ~~economy~~

Classification principle: *Car-producing countries*

1.   Dogs

Miniature poodle   Great Dane   Doberman   Saint Bernard

Classification principle: _____

2.   Food

Soda pop   Hamburgers   French fries   Fresh fruit

Classification principle: _____

3.   Books

Paperback   Hardcover   Best-sellers   Online

Classification principle: _____

4.   Sports

Cycling   Rock climbing   Bungee jumping   Skydiving

Classification principle: _____

5.   Items in my home

Nice photograph   Broken chair   Clothing that does not fit   Book I'll never read

Classification principle: _____

Make a Point

To make interesting classification paragraphs, try to express an attitude, opinion, or feeling about the topic. For example, you can write a paragraph about types of diets, but it is more interesting if you make a point about the types of diets.

Poor: Types of diets

Better: Types of **dangerous** diets

Types of **effective** diets

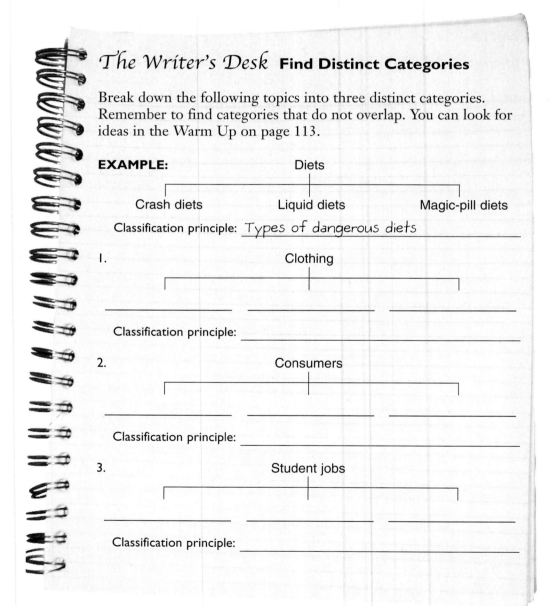

The Writer's Desk **Find Distinct Categories**

Break down the following topics into three distinct categories. Remember to find categories that do not overlap. You can look for ideas in the Warm Up on page 113.

EXAMPLE: Diets

Crash diets   Liquid diets   Magic-pill diets

Classification principle: *Types of dangerous diets*

1.   Clothing

Classification principle:

2.   Consumers

Classification principle:

3.   Student jobs

Classification principle:

DEVELOPING

The Topic Sentence

The topic sentence in a classification paragraph clearly indicates what a writer will classify. It also includes the controlling idea, which is the classification principle that you use.

ESSAY LINK

In a classification essay, the thesis statement expresses the controlling idea or classification principle.

Several types of students can completely disrupt a classroom.

Topic:	Students
Classification principle:	Disruptive types

You can also mention the types of categories in your topic sentence.

The most annoying telephone calls are surveys, prank calls, and wrong numbers.

Topic:	Telephone calls
Classification principle:	Types of annoying calls

The Writer's Desk **Write Topic Sentences**

Look again at what you wrote in the Warm Up on page 113. Also look at the classification charts that you made for each topic. Now write clear topic sentences. Remember that your topic sentence can include the different categories you will be discussing.

EXAMPLE: Diets

Dieters sometimes use dangerous methods to lose weight, such as the high-fat diet, the liquid diet, and the magic-pill diet.

1. Topic: Clothing

   Topic sentence: _____

   _____

2. Topic: Consumers

   Topic sentence: _____

   _____

3. Topic: Student jobs

   Topic sentence: _____

   _____

ESSAY LINK

You can make a detailed classification chart when you develop your classification essay. Each supporting idea would become a distinct paragraph.

The Supporting Ideas

After you have developed an effective topic sentence, generate supporting ideas. In a classification paragraph, you can list details about each of your categories.

The Paragraph Plan

You can make a standard paragraph plan. Another way to visualize your categories and your supporting ideas is to make a detailed classification chart. Break down the main topic into several categories, and then give details about each category.

Dieters sometimes use dangerous methods to lose weight, such as the high-fat diet, the liquid diet, and the magic pill diet.

High-fat diets	Liquid diets	Magic-pill diets
- point is to completely cut out carbohydrates - focus on animal and vegetable fats and oils - may cause heart disease	- drink only liquids for many days - milkshake diet - water diet - fruit juice diet - dangerous malnutrition	- pills reduce calories - fat-burning pills - appetite reduction pills - caffeine diet pills - herbal diet pills - deaths associated with pill diets

The Writer's Desk **Make a Detailed Classification Chart**

Choose one of the topic sentences that you wrote for the Writer's Desk on page 119, and make a detailed classification chart. Arrange the supporting details in a logical order. You can refer to the information you generated in the Warm Up.

Topic sentence: _____

_____

Use the Chart as a Plan

Your classification chart can also serve as your paragraph plan. Like a paragraph plan, your chart contains your topic sentence, your categories, and details about each category.

The First Draft

After you outline your ideas in a classification chart or plan, you are ready to write the first draft. Remember to write complete sentences. You might include transitional words or expressions to help your ideas flow smoothly.

Transitional Words and Expressions

Some classification paragraphs use transitional words and expressions to show which category is most important and to signal a movement from one category to the next. The next transitions are very useful in classification writing.

To Show Importance	To Show Types of Categories
above all	one kind . . . another kind
clearly	the first/second type
the most important	the first/second kind
most of all	the last category
particularly	

The Writer's Desk **Write the First Draft**

Write the first draft of your classification paragraph. Before you write, carefully review your detailed classification chart and make any necessary changes.

REVISING AND EDITING

Revise and Edit a Classification Paragraph

When you finish writing a classification paragraph, carefully review your work and revise it to make sure that the categories do not overlap. Check to make sure that you have organized your paragraph logically, and remove any irrelevant details.

PRACTICE 3

Read the next student paragraph and answer the questions.

Dieters sometimes use dangerous methods to lose weight, such as high-fat diets, liquid diets, fad diets, and the magic pill diets. With high-fat diets, the point is to cut out carbohydrates. The dieter can eat as much animal protein and fat as he or she likes. However, this diet can cause high cholesterol. Another dangerous weight-loss method is the liquid diet. People have liquid meals, but if they continue this diet for a long time, they can become malnourished. One more common type of diet is the fad diet. Somebody promotes a new, improved weight-loss method, and people blindly follow this latest diet fad. For example, in the Atkins diet, dieters limit their intake of carbohydrates, or in the liquid protein diet, you just drink a protein beverage. The last type of diet, magic pills. People rely on pills such as caffeine or appetite-reduction pills to lose weight. The fen-phen diet was very popular for a while, but the pills sometimes had fatal side effects.

Revising

1. What is the classification principle in this paragraph? _____

2. What are the four categories? _____

   _____

3. Which category is not valid? _____

   Explain why. _____

   _____

4. This paragraph does not have a concluding sentence. Write a concluding sentence in the space. The concluding sentence can restate the main idea of the paragraph.

   _____

   _____

Editing

5. A fragment lacks a subject or verb and is an incomplete sentence. Identify and correct one fragment. (You can find more information about fragments in Chapter 20.)

6. One sentence contains a pronoun shift. The noun and the subsequent pronoun are not consistent. Identify and correct the pronoun shift. (You can find more information about pronoun consistency in Chapter 28.)

The Writer's Desk Revise and Edit Your Paragraph

Revise and edit the paragraph that you wrote for the previous Writer's Desk. Ensure that your paragraph has unity, adequate support, and coherence. Also correct any errors in grammar, spelling, punctuation, and mechanics.

REFLECT ON IT

Think about what you have learned in this chapter. If you do not know an answer, review that topic.

1. What is classification? _____
   _____

2. What is the classification principle? _____
   _____

3. Give examples of various classification principles that you can use to classify the following items.
   EXAMPLE: Cars _Countries of origin, degrees of fuel efficiency, price_
   a. Animals _____
   b. Sports _____

4. Now choose one classification principle for each item in question 3. Write down three possible categories for that item.
   EXAMPLE: Cars
   Classification principle: _Country of origin_
   Categories: _American cars, European cars, Japanese cars_
   a. Animals
      Classification principle: _____
      Categories: _____
   b. Sports
      Classification principle: _____
      Categories: _____

5. Why is it useful to make a classification chart? _____
   _____

The Writer's Room

Topics for Classification Paragraphs

Writing Activity 1

Choose any of the following topics, or choose your own topic. Then write a classification paragraph.

WRITING LINK

More Classification Writing Topics
Chapter 21, Writer's Room topic 4 (page 328)
Chapter 24, Writer's Room topic 2 (page 367)
Chapter 35, Writer's Room topic 3 (page 511)

General Topics

Types of . . .

1. parents
2. problems in a relationship
3. friends
4. magazines
5. games
6. sports

College and Work-Related Topics

Types of . . .

7. campus fashions
8. housing
9. roommates
10. bosses
11. office equipment
12. co-workers

Writing Activity 2

Examine this photo, and think about some classification topics. For example, you might discuss types of risky behavior, dangerous jobs, entertainment involving animals, or culturally specific entertainment. Then write a classification paragraph based on the photo or your related topic.

READING LINK

More Classification Readings
"Fads" by David A. Locher (page 554)
"Dealing with People" by Greg McGrew (page 533)

CLASSIFICATION PARAGRAPH CHECKLIST

As you write your classification paragraph, review the checklist on the inside front cover. Also ask yourself the following questions.

Does my topic sentence explain the categories that will be discussed?

Do I use a common classification principle to unite the various items?

Do I offer sufficient details to explain each category?

Do I arrange the categories in a logical manner?

Does all of the supporting information relate to the categories that are being discussed?

Do I include categories that do not overlap?

See Chapter 9 of the Visualizing Writing CD for an additional mini-lecture on **Classification.**

CHAPTER 10

Comparison and Contrast

> *Life is often compared to a marathon, but I think it is more like a sprint; there are long stretches of hard work punctuated by brief moments in which we are given the opportunity to perform at our best.*
>
> —MICHAEL JOHNSON
> *American sprinter (b. 1967)*

CONTENTS

Exploring
- Explore Topics
- What Is Comparison and Contrast?
- The Comparison and Contrast Paragraph

Developing
- The Topic Sentence
- The Supporting Ideas
- The Paragraph Plan
- The First Draft

Revising and Editing
- Revise and Edit a Comparison and Contrast Paragraph

Shoppers compare prices to obtain the best value for their money. In this chapter, you will practice comparing and contrasting.

EXPLORING

Explore Topics

In the Warm Up, you will try an exploring strategy to generate ideas about different topics.

The Writer's Desk **Warm Up**

Think about the following questions, and write down the first ideas that come to your mind. Try to think of two to three ideas for each topic.

EXAMPLE: What are some key features of living alone and living with others?

Living alone	**Living with others**
don't have to share	must compromise
can do what you want whenever	share the TV
sometimes it's lonely	share the bathroom; schedule showers

1. What are some key features of high school and college?

High school	**College**
_____	_____
_____	_____
_____	_____

2. What were your goals when you were a child? What are your goals today?

Goals in childhood	**Goals today**
_____	_____
_____	_____
_____	_____

3. Write down the names of two people who are very close to you. You might think of friends or family members. Then list some interesting characteristics of each person.

Person 1: _____	**Person 2:** _____
_____	_____
_____	_____
_____	_____

What Is Comparison and Contrast?

When you want to decide between options, you compare and contrast. You **compare** to find similarities and **contrast** to find differences. The exercise of comparing and contrasting can help you make judgments about things. It can also help you better understand familiar things.

You often compare and contrast. At home, when you watch TV, you might compare and contrast different programs. At college, you might compare and contrast different psychological or political theories. On the job, you might need to compare and contrast computer operating systems, shipping services, or sales figures.

The Comparison and Contrast Paragraph

In a comparison and contrast paragraph, you can compare and contrast two different subjects, or you can compare and contrast different aspects of a single subject. For example, you might contrast married life and single life, or you might write only about marriage but contrast expectations people have before they get married versus what realistically happens after marriage.

When you write a comparison or contrast paragraph, remember to think about your specific purpose.

- **Your purpose could be to make judgments about two things.** For example, you might compare and contrast two restaurants in order to convince your readers that one is preferable.
- **Your purpose could be to describe or understand two familiar things.** For example, you might compare two stories to help your readers understand their thematic similarities.

Comparison and Contrast Patterns

Comparison and contrast texts follow two common patterns. One pattern is to present the details point by point. Another is to present one topic and then the other topic.

When you are thinking about ideas for writing a comparison and contrast paragraph, you can choose one of two methods to organize your supporting ideas: point by point or topic by topic.

ESSAY LINK

To write a comparison and contrast essay, organize *each paragraph* in point-by-point or topic-by-topic form.

Point by Point

Present one point about Topic A and then one point about Topic B. Keep following this pattern until you have a few points for each topic. You go back and forth from one side to the other like tennis players hitting a ball back and forth across a net.

Point A   Point B   Point A   Point B   Point A   Point B

Topic by Topic

Present all points related to Topic A in the first few sentences, and then present all points related to Topic B in the last few sentences. So, you present one side and then the other side, just as lawyers might in the closing arguments of a court case.

All of Topic A   All of Topic B

KYLE'S EXAMPLE

Kyle is trying to decide whether he should take a job in another city or stay at his current job in his hometown. His goal is to decide whether he should move or stay where he is. Kyle could organize his information using a point-by-point or topic-by-topic method.

Point by Point		Topic by Topic	
Job A	Low salary	Job A	Low salary
Job B	Good salary		Parents nearby
Job A	Parents nearby		Like my colleagues
Job B	Parents far away		
Job A	Like my colleagues	Job B	Better salary
Job B	Don't know colleagues		Parents far away
			Don't know colleagues

The following *Comparison and Contrast at Work* paragraph uses a point-by-point pattern to contrast two types of people.

Comparison and Contrast at Work

In this paragraph, Dawn Rosenberg McKay, a professional career planner, contrasts a mentor and a protégé.

The mentor is typically more experienced than his or her protégé. He or she possesses the wisdom that only experience can provide. The protégé is someone who is looking to move up the career ladder, usually following in the footsteps of the mentor. The relationship benefits both mentor and protégé. The protégé receives guidance and helpful advice. Invitations to industry events and introductions to industry higher-ups may be forthcoming. The mentor benefits from the opportunity to strengthen his or her leadership skills.

PRACTICE I

Read the next two paragraphs and answer the questions.

A.   Fashion is fashion and teen fashion is meant to shock. According to my son, the girls in his school like to wear decorative thongs and let them peek out from over the tops of their low-slung jeans "for all the boys to see in English class." Their *t*-shirts are tiny, about the size of face cloths. Covering up the back is optional. Oddly, it is my son who finds this style of dressing shocking (among other things). It is not a flattering fashion, for sure, but I dare not complain. In high school I wore a micro miniskirt, and I am sure the boys could see my panties as I climbed the stairs in front of them. I seldom wore a bra (which bothered a friend's father so much, I was not allowed into her house). So, when my son brings home his first near-naked girlfriend, I will not act shocked; I will merely crack a conspiratorial smile.

—Dorothy Nixon, "Teen Fashion"

1. Underline the topic sentence.

2. What aspects of fashion does the author compare? _____

   _____

3. What pattern of comparison does the author follow? Circle the correct answer.

   a. Point by point   b. Topic by topic

4. What does this paragraph focus on? Circle the correct answer.
    a. Similarities   b. Differences

B.   Women's sports lag behind men's in media, prize money, and salaries. Some recent comparisons tell the story. The Women's Sport Foundation, a charitable educational organization established in 1974 by Billie Jean King, reports that over ninety percent of all print column inches and hours of televised sports still goes to men's sports. It has only been since 1991 that women's sports received more coverage than horse and dog racing. On the money front, the average prize earnings of the top ten professional male athletes were at least double that of their female counterparts in tennis, bowling, golf, skiing and beach volleyball. There is a huge difference in salaries as well. In professional basketball, the average salary of male players during the 1995–1996 season was 140 times higher than the average salary of female players in the now-**defunct** American Basketball League during its 1996–1997 season. Well, I think you get the picture, and it is not pretty. Now, if we could turn back Father Time and compare the women's games of today to the same developmental period in men's sports, a comparison might seem more legitimate.

—Ellen Zavian, "Men's and Women's Sports? No Comparison!" *USA Today*

defunct: no longer existing

5. Underline the topic sentence.

6. What does this paragraph compare? _____

    _____

7. What pattern of comparison does the author follow? Circle the best answer.
    a. Point by point   b. Topic by topic

8. What does the author focus on? Circle the correct answer.
    a. Similarities   b. Differences

Focus on Similarities, Differences, or Both

After you have chosen a topic and determined your purpose, decide whether you want to focus on comparing (looking at similarities), contrasting (looking at differences), or both. In a paragraph, it is usually best to focus on either comparing or contrasting. In a larger essay, you could more easily do both.

The Writer's Desk Find Similarities and Differences

Write some similarities and differences for the next three pairs of topics.

EXAMPLE: Living alone versus living with others

Similarities	**Differences**	
Living alone and with others	Living alone	Living with others
must pay for necessities	have freedom	must compromise
clean up after myself	lonely	people to talk to
learn to balance budget	do all housework	can share jobs
	quiet	others' noise
	expensive	share expenses

I would choose to write a paragraph about _differences_ .

1.	**Similarities**	**Differences**	
	High school and college	High school	College
	_____	_____	_____
	_____	_____	_____
	_____	_____	_____
	_____	_____	_____
	_____		

I would choose to write a paragraph about _____.

2.	**Similarities**	**Differences**	
	Child and adult goals	Childhood goals	Goals today
	_____	_____	_____
	_____	_____	_____
	_____	_____	_____
	_____	_____	_____
	_____		

I would choose to write a paragraph about _____.

3.	**Similarities**	**Differences**	
	Two people who are close to me:	Person 1:	Person 2:
		_____	_____
	_____	_____	_____
	_____	_____	_____
	_____	_____	_____
	_____	_____	_____

I would choose to write a paragraph about _____.

ESSAY LINK

In a comparison and contrast essay, the thesis statement expresses the main point of the essay.

DEVELOPING

The Topic Sentence

In a comparison and contrast paragraph, the topic sentence indicates what is being compared and contrasted and expresses a controlling idea.

> Although all dogs make good house pets, large dogs are much more useful than small dogs.
>
> Topic being compared or contrasted: Large dogs vs. small dogs
> Controlling idea: One is more useful than the other.

PRACTICE 2

Read each topic sentence, and then answer the questions that follow. State whether the paragraph would focus on similarities or differences.

EXAMPLE:

Although coffee and tea can both be caffeinated, tea is a much healthier drink than coffee.

    a. What is being compared? _Coffee and tea_

    b. What is the controlling idea? _One is healthier than the other._

    c. What will the paragraph focus on? Circle the correct answer.

    Similarities   (Differences)

1. Many media pundits complain about reality television; however, reality shows are just as good as regular scripted shows.

    a. What is being compared? _____

    _____

    b. What is the controlling idea? _____

    _____

    c. What will the paragraph focus on? Circle the correct answer.

    Similarities   Differences

2. Before the baby comes, people expect a beautiful world of soft coos and sweet smells, but the reality is quite different.

    a. What is being compared? _____

    _____

    b. What is the controlling idea? _____

    _____

    c. What will the paragraph focus on? Circle the correct answer.

    Similarities   Differences

3. Teenagers are as difficult to raise as toddlers.

  a. What is being compared? _____

  _____

  b. What is the controlling idea? _____

  _____

  c. What will the paragraph focus on? Circle the correct answer.

  Similarities   Differences

The Writer's Desk   Write Topic Sentences

For each topic, write whether you will focus on similarities or differences. Then, write a topic sentence for each one. You can look for ideas in the Warm Up or in Writer's Desk: Finding Similarities and Differences on pages 130–131. Your topic sentence should include what you are comparing and contrasting, as well as a controlling idea.

Topic: Living alone and living with others

Focus: *Differences*

Topic sentence: *Although many people like the freedom and privacy of living alone, living with other people has its merits.*

1. Topic: High school and college

  Focus: _____

  Topic sentence: _____

  _____

2. Topic: Goals in childhood and goals in adulthood

  Focus: _____

  Topic sentence: _____

  _____

3. Topic: Two people who are close to me

  Focus: _____

  Topic sentence: _____

  _____

The Supporting Ideas

After you have developed an effective topic sentence, generate supporting ideas. In a comparison and contrast paragraph, think of examples that help clarify the similarities or differences.

The Paragraph Plan

ESSAY LINK

In a comparison and contrast essay, place the thesis statement in the introduction. Each supporting idea becomes a distinct paragraph with its own topic sentence.

Before you write a comparison and contrast paragraph, it is a good idea to make a paragraph plan. Decide which pattern you will follow: point by point or topic by topic. "**A**" and "**B**" written alongside your topics can indicate which side they support. Then add supporting details. Make sure that each detail supports the topic sentence.

TOPIC SENTENCE: <u>Although many people like the freedom and privacy of living alone, living with other people has its merits.</u>

Point by Point	Topic by Topic
A With others, you can share expenses. **Details:** phone, electricity, etc., costs are less for each person	**A** With others, you can share expenses. **Details:** phone, electricity, etc., costs are less for each person
B Alone, you must pay for everything yourself. **Details:** can be very expensive	**A** With others, there is someone to talk to. **Details:** at end of day, you can discuss experiences
A With others, there is someone to talk to. **Details:** at end of day, you can discuss experiences	**A** With others, you must compromise. **Details:** if there are conflicts, you must find resolution
B Alone, you can sometimes be lonely. **Details:** nobody to come home to	**B** Alone, you must pay for everything yourself. **Details:** can be very expensive
A With others, you must compromise. **Details:** if there are conflicts, you must find resolution	**B** Alone, you can sometimes be lonely. **Details:** nobody to come home to
B Alone, you can do what you want, when you want. **Details:** no worry about making noise	**B** Alone, you can do what you want, when you want. **Details:** no worry about making noise

The Writer's Desk Write a Paragraph Plan

Write a detailed paragraph plan in a point-by-point or side-by-side pattern. You can refer to the information you generated in previous Writer's Desk exercises. You can use the letters **A** and **B** to indicate which side you are discussing in your plan. Include details about each supporting idea.

Topic sentence: _____

_____

Support 1: _____

  Details: _____

_____

Support 2: _____

  Details: _____

_____

Support 3: _____

  Details: _____

_____

Support 4: _____

  Details: _____

_____

Support 5: _____

  Details: _____

_____

Support 6: _____

  Details: _____

_____

The First Draft

After you outline your ideas in a plan, you are ready to write the first draft. Remember to write complete sentences. You might include transitional words or expressions to help your ideas flow smoothly.

Transitional Words and Expressions

In comparison and contrast paragraphs, there are some transitional words and expressions that you might use to explain either similarities or differences.

To Show Similarities		**To Show Differences**	
additionally	in addition	conversely	nevertheless
at the same time	in the same way	however	on the contrary
equally	similarly	in contrast	then again

The Writer's Desk **Write the First Draft**

Write the first draft of your comparison and contrast paragraph. Before you write, carefully review your paragraph plan to see if you have enough support for your points and topics.

REVISING AND EDITING

Revise and Edit a Comparison and Contrast Paragraph

When you finish writing a comparison and contrast paragraph, carefully review your work and revise it to make the comparison or contrast as clear as possible to your readers. Check that you have organized your paragraph logically, and remove any irrelevant details.

PRACTICE 3

Read the next student paragraph and answer the questions.

Although many people like the freedom and privacy of living alone, living with other people has its merits. When you live alone, there are advantages. For example, you can do what you want when you want, and you do not have to worry about other people's feelings or schedules. However, there are also disadvantages to living alone. You had to pay for everything, and it can be very expensive. It can also be lonely to live alone. At the end of the day, there is nobody to come home to. When you live with others, the advantages are great. You can share expenses of items such as phone and utility bills. Also, you have the warmth of human companionship. Of course, you must make compromises when you share a living space. For example, if your roommate do shift work, you must be quiet when he or she is sleeping. Nonetheless, living with others is preferable to living alone.

Revising

1. In the topic sentence, what is the student comparing or contrasting? _____

   _____

2. What does the writer focus on? Circle the correct answer.
   a. Similarities   b. Differences

3. What pattern does the writer use to organize this paragraph? Circle the correct answer.
   a. Point by point   b. Topic by topic

4. Underline five transitional expressions that appear at the beginning of sentences.

Editing

5. There is one tense inconsistency in the paragraph. Cross out and correct the error. (For more information about tense consistency, see Chapter 26.)

6. Identify and correct one subject-verb agreement error. (For more information about subject-verb agreement, see Chapter 25.)

The Writer's Desk   Revise and Edit Your Paragraph

Revise and edit the paragraph that you wrote for the previous Writer's Desk. Ensure that your paragraph has unity, adequate support, and coherence. Also correct any errors in grammar, spelling, punctuation, and mechanics.

REFLECT ON IT

Think about what you have learned in this chapter. If you do not know an answer, review that topic.

1. Define the words *comparing* and *contrasting*.
   a. Comparing: _____
   b. Contrasting: _____

2. Explain the following comparison and contrast patterns.
   a. Point by point: _____

   _____

   b. Topic by topic: _____

   _____

The Writer's Room   **Topics for Comparison and Contrast Paragraphs**

WRITING LINK

More Comparison and Contrast Writing Topics
Chapter 21, Writer's Room topic 2 (page 328)
Chapter 28, Writer's Room topic 3 (page 424)
Chapter 32, Writer's Room topic 1 (page 476)

Writing Activity 1

Choose any of the following topics, or choose your own topic. Then write a comparison and contrast paragraph.

General Topics

Compare or contrast . . .

1. two singers
2. people from two different regions
3. your current home and a home that you lived in before
4. expectations about marriage and the reality of marriage
5. real-life heroes and movie heroes
6. a clean person and a messy person

College and Work-Related Topics

Compare or contrast . . .

7. young college students and older college students
8. two college courses
9. two career options
10. working indoors and working outdoors
11. leaving a child in day care and leaving a child with a family member
12. working mainly with your hands and working mainly with your head

Writing Activity 2

Examine these photos, and think about things that you could compare and contrast. Some ideas might be two types of fashion, two generations, two youth subcultures, or two types of rebellion. Then write a comparison and contrast paragraph.

READING LINK

More Comparison and Contrast Readings
"Body Over Mind" by Mitch Albom (page 572)
"Religious Faith Versus Spirituality" by Neil Bissoondath (page 589)

1920s flappers

James Dean, 1950s rebel

COMPARISON AND CONTRAST PARAGRAPH CHECKLIST

As you write your comparison and contrast paragraph, review the checklist on the inside front cover. Also ask yourself the following questions.

Does my topic sentence explain what I am comparing and/or contrasting?

Does my topic sentence make a point about the comparison?

Does my paragraph have a point-by-point or topic-by-topic pattern?

Does my paragraph focus on either similarities or differences?

Do all of my supporting examples clearly relate to the topics that I am comparing or contrasting?

 See Chapter 10 of the Visualizing Writing CD for an additional mini-lecture on **Comparison and Contrast.**

CHAPTER 11

Cause and Effect

> *Do not go where the path may lead; go instead where there is no path and leave a trail.*
>
> —RALPH WALDO EMERSON
> *American essayist and poet (1803–1882)*

CONTENTS

Exploring
- Explore Topics
- What Is Cause and Effect?
- The Cause and Effect Paragraph

Developing
- The Topic Sentence
- The Supporting Ideas
- The Paragraph Plan
- The First Draft

Revising and Editing
- Revise and Edit a Cause and Effect Paragraph

What causes dirty air, water, and soil? What are the effects of pollution? Cause and effect writing helps explain the answers to these types of questions.

EXPLORING

Explore Topics

In the Warm Up, you will try an exploring strategy to generate ideas about different topics.

The Writer's Desk **Warm Up**

Think about the following questions, and write down the first ideas that come to your mind. Try to think of two or three ideas for each topic.

EXAMPLE: Why have governments banned smoking in the workplace?

Secondhand smoke is dangerous for nonsmokers.

Some people have lung problems such as asthma.

Antismoking groups lobby the government for these laws.

1. What are some different ways that people cheat?

    _____

    _____

    _____

2. List a few reasons why some businesses fail.

    _____

    _____

    _____

3. When you were an adolescent, did you rebel in any way? What types of things did you do?

    _____

    _____

    _____

What Is Cause and Effect?

Cause and effect writing explains why an event happened or what the consequences of such an event were. A cause and effect paragraph can focus on causes, effects, or both.

You often analyze the causes or effects of something. At home, you may worry about what causes your siblings or your own children to behave in a certain manner, or you may wonder about the effects of certain foods on your health. In a U.S. history course, you might analyze the causes of the Civil War, or you might write about the effects of industrialization on American society. At work, you may wonder about the effects of a promotion or a pay cut.

The Cause and Effect Paragraph

When you write a cause and effect paragraph, focus on two main points.

1. **Indicate whether you are focusing on causes, effects, or both.** Because a paragraph is not very long, it is often easier to focus on either causes or effects. If you do decide to focus on both causes and effects, make sure that your topic sentence announces your purpose to the reader.

2. **Make sure that your causes and effects are valid.** Determine real causes and effects and do not simply list things that happened before or after the event. Also verify that your assumptions are logical.

Illogical: The product does not work because it is inexpensive.

(This statement is illogical; quality is not always dictated by price.)

Better: The product does not work because it is constructed with poor-quality materials.

The following *Cause and Effect at Work* paragraph discusses causes and effects in a workplace situation.

Cause and Effect at Work

In this memo from the file of a fourth-grade student, early childhood educator Luisa Suarez explains some causes and effects of the child's behavioral and learning problems.

Mark frequently expresses his dislike of school and reading. He continues to read at a second-grade level and is behind his classmates in the acquisition of knowledge expected from fourth-grade students. In interviews with the child, he has stated that he never reads at home and spends most of his time watching television. Because he is so far behind his peers in the classroom, he is embarrassed to show his lack of reading skills for fear of ridicule. It is easier for him to "act out," thus distracting others from his deficiency in reading. He displays a low level of self-confidence and appears to have given up trying.

PRACTICE I

Read the next paragraph and answer the questions.

When I played football, I learned to be an animal. Being an animal meant being fanatically aggressive and ruthlessly competitive. If I saw an arm in front of me, I trampled it. Whenever blood was spilled, I nodded approval. Broken bones (not mine of course) were secretly seen as little victories within the bigger struggle. The coaches taught me to "punish the other man," but little did I suspect that I was devastating my own body at the same time. There were broken noses, ribs, fingers, toes and teeth, torn muscles and ligaments, bruises, bad knees, and busted lips, and the gradual pulverizing of my spinal column that, by the time my jock career was long over at age 30, had resulted in seven years of near-constant pain. It was a long road to the surgeon's office.

—Don Sabo, "Pigskin, Patriarch, and Pain"

1. Underline the topic sentence.

2. What does this paragraph focus on? Circle the best answer.

   a. Causes   b. Effects

3. Who is the audience? _____

4. List the supporting details.

   _____

   _____

   _____

   _____

   _____

Identifying Causes and Effects

Imagine that you have to write a cause and effect paragraph about employee absenteeism. You might brainstorm and think of as many causes and effects as possible. Here are some examples:

Causes
- child is sick
- employee is sick
- personal problems such as marital strife, depression
- lack of motivation

Effects
- other employees do more
- may lose job
- could get demoted
- develop financial problems

The Writer's Desk **Identify Causes and Effects**

Write some possible causes and effects for the following topics. Then decide whether your paragraph will focus on causes or effects.

EXAMPLE: Smoke-free work zones

Causes	Effects
workers complain about smoke	employees smoke in entrances
new legislation	cigarette litter outside building
lobby groups ask for smoke-free zones	smokers influence nonsmokers
lack of ventilation in offices	smokers take long breaks

Focus on: effects

1. Cheating

Causes	Effects
_____	_____
_____	_____
_____	_____
_____	_____

Focus on: _____

2. Businesses failure

Causes	Effects
_____	_____
_____	_____
_____	_____
_____	_____

Focus on: _____

3. Teenage rebellion

Causes	Effects
_____	_____
_____	_____
_____	_____
_____	_____

Focus on: _____

DEVELOPING

The Topic Sentence

The topic sentence in a cause and effect paragraph must clearly demonstrate whether the focus is on causes, effects, or both. Also, make sure that you have clearly indicated your controlling idea. For example, read the topic sentences. Notice that the controlling idea is underlined.

ESSAY LINK

In a cause and effect essay, the thesis statement expresses whether the essay will focus on causes, effects, or both.

topic   controlling idea (causes)
The Civil War was fought <u>for many reasons</u>.

topic   controlling idea (effects)
The Civil War <u>changed the values</u> of American society in a profound way.

topic   controlling idea (causes and effects)

The Civil War, which was fought <u>for many reasons,</u> <u>changed the</u> <u>values</u> of American society in a profound way.

PRACTICE 2

Look carefully at the following sets of topic sentences. Decide whether each sentence focuses on causes, effects, or both. Look for key words that give you clues, and circle the best answer.

1. My family has suffered serious consequences because of new technology.

   a. Causes   b. Effects   c. Both

2. The Chernobyl nuclear accident led to problems in the environment, as well as in people's mental and physical health.

   a. Causes   b. Effects   c. Both

3. The Chernobyl nuclear accident happened due to a lack of safety procedures, a faulty design, and poor communication between team members.

   a. Causes   b. Effects   c. Both

4. Because of many problems at the Chernobyl nuclear site, the environment in the Ukraine has changed forever.

   a. Causes   b. Effects   c. Both

 Do Not Confuse *Effect* **and** *Affect*

Generally, *affect* is used as a verb, and *effect* is used as a noun. *Affect* (verb) means "to influence or change," and *effect* (noun) means "result."

verb
How will the new drug <u>affect</u> pregnant women?

noun
What <u>effects</u> will the new drug have on pregnant women?

Effect can also be used as a verb that means "to cause or to bring about." It generally has the following meanings: "to effect a change" or "to effect a plan."

verb
The union members demonstrated to <u>effect</u> changes in their working conditions.

 The Writer's Desk **Write Topic Sentences**

Write a topic sentence for each of the following topics. You can look for ideas in the Warm Up. You can also use the information you generated in the Writer's Desk: Identify Causes and Effects on page 143. Determine whether you will focus on the causes, effects, or both in your paragraph.

EXAMPLE: Smoke-free work zones

Topic sentence: *Smoke-free work zones, implemented for obvious reasons, have had surprising consequences for employees.*

1. Topic: Cheating

   Topic sentence: _____

   _____

2. Topic: A business failure

   Topic sentence: _____

   _____

3. Topic: Teenage rebellion

   Topic sentence: _____

   _____

The Supporting Ideas

After you have developed an effective topic sentence, generate supporting ideas. When planning a cause and effect paragraph, think of examples that clearly show the causes or effects. Then arrange your examples in emphatic order. **Emphatic order** means that you can place your examples from the most to the least important or from the least to the most important.

Hint   **Do Not Oversimplify**

Avoid attributing a simple or general cause to a complex issue. When you use expressions such as *it appears that* or *a possible cause is,* you show that you are aware of the complex factors involved in the situation.

Oversimplification:	The high murder rate in cities is caused by easily obtained firearms.
	(This is an oversimplification of a complicated problem.)
Better:	A possible cause of the high murder rate in cities is the abundance of easily obtained firearms.

The Writer's Desk **Generate Supporting Ideas**

Choose one of the topic sentences from the Writer's Desk on pages 145–146. Then list either causes or effects.

EXAMPLE: Smoke-free work zones, implemented for obvious reasons, have had surprising consequences for employees.

　　polluted entrances of buildings
　　smokers need long breaks
　　smokers influence nonsmokers

Topic sentence: _____

_____

Supports: _____

_____

_____

The Paragraph Plan

In many courses, instructors ask students to write about the causes or effects of a particular subject. It is a good idea to plan your paragraph before you write your final version. Also think about the order of ideas. Arrange the supporting details in a logical order. As you make your plan, ensure that you focus on causes, effects, or both.

ESSAY LINK

In a cause and effect essay, place the thesis statement in the introduction. Then use body paragraphs, each with its own topic sentence, to support the thesis statement.

TOPIC SENTENCE:	Smoke-free work zones, implemented for obvious reasons, have had surprising consequences for employees.
Support 1:	Smokers stand at entrances to have their cigarettes.
Details:	—drop their cigarette butts on the ground —heavy smoke at the entrances
Support 2:	Smokers take more breaks.
Details:	—need frequent cigarette breaks —not fair to others who must do extra work
Support 3:	Smoking culture influences nonsmokers.
Details:	—nonsmokers take breaks with their smoking friends —some nonsmokers become smokers

The Writer's Desk   **Write a Paragraph Plan**

Refer to the information you generated in previous Writer's Desk exercises and create a paragraph plan. If you think of new details that will explain your point more effectively, include them here.

Topic sentence: _____

_____

Support 1: _____
Details: _____
_____
_____

Support 2: _____
Details: _____
_____
_____

Support 3: _____
Details: _____
_____
_____

The First Draft

After you outline your ideas in a plan, you are ready to write the first draft. Remember to write complete sentences. You might include transitional words or expressions to help your ideas flow smoothly.

Transitional Words and Expressions

The following transitional expressions are useful for showing causes and effects.

To Show Causes	To Show Effects
for this reason	accordingly
the first cause	as a result
the most important cause	consequently

The Writer's Desk **Write the First Draft**

Write the first draft of your cause and effect paragraph. Before you write, carefully review your paragraph plan and make any necessary changes.

REVISING AND EDITING

Revise and Edit a Cause and Effect Paragraph

When you finish writing a cause and effect paragraph, review your work and revise it to make the examples as clear as possible to your readers. Make sure that your sentences relate to the topic sentence and flow together smoothly.

PRACTICE 3

Read the next student paragraph and answer the questions.

> Smoke-free work zones, implemented for obvious reasons, have had surprising consequences for employees. First, smokers light up outside the main entrances of buildings, and nonsmokers must pass through a cloud of heavy smoke to get inside. Additionally, the ground outside entrances is littered with cigarette butts, which smokers do not consider as pollution. Moreover, smokers get more breaks because they frequently leave their workstations to have cigarettes. Some people smoke cigars, and others smoke pipes. The nonsmokers must work more harder to cover for their smoking colleagues, and this makes the nonsmokers resentful. An other surprising consequence is that the smoking culture influences nonsmokers. Former smokers, or those who have never smoked, sometimes get into the habit of smoking in order to socialize with their colleagues during the many breaks. Although no-smoking rules are in the public interest, the consequences of such rules should be examined more thoroughly.

Revising

1. Does the paragraph focus on causes, effects, or both? _____

2. List the causes or effects given. _____

   _____

   _____

   _____

3. There is one sentence in the paragraph that does not really relate to the topic sentence. Cross out that sentence.

Editing

4. There is one error with the comparative form. An adverb is incorrectly formed. Correct the error directly on the text. (For more information about adjectives and adverbs, see Chapter 29.)

5. This paragraph contains two misspelled words. Identify and correct them.

The Writer's Desk Revise and Edit Your Paragraph

Revise and edit the paragraph that you wrote for the Writer's Desk on page 149. Ensure that your paragraph has unity, adequate support, and coherence. Also correct any errors in grammar, spelling, punctuation, and mechanics.

REFLECT ON IT

Think about what you have learned in this chapter. If you do not know an answer, review that topic.

1. What is the difference between the words *affect* and *effect?*

   Affect: _____

   Effect: _____

2. Brainstorm to think of three possible causes for each option.

   a. Starting to smoke _____

   _____

   b. A car crash _____

   _____

3. Brainstorm to think of three possible effects for each option.

   a. Pollution: _____

   _____

   b. War: _____

   _____

The Writer's Room · Topics for Cause and Effect Paragraphs

Writing Activity 1

Choose any of the following topics, or choose your own topic. Then write a cause and effect paragraph.

General Topics

Causes and/or effects of . . .

1. having a close friendship
2. having a caffeine addiction
3. getting a higher education
4. having a poor body image
5. spoiling a child
6. joining a sports team

College and Work-Related Topics

Causes and/or effects of . . .

7. having low (or high) marks in college
8. not keeping up with college workload
9. quitting a job
10. working with a family member
11. working at home
12. getting a promotion

WRITING LINK

More Cause and Effect Writing Topics
Chapter 19, Writer's Room topic 2 (page 305)
Chapter 26, Writer's Room topic 3. (page 388)
Chapter 35, Writer's Room topic 2. (page 511)

Writing Activity 2

Think about a day when you felt frustrated. What causes you to feel like screaming? What are the effects when you scream at someone or when someone screams at you? Write a paragraph about the causes or effects of screaming.

READING LINK

More Cause and Effect Readings
"Dying to Be Bigger" by H.D. (page 575)
"Growing Up in Cyberspace" by Brent Staples (page 548)

CAUSE AND EFFECT PARAGRAPH CHECKLIST

As you write your cause and effect paragraph, review the checklist on the inside front cover. Also ask yourself the following questions.

☐ Does my topic sentence indicate clearly that my paragraph focuses on causes, effects, or both?

☐ Do I have adequate supporting examples of causes and/or effects?

☐ Do I make logical and valid points?

☐ Do I use the terms *effect* and/or *affect* correctly?

 See Chapter 11 of the Visualizing Writing CD for an additional mini-lecture on **Cause and Effect.**

Argument

> *Do not fear to be eccentric in opinion, for every opinion now accepted was once eccentric.*
>
> —BERTRAND RUSSELL
> *British author and philosopher (1872–1970)*

CONTENTS

Exploring
- Explore Topics
- What Is Argument?
- The Argument Paragraph

Developing
- The Topic Sentence
- The Supporting Ideas
- The Paragraph Plan
- The First Draft

Revising and Editing
- Revise and Edit an Argument Paragraph

Lawyers have to make effective arguments to persuade a judge and jury. In argument writing, you try to convince readers to agree with your point of view.

EXPLORING

Explore Topics

In the Warm Up, you will try an exploring strategy to generate ideas about different topics.

The Writer's Desk Warm Up

Think about the following questions, and write down the first ideas that come to mind. Try to think of two or three ideas for each topic.

EXAMPLE: Should public schools require students to wear uniforms?

Yes, I think so. Then rich kids do not stand out so much, and neither do poor ones. Everyone dresses the same. The kids look more serious. But some kids will hate this rule. They'll try to break the rule somehow.

1. Sometimes minors steal, vandalize, go joyriding, and do other illegal acts. Should parents pay for damages when their children break the law?

   _____

   _____

   _____

2. In some countries, all youths must do two years of military service. What do you think about compulsory military service?

   _____

   _____

3. What are some of the major controversial issues in your neighborhood, at your workplace, at your college, or in the news these days?

   _____

   _____

   _____

What Is Argument?

When you use **argument,** you take a position on an issue and try to defend your position. You try to convince somebody that your point of view is the best one.

Argument is both a writing pattern and a purpose for writing. In fact, it is one of the most common aims, or purposes, in most college and work-related writing. For example, in Chapter 10, there is a paragraph about teen fashion, and the author uses comparison and contrast as the predominant pattern. At the same time, the author uses argument to convince the reader that fashions have not become more shocking over the years. Therefore, in most of your college and work-related writing, your purpose is to persuade the reader that your ideas are compelling and legitimate.

You use argument every day. You might write a persuasive letter to a newspaper to express your views about public policy. At college, in a sociology class, you might take a position on capital punishment or on gun control. At work, you might have to convince your manager to give you a raise.

Argument at Work

In this memo to a residential program manager, Kamal Natu, a family service worker, uses argument writing to explain why she recommends a children's group home.

My client, a six-year-old boy, should immediately receive part-time placement in a children's group home. He is severely brain damaged and is delayed in every normal area of development, including sensory, social, and emotional functions. He also has a gross deficit in language communication and great difficulties in responding to his enironment. The family needs support to look after him on weekends and during stressful periods. Because of the great demands put on the parents looking after my client, family members cannot enjoy interactions such as eating meals, reading books, playing games, and so on. To relieve some pressure from the family and to look after the boy's needs, weekend placement in a group home for my client is necessary.

The Argument Paragraph

When you write an argument paragraph, remember the following four points.

ESSAY LINK

When you write argument essays, also keep these four points in mind.

- **Choose a subject that you know something about.** It would be very difficult to write a good text about space research funds, capital punishment, or conditions in federal prisons, for example, if you have never had experience with, or read about, these issues. On the other hand, if you, or someone close to you, cannot find good day care, then you could likely write a very effective paper about the necessity of having better day-care services.
- **Consider your readers.** What do your readers already know about the topic? Will they likely agree or disagree with you? Do they have specific concerns? Consider what kind of evidence would be most effective with your audience.
- **Know your purpose.** In argument writing, your main purpose is to persuade the reader to agree with you. Your specific purpose is more focused. You may want the reader to take action, you may want to support a view-point, you may want to counter somebody else's argument, or you may want to offer a solution to a problem. Ask yourself what your specific purpose is.
- **Take a strong position and provide supporting evidence.** The first thing to do in the body of your paragraph is to prove that there is, indeed, a problem. Then back up your point of view with a combination of facts, statistics, examples, and informed opinions.

Be Passionate!

When you are planning your argument paragraph, try to find a topic that you feel passionate about. If you care about your topic, and if you express your enthusiasm, your audience will be more likely to care about it, too.

PRACTICE 1

Read the next paragraph and answer the questions.

Ordinary families would benefit greatly from a plan that provided health insurance to those now uninsured. It is true that at any given moment most middle-income families have insurance, but people lose their jobs, companies go bankrupt, and benefits get suddenly slashed. Over any given two-year period, roughly a third of Americans spend some time without health insurance; over longer periods, the risk of losing health insurance is very significant for most families. When a family without health insurance suffers illness, the results are often catastrophic—either serious conditions go untreated or the family faces financial ruin. Our inadequate insurance system is one important reason why America, the richest country in the world, has lower life expectancy and higher child mortality than most other advanced nations. If American families knew what was good for them, then most of them—all but a small, affluent minority—would cheerfully give up any tax cuts in return for a guarantee that health care would be there when needed. And even the affluent might prefer to live in a society where no sick child was left behind.

—Paul Krugman, *New York Times* editorial

1. Underline the topic sentence.

2. Who is the author's audience? _____

3. What is the author's specific purpose? _____

_____

_____

4. What health-care issues might concern the audience?

_____

_____

_____

_____

5. Underline some examples that the author gives to show that there is a problem.

6. Look at the author's supporting evidence, and circle a statistic.

The Topic Sentence

In the topic sentence of an argument paragraph, state your position on the issue.

Topic + Controlling idea (your position on the issue)

controlling idea   topic

<u>Our government should severely punish</u> **corporate executives who commit fraud.**

Your topic sentence should be a debatable statement. It should not be a fact or a statement of opinion.

Fact:	In some public schools, students wear uniforms.
	(This is a fact. It cannot be debated.)
Opinion:	I think that it is a good idea for public school students to wear uniforms.
	(This is a statement of opinion. Nobody can deny that you like school uniforms. Therefore, do not use phrases such as *In my opinion, I think,* or *I believe* in your topic sentence.)
Argument:	Public school students should wear uniforms.
	(This is a debatable statement.)

PRACTICE 2

Evaluate the following statements. Write *F* for a fact, *O* for an opinion, or *A* for a debatable argument.

1. I think that the drinking age is too high in New York State. _____

2. The legal drinking age is too high in New York State. _____

3. The legal drinking age should be lowered to eighteen in all states. _____

4. In Canada, the legal drinking age is eighteen in most provinces. _____

5. In my opinion, some college students drink too much. _____

6. Some students engage in binge drinking on our college campus. _____

7. The proposed "No Binge Drinking" campaign should be scrapped because underage drinking is not a serious problem in our college. _____

8. I believe that most students are responsible and do not abuse alcohol. _____

Be Direct

You may feel reluctant to state your point of view directly. You may feel that it is impolite to do so. However, in academic writing, it is perfectly acceptable, and even desirable, to state an argument in a direct manner.

In argument writing, you can make your topic debatable by using *should, must,* or *ought to* in the topic sentence or thesis statement.

Although daily prayer is important for many people in the United States, it **should** not take place in the classroom.

The Writer's Desk **Write Topic Sentences**

Write a topic sentence for the next topics. You can look for ideas in the Warm Up on page 153. Make sure that each topic sentence clearly expresses your position on the issue.

EXAMPLE: <u>Uniforms should be mandatory in public</u>
<u>schools.</u>

1. Topic: Parents paying for children's crime sprees

   Topic sentence: _____

   _____

2. Topic: Compulsory military service

   Topic sentence: _____

   _____

3. Topic: A controversial issue in the news, in your neighborhood, at work, or at college

   Topic sentence: _____

   _____

ESSAY LINK

In an argument essay, body paragraphs should contain supporting details such as examples, facts, informed opinions, logical consequences, or answers to the opposition.

The Supporting Ideas

When you write an argument paragraph, it is important to support your point of view with examples, facts, statistics, and informed opinions. It is also effective to think about some answers you can give to counter the opposition's point of view, and you can consider the long-term consequences if something does not occur. Therefore, try to use several types of supporting evidence.

- **Examples** are pieces of information that illustrate your main argument. For instance, if you want to argue that there are not enough day-care centers in your area, you can explain that one center has over one hundred children on its waiting list.

Another type of example is the **anecdote.** To support your main point, you can write about a true event or tell a personal story. For example, if you think that rebellious teenagers hurt their families, you might tell a personal story about your brother's involvement with a gang.

- **Facts** are statements that can be verified in some way. For example, the following statement is a fact: "According to the World Health Organization, secondhand smoke can cause cancer in nonsmokers." **Statistics** are another type of fact. When you use statistics, ensure that the source is reliable, and remember to mention the source. For example, if you want to argue that underage drinking is a problem, you could mention the following statistic from the *Journal of the American Medical Association:* "Underage drinkers consume about 20 percent of all the alcohol imbibed in this country."

- Sometimes experts in a field express an **informed opinion** about an issue. An expert's opinion can give added weight to your argument. For example, if you want to argue that the courts treat youths who commit crimes too harshly or leniently, then you might quote a judge who deals with juvenile criminals. If you want to argue that secondhand smoke is dangerous, then you might quote a lung specialist or a health organization.

- Solutions to problems can carry **logical consequences.** When you plan an argument, think about long-term consequences if something does or does not happen. For example, in response to the terrorist attacks of September 11, 2001, many governments enacted antiterrorism legislation. However, in some cases, the new laws could be used to suppress legitimate dissent or free speech. Also, those new laws could be misused or misinterpreted by future governments.

- In argument writing, try to **answer the opposition.** For example, if you want to argue that drinking laws are ineffective, you might think about the arguments that your opposition might make. Then you might write, "Drinking age laws do a fine job of keeping young people out of clubs and bars; however, these laws do nothing to keep young people from getting access to alcohol from other places." Try to refute some of the strongest arguments of the opposition.

 Avoid Circular Reasoning

When you write an argument paragraph, ensure that your main point is supported with facts, examples, informed opinions, and so on. Do not use circular reasoning. Circular reasoning means that you restate your main point in various different ways.

Circular	The abundance of spam is not harmless; in fact, a lot of junk e-mail is offensive. People receive many copies of junk mail and the content offends them. Most people complain when they receive too much junk e-mail, and they feel especially unhappy when the junk e-mail has offensive images.
Not Circular	The abundance of spam is not harmless; in fact, a lot of junk e-mail is offensive. According to Odin Wortman of Internet Working Solutions, about thirty percent of e-mail is pornographic. Children and older people open such mail hoping for a message from a friend, only to see an offensive picture. Another thirty percent of junk mail advertises fraudulent schemes to get rich quick and hawks products of questionable value or safety.

Avoid Common Errors

When you write an argument paragraph or essay, avoid the following pitfalls.

Do not make generalizations. If you begin a statement with *Everyone knows* or *It is common knowledge*, then the reader may mistrust what you say. You cannot possibly know what everyone else knows. It is better to refer to specific sources.

Generalization:	Everyone knows that sending troops to Iraq was necessary.
Better:	Prominent politicians such as Donald Rumsfeld stated that sending troops to Iraq was necessary.

Use emotional arguments sparingly. Certainly, the strongest arguments can be emotional ones. Sometimes the most effective way to influence others is to appeal to their sense of justice, humanity, pride, or guilt. However, do not rely on emotional arguments. If you use emotionally charged words (for example, if you call someone *ignorant*) or if you try to appeal to base instincts (for example, if you appeal to people's fear of other ethnic groups), then you will seriously undermine your argument.

Emotional:	Bleeding-heart liberals did not want the United States to send troops to Iraq.
Better:	Many sectors of society, including several student activists, actors, educators, and business groups, did not want the United States to send troops to Iraq.

Do not make exaggerated claims. Make sure that your arguments are plausible.

Exaggerated:	If military forces had not captured Iraq's leader, Saddam Hussein, eventually the United States would have been destroyed.
Better:	If military forces had not captured Saddam Hussein, the tyrant would have continued to terrorize his people.

The Paragraph Plan

Before you write your argument paragraph, make a plan. Think of some supporting arguments, and think about details that can help illustrate each argument. Ensure that every example is valid and that it relates to the topic sentence. Also, arrange your ideas in a logical order.

TOPIC SENTENCE:	There should be mandatory uniforms in public schools.
Support 1:	Students will feel as if they belong.
Details:	—Uniforms will give a sense that students are united.
Support 2:	Uniforms will equalize rich and poor students.
Details:	—Rich students cannot show off their expensive clothing. —Poor students will not stand out so much.
Support 3:	Uniforms are convenient.
Details:	—Instead of a large wardrobe, two or three uniforms serve for school. —Students do not waste time deciding what to wear each day.

The Writer's Desk **Write a Paragraph Plan**

Choose one of the topic sentences that you wrote for the Writer's Desk on page 158, and write a detailed paragraph plan. You can refer to the information you generated in previous Writer's Desk exercises, and if you think of examples that will explain your point more effectively, include them here.

Subject: _____

Topic sentence: _____

_____

_____

Support 1: _____

Details: _____

_____

_____

Support 2: _____

Details: _____

_____

_____

Support 3: _____

Details: _____

_____

_____

The First Draft

After you outline your ideas in a plan, you are ready to write the first draft. Remember to write complete sentences. You might include transitional words or expressions to help your ideas flow smoothly.

Transitional Words and Expressions

The following transitional words and expressions can introduce an answer to the opposition or the support for an argument.

To Answer the Opposition	To Support Your Argument
admittedly	certainly
however	consequently

(continued)

To Answer the Opposition	To Support Your Argument
nevertheless	furthermore
of course	in fact
on one hand/on the other hand	obviously
undoubtedly	of course

The Writer's Desk **Write the First Draft**

Write the first draft of your argument paragraph. Before you write, carefully review your paragraph plan and make any necessary changes.

REVISING AND EDITING

Revise and Edit an Argument Paragraph

When you finish writing an argument paragraph, carefully review your work and revise it to make the supporting examples as clear as possible to your readers. Check that the order of ideas is logical, and remove any irrelevant details.

PRACTICE 4

Read the next student paragraph and answer the questions.

> In public schools, some students wear inappropriate clothing such as low-cut jeans and dirty baseball caps, and they look idiotic. To solve the problem, there should be mandatory uniforms in public schools. When schools make uniforms compulsory, most students develop a stronger sense of loyalty to their school. With uniforms, rich students are no longer able to display their wealth by wearing expensive clothing, and poor students do not need to buy the latest fashions. Nobody would feel no pressure to have brand-name clothing. School uniforms are also convenient and less costly. Students would no longer have to spend money on a large wardrobe, and two or three uniforms could serve for the whole school year. Also, students are gonna waste less time deciding what to wear each day. If schools do not make uniforms compulsory, students will wear bathing suits to school, and the corridors could become filled with anarchy. Definitely it is a good idea to force students to wear school uniforms.

Revising

1. Underline the topic sentence. Remember that the topic sentence is not always the first sentence in the paragraph.

2. The writer uses emotionally charged words and exaggerates. Give examples of each of these problems.

   Emotionally charged word: _____

   Exaggeration: _____

   _____

3. List the three arguments that support the topic sentence.

   _____

   _____

   _____

Editing

4. In this paragraph there is one nonstandard verb, which is a verb that people say but should not write. Underline the error and write the correct form in the space below. (For more information about nonstandard verb forms, see Chapter 24.)

   Correction: _____

5. This paragraph contains a double negative. Underline the error and write the correct phrase in the space. (For more information about double negatives, see Chapter 22.)

   Correction: _____

The Writer's Desk **Revise and Edit Your Paragraph**

Revise and edit the paragraph that you wrote for the previous Writer's Desk. Ensure that your paragraph has unity, adequate support, and coherence. Also correct any errors in grammar, spelling, punctuation, and mechanics.

REFLECT ON IT

Think about what you have learned in this chapter. If you do not know an answer, review that topic.

1. What is the main purpose of an argument paragraph or essay?

   _____

2. What is the difference between a statement of opinion and a statement of argument?

   _____

   _____

(continued)

PART III

The Essay

What Is an Essay?

An *essay* is a series of paragraphs. Essays differ in length, style, and subject, but the structure of an essay generally consists of an *introductory paragraph,* several *body paragraphs,* and a *concluding paragraph.*

Before you begin reading the next chapters, become familiar with the parts of the common five-paragraph essay.

Each body paragraph begins with a topic sentence.

The introductory paragraph introduces the essay's topic and contains its thesis statement.

The title gives a hint about the essay's topic.

The thesis statement contains the essay's topic and its controlling idea.

Alternative Culture

In an era when alternative has become mainstream, what's an angst-ridden teenager to do? Dying hair punk colors has become passé. Goths with white face powder, dark lipstick, and lots of eyeliner no longer attract even a second glance. Everyone listens to "alternative" music. It has become increasingly hard for a teenager to rebel against the mainstream.

In other eras, youths had something to rebel about. The 1960s had the hippie era, as young adults rebelled by protesting against injustice, the Vietnam War, and the restrictions of society. LSD, marijuana, and free love reigned. Flash forward to the 1970s, when the punk movement came into existence with bands such as the Sex Pistols, and unemployed youths railed against consumerism. Kurt Cobain in the early 1990s became the rallying cry for a new generation of teenagers disillusioned with the confines of society. But what about now?

Furthermore, bizarre fashion statements have become acceptable. Previously, rebellious teenagers had to resort to shopping in thrift stores or making their own clothes to attain their desired fashion statement. Luckily (or unluckily) for them, society now makes it easy to dress like an individual. Companies make jeans that already have holes in them so they do not have to wait around to have that punk look. If they want to look different, they can try Urban Outfitters, the trendy chain store for people who are fed up with trendy chain stores, where they can look "unique" just like everone else who shops there.

With this watering down of alternative culture, it has become harder and harder to shock anyone or gain any notorious press. Marilyn Manson, the press's former whipping boy and scapegoat for music as a cause of violence in society (witness the aftermath of the Columbine shootings), has faded from the public's view. Then Eminem became a strange symbol for the increasingly difficult quest to be different from everyone else and to shock society into paying attention. He got some press for his song about killing his wife, but today, nobody is paying attention.

Perhaps to be truly alternative, adolescents must think for themselves. They must be themselves, no matter what they might be. They can dress as punk or as preppy as they like. They should not let society's version of "alternative" control their actions. The truly cool can think for themselves.

The concluding paragraph brings the essay to a satisfactory close.

Each body paragraph contains details that support the thesis statement.

—*Veena Thomas, student*

Writing the Essay

> *Without words, without writing, and without books there would be no history, and there could be no concept of humanity.*
>
> —HERMANN HESSE
> *German author (1877–1962)*

CONTENTS

Exploring
- Explore Topics

Developing
- The Thesis Statement
- The Supporting Ideas
- The Essay Plan
- The Introduction
- The Conclusion
- The First Draft

Revising and Editing
- Revising and Editing the Essay
- The Essay Title
- The Final Draft

Completed in 1973, The Sydney Opera House in Australia has tons of concrete, steel, and glass supporting its structure. In the same way, an essay is a sturdy structure that is supported by a strong thesis statement and solid body paragraphs held together by plenty of facts and examples.

EXPLORING

Explore Topics

There are limitless topics for writing essays. Your knowledge and personal experiences will help you find topics and develop ideas when you write your essay.

When you are planning your essay, consider your topic, audience, and purpose. Your **topic** is who or what you are writing about. Your **audience** is your intended reader, and your **purpose** is your reason for writing. Do you hope to entertain, inform, or persuade the reader?

Narrowing the Topic

Your instructor may assign you a topic for your essay, or you may need to think of your own. In either case, you need to narrow your topic (make it more specific) to ensure that it suits your purpose for writing and fits the size of the assignment. To narrow your topic, you can use some exploring methods such as questioning or brainstorming.

WRITING LINK

For more information about exploring strategies, see Chapter 1.

When you narrow your topic, keep in mind that an essay contains several paragraphs; therefore, an essay topic can be broader than a paragraph topic. In the next examples, you will notice that the essay topic is narrow but is slightly larger than the paragraph topic.

Broad Topic	**Paragraph Topic**	**Essay Topic**
Job interview	Dressing for the interview	Preparing for the interview
Rituals	College orientation week	Initiation rituals

 Choosing an Essay Topic

Paragraphs and essays can also be about the same topic. However, an essay has more details and concrete examples to support its thesis.

Do not make the mistake of choosing an essay topic that is too broad. Essays that try to cover a large topic risk being superficial and overly general. Make sure that your topic is specific enough that you can cover it in an essay.

OCTAVIO NARROWS HIS TOPIC

Student writer Octavio Sanchez used both brainstorming and questioning to narrow his broad topic, "live entertainment." His audience was his English instructor, and the purpose of his assignment was to persuade.

– should beautiful old theaters be restored?
– ban street performers
– permit artists to sell portraits on the streets
– why clowns are creepy
– bad circuses
– treatment of circus animals
– what is talent?
– the best types of nightclubs

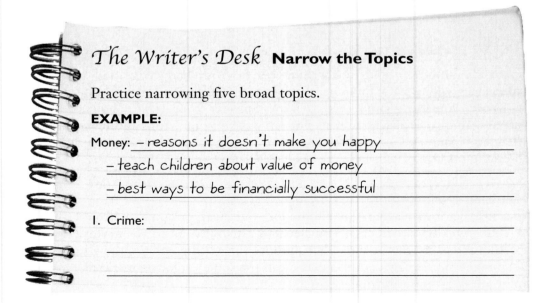

The Writer's Desk **Narrow the Topics**

Practice narrowing five broad topics.

EXAMPLE:

Money: – reasons it doesn't make you happy

– teach children about value of money

– best ways to be financially successful

1. Crime: _____

_____

_____

2. Volunteer work: _____

_____

_____

3. Fashion: _____

_____

_____

4. Advertising: _____

_____

_____

5. Education: _____

_____

_____

DEVELOPING

The Thesis Statement

Once you have narrowed the topic of your essay, develop your thesis statement. The **thesis statement**—like the topic sentence in a paragraph—introduces the topic of the essay and arouses the interest of the reader.

Characteristics of a Good Thesis Statement

A thesis statement has three important characteristics.

- It expresses the main topic of the essay.
- It contains a controlling idea.
- It is a complete sentence that usually appears in the essay's introductory paragraph.

Here is an example of an effective thesis statement.

topic   controlling idea
Marriage has lost its importance for many young people in our society.

Writing an Effective Thesis Statement

When you develop your thesis statement, ask yourself the following questions.

1. **Is my thesis statement a complete statement that has a controlling idea?**
   Your thesis statement should always reveal a complete thought and make a point about the topic. It should not announce the topic or express a widely known fact.

Incomplete:	Gambling problems.
	(This statement is not complete.)
Announcement:	I will write about lotteries.
	(This statement announces the topic but says nothing relevant about the topic. Do not use expressions such as *I will write about . . .* or *My topic is . . .*)
Thesis statement:	A lottery win will not necessarily lead to happiness.

2. **Does my thesis statement make a valid and supportable point?** Your thesis statement should express a valid point that you can support with evidence. It should not be a vaguely worded statement, and it should not be a highly questionable generalization.

Vague:	Workplace relationships are harmful.
	(For whom are they harmful?)
Invalid point:	Women earn less money than men.
	(Is this really true for all women in all professions? This generalization might be hard to prove.)
Thesis statement:	Before co-workers become romantically involved, they should carefully consider possible problems.

3. **Can I support my thesis statement in an essay?** Your thesis statement should express an idea that you can support in an essay. It should not be too broad or too narrow.

Too broad:	There are many museums in the world.
	(It would be difficult to write an essay about this topic.)
Too narrow:	The Spy Museum is in Washington.
	(What more is there to say?)
Topic sentence:	Washington's Spy Museum contains fascinating artifacts related to the secret world of espionage.

 Give Specific Details

Give enough details to make your thesis statement interesting. Your instructor may want you to guide the reader through your main points. To do this, mention both your main point and your supporting points in your thesis statement. In other words, your thesis statement provides a map for the readers to follow.

Weak: My first job taught me many things.

Better: My first job taught me about responsibility, organization, and the importance of teamwork.

PRACTICE I

Identify the problem in each thesis statement. Then revise each statement to make it more interesting and complete.

Announces	Invalid	Broad
Incomplete	Vague	Narrow

EXAMPLE:

I will write about human misery on television news.

Problem: _Announces_

Revised statement: _Television news programs should not treat personal tragedies as big news._

1. I think that college friendships are important.

   Problem: _____

   Revised statement: _____

   _____

2. Scholarships go to athletes, so academic excellence is not appreciated in colleges.

   Problem: _____

   Revised statement: _____

   _____

3. Scientific discoveries have changed the world.

   Problem: _____

   Revised statement: _____

   _____

4. The streets are becoming more dangerous.

   Problem: _____

   Revised statement: _____

   _____

5. How to discipline children.

   Problem: _____

   Revised statement: _____

   _____

6. This essay will talk about security and privacy on the Internet.

   Problem: _____

   Revised statement: _____

   _____

The Writer's Desk **Write Thesis Statements**

For each item, choose a narrowed topic from the Writer's Desk on page 170. Then write an interesting thesis statement. Remember that each thesis statement should contain a controlling idea.

EXAMPLE: Topic: Money

Narrowed topic: _Winning a lottery_

Thesis statement: _Rather than improving your life, a lottery win can lead to feelings of guilt, paranoia, and boredom._

1. Topic: Crime

   Narrowed topic: _____

   Thesis statement: _____

   _____

2. Topic: Volunteer work

   Narrowed topic: _____

   Thesis statement: _____

   _____

3. Topic: Fashion

   Narrowed topic: _____

   Thesis statement: _____

   _____

4. Topic: Advertising

   Narrowed topic: _____

   Thesis statement: _____

   _____

5. Topic: Education

   Narrowed topic: _____

   Thesis statement: _____

   _____

The Supporting Ideas

The thesis statement expresses the main idea of the entire essay. In the following illustration, you can see how the ideas flow in an essay. Topic sentences relate to the thesis statement, and details support the topic sentences; therefore, every single idea in the essay is unified and supports the thesis.

PRACTICE 2

Read the following essay. After you have finished reading, do the following:

1. Create an effective thesis statement. It should sum up the point of the entire essay.

2. Write a topic sentence at the beginning of each body paragraph. The topic sentence should sum up the main point of the paragraph in an interesting way.

Introduction:

    Danger has always been synonymous with travel. In past centuries, pirates on the high seas attacked passing ships. Land travelers were not much safer; bandits could attack their covered carriages. Even trains were not safe; in 1877 the masked outlaw Sam Bass held up a train in Nebraska and robbed the passengers. Today, with modern communication and with high-speed trains and planes, travel is quick and relatively risk-free. Nonetheless, there are still certain hazards inherent in traveling.

Thesis statement: _____

_____

Body paragraph 1 topic sentence: _____

_____

    For example, before you arrive in a new town, find an address and phone number for affordable lodging, and book a room for your first night. If you are a budget traveler, you can always find cheaper accommodations the next day. If you are going to visit a large city, plan to arrive during the daylight hours. It is dangerous to arrive at night and then try to find your way around. Also, make sure that you have a map of your destination. You can download maps on the Internet.

Body paragraph 2 topic sentence: _____

_____

    Do not flash your money in public places. You might wear a money belt under your clothing. One innovative solution is to sew long, extended pockets on the insides of your clothes; you could keep your checks and passport there. In a small, easily accessible purse or wallet, keep small amounts of local currency for your daily spending.

Body paragraph 3 topic sentence: _____

_____

For example, you could bring along a first aid kit that includes bandages and pain relievers. Wear hats in very hot, sunny places. If you are visiting a tropical country, make sure you have the proper vaccinations. Be careful about where you eat and what you eat, and buy bottled drinking water. Your health is important. Obviously, if you get sick, you are not going to enjoy your trip.

Conclusion:
Although robberies can happen, it is unlikely that someone will physically hurt you. If you take risks with your health, if you are careless with your money and passports, or if you underestimate thieves, you may have an unpleasant experience. Of course, if you are careful, you should have a perfectly safe and exciting trip.

Generating Supporting Ideas

An effective essay has **unity** when the body paragraphs support the thesis statement. When you develop supporting ideas, make sure that they all focus on the central point that you are making in the thesis statement. To generate ideas for body paragraphs, you could use exploring strategies such as brainstorming, clustering, or freewriting.

OCTAVIO'S SUPPORTING IDEAS

Octavio created a list to support his thesis statement. Then he reread his supporting points and removed ideas that he did not want to develop in his essay.

THESIS STATEMENT: Circuses should be banned from using large animals such as tigers, bears, and elephants.

Supporting points:

— animals may get hurt in training and during the show

— tigers may be muzzled or even drugged

— whips and electric prods are used on animals

— animals are a danger to public and trainers

— ~~not good education for children~~

— some animals go on rampages

— animals are kept in confined spaces

— moved around in hot trailers or trains

— no room to roam

— ~~circus animals are not that interesting to see~~

The Writer's Desk List Supporting Ideas

Choose two of your thesis statements from the previous Writer's Desk on page 174, and create two lists of possible supporting ideas.

Thesis 1: _____   Thesis 2: _____

_____   _____

Support: _____   Support: _____

_____   _____

_____   _____

_____   _____

_____   _____

_____   _____

_____   _____

_____   _____

_____   _____

_____   _____

Organizing Your Ideas

After you have examined your list of supporting ideas, choose three or four that are most compelling and most clearly support your statement. Highlight your favorite ideas, and then group together related ideas. Finally, make your essay as clear and coherent as possible by organizing your ideas in a logical manner using time, space, or emphatic order.

WRITING LINK

For more information about time, space, and emphatic order, see Chapter 2, "Developing."

OCTAVIO'S EXAMPLE

Octavio underlined his three best supporting points, and he grouped related ideas using emphatic order.

2
- animals may get hurt in training and during the show
- dangerous animals may be muzzled or even drugged
- whips and electric prods are used on animals

3
- animals are a danger to public and trainers
- not good education for children
- some animals go on a rampage

1
- animals are kept in confined spaces
- moved around in hot trailers or trains
- no room to roam
- circus animals are not that interesting to see

The Writer's Desk **Organize Your Ideas**

Look at the list you produced in the previous Writer's Desk, and then follow these steps.

1. Highlight at least three ideas from your list that you think are most compelling and most clearly illustrate the point you are making in your thesis statement.

2. Group together any related ideas with the three supporting ideas.

3. Organize your ideas using time, space, or emphatic order.

The Essay Plan

An **essay plan** or an **outline** can help you organize your thesis statement and supporting ideas before writing your first draft. To create an essay plan, follow these steps.

- Look at your list of ideas and identify the best supporting ideas.
- Write topic sentences that express the main supporting ideas.
- Add details under each topic sentence.

In the planning stage, you do not have to develop your introduction and conclusion. It is sufficient to simply write your thesis statement and an idea for your conclusion. Later, when you develop your essay, you can develop the introduction and conclusion.

OCTAVIO'S ESSAY PLAN

Octavio wrote topic sentences and supporting examples and organized his ideas into a plan. Notice that he begins with his thesis statement, and he indents his supporting ideas.

THESIS STATEMENT:	<u>Circuses should be banned from using large animals such as tigers, bears, and elephants.</u>
Body paragraph 1:	Travel is hard on the animals. —They are moved around in hot trailers or trains. —They are kept in small cages.
Body paragraph 2:	Animals may get hurt in training or during the show. —Tigers and bears are muzzled or drugged. —Trainers use electric prods and whips.
Body paragraph 3:	The animals are a danger to the public and trainers. —Some animals go on rampages. —Some attack and kill their trainers.
Concluding idea:	Circuses do not need wild animals in order to be successful.

Writing a Formal Essay Plan

Most of the time, a basic essay plan is sufficient. However, in some of your courses, your instructor may ask you to make a formal plan. A formal plan uses Roman numerals and letters to identify main and supporting ideas.

Thesis statement: _____

    I. _____

        A. _____

        B. _____

   II. _____

        A. _____

        B. _____

  III. _____

        A. _____

        B. _____

Concluding idea: _____

PRACTICE 3

Create an essay plan based on Veena Thomas's essay "Alternative Culture" on page 168.

_____

_____

_____

_____

_____

_____

_____

_____

_____

_____

_____

_____

_____

_____

PRACTICE 4

Complete the following essay plan. Add details under each supporting point.
Make sure that the details relate to the topic sentence.

Thesis statement: Rather than improving your life, a lottery win can
lead to feelings of guilt, paranoia, and boredom.

I.   Feelings of guilt are common in newly rich people.

Details: A. _____

_____

B. _____

_____

C. _____

_____

II. Lottery winners often become paranoid.

Details: A. _____

_____

B. _____

_____

C. _____

_____

III. After lottery winners quit their jobs, they commonly complain
of boredom.

Details: A. _____

_____

B. _____

_____

C. _____

_____

Concluding idea: _____

_____

_____

The Writer's Desk   **Write an Essay Plan**

Write an essay plan using one of your thesis statements and supporting details you came up with in the previous Writer's Desk on page 178.

Thesis statement: _____

_____

I. _____

Details: A. _____

B. _____

C. _____

II. _____

Details: A. _____

B. _____

C. _____

III. _____

Details: A. _____

B. _____

C. _____

Concluding idea: _____

_____

The Introduction

After you have made an essay plan, you develop the sections of your essay by creating an effective introduction, linking paragraphs, and a conclusion.

The **introductory paragraph** introduces the subject of your essay and contains the thesis statement. A strong introduction will capture the reader's attention and make him or her want to read on. Introductions may have a lead-in, and they can be developed in several different ways.

The Lead-In

You can begin the introduction with an attention-grabbing opening sentence, or lead-in. There are three common types of lead-ins.

- Quotation
- Surprising or provocative statement
- Question

Introduction Styles

You can develop the introduction in several different ways. Experiment with any of these introduction styles.

- **Give general or historical background information.** The general or historical information gradually leads to your thesis. For example, in an essay about winning a lottery, you could begin by giving a brief history of lotteries.
- **Tell an interesting anecdote.** Open your essay with a story that leads to your thesis statement. For example, you might begin your lottery essay by telling the story of a real-life lottery winner.
- **Present a vivid description.** Give a detailed description, and then state your thesis. For example, you might describe the moment when a lottery winner realizes that he or she has won.
- **Present an opposing position.** Open your essay with an idea that contradicts a common belief, and build to your thesis. For instance, if most people want to win the lottery, you could begin your essay by saying that you definitely do not want to be a millionaire.
- **Give a definition.** Define a term, and then state your thesis. For example, in an essay about the lottery, you could begin by defining *happiness*.

> **Placement of the Thesis Statement**
>
> Although a paragraph often begins with a topic sentence, an introduction does not begin with a thesis statement. Rather, most introductions begin with sentences that introduce the topic and lead the reader to the main point of the essay. In other words, the thesis statement is generally the last sentence in the introduction.

PRACTICE 5

In introductions A through E, the thesis statement is underlined. Read each introduction and then answer the questions that follow. Look at Octavio's example for some guidance.

OCTAVIO'S INTRODUCTION

"Welcome to the greatest show on earth!" The ringmaster's voice echoes through the circus tent. In the arena, a majestic elephant lifts itself onto its hind legs and walks carefully toward its trainer. The crowd murmurs with appreciation, unaware that the elephant may be an unwilling, neglected, or even abused participant in this spectacle. <u>Circuses should be banned from using large animals such as tigers, bears, and elephants.</u>

1. What type of lead-in does Octavio use? *Quotation*

2. What introduction style does he use?
   - (a.) Description
   - b. Definition
   - c. Background information
   - d. Opposing position

3. What is his essay about? *Abolishing the use of large animals in circuses*

A. "I never saw the blow to my head come from Huck. Bam! And I was on all fours, struggling for my equilibrium." These are the words of Kody Scott, a former member of a Los Angeles street gang. Kody is describing part of the initiation ritual he endured in order to join a local branch (or "set") of the Crips. First, he stole an automobile to demonstrate his "street smarts" and willingness to break the law. Then he allowed himself to be beaten, showing both that he was tough and that he was ready to do whatever the gang required of him. He completed the process by participating in a "military action"—killing a member of a rival gang. <u>Initiations like this are by no means rare in today's street gangs.</u> Kody, by the way, was just eleven years old.

—Linda L. Lindsey and Stephen Beach, "Joining the Crips," *Essentials of Sociology*

1. What type of lead-in does the author use? _____

2. What introduction style does the author use?
   a. Anecdote   b. Definition
   c. Background information   d. Opposing position

3. What is this essay about? _____

B. What is there about alternative medicine that sets it apart from ordinary medicine? The term refers to a remarkable heterogeneous group of theories and practices that are as disparate as homeopathy, therapeutic touch, imagery, and herbal medicine. What unites them? Eisenberg et al. defined alternative medicine (now often called complementary medicine) as "medical interventions not taught widely at U.S. medical schools or generally available at U.S. hospitals." <u>That is not a very satisfactory definition, especially since many alternative remedies have recently found their way into the medical mainstream.</u>

—Adapted from Marcia Angell and Jerome P. Kassirer, "Alternative Medicine: The Risks of Untested and Unregulated Remedies," *The New England Journal of Medicine*

4. What type of lead-in does the author use? _____

5. What introduction style does the author use?
   a. Anecdote   b. Definition
   c. Description   d. Opposing position

6. What is this essay about? _____

C. High school is a waste of time. In fact, it is a baby-sitting service for teens who are too old to be baby-sat. In England, fifteen-year-olds graduate and can choose technical or university streams of education. They are free to choose what to study, or they can stop schooling and get jobs. In short, they are treated like mature adults. In our country, we prolong the experience of forced schooling much longer than is necessary. <u>We should abolish high schools and introduce a system of technical or pre-university schooling.</u>

—Adelie Zang, Student

7. What type of lead-in does the author use? _____

8. What introduction style does the author use?
   a. Anecdote   b. Definition
   c. Background information   d. Opposing position

9. What is this essay about? _____

D. When I was 8 years old, I read a story about a boy who built a robot out of junkyard scraps. The robot in the story could move, talk, and think, just like a person. For some reason, I found the idea of building a robot very appealing, so I decided to build one of my own. I remember optimistically collecting body parts: pipes for arms and legs, motors for muscles, light bulbs for eyes, and a big tin can for the head, fully expecting to assemble the pieces into a working mechanical man. After nearly electrocuting myself a few times, I began to get my parts to move, light up, and make noises. I felt I was making progress. If I only had the right tools and the right parts, I was sure that I could build a machine that could think.

—Danny Hillis, "Can They Feel Your Pain?"

10. What introduction style does the author use?
    a. Anecdote   b. Definition
    c. Background information   d. Opposing position

11. What is this essay about? _____

E. The story of how Christianity ultimately conquered the Roman Empire is one of the most remarkable in history. Christianity faced the hostility of the established religious institutions of its native Judea and had to compete not only against the official cults of Rome and the sophisticated philosophies of the educated classes, but also against "mystery" religions like the cults of Mithra, Isis, and Osiris. The Christians also suffered formal persecution, yet Christianity finally became the official religion of the empire.

—Albert M. Craig et al., *The Heritage of World Civilizations*

12. What introduction style does the author use?
    a. Description   b. Definition
    c. Historical information d. Opposing position

13. What is this essay about? _____

The Writer's Desk **Write Two Introductions**

In the previous Writer's Desk on page 181, you made an essay plan. Now, write two different styles of introductions for your essay. Use the same thesis statement in both introductions. Later, you can choose the best introduction for your essay.

The Conclusion

A **conclusion** is a final paragraph that rephrases the thesis statement and summarizes the main points in the essay. To make your conclusion more interesting and original, you could close with a prediction, a suggestion, a quotation, or a call to action.

OCTAVIO'S CONCLUSION

Octavio concluded his essay by restating his main points.

> Clearly, large animals suffer when they are enclosed, carted around from town to town, and forced to perform for crowds of humans. Perhaps traditional circuses should consider the example of Cirque du Soleil, which does not use any large animals in its shows, yet it is one of the world's most profitable and popular circuses.

He could then close his essay with one of the following:

Prediction:	If animal-free circuses continue to thrive, then perhaps we will see a day when lions, tigers, elephants, and bears are not forced to perform in circus rings.
Suggestion:	The best way to change practices of circuses is to avoid those that use large animals.
Quotation:	According to Mahatma Gandhi, "A nation's moral progress can be judged by the way it treats its animals."
Call to action:	If you feel strongly about the use of large animals in circuses, you could write letters about the issue to local and state politicians.

PRACTICE 6

Read the following conclusions and answer the questions.

> A. As soon as smoking is banned in all public places, we will see the benefits. Our hospitals will treat fewer smoking-related illnesses, and this will save money. Non-smokers will be saved from noxious fumes, and smokers, who will be forced to smoke outdoors, might feel a greater desire to give up the habit. In the future, we will have a world where a non-smoker can go through life without having to breathe in someone else's cigarette smoke.
>
> —Jordan Lamott, "Butt Out!"

1. What method does the author use to end the conclusion?
   a. Prediction   b. Suggestion
   c. Quotation   d. Call to action

> B. Ultimately, spam is annoying, offensive, time consuming, and expensive. There is nothing good to say about it. Spam marketers will argue that we get junk in our mail, and that cannot be denied, but we

do not get crates of junk mail every week. If we did, paper junk mail would be banned in a hurry. The only real solution is for governments around the world to work together in order to make spam production illegal. Governments must actively hunt down and prosecute spammers.

—Adela Fonseca, "Ban Spam"

2. What method does the author use to end the conclusion?
    a. Prediction
    b. Suggestion
    c. Quotation
    d. Call to action

C. Every once in a while the marketing wizards pay lip service to today's expanding career options for women and give us a Scientist Barbie complete with a tiny chemistry set as an accessory. But heaven forbid should little Johnnie plead for his parents to buy him that Scientist Barbie. After all, it is acceptable for girls to foray, occasionally, into the world of boy-style play, but for boys the opposite "sissified" behavior is taboo. Why is this? One commentator, D. R. Shaffer, says, "The major task for young girls is to learn how not to be babies, whereas young boys must learn how not to be girls."

—Dorothy Nixon, "Put GI Barbie in the Bargain Bin"

3. What method does the author use to end the conclusion?
    a. Prediction
    b. Suggestion
    c. Quotation
    d. Call to action

 Avoiding Conclusion Problems

In your conclusion, do not contradict your main point, and do not introduce new or irrelevant information.

 The Writer's Desk **Write a Conclusion**

In previous Writer's Desks, you wrote an introduction and an essay plan. Now write a conclusion for your essay.

The First Draft

After creating an introduction and conclusion, and after arranging the supporting ideas in a logical order, you are ready to write your first draft. The first draft includes your introduction, several body paragraphs, and your concluding paragraph.

The Writer's Desk **Write the First Draft**

In previous Writer's Desks, you wrote an introduction, a conclusion, and an essay plan. Now write the first draft of your essay.

REVISING AND EDITING

Revising and Editing the Essay

Revising your essay is an extremely important step in the writing process. When you revise your essay, you modify it to make it stronger and more convincing. You do this by reading the essay critically, looking for faulty logic, poor organization, or poor sentence style. Then you reorganize and rewrite it, making any necessary changes.

   Editing is the last stage in writing. When you edit, you proofread your writing and make sure that it is free of errors.

Revising for Unity

To revise for **unity,** verify that all of your body paragraphs support the thesis statement. Also look carefully at each body paragraph: ensure that the sentences support the topic sentence.

> **WRITING LINK**
>
> To practice revising for unity and support, see Chapter 3, "Revising and Editing."

 Avoiding Unity Problems

Here are two common errors to check for as you revise your body paragraphs.

• **Rambling paragraphs**   The paragraphs in the essay ramble on. Each paragraph has several topics, and there is no clearly identifiable topic sentence.

• **Artifical breaks**   A long paragraph is split into smaller paragraphs arbitrarily, and each smaller paragraph lacks a central focus.

To correct either of these errors, revise each body paragraph until it has *one* main idea that supports the thesis statement.

Revising for Adequate Support

When you revise for adequate **support,** ensure that there are enough details and examples to make your essay strong and convincing.

Revising for Coherence

When you revise for **coherence,** ensure that paragraphs flow smoothly and logically. To guide the reader from one idea to the next, or from one paragraph to the next, try using **paragraph links.**

You can develop connections between paragraphs using three methods.

1. **Repeat words or phrases from the thesis statement in each body paragraph.** In the next example, *violent* and *violence* are repeated words.

Thesis statement:	Although some will argue that <u>violent</u> movies are simply a reflection of a <u>violent</u> society, these movies actually cause a lot of the <u>violence</u> around us.
Body paragraph 1:	Action movie heroes train children to solve problems with <u>violence</u>.
Body paragraph 2:	<u>Violent movies</u> are "how to" films for many sick individuals.

2. **Refer to the main idea in the previous paragraph, and link it to your current topic sentence.** In body paragraph 2, the writer reminds the reader of the first point (the newly rich feel useless) and then introduces the next point.

Thesis statement:	A cash windfall may cause more problems than it solves.
Body paragraph 1:	The newly rich often lose their desire to become productive citizens, and they end up <u>feeling useless</u>.
Body paragraph 2:	Apart from <u>feeling useless</u>, many heirs and lottery winners also tend to feel guilty about their wealth.

3. **Use a transitional word or phrase to lead the reader to your next idea.**

Body paragraph 2:	<u>Furthermore</u>, the newly rich often feel guilty about their wealth.

WRITING LINK

Furthermore is a transition. For a list of transitions, see pages 43–44 in Chapter 3.

OCTAVIO'S ESSAY

Octavio examined his essay to see if it had unity, adequate support, and coherence. Review the notes that Octavio made in the margin of his essay.

"Welcome to the greatest show on earth!" The ringmaster's voice echoes through the circus tent. In the arena, a majestic elephant lifts itself onto its hind legs and walks carefully toward its trainer. The crowd murmurs with appreciation, unaware that the elephant may be an unwilling, neglected, or even abused participant in this spectacle. <u>Circuses should be banned from using large animals such as tigers, bears, and elephants.</u>

Add transition: First?

<u>Large animals are kept in tiny, confined spaces.</u> On circus grounds, large animals are restrained in small cages where they barely have room to lie down. When the animals travel, they are confined to hot trailers or trains, and sometimes they must spend days in such conditions.

Needs more details.

<u>Animals may get hurt in training and during the show.</u> While preparing the animals for the show, trainers use electric prods and whips. <u>It is important that trainers be dominant.</u> Trainers want to show the animals that they are in control, but trainers often hurt animals during practice exercises.

Add transition: Furthermore?

Unity: does this idea belong?

Large circus animals are a danger to the public and to enter-tainers. In some circuses, elephants have gone on rampages and attacked or even killed others. Tigers have turned on trainers. After such attacks happen, people wonder why the animals suddenly turned wild. Wild animals are not meant to be performing pets.

Clearly, large animals suffer when they are enclosed, carted around from town to town, and forced to perform for crowds of humans. Perhaps traditional circuses should consider the example of Cirque du Soleil, which does not use any large animals in its shows, yet it is one of the world's most profitable and popular circuses. If animal-free circuses continue to thrive, then perhaps we will see a day when lions, tigers, elephants, and bears are not forced to perform in circus rings.

Add link?

Needs specific example.

Is the order logical?

Is this a good example? Are there more?

Revising for Style

Another important step in the revision process is to ensure that you have varied your sentences and that you have used concise wording. When you revise for sentence style, ask yourself the following questions.

- Do I use a variety of sentence patterns? (To practice using sentence variety, see Chapter 19.)
- Do I use exact language? (To learn about slang, wordiness, and overused expressions, see Chapter 31.)
- Are my sentences parallel in structure? (To practice revising for parallel structure, see Chapter 21.)

Editing

When you edit, you proofread your essay and correct any errors in punctuation, spelling, grammar, and mechanics. There is an editing guide on the inside back cover of this book that provides you with a list of things to check for when you proofread your text.

ESSAY LINK

To practice your editing skills, see Chapter 36, "Editing Paragraphs and Essays."

The Writer's Desk Revising and Editing Your Essay

In the previous Writer's Desk in this chapter, you wrote the first draft of an essay. Now revise and edit your essay. You can refer to the checklist at the end of this chapter.

The Essay Title

It is a good idea to think of a title after you have completed your essay because then you will have a more complete impression of your essay's main point. The most effective titles are brief, depict the topic and purpose of the essay, and attract the reader's attention.

ESSAY LINK

For more information about punctuating titles, see page 498 in Chapter 34.

When you write your title, place it at the top center of your page. Capitalize the first word of your title, and capitalize the main words except for prepositions (*in, at, for, to,* etc.) and articles (*a, an, the*). Leave about an inch of space between the title and the introductory paragraph.

Descriptive Titles

Descriptive titles are the most common titles in academic essays. They depict the topic of the essay clearly and concisely. Sometimes, the author takes key words from the thesis statement and uses them in the title. Here are some descriptive titles.

The Importance of Multiculturalism in a Democratic Society

Why Mothers and Fathers Should Take Parenting Seriously

Titles Related to the Writing Pattern

You can also relate your title directly to the writing pattern of your essay. Here are examples of titles for different writing patterns.

Illustration:	The Problems with Elections
Narration:	My Visit to Las Vegas
Description:	Graduation Day
Process:	How to Dress for an Interview
Definition:	What It Means to Be Brave
Classification:	Three Types of Hackers
Comparison and contrast:	Fast Food vs. Gourmet Food
Cause and effect:	Why People Enter Beauty Pageants
Argument:	Barbie Should Have a New Look

 Avoiding Title Pitfalls

When you write your title, watch out for problems.

• Do not view your title as a substitute for a thesis statement.

• Do not put quotation marks around the title of your essay.

• Do not write a really long title because it can be confusing.

PRACTICE 7

1. List some possible titles for the essay about travel in Practice 2 (page 175).

_____

_____

2. List some possible titles for Octavio's essay about circus animals (page 188).

_____

_____

The Final Draft

When you have finished making the revisions on the first draft of your essay, write the final copy. This copy should include all the changes that you have made during the revision phase of your work. You should proofread the final copy of your work to check for grammar, spelling, mechanics, and punctuation errors.

The Writer's Desk **Writing Your Final Draft**

At this point, you have developed, revised, and edited your essay. Now write the final draft. Before you hand it to your instructor, proofread it one last time to ensure that you have found as many errors as possible.

REFLECT ON IT

Think about what you have learned in this unit. If you do not know an answer, review that topic.

1. What is a thesis statement? _____

_____

2. What are the five different introduction styles?

_____   _____

_____   _____

_____

3. What are the four different ways to end a conclusion?

_____   _____

_____   _____

4. What are the three different ways you can link body paragraphs?

_____

_____

_____

The Writer's Room   **Essay Topics**

Writing Activity 1

Choose any of the following topics, or choose your own topic. Then write an essay. Remember to follow the writing process.

General Topics

1. values
2. having a roommate
3. differences between generations
4. violence
5. peer pressure

College and Work-Related Topics

6. juggling college and family life
7. having a job and going to college
8. extracurricular activities at college
9. a stressful work environment
10. an important issue in the workplace

 REVISING AND EDITING CHECKLIST FOR ESSAYS

Revising

☐ Does my essay have a compelling introduction and conclusion?

☐ Does my introduction have a clear thesis statement?

☐ Does each body paragraph contain a topic sentence?

☐ Does each body paragraph's topic sentence relate to the thesis statement?

☐ Does each body paragraph contain specific details that support the topic sentence?

☐ Do all of the sentences in each paragraph relate to its topic sentence?

☐ Do I use transitions to smoothly and logically connect ideas?

☐ Do I use a variety of sentence styles?

Editing

☐ Do I have any errors in grammar, spelling, punctuation, and capitalization?

 See Chapter 13 of the Visualizing Writing CD for additional mini-lectures on **Titles**, **Introductions**, **The Thesis Statement**, **Supporting Ideas**, and **Conclusions**.

Essay Patterns

CHAPTER 14

" *The act of writing is the act of discovering what you believe.* "

—DAVID HARE
American playright (1947–)

CONTENTS

- The Illustration Essay
- The Narrative Essay
- The Descriptive Essay
- The Process Essay
- The Definition Essay
- The Classification Essay
- The Comparison and Contrast Essay
- The Cause and Effect Essay
- The Argument Essay

Fashion designers choose fabric patterns that are appropriate for the articles of clothing that they wish to make. In the same way, writers choose essay patterns that best suit their purposes for writing.

In Chapters 4 through 12, you read about and practiced using nine different paragraph patterns. In this chapter, you will learn how to apply those patterns when writing essays. Before you begin working through this chapter, take a moment to review nine writing patterns.

Pattern	Definition
Illustration	To illustrate or prove a point using specific examples
Narration	To narrate or tell a story about a sequence of events that happened
Description	To describe using vivid details and images that appeal to the reader's senses
Process	To inform the reader about how to do something, how something works, or how something happened
Definition	To define or explain what a term or concept means by providing relevant examples
Classification	To classify or sort a topic to help readers understand different qualities about that topic

(continued)

Pattern	Definition
Comparison and contrast	To present information about similarities (compare) or differences (contrast)
Cause and effect	To explain why an event happened (the cause) or what the consequences of the event were (the effects)
Argument	To argue or to take a position on an issue and offer reasons for your position

Most college essay assignments have one dominating essay pattern. However, you can use several essay patterns to fulfill your purpose. For example, imagine that you want to write a cause and effect essay about youth crime, and the purpose of the essay is to inform. The supporting paragraphs might include a definition of youth crime and a narrative about an adolescent with a criminal record. You might incorporate different writing patterns, but the dominant pattern would still be cause and effect.

Each time you write an essay, remember to follow the writing process that you learned in Chapter 13, "Writing the Essay."

PARAGRAPH LINK

For more information about developing ideas with examples, refer to Chapter 4, "Illustration."

The Illustration Essay

When writing an illustration essay, you use specific examples to illustrate or clarify your main point. Illustration writing is a pattern that you frequently use in college essays and exams because you must support your main idea with examples.

The Thesis Statement

The thesis statement in an illustration essay controls the direction of the body paragraphs. It includes the topic and a controlling idea about the topic.

topic   controlling idea
A second language <u>provides students with several important advantages</u>.

The Supporting Ideas

In an illustration essay, the body paragraphs contain examples that support the thesis statement. You can develop each body paragraph in two different ways. To give your essay variety, you could use both a series of examples and extended examples.

- **Use a series of examples** that support the paragraph's topic sentence. For example, in an essay about bad driving, one body paragraph could be about drivers who do not pay attention to the road. The paragraph could list the things that those drivers do, such as looking through CDs, using a cell phone, eating, and putting on makeup.

- **Use an extended example** to support the paragraph's topic sentence. The example could be an anecdote or a description of an event. In an essay about bad driving, for example, one paragraph could contain an anecdote about a driver who always wanted to be faster than other drivers.

An Illustration Essay Plan

Read the next essay plan and answer the questions.

Introduction
Thesis statement: New technologies have had a profound impact on self-employed workers.

I. Hand-held organizers help such workers maintain a portable office.
   A. stores e-mails, schedules, phone lists, and more
   B. models are lightweight and fit in a pocket
   C. messenger services provide means to communicate in real time
II. Portable computers provide workers with the ability to do complicated things anywhere.
   A. can format and design documents using graphs, tables, and art
   B. can write, revise, and edit simultaneously
   C. no need to carry large paper files; computers can store hundreds of files
   D. can access Internet while traveling
III. Computer printers have useful features for the self-employed worker.
   A. integrated scanners and photocopiers
   B. fax machine allows easy sending and receiving of messages
   C. laser printers can quickly print out large volumes of documents

Conclusion: As technologies evolve, more people will work at home.

PRACTICE I

1. Circle the topic and underline the controlling idea in the thesis statement.

2. How does the writer develop each body paragraph? Circle the best answer.
    a. With an extended example   b. With a series of examples

3. Write another topic sentence that could support the writer's thesis statement.

   _____

   _____

An Illustration Essay

Read the next essay by journalist Stephen Lautens and answer the questions.

Down Time

1   As I write this, my phone is ringing. I am also doing my Internet banking and refilling the fax machine with paper. How did we all get so busy? We eat our breakfast and check our voice mail on the drive to work. The ATM line is the perfect place to call an estranged relative or answer our pager. What we have done is successfully eliminated the concept of spare time. It seems like we are not happy unless we have filled every waking moment of our lives with something to do.

2   My father knew how to relax. I remember him sitting on the big green couch under a reading lamp for hours at a time, carefully going through the newspaper. It was as if time stood still. Sometimes he would just listen to music. It is amazing because all he was doing was listening to music—not trying to balance his checkbook and make a stock trade at the same time.

3   Some of my best times as a kid were days when I had nothing planned. Nothing was sweeter than the first day of the vast summer holiday, without a single thing to fill it. My mother tried **valiantly** to send us off to camp, but I refused to go. I took goofing around very seriously. Much to my mother's dismay, I never had any interest in hockey, soccer, or any other organized sport that made me get up early or lose any teeth.

4   Technology has given us some terrific benefits, but now we feel that we are wasting valuable time unless we are doing six things at once. I am not knocking vaccines, airbags, or NSYNC CDs, but there is something wrong when everyone has to have a website. (I am guilty as charged.) We feel we have to be an expert on the high-tech stocks—otherwise how can we expect to be a dot-com millionaire by the age of twelve? Electronic appointment books are being marketed for children so they can schedule their play dates. No doubt they can also keep track of all the other six-year-olds' e-mail addresses and cell phone numbers. There is a TV commercial on right now where a little boy puts his playmates on a conference call, which is probably good practice for the day when he has to eat his lunch at his desk with a phone in his ear.

5   Now when I get a few days off, it is so packed with errands and obligations that I am worn out by Monday morning. Maybe it is just part of growing up. If it is, I do not recommend it to anyone. Do not get me wrong. I like to be busy, but we have forgotten the need to slow down. We feel the need to be connected all the time. So go ahead. Turn off the phone and have a nap. I guarantee the world will still be there when you wake up, and it will look better too.

valiantly: bravely

PRACTICE 2

1. Underline the thesis statement of the essay.

2. Underline the topic sentence in each body paragraph.

3. In which paragraph(s) does the author make an extended example?

   _____

4. In which paragraph(s) does the author list ideas to illustrate his point?

   _____

5. What suggestion does the author make in the conclusion of the essay?

   _____

   _____

The Writer's Room   **Topics for Illustration Essays**

PARAGRAPH LINK

You could also develop an essay about one of the topics found in Chapter 4, "Illustration."

Writing Activity 1

Write an illustration essay about one of the following topics.

General Topics

1. the junk in your home
2. characteristics of a good friend
3. entertainment activities
4. useless products or inventions
5. accomplishments of a cultural icon
6. commercialization of holidays

College and Work-Related Topics

7. reasons to take time off before starting college
8. qualities of an ideal workplace
9. skills that you need for your job
10. qualities of co-workers who are easy or difficult to get along with
11. important things to know about doing your job
12. your employment history

Writing Activity 2

Read the following quotations. Find one that you agree or disagree with, or find one that inspires you in some way. Then write an illustration essay based on the quotation.

> Sports serve society by providing vivid examples of excellence.
> —George F. Will, American editor and columnist

> After climbing a great hill, one only finds that there are many more hills to climb.
> —Nelson Mandela, former South African president

> Everything has its beauty, but not everyone sees it.
> —Confucius, ancient Chinese philosopher and educator

> Everyone I meet is in some way my superior.
> —Ralph Waldo Emerson, American author

> Creativity comes from looking for the unexpected and stepping outside your experience. Computers simply cannot do that.
> —Masaru Ibuka, Japanese businessman

✓ ILLUSTRATION ESSAY CHECKLIST

As you write your illustration essay, review the essay checklist on the inside front cover. Also ask yourself the following questions.

☐ Does my thesis statement include a topic that I can support with examples?

☐ Does my thesis statement make a point about the topic?

(continued)

> Do my body paragraphs contain sufficient examples that clearly support the thesis statement?
>
> Do I smoothly and logically connect the examples?

PARAGRAPH LINK

For more information about narrative writing, refer to Chapter 5, "Narration."

The Narrative Essay

When you write a narrative essay, you tell a story about what happened, and you generally explain events in the order in which they occurred.

There are two main types of narrative writing. In **first-person narration**, you describe a personal experience using *I* or *we*. In **third-person narration**, you describe what happened to somebody else, and you use *he*, *she*, or *they*.

The Thesis Statement

The thesis statement controls the direction of the body paragraphs. To create a meaningful thesis statement for a narrative essay, you could ask yourself what you learned, how you changed, or how the event is important.

controlling idea   topic
<u>Something terrible happened</u> **that summer I turned fifteen.**

The Supporting Ideas

Here are some tips to remember as you develop a narrative essay.

- Make sure that it has a point. Do not simply recount what happened. Try to indicate why the events are important.
- Organize the events in time order (the order in which they occurred). You could also reverse the order of events by beginning your essay with the outcome of the events, and then explaining what happened that led to the outcome.
- Make your narrative essay more interesting by using some descriptive language. For example, you could use images that appeal to the senses.

To be as complete as possible, a good narrative essay should provide answers to most of the following questions.

- *Who* is the essay about?
- *What* happened?
- *When* did it happen?
- *Where* did it happen?
- *Why* did it happen?
- *How* did it happen?

Using Quotations

One effective way to enhance your narrative essay is to use dialogue. Include direct and/or indirect quotations.

A **direct quotation** contains the exact words of an author, and the quotation is set off with quotation marks. When you include the exact words of more than one person, you must start a new paragraph each time the speaker changes.

> Sara looked at me sadly. "Why did you betray me?"
>
> "I didn't mean to do it," I answered.
>
> She looked down at her hands and said, "I don't think I can ever forgive you."

An **indirect quotation** keeps the author's meaning but is not set off by quotation marks.

> Sara asked why I had betrayed her.

 GRAMMAR LINK

For information about punctuating quotations, see Chapter 34.

A Narrative Essay Plan

Read the next essay plan and answer the questions that follow.

Introduction
Thesis statement: Stephen Glass, a promising young writer in Washington, D.C., shocked the world of journalism with his fabricated stories.

I. After his first small falsehood, his lying escalated.
    A. invented a quotation in 1995
    B. invented sources to back up his stories
    C. knew about fact checkers, so he created false memos, meeting notes, etc.
    D. soon entire stories filled with lies
II. Glass's career came to a crashing end.
    A. *Forbes* magazine wanted to follow up a Glass story about hackers
    B. Glass unable to produce documents about sources
    C. invented more lies to cover up his initial lies
    D. realizing Glass was unethical, editor of *New Republic* fired him in 1998
III. The Glass scandal erupted, shocking publishers and readers.
    A. story became front-page news
    B. editors' competency was questioned
    C. fact checkers exposed as not being thorough enough
    D. readers wondered if journalists could be trusted

Conclusion: The world of journalism is still recovering from the Glass scandal.

PRACTICE 3

1. Who is this essay plan about? _____

2. What happened? _____

3. When and where did this happen? _____

4. What type of narration is this? Circle the best answer.
   a. First person   b. Third person

A Narrative Essay

In the next essay, Jeff Kemp recounts what happened during his early years as a professional football player. Read the essay and answer the questions.

A Lesson in Humility

1   We live in an age when, too often, rules are scorned, values are turned upside down, principles are replaced by **expediency,** and character is sacrificed for popularity. Individual athletes are sometimes the worst offenders, but not as often as one might think. In fact, sports teach important moral lessons that athletes can apply on and off the playing field.

2   Many people dream of being a professional athlete. For me, the dream seemed to be within reach because my father, Jack Kemp, an outstanding quarterback, played for the American Football League's Buffalo Bills (prior to the AFL's 1970 merger with the National Football League). The trouble was, I was not very good! I was a third-string football player through most of junior high and high school and for two years at Dartmouth College. I was not anyone's idea of a "hot prospect." After graduation, I was passed over by NFL scouts. When I finally was asked to join the Los Angeles Rams in 1981 as a free agent, I was **designated** as fifth-string quarterback.

3   It was a 50-to-1 shot that I would survive training camp. Rookies were the only players required to show up for the first week of camp. There were dozens competing for the few spots open on the team. After two days, a young boy approached me as I was walking off the field. He asked if he could carry my helmet to the locker room. It was a long way, but I said, "Sure, I think you can handle that." The next morning, he showed up before practice and offered to carry my helmet and shoulder pads, and he was there again after practice offering the same service. So it went for the rest of the week.

4   On the last day, as we were departing the field, my young assistant said, "Jeff, can I ask you a question?" (We were on a first-name basis by then.)

5   I thought, "This is my first fan! He is going to ask me for an autograph."

6   He then inquired, "When do the good football players come to camp?" Right then and there, I learned a lesson in humility from a seven-year-old boy.

7   In my first three NFL seasons, I was forced to learn the same lesson over and over again. During that time, I threw just 31 passes. Nevertheless, by 1984, I had managed to outlast the five NFL quarterbacks who had been ahead of

expediency: convenience; self-interest

designated: selected

me. With the Rams' record standing at 1–2, I took over for injured quarterback Vince Ferragamo and earned my first start against the Cincinnati Bengals, eventually leading the Rams to nine more victories and a playoff berth.

8   The next season, I returned to the bench as a backup quarterback. Humility, I was compelled to remind myself, was a good thing. It helped me appreciate what I had and avoid dwelling on what I did not have. It prevented complaining, which drains the spirit and unity of any group. It also led me to persevere and be ready whenever opportunity presented itself.

PRACTICE 4

1. What type of narration is this text? Circle the best answer.
   a. First person   b. Third person

2. Underline the thesis statement of the essay.

3. What introduction style does Kemp use? Circle the best answer.
   a. Definition   b. Anecdote
   c. General information   d. Historical information

4. List the main events that Kemp recounts in his essay.

   _____

   _____

   _____

   _____

   _____

   _____

   _____

5. What organizational method does Kemp use? Circle the best answer.
   a. Time order   b. Space order   c. Emphatic order

6. Write down one example of an indirect quotation from the essay.

   _____

7. Write down one example of a direct quotation from the essay.

   _____

8. Narrative writers do more than simply list a series of events. Kemp explains why the events were meaningful. What did Kemp learn?

   _____

   _____

PARAGRAPH LINK

You could also develop one of the topics found in Chapter 5, "Narration."

 The Writer's Room   **Topics for Narrative Essays**

Writing Activity 1

Write a narrative essay about one of the following topics.

General Topics

1. a family legend
2. an illuminating moment
3. a surprising coincidence
4. a poor financial decision
5. an important event in the world
6. when you learned to do something new

College and Work-Related Topics

7. life lessons that college teaches you
8. what your previous job taught you
9. your best or worst job
10. a good or bad experience with a bank
11. when you worked with a team
12. a scandal at work or college

Writing Activity 2

Read the following quotations. Find one that you agree or disagree with, or find one that inspires you in some way. Then write a narrative essay based on the quotation.

> Drama is life with the dull bits cut out.
>
> —Alfred Hitchcock, British filmmaker

> When your mouth stumbles, it's worse than feet.
>
> —Oji proverb

> Those who cannot remember the past are condemned to repeat it.
>
> —George Santayana, Spanish poet and philosopher

> If you tell the truth, then you don't have to remember everything.
>
> —Mark Twain, American author

> We can draw lessons from the past, but we cannot live in it.
>
> —Lyndon B. Johnson, American politician

 NARRATIVE ESSAY CHECKLIST

As you write your narrative essay, review the essay checklist on the inside front cover. Also ask yourself the following questions.

☐ Does my thesis statement clearly express the topic of the narration, and does it make a point about that topic?

☐ Does my essay answer most of the following questions: *who, what, when, where, why, how?*

☐ Do I use transitional expressions that help clarify the order of events?

☐ Do I include details to make my narration more interesting?

The Descriptive Essay

When writing a descriptive essay, use words to create a vivid impression of a subject. Use details that appeal to the five senses: sight, smell, hearing, taste, and touch. You want your readers to be able to imagine all that you are describing.

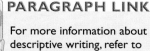

PARAGRAPH LINK

For more information about descriptive writing, refer to Chapter 6, "Description."

The Thesis Statement

In a descriptive essay, the thesis statement includes what you are describing and makes a point about the topic.

topic   controlling idea

Walking down the streets of New York, I was filled with a sense of wonder.

The Supporting Ideas

When you develop your descriptive essay, make sure it has a **dominant impression.** The dominant impression is the overall feeling that you wish to convey. For example, the essay could convey an impression of tension, joy, nervousness, or anger.

You can place the details of a descriptive essay in space order, time order, or emphatic order. The order that you use depends on the topic of your essay. For example, if you describe a place, you can use space order, and if you describe a difficult moment, you can use time order.

 Using Figurative Devices

When writing a descriptive essay, you can use figurative devices such as simile, metaphor, or personification. These devices use comparisons and images to add vivid details to your writing.

- A **simile** is a comparison using *like* or *as*.

    Just imagine me with no flaws

    like a parking lot with no cars . . .   —Mya, "Movin' On"

    My son's constant whining felt like a jackhammer on my skull.

- A **metaphor** is a comparison that does not use *like* or *as*.

    I'm a genie in a bottle . . .   —Christina Aguilera, "Genie in a Bottle"

    The mind is a battlefield.

- **Personification** is the act of attributing human qualities to an inanimate object or animal.

    The wind kicked the leaves.   —Kurt Vonnegut, Jr., "Next Door"

    The sauce hissed on the stove.

PRACTICE 5

Practice using figurative language. Use one of the following to describe each item: simile, metaphor, or personification. If you are comparing two things, try to use an unusual comparison.

EXAMPLE:

Surprising: *Her sudden appearance was as surprising as a 4 a.m. phone call. (simile)*

1. Truck: _____

2. Road: _____

3. Crowd: _____

4. Annoying: _____

5. Relaxed: _____

A Descriptive Essay Plan

Read the next essay plan and answer the questions that follow.

> ### Introduction
> Thesis statement: Walking down the streets of Manhattan, I was filled with a sense of wonder.
>
> I. Times Square was buzzing with bright lights, bustling crowds, and eclectic sounds.
>   A. the lights on the billboards
>   B. the theaters on every corner
>   C. the chatter of many different languages
>   D. the salty pretzels on my tongue
> II. Central Park was an oasis in the center of Manhattan
>   A. the joggers on the running paths
>   B. the hansom drivers with their beautiful horses
>   C. the smell of the hot dogs and sausages
>   D. the saxophone player, the bird lady, and the mime
> III. Battery Park, on the southern tip of the island, was impressive.
>   A. the roar of the waves crashing
>   B. the chilly wind on my face
>   C. the Statue of Liberty in the distance
>   D. the shouts of the vendors
>
> **Conclusion:** "Outside America, New York is America, and its skyscraper a symbol of the spirit of America" (Thomas Adams, 1931).

PRACTICE 6

1. This essay plan contains imagery that appeals to the senses. Find one example of imagery for each sense.

   a. Sight: _____

   _____

b. Sound: _____

_____

c. Smell: _____

_____

d. Taste: _____

_____

e. Touch: _____

_____

2. Which type of imagery is most prevalent? _____

3. What is the dominant impression of this essay? Circle the best answer.
   a. Desire   b. Suspicion
   c. Joy and awe   d. Sadness

A Descriptive Essay

Read the following essay by Rahul Goswami, a journalist for *Orientation: Middle East*, and answer the questions. Pay close attention to the descriptive details.

Monsoon Time

1   My father used to tell me about the **monsoon** in Bangladesh. He was born in Handiyal, a village in the north-central district of the country. Behind his parents' house was a river, the Padma, a part of the immense water system that crisscrosses Bangladesh. Big even during the sweltering dry months, the Padma would become an inland ocean at the height of the monsoon. My father would talk about the river swelling day after day as the rain drove down. He loved the monsoon, despite the inevitable annual floods, the misery, and the hardship.

2   Years later, I moved to Dubai, where I lived until just recently. It is a modern metropolis—built on the edge of the great Arabian sand sea— glittering with glazed glass and proud of its impeccably maintained highways. It **scarcely** ever rains here. On perhaps five days a year, a few millimeters of rain will reluctantly descend. More frequent are the sandstorms, which clog drains that are tested no more than annually. This past year was my first full one in Dubai and the first time in my life I have missed an entire monsoon.

3   By June in India, when the first wet **squalls** explode over Bombay, one has been anticipating the rain for a month and more. Then in July, the massive, heavy cloud systems have settled immovably over the subcontinent, and they let fall torrents of rain, day after day. Indoors a **patina** of moisture coats everything, clothes will not dry, and head colds make one miserable. Outside, the city struggles with its everyday routines. Suburban trains do not run, their tracks submerged under feet of muddy water. City drains, routinely untended and choked with tons of garbage, refuse to do their work. Housing colonies turn into **archipelagos.** Mosquitoes assume fearsome proportions.

monsoon: rainy season in South Asia

scarcely: hardly; rarely

squalls: sudden violent gusts of wind

patina: a gloss or layer

archipelagos: a group of small islands

4 By August, the monsoon has dulled the world. Trees appear a uniform drab green, the sea stays gray and forbidding, and the city stinks. When, in September, the rains have at last weakened into ineffectual evening drizzles, one is relieved.

5 The monsoon season has, I discovered, a rhythm that the mind and body grow accustomed to. In Dubai last June, when the temperature reached 48° Celsius, I would catch myself glancing at the sky, wondering idly if there was a hint of interesting cloud. My rational self knew there could not be a monsoon here, but the subconscious would not be denied. Some mornings I would awake in my darkened, air-conditioned room and imagine rain drumming on the window. It was an illusion that persisted several seconds into wakefulness, and even after I rose I would resist drawing the curtain aside, preferring instead to retreat to the even darker bathroom. Then I'd tell myself there is no rain, and I'd lace my shoes and step outside into the pitiless heat of Arabia.

6 Late in July, I noticed that the illusions persisted at work, too. With the window blinds down and the central air-conditioning humming along at a cool 22° Celsius, I occasionally caught myself wondering whether I'd find a cab that would be willing to drive me home in the rain. After all, it must be raining outside by now. At these times it took some courage to walk into the passageway between the office suites, face the window, stare at the Dubai skyline carelessly shimmering in the late evening sun, and remind myself that the monsoon lay on the other side of the Indian Ocean.

7 The sounds of rain would still visit, sometimes surprising, always comforting, while outside Dubai still blazed with heat and light. August slipped into September and as the body readjusted itself, the mind played along. As the Gulf's fall months began, the harsh absence of monsoon faded. I no longer looked for that high and lonely cloud in the sky. The time for rain had passed, and I wondered whether next year my longing would be the same.

PRACTICE 7

1. The writer begins by comparing the monsoon in Bangladesh with the dry climate in Dubai. He places his thesis statement in paragraph 2. Underline the thesis statement.

2. How does the writer describe Dubai? Write some descriptive words and phrases that he uses.

   _____

   _____

   _____

3. How does the writer describe Bombay during the monsoon season? Write some descriptive words and phrases that he uses.

   _____

   _____

   _____

4. What is the dominant impression in Goswami's essay? Circle the best answer.

    a. Joy   b. Tension   c. Homesickness

    d. Anger   e. Despair

5. The writer appeals to more than one sense. Give an example for each type of imagery.

    a. Sight: _____

    _____

    b. Sound: _____

    _____

    c. Smell: _____

    _____

 The Writer's Room **Topics for Descriptive Essays**

Writing Activity 1

Write a descriptive essay about one of the following topics.

General Topics

1. a celebration
2. a future car or house
3. a painting or photograph
4. a shopping area
5. a physical and psychological self-portrait
6. a train or bus station, or a hospital waiting room

College and Work-Related Topics

7. your first impressions of college
8. relaxing areas on campus
9. a past or current workplace
10. your college or workplace cafeteria or food court
11. a memorable person with whom you have worked
12. a pleasant or unpleasant task

PARAGRAPH LINK

You could also develop one of the topics in Chapter 6, "Description."

Writing Activity 2

Read the following quotations. Find one that you agree or disagree with, or find one that inspires you in some way. Then write a descriptive essay based on the quotation.

> The real voyage of discovery consists not in seeking new landscapes but in having new eyes.
>
> —Marcel Proust, French author

> There is no need to go to India or anywhere else to find peace. You will find that deep place of silence right in your room, your garden, or even your bathtub.
>
> —Elisabeth Kubler-Ross, Swiss author

Speak when you are angry—and you will make the best speech you'll ever regret.

—Laurence J. Peter, American educator and author

All sanity depends on this: that it should be a delight to feel heat strike the skin, a delight to stand upright, knowing the bones are moving easily under the flesh.

—Doris Lessing, British author

Iron rusts from disuse, and stagnant water loses its purity and in cold weather becomes frozen; even so does inaction sap the vigor of the mind.

—Leonardo Da Vinci, Italian artist and inventor

DESCRIPTIVE ESSAY CHECKLIST

As you write your descriptive essay, review the essay checklist on the inside front cover. Also ask yourself the following questions.

- Does my thesis statement clearly show what I will describe in the rest of the essay?

- Does my thesis statement make a point about the topic?

- Does my essay have a dominant impression?

- Does each body paragraph contain supporting details that appeal to the reader's senses?

- Do I use figurative language (simile, metaphor, or personification)?

PARAGRAPH LINK

For more information about process writing, refer to Chapter 7, "Process."

The Process Essay

A **process** is a series of steps done in chronological order. When you write a process essay, you explain how to do something, how something happens, or how something works. There are two main types of process essays.

1. **Complete a process.** Explain how to complete a particular task. For example, you might explain how to create a sculpture or how to give first aid to a choking victim. Each step you describe helps the reader complete the process.

2. **Understand a process.** Explain how something works or how something happens. In other words, the goal is to help the reader understand a process rather than do a process. For example, you might explain how a law is passed or explain how a previous war began.

The Thesis Statement

The thesis statement in a process essay includes the process you are describing and a controlling idea. In the introduction of a process essay, you should also mention any tools or supplies that the reader would need to complete the process.

topic   controlling idea
Choosing a college <u>requires some careful thinking and planning</u>.

topic   controlling idea
Pregnancy <u>consists of several stages</u>.

 List Specific Steps

You can write a thesis statement that contains a map, or guide, to the details that you will present in your essay. To guide your readers, you could mention the main steps in your thesis statement.

topic   controlling idea
It is possible to quit smoking <u>if you focus on your goal</u>, <u>find alternative relaxing activities</u>, and <u>enlist the support of friends and family</u>.

The Supporting Ideas

The body paragraphs in a process essay should explain the steps in the process. Each body paragraph should include details and examples to explain each step.

 Using Commands

When writing a "complete a process" essay, you can use commands when you explain each step in the process. It is not necessary to write *you should*.

command
First, **introduce** yourself to your roommate.

command
Ask your roommate about his or her pet peeves.

A Process Essay Plan

Read the next essay plan and answer the questions that follow.

Introduction
Thesis statement: By introducing yourself, joining groups, and organizing events, you will have a better chance of making friends in a new neighborhood.

I. Introduce yourself to your neighbors.
    A. Find a good moment.
    B. Explain that you are new to the neighborhood.
    C. Ask a few questions about the area.
II. Have an outdoor party and invite your neighbors.
    A. Find a pretext (holiday, birthday).
    B. Keep the party casual (the point is to have a relaxing time).
    C. Do not worry if some neighbors turn you down.
    D. Aim to find at least one good friend in your area.

(continued)

III. Get involved in your community.
  A. Volunteer to work at the library.
  B. Become politically active in local elections.
Conclusion: With a bit of effort, you can make friends in any neighborhood.

PRACTICE 8

1. What kind of process essay is this? Circle the best answer.
   a. Complete a process   b. Understand a process

2. Add another supporting idea to body paragraph 3.

   _____

   _____

3. What organizational method does the writer use? Circle the best answer.
   a. Time   b. Space   c. Emphatic

A Process Essay

In the next essay, Jake Sibley, a musician who maintains an online music site, explains how to become a successful musician. Read the essay and answer the questions.

Steps to Music Success

1   Before you can achieve anything, you must first imagine it. If you are serious about becoming a successful musician, it will serve you well to be looking not only at the next step, but also looking down the road to where you ultimately want to be. There is no question that regularly revisiting the fundamentals is critical to success in any long-term **endeavor.** With that in mind, there are some basic things to consider while pursuing your musical dreams.

2   First, setting specific goals and giving them regular attention is **vital** to achieving success at any level. Goals give direction to your action. Furthermore, achieving goals is a tasty reward that will build your esteem and motivate you to reach even higher. So pick your endpoint, and then write down the steps to get there. If you are just beginning in music, then resolve to take lessons. If you are taking lessons, then resolve to get in a performing band. If you are already performing, then resolve to join a paid project. There is no reason that can keep you from reaching your dream. You just have to plan it and then do it.

3   It is also important to spend time, not money, on your dream. Most likely you have seen rookie musicians with stacks of absurdly expensive gear. Certainly I am guilty of walking into a music store and **ogling** the top-end instruments, convinced that if I could afford that equipment, my sound would improve by leaps and bounds: "If I had that guitar, I would practice *every day.*" If you are not practicing every day already, a new guitar won't change that. The only investment that will improve your success as musicians is *time*— time spent practicing, time spent learning, and time spent pursuing your goals. The lure of expensive gear is a tempting but false road to better musicianship.

endeavor: attempt

vital: extremely important

ogling: staring at with desire

4   Furthermore, if you really want to improve, play with others. Music is a form of conversation between human beings. It may well be the oldest language, used for millennia by musically inclined people to jointly convey their own rage, sorrow, hope, and joy to other human beings. Learning music without this community is as futile as learning to play football by yourself. Although hours spent alone with your instrument are certainly necessary for success, engaging in musical conversations and performances is an equally vital element to your progress. A very common weakness among amateur musicians is their inability to make music with other artists—a flaw that can be easily remedied with experience. Even if you are a beginner, get out and play with others and stage a few performances if you can. Without even realizing it, you will begin to assimilate fundamental lessons about listening, interacting, and performing in a live setting that are critical to your future success.

5   Finally, practice, practice, practice! There is simply no other way to ensure your own progress as a musician. Have you been spending hours on the Internet, combing for information on how to market your music, or cheaply record a CD, or win a music competition? That's great, but have you been spending as least as much time alone with your instrument? If not, you should reconsider your priorities. If you are not practicing several times a week at least, the music you market, or record cheaply, or submit to a competition is not going to get very far. As a musician seeking success at any level, practicing your instrument should be your number-one priority.

6   If you're serious about music, keep focused on your goal. Take the time to learn your craft, and share your gift with others. Do not let anyone else hold you back from what you know you can achieve.

PRACTICE 9

1. Underline the thesis statement of the essay.

2. What type of process essay is this? Circle the best answer.
    a. Complete a process
    b. Understand a process

3. In process essays, the support is generally a series of steps. List the steps to music success.

    _____

    _____

    _____

    _____

    _____

4. What organizational method does the author use?
    a. Time order   b. Emphatic order   c. Space order

5. Write down the transitional expressions that Sibley uses to introduce each new paragraph.

    _____

    _____

6. Who is the audience for this essay? _____

7. How could this essay have relevance for people who never play music?

   _____

   _____

 The Writer's Room   **Topics for Process Essays**

PARAGRAPH LINK

You could also develop one of the topics in Chapter 7, "Process."

Writing Activity 1

Write a process essay about one of the following topics.

General Topics

1. how to be happy
2. how to be healthy
3. how to learn a new language
4. how to find a good roommate
5. how something works
6. how to deal with a problematic teenager

College and Work-Related Topics

7. how to manage your time
8. how education can change lives
9. how to plan a project
10. how to do your job
11. how to get ahead in your job
12. how to find satisfaction in your work life

Writing Activity 2

Read the following quotations. Find one that you agree or disagree with or one that inspires you in some way. Then write a process essay based on the quotation.

> Treat the earth well. It was not given to you by your parents; it was loaned to you by your children.
>
> —Native American proverb

> If you judge people, you have no time to love them.
>
> —Mother Teresa, Catholic nun

> Know how to listen, and you will profit even from those who talk badly.
>
> —Plutarch, ancient Greek philosopher

> Every child is an artist. The problem is how to remain an artist once he [or she] grows up.
>
> —Pablo Picasso, Spanish artist

> If you can spend a perfectly useless afternoon in a perfectly useless manner, you have learned how to live.
>
> —Lin Yutang, Chinese author

> ## ✔ PROCESS ESSAY CHECKLIST
>
> As you write your process essay, review the essay checklist on the inside front cover. Also ask yourself the following questions.
>
> ☐ Does my thesis statement make a point about the process?
>
> ☐ Does my essay explain how to do something, how something works, or how something happened?
>
> ☐ Do I include all of the steps in the process?
>
> ☐ Do I clearly explain the steps in the process or in the event?
>
> ☐ Do I mention any tools or equipment that my readers need to complete or understand the process?

The Definition Essay

A definition tells you what something means. When you write a **definition essay,** you give your personal definition of a term or concept. Although you can define most terms in a few sentences, you may need to offer extended definitions for words that are particularly complex. For example, you could write an essay or even an entire book about the term *love*. The way that you interpret love is unique, and you would bring your own opinions, experiences, and impressions to your definition essay.

PARAGRAPH LINK

For more information about definition writing, refer to Chapter 8, "Definition."

The Thesis Statement

In your thesis statement, indicate what you are defining, and include a definition of the term. Look at the three ways you might define a term in your thesis statement.

1. **Definition by synonym.** You could give a synonym for the term.

   term   +   synonym
   Some consumers insist that Frankenfood, or genetically modified food, be labeled.

2. **Definition by category.** Decide what larger group the term belongs to, and then determine the unique characteristics that set the term apart from others in that category.

   term   +   category   +   detail
   A groupie is a fanatical devotee of a musician or band.

3. **Definition by negation.** Explain what the term is not, and then explain what it is.

   term   +   what it is not   +   what it is
   Stalkers are not misguided romantics; they are dangerous predators.

The Supporting Ideas

In a definition essay, you can support your main point using a variety of writing patterns. For example, in a definition essay about democracy, one supporting paragraph could give historical background about democracy, another could include a description of a functioning democracy, and a third paragraph could compare different styles of democracy. The different writing patterns would all support the overriding pattern, which is definition.

 Enhancing a Definition

One way to enhance a definition essay is to begin with a provocative statement about the term. Then in the body of your essay, develop your definition more thoroughly. This technique arouses the interest of the readers and makes them want to continue reading. For example, the next statement questions a common belief.

According to Dr. W. Roland, attention deficit disorder is an invented disease.

A Definition Essay Plan

Read the next essay plan and answer the questions that follow.

Introduction

Thesis statement: Depression is not just the blues; it is a serious health problem.

I. A depressed person cannot just "snap out of it."
 A. is not a sign of self-indulgence
 B. some people battle the illness for years and need specific treatment
 C. offer the example of Katie Rowen, who has been hospitalized several times
 D. quotations from people suffering from depression: William Styron says, "Nightfall seemed more somber"; Mike Wallace calls it "endless darkness"

II. Symptoms are not always obvious and can be overlooked.
 A. excess fatigue, lack of energy
 B. unexplained bouts of sadness
 C. extremely irritable for no obvious reason
 D. academic and work performance suffer

III. Depression has impacts on a person's physical and emotional life.
 A. may neglect nutrition, leading to excess weight gain or weight loss
 B. may neglect appearance and hygiene
 C. may alienate family and co-workers
 D. may suffer job loss, leading to financial consequences

Conclusion: Depression is a serious illness that affects many people in our society.

PRACTICE 10

1. What type of definition does the writer use in the thesis statement? Circle the best answer.
 a. Definition by synonym   b. Definition by category
 c. Definition by negation

2. The writer uses many types of supporting details. Underline a quotation, and circle an anecdote.

3. What organizational strategy does the writer use? Circle the best answer.

   a. Time order   b. Emphatic order   c. Space order

A Definition Essay

In the next essay, student writer Diego Pelaez defines a sports fanatic. Read the essay and answer the questions.

Sports Fanatics

1   The opposing team's greatest player received the ball with time running low. His team down a point, he went to work on his defender. Faking a rush to the basket, he stepped back and rose for the deciding jump shot of the game. He released the ball with a good arc, and sure enough, it found its target, winning the game and the championship. I watched silently and shared the sorrow of the team, for I am a sports fanatic. When a beloved team loses, the true sports fanatic feels like he or she has been through a personal tragedy. For sports fanatics, the game is not just a game; it is one of life's most significant events.

2   Sports fanatics never hesitate to show devotion to the team, for devotion is what separates a true sports fanatic from the average, casual sports fan. The casual fan may express **complacency** when the team loses. A sports fanatic feels each defeat with stretches of sorrow and answers each victory with **jubilation.** When my team lost that championship game, I was **despondent** for over a week. I kept going over the game in my head, imagining what might have happened had the game ended a few seconds earlier.

complacency: contentment

jubilation: extreme joy

despondent: miserable

3   Statistics are a vital part to the full understanding of any sport, and sports fanatics know this fact. Fanatics learn everything that they can about the game. They can usually rattle off at least a few statistics that can make regular people question their use of their spare time. Yet despite the opinions of others, true sports fans wear their ability to memorize statistics as a badge of honor and as proof of their undying dedication. For example, when I meet a fellow fanatic, I excitedly recite numbers, names, and dates, often competing to show that I have amassed more information about my favorite sport than others.

4   True sports fanatics are not crazy; they simply have an **avid** fantasy life. Millions of kids imitate Joe Montana or Michael Jordan, dreaming of becoming a major leaguer. Even if the sports fanatic is a poor player, he or she has usually played the game in order to fully understand the sport. In essence, the thrill of the sports fanatic is to **live vicariously** through the people talented enough to achieve the fanatic's childhood dreams. I spend many pleasurable moments imagining that I can hear the roar of the crowd when I make that winning jump shot.

avid: full, enthusiastic

live vicariously: to imagine participating in someone else's experience

5   The sports fanatic is a hard creature to understand. Others may wonder why die-hard fans care so much about sports. The point is, fanatics have a purpose in life: they truly care about something, and they express their devotion wholeheartedly. Some of the greatest athletes are sports fanatics too. Growing up, Michael Jordan was passionate about baseball and basketball. Wayne Gretzky spent his childhood absorbing everything that he could about hockey. So instead of regarding sports fanatics as crazy, people should commend them for their commitment and love of the game.

PRACTICE 11

1. Underline the thesis statement of the essay.

2. What introduction style does the writer use in this essay? Circle the best answer.

   a. Anecdote   b. Historical information   c. Shocking statement

3. In paragraph 2, the writer compares a fanatic with a casual fan. What is the main difference between the two?

   _____

   _____

4. Using your own words, list the main supporting ideas in this essay.

   a. _____

   b. _____

   c. _____

5. Look in the essay, and find an example of definition by negation. Write it here.

   _____

   _____

6. What method does the writer use to end this essay? Circle the best answer.

   a. Quotation   b. Suggestion   c. Prediction

 The Writer's Room **Topics for Definition Essays**

PARAGRAPH LINK

You could also develop one of the topics found in Chapter 8, "Definition."

Writing Activity 1

Write a definition essay about one of the following topics.

General Topics

1. propaganda
2. a pacifist
3. street smarts
4. a control freak
5. a blog
6. a generation gap

College and Work-Related Topics

7. a McJob
8. a perfectionist
9. a whistle-blower
10. an ineffective boss
11. affirmative action
12. downsizing

Writing Activity 2

Read the following quotations. Find one that you agree or disagree with, or find one that inspires you in some way, and use it as the basis for a definition essay.

A cult is a religion with no political power.

—Tom Wolfe, American author

Tact is the ability to describe others as they see themselves.

—Abraham Lincoln, former American president

One of the keys to happiness is a bad memory.

—Rita Mae Brown, American activist

A leader who does not hesitate before he sends his nation into battle is not fit to be a leader.

—Golda Meir, former Israeli prime minister

Opportunity is missed by most people because it is dressed in overalls and looks like work.

—Thomas A. Edison, American inventor

✔ DEFINITION ESSAY CHECKLIST

As you write your definition essay, review the essay checklist on the inside front cover. Also ask yourself the following questions.

☐ Does my thesis statement explain what term I am defining?

☐ Does each topic sentence clearly show some aspect of the definition?

☐ Do my supporting paragraphs include examples that help illustrate the definition?

☐ Do I use concise language in my definition?

The Classification Essay

Classifying means "to sort a subject into more understandable categories." When you are planning a classification essay, find a topic that you can divide into categories. Each of the categories must be part of a larger group, yet they must also be distinct. For example, if your essay is about types of lawyers, you might sort them into criminal lawyers, divorce lawyers, and corporate lawyers.

PARAGRAPH LINK

For more information about classification writing, refer to Chapter 9, "Classification."

The Thesis Statement

The thesis statement in a classification essay mentions the categories of the subject and contains a controlling idea. In this type of essay, the controlling idea is your classification principle, which is the overall method that you use to sort the items. For example, if your essay topic is "children," you might sort them according to their stages of development, their birth order, or their social classes.

controlling idea (classification principle)   topic
<u>Birth order has a profound influence on</u> **the personalities of children.**

List Specific Categories

You can guide your reader by listing the specific categories you will cover in your thesis statement.

topic   controlling idea

Children learn gender roles <u>through the family, the school, and the media.</u>

The Supporting Ideas

In a classification essay, each body paragraph covers one category. To organize your categories and supporting details, you can use a classification chart or a more traditional classification essay plan.

A Classification Chart

A classification chart helps you plan your ideas by providing a visual representation of how you wish to classify a subject. In this sample chart, the thesis statement appears at the top, and all of the categories branch from it.

Historically, three types of marital unions have been practiced around the world.

Monogamy	Polygyny	Polyandry
- marriage between one man and one woman - most commonly accepted - because of divorce, some practice serial monogamy	- males may have more than one wife - common in preindustrial societies - practiced today by some religious groups	- females may have more than one husband - was common in some tribal societies in India - rare to nonexistent today

A Classification Essay Plan

A classification essay plan also helps you organize your essay's categories and details. Read the next essay plan and answer the questions.

Introduction

Thesis statement: There are three main types of bad jokes: overused children's jokes, practical jokes, and insulting jokes.

I. Overused children's jokes bore the listener.
  A. knock-knock jokes
  B. "what is it" jokes
  C. "why did the chicken cross the road" jokes
  D. silly riddles
II. Practical jokes humiliate the victims.
  A. whoopee cushions
  B. plastic wrap on the toilet seat
  C. paint can over the door
  D. "kick me" note on a person's back

III. Insulting jokes can seriously hurt or offend others.
    A. jokes about ethnic groups or religious groups
    B. jokes about a person's appearance (big nose jokes, blond jokes)
    C. jokes about a profession (lawyer jokes)

Conclusion: As long as people laugh at them, bad jokes will continue to be repeated.

PRACTICE 12

1. What is the classification principle? That is, what main principle unifies the three categories?

    _____

2. Why is each type of joke considered bad? Underline the reason in each topic sentence.

3. The author organizes the main ideas in emphatic order. How are they arranged? Circle the best answer.

    a. From most to least offensive   b. From least to most offensive

4. How does the writer support the main ideas? Circle the best answer.

    a. Examples   b. Anecdotes   c. Statistics

A Classification Essay

Read the next essay by student writer Naomi Ihara and answer the questions.

ATM Fraud

1   In the 1980s, automated teller machines started appearing in bank entrances, gas stations, and grocery stores. As fast as the machines appeared, so did criminals who were intent on finding ways to rob the **ATMs.** Today, there are three very effective types of bank machine crimes occurring across the nation: no-tech, low-tech, and high-tech.

ATMs: automated teller machines

2   Criminals who attempt no-tech crimes use simple methods to defraud others. For example, a thief may stand near a bank machine and intently watch people punching in their **PIN** codes. After reading the code, the thief follows the victim and waits for the right moment to attack. Then the thief snatches the victim's purse or wallet in order to get the card. With the debit card and the code, the crook can empty the victim's account. Another method is to look through recycling waste for receipts and bank statements. With a name, birth date, and personal banking information, a thief can steal someone's identity and try to get a new bank card issued in the victim's name. These types of criminals are the most likely to be caught.

PIN: personal identification number

3   Several low-tech methods of defrauding customers exist. One method involves the use of an inexpensive plastic sleeve that is inserted into the debit card slot. Later, after inserting a debit card, the customer attempts to punch in his or her personal identity number. The machine instructs the customer to re-enter the code because it cannot read the automatic strip on the card. The customer, who is being watched, makes several futile attempts and then leaves, assuming the machine has kept the card. A few minutes later,

a criminal removes the sleeve containing the card from the machine, re-enters the card, types in the victim's PIN code, and removes cash. Another low-tech method involves the use of a false cash dispenser cover. A thief removes the cover from one machine and places it on another. When customers attempt to remove cash, the false cover blocks the cash dispenser. Victims leave, assuming the machine has malfunctioned. Then the thief arrives, removes the false cover, and takes the money.

4   High-tech methods include the use of card readers and fake bank machines. The card readers are small devices that can be attached to an ATM machine. Anna C. Irwin, in an article for the Maryville, Tennessee paper, *The Daily Times*, recounts the story of Mike and Roxanne Coffey. They arrived at a machine and read a notice telling them that due to recent fraud attempts, they should use an electronic reader beside the machine. They did so, and then noticed that the reader was not properly attached to the wall. They alerted the bank and were told that the machine was not bank property. Apparently, such card readers give criminals all the data they need to make and use false bankcards. Furthermore, in some areas, police have discovered fake bank machines sitting in entrances to retail outlets. Customers insert their cards into the fake machines, unknowingly giving criminals their card and PIN information.

5   According to the American Bankers Association, banks lose over fifty million dollars per year due to debit card fraud. Although most banks quickly reimburse customers who are victims of such scams, not all do. Some customers report having to fight with bank employees for months over unexplained withdrawals from their accounts. It is always a good idea to be vigilant when using a bank machine. If something seems odd, trust your instincts and report it.

PRACTICE 13

1. Underline the thesis statement of the essay.

2. What is the essay's classification principle? _____

_____

3. The author lists three main categories. What are they?

_____

4. Underline the topic sentences in the body paragraphs.

5. To better understand how the author organizes this essay, make a classification chart. Write the categories on the lines and examples in the boxes.

Types of ATM Fraud

The Writer's Room — Topics for Classification Essays

Writing Activity 1

Write a classification essay about one of the following topics.

General Topics

1. addictions
2. transportation
3. extreme sports
4. things that cause allergic reactions
5. youth subcultures
6. punishment

College and Work-Related Topics

7. professions
8. art
9. work-related expenses
10. success
11. conversational topics at work
12. fashions in the workplace

PARAGRAPH LINK

You could also develop one of the topics found in Chapter 9, "Classification."

Writing Activity 2

Read the following quotations. Find one that you agree or disagree with, or find one that inspires you in some way. Then write a classification essay based on the quotation.

> Work saves us from three great evils: boredom, vice, and need.
> —Voltaire, French author and philosopher

> There are three kinds of lies: lies, damned lies, and statistics.
> —Benjamin Disraeli, British politician

> Nothing is particularly hard if you divide it into small jobs.
> —Henry Ford, American inventor

> There appears to be three types of politicians: leaders, lobbyists, and professionals.
> —R. Ravimohan, Indian journalist

> Never bear more than one trouble at a time. Some people bear three kinds—all they have had, all they have now, and all they expect to have.
> —Edward Everett Hale, American author and clergyman

✔ CLASSIFICATION ESSAY CHECKLIST

As you write your classification essay, review the essay checklist on the inside front cover. Then ask yourself the following questions.

☐ Do I clearly identify which categories I will discuss in my thesis statement?

☐ Do I use a common classification principle to unite the various items?

(continued)

Do I include categories that do not overlap?

Do I clearly explain one of the categories in each body paragraph?

Do I use sufficient details to explain each category?

Do I arrange the categories in a logical manner?

PARAGRAPH LINK

For more information about this pattern, refer to Chapter 10, "Comparison and Contrast."

The Comparison and Contrast Essay

You **compare** when you want to find similarities and **contrast** when you want to find differences. When writing a comparison and contrast essay, you explain how people, places, things, or ideas are the same or different to prove a specific point.

Before you write, you must make a decision about whether you will focus on similarities, differences, or both. As you explore your topic, it is a good idea to make a list of both similarities and differences. Later, you could use some of the ideas in your essay plan.

The Thesis Statement

The thesis statement in a comparison and contrast essay indicates if you are making comparisons, contrasts, or both. When you write a thesis statement, indicate what you are comparing or contrasting and the controlling idea.

Although neat people have a very nice environment, messy people are more relaxed.

Topics being contrasted: Neat people and messy people

Controlling idea: Messy people are more relaxed

Alice's daughter wants to be her own person, but she is basically very similar to her mother.

Topics being compared: Mother and daughter

Controlling idea: Very similar personalities

The Supporting Ideas

In a comparison and contrast essay, you can develop your body paragraphs in two different ways.

1. In a **point-by-point** development, you present *one* point about Topic A and then *one* point about Topic B. You keep following this pattern until you have a few points for each topic.

    Point A   Point B   Point A   Point B   Point A   Point B

2. In a **topic-by-topic** development, you discuss one topic in detail, and then you discuss the other topic in detail.

    All of Topic A   All of Topic B

A Comparison and Contrast Essay Plan

Read the next essay plan and answer the questions.

Introduction

Thesis statement: Although I earned a lot when I was an accountant, I am much happier just working in a bank.

I.   When I worked as an accountant, my family life suffered.
    A. Before, I yelled at my children because of stress.
    B. I worked evenings and weekends visiting clients.
    C. I didn't give my spouse any attention.
    D. I didn't take time to do family things.

II. My health was in danger when I was an accountant.
    A. I got panic attacks during tax time.
    B. My blood pressure rocketed when clients yelled at me.
    C. If I made a mistake, I felt physically ill with guilt.
    D. I drank and smoked more to cope with stress.

III. Now in my new bank job, I have less stress and my family life is better.
    A. Now I work only 9 to 5, and no weekends or evenings.
    B. We do family activities every Sunday.
    C. Now my bank clients are happy to see me.
    D. My days are relaxed, and my co-workers are pleasant.
    E. My health is better, and I no longer have panic attacks.

Conclusion: Do not sacrifice your family for your job.

PRACTICE 14

1. The writer compares and contrasts two things in this essay plan. What are they?

    _____

    _____

2. Look at the thesis statement. What is the controlling idea?

    _____

    _____

3. What will this essay focus on? Circle the best answer.
    a. Similarities   b. Differences

4. Look at paragraphs 1 through 3. What comparison and contrast style does the writer use? Circle the best answer.
    a. Point by point   b. Topic by topic

A Comparison and Contrast Essay

In the next essay, college student Emily Hotte compares two eras. Read the essay and answer the questions.

The Unchanging Generation

1　　In the 1920s, life was more difficult for most people than it is today. There were no electric washers, dryers, or dishwashers. Racism was more rampant, and so was sexism. Women were expected to work in the home, and few universities accepted female students. Entertainment was different, too. People listened to radios and watched silent films. They did not have televisions, MP3 players, computers, or cellular phones. Yet in spite of these differences, young people in the 1920s were very much like young people today.

2　　Today, young people want to be popular, and they go to great lengths to fit in with their friends, yet this was also true in the 1920s. F. Scott Fitzgerald wrote stories and novels that describe the 1920s, and he portrays a world where young people are divided among those who are popular and those who are not. In his short story "Bernice Bobs Her Hair," the main character is a shy, socially awkward girl who feels a "vague pain that she was not at present engaged in being popular" (26). In a desperate effort to make friends, Bernice changes her style and modifies her personality in order to be accepted by her peers. Today's youths also worry about popularity. Those who are not part of the "in" crowd are often ridiculed and rejected, and those at the top of the social hierarchy are imitated, envied, and admired. In several highly publicized cases of school violence, the perpetrators complained of being unpopular outcasts who were bullied by more popular students.

3　　Teens of the 1920s, like teens today, tried to distinguish themselves from previous generations. In the 1920s, young "flapper" women stopped wearing corsets; they wore skirts that showed their legs; and, in an act of extreme rebellion, they cut their long hair short. In Fitzgerald's story, Bernice calls bobbed hair on women "immoral" but then notes that "you've either got to amuse people or feed 'em or shock 'em" (21). Today, teenagers also differentiate themselves from their elders in an attempt to forge their own identities and create a sense of independence. To the chagrin of their parents, teens color their hair distinctive shades and tattoo or pierce body parts. Some commentators lament the deplorable state of youth fashion, complaining that their daughters expose too much skin and their sons wear poorly fitting clothing.

4　　In contemporary subcultures, music is an element that can bond youths together but enrage parents, and the same was true in the 1920s. Fitzgerald called the 1920s the "Jazz Age" and said that youths were a jazz-nourished generation. Jazz, which was created by African Americans, was noted for its forceful rhythms and improvisations. Many parents associated the music with immoral behavior; however, that did not stop armies of kids from crowding jazz clubs. Today, virtually all youth subcultures identify with a particular music style. Punk, alternative, rap, and hip-hop are just some musical styles associated with various youth groups. Often, the music, with its violent or sexual lyrics, enrages older generations. In fact, in the early 2000s, a Senate subcommittee looked at the impact of violent lyrics on urban youths.

5　　Although many things have changed since the 1920s, the characteristics of adolescents have remained fundamentally the same. Rebellious youths in the 1920s attacked social conventions by adopting new and shocking styles and by dancing to music that was considered **licentious**. Today, youths do much the same things. Perhaps the association of youth and rebellion is simply part of the human condition. In fact, about two thousand years ago,

licentious: immoral or shameful

Seneca, a Roman philosopher and statesman, said, "It is a youthful failing to be unable to control one's impulses."

PRACTICE 15

1. Underline the thesis statement of the essay.

2. In the thesis statement, what two things does the writer compare?

   _____

3. What does this essay focus on? Circle the best answer.
   a. Similarities   b. Differences

4. What pattern of comparison does the writer follow in paragraph 2? Circle the best answer.
   a. Point by point   b. Topic by topic

5. Using your own words, list the writer's main supporting points.

   _____

   _____

   _____

6. In the conclusion, how does the quotation support the writer's main point?

   _____

   _____

 The Writer's Room **Topics for Comparison and Contrast Essays**

Writing Activity 1

Write a comparison and contrast essay about one of the following topics.

General Topics

Compare and/or contrast . . .

1. a liberal and a conservative

2. expectations about parenthood vs. the reality of parenthood

3. two sides of a controversial issue

4. living together and getting married

5. manners today and manners fifty years ago

6. a book and a film about the same topic

College and Work-Related Topics

Compare and/or contrast . . .

7. male and female college athletes

8. working with others and working alone

9. a good manager and a bad manager

10. a stay-at-home parent and an employed parent

11. student life and professional life

12. expectations about a job and the reality of that job

PARAGRAPH LINK

You could also develop one of the topics found in Chapter 10, "Comparison and Contrast."

Writing Activity 2

Read the following quotations. Find one that you agree or disagree with, or find one that sparks your imagination. Then write a comparison and contrast essay based on the quotation.

My grandfather once told me that there are two kinds of people: those who work, and those who take the credit. He told me to try to be in the first group; there was less competition there.

—Indira Gandhi, Indian politician

People are more violently opposed to fur than leather because it is safer to harass rich women than motorcycle gangs.

—Unknown

Happy families are all alike. Every unhappy family is unhappy in its own way.

—Leo Tolstoy, Russian author

Commandments for wives:

1. Don't bother your husband with petty troubles and complaints when he comes home from work.
2. Let him relax before dinner, and discuss family problems after the "inner man" has been satisfied.

Commandments for husbands:

1. Remember your wife wants to be treated as your sweetheart.
2. Compliment her new dress, hair-do, and cooking.

—Edward Podolsky, American author of 1947 self-help manual

The first half of our lives is ruined by our parents, and the second half is ruined by our children.

—Clarence Darrow, American defense lawyer

COMPARISON AND CONTRAST ESSAY CHECKLIST

As you write your comparison and contrast essay, review the essay checklist on the inside front cover. Also ask yourself the following questions.

☐ Does my thesis statement explain what I am comparing or contrasting?

☐ Does my thesis statement make a point about my topic?

☐ Does my essay focus on either similarities or differences?

☐ Does my essay include point-by-point and/or topic-by-topic patterns?

☐ Do all of my supporting examples clearly relate to the topics that are being compared or contrasted?

☐ Do I use transitions that will help readers follow my ideas?

The Cause and Effect Essay

When writing a cause and effect essay, you explain why an event happened or what the consequences of such an event were.

PARAGRAPH LINK

For more information about this pattern, refer to Chapter 11, "Cause and Effect."

The Thesis Statement

The thesis statement in a cause and effect essay contains the topic and the controlling idea. The controlling idea indicates whether the essay will focus on causes, effects, or both.

topic   controlling idea (causes)
Chronic insomnia is caused by many factors.

topic   controlling idea (effects)
Chronic insomnia can have a serious impact on a person's health.

topic   controlling idea (causes and effects)
Chronic insomnia, which is caused by many factors, can have a serious impact on a person's health.

 Thinking About Effects

If you are writing about the effects of something, you might think about both the short-term and long-term effects. By doing so, you will generate more ideas for the body of your essay. You will also be able to structure your essay more effectively by moving from short-term to long-term effects.

For example, look at the short- and long-term effects of a smoke-free work zone.

Short term: Inside air is cleaner.

                     The smokers get more coffee breaks.

Long term: Fewer smoke-related illnesses occur in nonsmokers.

                     Some smokers might quit smoking.

PRACTICE 16

Look at the following thesis statements. As you read each sentence, ask yourself whether it focuses on causes, effects, or both. Circle the best answers.

1. Youths join street gangs because they crave excitement, want to belong to a group, and feel safer in a gang.
   a. Causes   b. Effects   c. Both

2. Now that I am a vegetarian, I have more energy, fewer health problems, and greater self-respect.
   a. Causes   b. Effects   c. Both

3. Because of world demand for wood, meat, and gold, the depletion of natural resources in the Amazon jungle is progressing at an alarming rate.
   a. Causes   b. Effects   c. Both

The Supporting Ideas

The body paragraphs in a cause and effect essay focus on either causes, effects, or both. Make sure that each body paragraph contains specific examples that clarify the cause and/or effect relationship.

A Cause and Effect Essay Plan

Read the next essay plan and answer the questions.

Introduction

Thesis statement: I have become a vegetarian for three important reasons.

I.   I cannot justify killing something with a nervous system.
  A.   I do not want to hurt living creatures.
  B.   Animals with a nervous system suffer horribly when they are killed for food.
  C.   Methods used in slaughterhouses are inhumane.
II. A vegetarian diet is healthier than a meat-based diet.
  A.   In modern agricultural practices, steroids are given to farm animals.
  B.   Meat products have higher cholesterol levels than plant and grain products.
  C.   Vegetables and beans ensure an adequate supply of nutrients and proteins.
III. A vegetarian diet is inexpensive.
  A.   Vegetables are cheaper than meat.
  B.   It is cheaper to produce one pound of vegetables than one pound of beef.
  C.   People can grow their own vegetables.

Conclusion: A vegetarian diet is a healthy alternative.

PRACTICE 17

1.   In the thesis statement, circle the topic and underline the controlling idea.

2.   Does this essay focus on causes or effects? _____

3.   Who is the audience for this essay? _____

A Cause and Effect Essay

Read the next essay by student writer Jim Baek and then answer the questions that follow.

Why Small Businesses Fail

1   Last spring, Pablo Ortiz rented a tiny pizzeria in his neighborhood to turn it into a taco restaurant. Full of enthusiasm, he bought supplies, paid for advertisements, and posted a large menu in the window of his new venture, called Taco Heaven. Ten months later, Taco Heaven closed, and Ortiz declared bankruptcy. He was not alone. The Small Business Administration Office

reports that close to half of all new businesses fail within the first five years. Causes of small business failures are numerous.

2   First, inexperienced business owners often neglect to do market research to find out if community members are interested in the product. In Ortiz's case, he thought that area residents would appreciate the chance to buy hearty chicken or pork tacos. However, locals were used to paying $2 for a slice of pizza and were unwilling to spend $3 for a homemade taco.

3   Second, inadequate pricing can hurt new businesses. Maggie Stevens, owner of a successful restaurant in Los Angeles, sells stuffed Belgian waffles to an eager clientele. Before pricing her waffles, she calculated the exact cost of each plate, right down to the strawberry that adorned the waffle and the touch of cream next to it. She also considered other costs beyond that of the ingredients, including the cost of labor and food spoilage. Her final price for each dish was 60 percent higher than her base cost. Ortiz, on the other hand, had absolutely no idea what he really spent to make each taco. He ended up underpricing his product and losing money.

4   Additionally, many small business owners have insufficient funds to run their ventures successfully. According to accountant Louis Polk, most small businesses operate for four years before they break even, let alone actually make money. Therefore, owners need a cash reserve to get through the first slow years. Ortiz, expecting to make a decent profit right away, did not realize that he would have to use up his savings to keep his business afloat.

5   Finally, inexperienced merchants may underestimate the sheer volume of work involved in running a business. Ortiz admits he was very naive about the workload. Taco Heaven had to be open 15 hours a day, 7 days a week. Ortiz also had to shop for ingredients and do the accounting. After months of grueling work and little to no pay, he burned out.

6   People who plan to open small businesses should become informed, especially about potential pitfalls. Inexperience, lack of proper planning, and insufficient funds can combine to create a business failure.

PRACTICE 18

1. Underline the thesis statement of the essay.

2. Does this essay focus on causes, effects, or both? _____

3. Give an example from the essay of the following:

     a. statistic _____

     _____

     b. anecdote _____

     _____

4. Using your own words, list the four supporting points.

     _____

     _____

     _____

     _____

The Writer's Room
Topics for Cause and Effect Essays

PARAGRAPH LINK

You could also develop one of the topics found in Chapter 11, "Cause and Effect."

Writing Activity I

Write a cause and effect essay about one of the following topics.

General Topics

Causes and/or effects of . . .

1. a new law or policy
2. stress
3. going to war
4. getting a divorce
5. voting or not voting
6. leaving your home or homeland

College and Work-Related Topics

Causes and/or effects of . . .

7. being a parent and college student
8. taking time off before college
9. having an office romance
10. working with a friend
11. gossiping in the office
12. changing jobs or career paths

Writing Activity 2

Read the following quotations. Find one that you agree or disagree with or one that inspires you in some way, and use it as the basis for a cause and effect essay.

> When a man tells you that he got rich through hard work, ask him, "Whose?"
>
> —Don Marquis, American humorist

> Another possible source of guidance for teenagers is television, but television's message has always been that the need for truth, wisdom and world peace pales by comparison with the need for toothpaste that offers whiter teeth and fresher breath.
>
> —Dave Barry, American author and humorist

> Sometimes when we are generous in barely detectible ways, it can change someone else's life forever.
>
> —Margaret Cho, American comedian

> All human actions have one or more of these seven causes: chance, nature, compulsion, habit, reason, passion, and desire.
>
> —Aristotle, ancient Greek philosopher

> One of the symptoms of an approaching nervous breakdown is the belief that one's work is terribly important.
>
> —Bertrand Russell, British author and philosopher

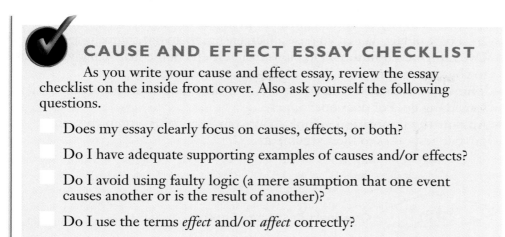

CAUSE AND EFFECT ESSAY CHECKLIST

As you write your cause and effect essay, review the essay checklist on the inside front cover. Also ask yourself the following questions.

- Does my essay clearly focus on causes, effects, or both?

- Do I have adequate supporting examples of causes and/or effects?

- Do I avoid using faulty logic (a mere asumption that one event causes another or is the result of another)?

- Do I use the terms *effect* and/or *affect* correctly?

The Argument Essay

When you write an **argument essay,** you take a position on an issue, and you try to defend your position. In other words, you try to persuade your readers to accept your point of view.

PARAGRAPH LINK

For more information about argument writing, refer to Chapter 12, "Argument."

The Thesis Statement

The thesis statement in an argument essay mentions the subject and a debatable point of view about the subject. Do not include phrases such as *in my opinion, I think*, or *I am going to talk about* in your thesis statement.

controlling idea   topic
Our college needs to provide **a nightly walk-home service for students.**

 List Specific Arguments

Your thesis statement can further guide your readers by listing the specific arguments you will make in your essay.

controlling idea   topic   (arguments)   1
Colleges should implement **work terms** to help students acquire job skills,
                          2   3
make professional contacts, and earn money for expenses.

The Supporting Ideas

In the body of your essay, give convincing arguments. Try to use several types of supporting evidence.

PARAGRAPH LINK

For more detailed information about types of evidence, see pages 158–159 in Chapter 12, "Argument."

- **Include anecdotes.** Specific experiences or pieces of information can support your point of view.

- **Add facts.** Facts are statements that can be verified in some way. **Statistics** are a type of fact. When you use a fact, ensure that your source is reliable.
- **Use informed opinions.** Opinions from experts in the field can give weight to your argument.
- **Think about logical consequences.** Consider long-term consequences if something does or does not happen.
- **Answer the opposition.** Think about your opponents' arguments, and provide responses to their arguments.

RESEARCH LINK

For more information about doing research, see Chapter 15, "Enhancing Your Writing with Research."

 Quoting a Respected Source

One way to enhance your essay is to include a quotation from a respected source. Find a quotation from somebody in a field that is directly related to your topic. When you include the quotation as supporting evidence, remember to mention the source.

According to Dr. Tom Houston, co-director of the American Medical Association's SmokeLess States campaign, secondhand smoke "can lead to serious health consequences, ranging from ear infections and pneumonia to asthma."

An Argument Essay Plan

Read the next essay plan and answer the questions.

Introduction

Thesis statement: America should institute longer vacation time for employees.

I. Paid vacations in America are much shorter than they are in other countries.
   A. My friend Jay complains because he has only one week of paid vacation.
   B. According to Perri Capell (*Wall Street Journal*), many American employees get only a one-week vacation during their first year of work.
   C. Most European countries give employees five weeks of vacation time during their first year of work.
   D. My sister lives in London and gets five weeks off each year.
II. Longer vacations allow employees to have a family life.
   A. Employees with children need time for the children.
   B. With current rules, many children must spend the summer in day camps.
   C. One week is not enough time to have adequate family holidays.
III. Employees with too little time off may burn out.
   A. According to psychologist Brenda Armour, "employees face stress-related illnesses because they don't get enough time off."
   B. Add anecdote about Ted M., who had a nervous breakdown.
   C. The physical health of employees goes down when they lack vacation time.

Conclusion: To improve the health and the morale of employees, the government needs to legislate more leisure time.

PRACTICE 19

1. Circle the topic and underline the controlling idea in the thesis statement.

2. The author uses many types of supporting material.
   a. Underline three anecdotes.   b. Circle two informed opinions.

3. Write a few lines that could appear in the introduction before the thesis statement. (For ideas about how to write an introduction, look in Chapter 13, "Writing the Essay.")

_____

_____

_____

_____

An Argument Essay

In the next essay, student writer Adela Fonseca argues that junk e-mail is a serious problem needing attention from government officials. Read the essay and answer the questions.

Ban Spam

1   Like most young people, I grew up with a mouse between my fingers. I have used computers almost since I could talk. In the early years of the Internet, I received the odd piece of junk mail, and it was not a big deal to erase one or two spams a month. During the last few years, though, it is as if junk-mail salespeople have hijacked the information highway. Where once there were two or three junk e-mails, there are now, literally, billions. They clog the arteries of my Internet highway, **obscuring** legitimate mail. Spam continues to grow at an alarming rate. Although the U.S. government has enacted some legislation aimed at dealing with spam, it has not stopped the problem. Spam is a global problem, and it needs a global solution. Governments need to work together and severely punish those who send junk e-mail because spam is irritating, offensive, and time-consuming.

obscuring: making unclear

2   First of all, spam is incredibly annoying. In the past, the e-mail inbox was a personal world where people could communicate with family and friends. Now it is like a minefield. For example, college student Eric Chu says that when he returned home after spending a week on vacation, he immediately checked his e-mail and found over eighty messages in his inbox. Chu knew that most of the mail would be pure junk. "I scanned the headings and deleted them, one by one. Most of the junk mail had fake sender names like 'Marie' or 'Gail,' and I almost deleted a message from an old friend who had found me," he says. Once upon a time most people looked forward to opening their e-mail boxes. Now many do so with a feeling of frustration and helplessness.

3   Furthermore, the **abundance** of spam is not harmless; in fact, a lot of junk e-mail is offensive. According to Odin Wortman of Internet Working Solutions, about thirty percent of spam is pornographic. Children and older people open such mail hoping for a message from a friend, only to see an offensive picture. Another thirty percent of junk e-mail advertises fraudulent schemes to get rich quick and hawks products of questionable value or safety.

abundance: a lot of something, a good supply

4   Some people say that it is not a big deal to press the delete button. What they forget is that spam consumes a lot of personal and company resources. Some individuals pay hourly rates for phone services and the Internet, and they waste money sifting through spam. Across the country, office employees spend too much time deleting junk mail. Internet providers invest in expensive filtering software to plug holes that let spammers in, but most filtering software is not that effective. It is like trying to block a hole the size of Kansas with a pencil. If nothing is done about the problem, then in the future we may have to delete thousands of junk e-mails each week.

5   Ultimately, spam is annoying, offensive, time-consuming, and expensive. There is nothing good to say about it. Spam marketers will argue that we get junk in our mail, and that cannot be denied, but we do not get crates of junk mail every week. If we did, paper junk mail would be banned in a hurry. The only real solution is for governments around the world to work together to make spam production illegal. Governments must actively hunt down and prosecute spammers.

PRACTICE 20

1. Underline the thesis statement of the essay.

2. What introductory styles open this essay? Circle the best answer.
   a. Definition and anecdote
   b. Anecdote and general information
   c. General information and definition
   d. Historical background information

3. The thesis statement maps out the writer's main arguments. What are her three main arguments?

   _____

   _____

4. Underline the topic sentence in each body paragraph.

5. In the introduction, how does the author show that there is a problem?

   _____

   _____

   _____

6. Find an example in the essay for each of the following types of evidence.
   a. Statistic: _____

   _____

   b. Anecdote: _____

   _____

   c. Logical consequence: _____

   _____

d. Answer to the opposition: _____

_____

7. What are some transitional expressions that the writer uses?

_____

8. With what does the writer conclude her essay? Circle the best answer.
   a. Prediction   b. Quotation   c. Suggestion

The Writer's Room   **Topics for Argument Essays**

PARAGRAPH LINK

You could also develop one of the topics found in Chapter 12, "Argument."

Writing Activity 1

Write an argument essay about one of the following topics. Remember to narrow your topic and follow the writing process.

General Topics

1. state-sponsored gambling
2. beauty contests
3. gun control
4. an unfair law
5. war
6. the health-care system

College and Work-Related Topics

7. outsourcing of jobs
8. great reasons to choose your college
9. the cost of a university education
10. student activism
11. the retirement age
12. dress codes at work

Writing Activity 2

Read the following quotations. Find one that you agree or disagree with or one that inspires you in some way, and use it as the basis for an argument essay.

Advertising is legalized lying.
—H. G. Wells, British author

An eye for an eye leads to a world of the blind.
—Mahatma Gandhi, Indian activist

Peace is not merely a distant goal that we seek, but the means by which we arrive at that goal.
—Dr. Martin Luther King, Jr., American civil rights leader

The thing that impresses me the most about America is the way that parents obey their children.
—King Edward VIII, British monarch

Choice has always been a privilege of those who could afford to pay for it.
—Ellen Frankfort, American journalist

ARGUMENT ESSAY CHECKLIST

As you write your argument essay, review the essay checklist on the inside front cover. Also ask yourself the following questions.

Does my thesis statement clearly state my position on the issue?

Do I include facts, examples, statistics, logical consequences, or answers to my opponents in my body paragraphs?

Do my supporting arguments provide evidence that directly supports each topic sentence?

Do I use transitions that will help readers follow my ideas?

See Chapter 14 of the Visualizing Writing CD for additional mini-lectures on **Illustration**, **Narration**, **Description**, **Process**, **Definition**, **Classification**, **Comparison and Contrast**, **Cause and Effect**, and **Argument**.

Enhancing Your Writing with Research

CHAPTER 15

> *Research is formalized curiosity. It is poking and prying with a purpose.*
>
> —ZORA NEALE HURSTON
> *American playwright and author (1891–1960)*

CONTENTS

- What Is Research?
- Research for Academic Writing
- Evaluate Sources
- Add a Paraphrase, Summary, or Quotation
- Cite Sources

When we want to seek more information about something, we might talk to other people, look for resources in libraries, bookstores, and museums, or search the Internet. You can use the same tools when looking for details to include in your writing.

What Is Research?

When you **research,** you look for information that will help you better understand a subject. For example, when you plan to see a movie and you read movie reviews in the newspaper, you are engaging in research to make an informed decision. At college, you are often asked to quote outside sources in your essays. And, if you have ever looked for a job, you might have read the newspaper's classified ads, talked to employment counselors, or spoken to potential employers.

This chapter gives you some strategies for researching information and effectively adding it to your writing.

Research for Academic Writing

There is a formal type of writing called the research paper. However, many types of academic essays, especially those with the purpose of persuading, can benefit from research. Additional facts, quotations, and statistics can back up your arguments.

OCTAVIO'S PARAGRAPH WITHOUT RESEARCH

Student writer Octavio Sanchez prepared an argument for an essay about circus animals. His purpose was to persuade the reader that large animals should not be used in circuses.

> Large circus animals are a danger to the public and to entertainers. In some circuses, elephants have gone on rampages and attacked or even killed others. Tigers have turned on trainers. After such attacks happen, people wonder why the animal suddenly turned wild. Wild animals are not meant to be performing pets.

Octavio's paragraph, although interesting, is not entirely convincing. He refers to animal attacks but gives no evidence of them, and without references to specific incidents, the reader may be skeptical about his claims. Octavio decided to do some research and add quotations to his paragraph. He found many Internet sites about his topic that are run by animal-rights organizations, but he worried that his readers might be skeptical if he used those sources. He kept searching and found a government Web site with the title "Captive Elephant Accident Prevention Act." He also found information on the U.S. Department of Labor Web site in an article called "Dangerous Jobs." Octavio added this information to his paragraph.

OCTAVIO'S PARAGRAPH WITH RESEARCH

Octavio added an example of an elephant that went on a rampage. ➤

Octavio offered a statistic from a trustworthy source. ➤

Octavio cited a well-known incident that illustrates his point. ➤

> Large circus animals are a danger to the public and to entertainers. In some circuses, elephants have gone on rampages and attacked or even killed others. According to the government House Committee Web site, "In Palm Bay, Florida in 1992, an elephant named Janet went on a rampage while carrying children on her back" ("Captive"). Furthermore, according to the Bureau of Statistics for the U.S. Department of Labor, elephant trainers have a hazardous job, and "the relative risk is 68 times greater than for the typical worker" ("Dangerous"). Elephants are not the only dangerous circus animals. In 2003, the well-publicized tiger attack on Roy Horn, of Sigfried and Roy fame, indicates that even a highly trained and pampered tiger can be volatile. Wild animals are not meant to be performing pets.

Evaluate Sources

Today's technological advances in both print and electronic publishing make it easier than ever to access information. To find information, you can try any of these strategies.

- Look in magazines, encyclopedias, periodicals, and books written by experts.
- Ask a librarian to help you locate information using various research tools, such as online catalogues, CD-ROMs, and microforms.
- Search the Internet by plugging in key words about your topic and allowing a search engine to find related Web sites.

 Evaluate Internet Sources

The Internet is a valuable research tool. Many important magazines and newspapers publish on the Internet. However, be careful when you use Internet sources. Some sites contain misleading information, and some sites are maintained by people who have very strong and specific biases. Remember that the content of Internet sites is not always verified for accuracy.

When you find a source, ask yourself the following questions.

- Is the information relevant and directly related to my topic?

- Who is the author of the work? Is he or she an expert on the subject?

- Does the author clearly favor one viewpoint over another? Could the author have a financial or personal interest in the issue?

- Is the information current? (Check the date of publication of the material you are considering.)

- On different sites, do different authors supply the same information?

Web Addresses

When you evaluate Internet sites, you can often determine what type of organization runs the Web site by looking at the last three letters of the Uniform Resource Locator (URL) address.

URL Ending	Meaning	Example
.com	Company	www.nytimes.com
.edu	Educational institution	univ.phoenix.edu
.gov	Government	www.irs.gov
.net	Network	www.jobs.net
.org	Organization	www.magazines.org

Keeping Track of Sources

When you find interesting sources, make sure that you record the following information. Later, when you incorporate quotations or paraphrases into your work, you can quickly find the source of the information. (You will learn how to cite sources later in this chapter.)

Book, Magazine, Newspaper	Web site
Author's full name	Author's full name
Title of article	Title of article
Title of book, magazine, or newspaper	Title of Web site
Publishing information (name of publisher, city, and date of publication)	Date of publication or last printing
Pages used	Date you accessed the site
	Complete Web site address

RESEARCH LINK

To find out more about the MLA and its guidelines, visit the MLA Web site at www.mla.org

 Finding Complete Source Information

Source information is easy to find in most print publications. It is usually on the second or third page of the book, magazine, or newspaper. On many Internet sites, however, finding the same information can take more investigative work. When you research on the Internet, look for the home page to find the site's title. The Modern Language Association (MLA) recommends that you find and cite as much information as is available.

Add a Paraphrase, Summary, or Quotation

To add research to a piece of writing, you can paraphrase it, summarize it, or quote it.

- When you **paraphrase,** you use your own words to present someone's ideas.
- When you **summarize,** you briefly state the main ideas of another work.
- When you **quote,** you either directly state a person's exact words (with quotation marks) or report them (without quotation marks).

All of these are valid ways to incorporate research in your writing, as long as you give credit to the author or speaker.

 Avoid Plagiarism!

Plagiarism is the act of using someone else's words or ideas without giving that person credit. Plagiarism is a very serious offense and can result in expulsion from college or termination from work.

The following actions are examples of plagiarism.

- Buying another work and presenting it as your own

- Using another student's work and presenting it as your own

- Failing to use quotation marks or properly set off an author's exact words

- Using ideas from another source without citing that source

- Making slight modifications to an author's sentences, but presenting the work as your own

To avoid plagiarism, always cite the source when you borrow words, phrases, or ideas from an author. Include the author's name, the title of the work, and the page number (if it is available).

Paraphrasing and Summarizing

Although summarizing and paraphrasing have some similarities, they are not the same thing.

Similarities

When paraphrasing and summarizing, you should do the following:

- **Use your own words.** Do not use words or phrases from the original text. Try to restate the author's words in a new way.
- **Always maintain the original meaning or intent of the author.** Do not use the author's words out of context.
- **Avoid including your own opinions.** A paraphrase and a summary present an author's views. Do not include personal observations.
- **Mention the source.** Identify the author and title of the work.

DIFFERENCES

Paraphrases and summaries have different lengths and content.

- **Length**   A paraphrase contains close to the same number of words as the original passage. A summary is much shorter than the original passage.
- **Content**   A paraphrase contains the same information as the original piece, but in a restated form. A summary presents a global view and contains only the most important ideas in a restated form.

 Consider Your Audience

When you decide whether to paraphrase or summarize, think about your audience.

- Paraphrase if your audience needs detailed information about the subject.

- Summarize if the audience needs to know only general information.

PRACTICE 1

The next selection, written by Adam Liptak, appeared in the August 24, 2003 edition of the New York Times on page A16. Read the selection, the paraphrase, and the summary, and then answer the questions that follow.

Original Selection

Gerald Sanders, 48, will spend the rest of his life in an Alabama prison because he stole a $16 bicycle. He had a five-year history of burglaries, none of them involving violence, and that record was enough under the state's habitual offender law to require a judge to send him away forever. Since California enacted a law requiring tough sentences for many third offenses in 1994, the trend in many states has been toward long, fixed sentences, even for nonviolent crimes.

Paraphrase

Adam Liptak, in the <u>New York Times</u>, reports that an Alabama citizen who committed a minor crime has been sentenced to life imprisonment. Because of a bicycle theft and a series of previous robberies, Gerald Sanders will die in jail. Following California's lead, Alabama and numerous other states have enacted strict three-strike laws that punish habitual offenders, including those who are not violent (A16).

Summary

Numerous states have followed California's lead and enacted three-strike laws, giving long prison sentences to habitual offenders. This law applies even to those who do not use violence, according to Adam Liptak in the <u>New York Times</u> (A16).

1. In the paraphrase and summary, does the writer express an opinion? _____

2. In the paraphrase and summary, the writer gives three pieces of information about the source. What are they?

_____

_____

_____

_____

_____

_____

 Paraphrasing and Summarizing

When you paraphrase, do not look at the original document. After you finish writing, compare your version with the original and ensure that you have not used too many words from the original document.

When you summarize, look at the key ideas in the text, and rephrase them using your own words.

PRACTICE 2

Read the following selections and answer the questions. The original selection, written by Martin Seligman, appeared in the <u>APA Monitor</u> on page 97.

Original Selection

Unfortunately it turns out that hit men, genocidal maniacs, gang leaders and violent kids often have high self-esteem, not low self-esteem. A recipe for their violence is a mean streak combined with an unwarranted sense of self-worth. When such a boy comes across a girl or parents or schoolmates who communicate to him that he is not all that worthy, he lashes out.

Summary 1

In the APA Monitor, Martin Seligman says that hit men and genocidal maniacs often have high self-esteem. Their mean streak combines with an unwarranted sense of self-worth, and creates a recipe for violence (97).

1. How does this summary plagiarize the original piece of writing?

_____

_____

_____

_____

Summary 2

Violent youths, like hired assassins and other murderers, often have self-esteem that is too high. Such youths lash out when others question their worthiness.

2. How does this summary plagiarize the original piece of writing?

_____

_____

_____

_____

Hint **Mention Your Source**

When you paraphrase or summarize, remember to mention the name of the author and the title of the publication. If the page number is available, place it in parentheses.

PRACTICE 3

Paraphrase and summarize the original selection. Remember that a paraphrase respects the length and order of the original document, whereas a summary is a very condensed version of the original. The next selection, written by Carol R. Ember and Melvin Ember, appeared on page 239 of their book, Cultural Anthropology.

Original Selection

Religious beliefs and practices are found in all known contemporary societies, and archaeologists think they have found signs of religious belief associated with Homo sapiens who lived at least 60,000 years ago. People then deliberately buried their dead, and many graves contain the remains of food, tools, and other objects that were probably thought to be needed in an afterlife.

Paraphrase: _____

_____

_____

_____

_____

_____

_____

_____

_____

Summary: _____

_____

_____

_____

_____

GRAMMAR LINK

To find out more about using quotations, see Chapter 34.

Quoting Sources

An effective way to support your arguments is to include quotations. Use quotations to reveal the opinions of an expert or to include ideas that are particularly memorable and important. When quoting sources, remember to limit how many you use in a single paper and to vary your quotations by using both direct and indirect quotations.

Direct and Indirect Quotations

A **direct quotation** contains the exact words of an author, and the quotation is set off with quotation marks.

A survey released by the Police Foundation states, "There are enough guns in private hands to provide every adult in America with one."

An **indirect quotation** keeps the author's meaning but is not set off by quotation marks.

A survey released by the Police Foundation states that there are so many privately owned guns in the United States that every adult could be given one.

How to Introduce or Integrate a Quotation

Quotations should be integrated into sentences. To learn how to introduce or integrate quotations in your writing, read the following original selection and then view three common methods. The selection, written by John E. Farley, appeared on page 97 of his book, Sociology.

> **Original Selection**
>
> Human history abounds with legends of lost or deserted children who were raised by wild animals. Legend has it, for example, that Rome was founded by Romulus and Remus, who had been raised in the wild by a wolf.

1. **Phrase introduction** You can introduce the quotation with a phrase followed by a comma. Capitalize the first word in the quotation. Place the page number in parentheses.

   > In Sociology, John E. Farley writes, "Human history abounds with legends of lost or deserted children who were raised by wild animals" (97).

   Alternatively, you can place the phrase after the quotation. End the quotation with a comma instead of a period.

   > "Human history abounds with legends of lost or deserted children who were raised by wild animals," writes John E. Farley in Sociology (97).

2. **Sentence introduction** Introduce the quotation with a sentence followed by a colon. Capitalize the first word in the quotation.

   > In his book Sociology, John E. Farley suggests that such stories are not new: "Human history abounds with legends of lost or deserted children who were raised by wild animals" (97).

3. **Integrated quotation** Integrate the quotation as a part of your sentence. Place quotation marks around the source's exact words. Do not capitalize the first word in the quotation.

   > In Sociology, John E. Farley mentions a legend about the twin founders of Rome "who had been raised in the wild by a wolf" (97).

 Words That Introduce Quotations

One common way to introduce a quotation is to write, "The author says ..." However, there are a variety of other verbs that you can use.

admits	concludes	mentions	speculates
claims	explains	observes	suggests
comments	maintains	reports	warns

PRACTICE 4

Practice integrating quotations. Read the following selection and then write direct and indirect quotations. The selection, written by Daniel R. Brower appeared on page 371 of his book, <u>The World in the Twentieth Century</u>.

> The collapse of German communism began with the regime's desperate decision to grant complete freedom of travel to East Germans. On the night of November 9, the gates through the Berlin Wall were opened to all. The city became the center of an enormous celebration by East and West Berliners. Some of them climbed the wall itself to celebrate.

1. Write a direct quotation.

   _____

   _____

   _____

   _____

   _____

   _____

2. Write an indirect quotation.

   _____

   _____

   _____

   _____

   _____

   _____

Cite Sources

Each time you use another writer's words or ideas, you must **cite the source**, giving complete information about the original document from which you borrowed the material. You should mention the source both in the body of your work and on a Works Cited page.

 Choose a Documentation Style

The three most common styles for documenting sources are the Modern Language Association (MLA) format, <u>Chicago Manual of Style</u> (CMS) format, and the American Psychological Association (APA) format. Before writing a paper, check with your instructor to see which documentation style you should use and to learn where you can find more information about it.

Citing the Source in the Body of Your Essay

When you introduce a quotation or idea, try to mention the source directly in your paragraph or essay. The next few examples show how you can cite some common sources using MLA style.

1. **Mention the author and page number in parentheses.**
Put the author's last name and the page number in parentheses. Place the final period after the parentheses, not inside the quotation marks.

> Successful people fight to succeed: "They have determined that nothing will stop them from going forward" (Carson 224).

2. **Mention the page number in parentheses.**
If you mention the author's name in the introductory phrase, put only the page number in the parentheses. Place the final period after the parentheses.

> "Successful people don't have fewer problems," writes Ben Carson (224).

3. **Mention the Internet site.**
If your source is an Internet site and you do not know the name of the author, place the first word of the site's title in parentheses. Then, remember to write the complete citation on your Works Cited page. Again, place the final period after the parentheses.

> Furthermore, according to the Bureau of Statistics for the U.S. Department of Labor, elephant trainers have a hazardous job, and "the relative risk is 68 times greater than for the typical worker" ("Dangerous").

 Writing Titles for Borrowed Material

Place the title of a short work (article or short story) in quotation marks, and underline the title of a longer work (book, magazine, or newspaper). If you are using a computer, you can choose to italicize or underline the titles of longer works.

Underlined:	"The End of the Concorde," <u>Vanity Fair</u>
Italicized:	"The End of the Concorde," *Vanity Fair*

GRAMMAR LINK

To find out more about writing titles, see page 498 in Chapter 34.

Preparing a Works Cited Page

Sometimes called a References list or Bibliography, the Works Cited page gives details about each source you have used and appears at the end of your paper. To prepare a Works Cited page, use this format.

- Write Works Cited at the top of the page and center it.
- List each source alphabetically, using the last names of the authors.
- Indent the second line and all subsequent lines of each reference.

Useful Internet Sites

The following Web sites could be useful when you research on the Internet.

Statistics

Statistics from over one hundred government agencies   www.fedstats.gov
Bureau of Labor Statistics   www.stats.bls.gov

News Organizations

Addresses of hundreds of online magazines   newsdirectory.com
Access to newspapers from all over the world   www.newspapers.com
New York Times site for college students   www.nytimes.com/college

Other Sites

Job sites   www.monster.com
    www.jobs.org
Internet Public Library   www.ipl.org/reading
Online encyclopedias   www.encyclopedia.com
    www.britannica.com

Here are some examples of how to cite different types of publications. Notice that the first details are separated by periods, not commas.

Book

- **One author**

  Last name, First name. "Title of Article." <u>Title of Book</u>. Place of publication: Publisher, Year.

  Tan, Amy. <u>The Joy Luck Club</u>. New York: Random House, 1990.

- **Two or more authors**

  Ember, Carol R., and Melvin Ember. <u>Cultural Anthropology</u>. New Jersey: Prentice Hall, 2002.

Periodical

- **Magazine or newspaper**

  Last name, First name. "Title of Article." <u>Title of Magazine or Newspaper</u> Date: pages.

  Foster, Don. "The Message in the Anthrax." <u>Vanity Fair</u> Oct. 2003: 180-200.

■ **Print Journal**

> Last name, First name. "Title of Article." <u>Title of Journal</u> Volume
>   Number. Issue (Year): pages.

> Seligman, Martin. "The American Way of Blame." <u>APA Monitor</u> 29.7
>   (1998): 97.

Internet Site

■ If the information was published on the Internet, include as much of the
following information as you can find. Keep in mind that some sites do not
contain complete information; therefore, you may need to contact the site
administrator to obtain further details.

> Author. "Title of Article." <u>Title of Site or Online Publication</u>. Date of
>   publication. Date you accessed the site <network address>.

> Krystek, Lee. "Crop Circles." <u>Museum of Unnatural Mystery</u>. 2003. 16 May
>   2005 <http://www.unmuseum.org/cropcir.htm>.

■ If the author is not mentioned on the site, begin with the title and include as
much information as you can find. (Note that MLA style does not use periods
with the abbreviation *US*.)

> "Dangerous Jobs." <u>US Department of Labor</u>. 22 July 1997. 28 May 2004
>   <http://stats.bls.gov/iif/oshwc/cfar0020.pdf>.

PRACTICE 5

Imagine that you are using the following sources to write a paper arguing that
athletes can make good role models. Arrange the sources for a Works Cited page.

A quotation

The quotation is from a magazine article that Alan Paul wrote for
<u>Slam</u>, titled "Unfinished Business." The article, published in the
November 2003 issue, appeared on pages 74 to 78.

A quotation

The quotation is from a book called <u>American Sports</u> written by
Benjamin G. Rader. The book was published by Prentice Hall, New
Jersey, in 1999.

A paraphrase

The paraphrase is from a Web site titled <u>Muhammad Ali</u>. The text is written by Muhammad Ali. The site at <http://ali.com> was created in 2003 and was accessed on November 28, 2004.

Works Cited

_____

_____

_____

_____

_____

_____

_____

_____

REFLECT ON IT

Think about what you have learned in this chapter. If you do not know an answer, review that topic.

1. What are the differences between a paraphrase and a summary?

Paraphrase	**Summary**
_____	_____
_____	_____
_____	_____

2. What are the differences between direct and indirect quotations?

Direct	**Indirect**
_____	_____
_____	_____
_____	_____

3. What is a Works Cited page?

_____

_____

_____

_____

The Writer's Room   **Research**

Writing Activity 1

Choose a paragraph or an essay that you have written, and research your topic to get more detailed information. Then insert at least one paraphrase, summary, or quotation into your work. Remember to acknowledge your sources.

Writing Activity 2

Write an essay about one of the next topics. Your essay should include research (find at least three sources). Include a Works Cited page at the end of your assignment.

1. Write about a contemporary issue that is in the news. In your essay, give your opinion about the issue.

2. Write about your career choice. You could mention job opportunities in your field, and you could include statistical information.

3. Write about the importance of a college education. Does a college education help or hurt a person's career prospects? Find some facts, examples, or statistics to support your view.

 See Chapter 15 of the Visualizing Writing CD for additional mini-lectures on **Recognizing a Research Paper**, **Finding Sources**, and **Avoiding Plagiarism**.

PART IV

The Editing Handbook

Why Is Grammar So Important?

When you speak, you have tools such as tone of voice and body language to help you express your ideas. When you write, however, you have only words and punctuation to get your message across. Naturally, if your writing contains errors in style, grammar, and punctuation, you may distract readers from your message, and they may focus, instead, on your inability to communicate clearly. You increase your chances of succeeding in your academic and professional life when you write in clear standard English.

The chapters in this Editing Handbook can help you understand and correct important grammar concepts. Before you begin, review the images on the right. They may help you think about key grammar topics in different ways.

◀ **SECTION 1: Effective Sentences**
THEME: CULTURE

An artist combines colors and lines in a striking way to get the viewers' attention. Similarly, combining different types of sentences can make your writing more appealing.

SECTION 2: Common Sentence Errors ▶
THEME: PSYCHOLOGY

If a puzzle were missing a piece, or if a piece from another puzzle were added to it, the final image would be incomplete. In the same way, the parts of a sentence must be connected properly to provide the reader with a complete picture.

◀ **SECTION 3: Problems with Verbs**
THEME: ESPIONAGE

Every espionage tale needs a cast of characters and exciting action to round out the plot. In a sentence, the subject is the character and the verb is the action.

SECTION 4: Verb Agreement and Consistency ▶
THEME: COLLEGE LIFE

To fit into a lock, a key must have the correct shape. In the same way, for a sentence to function correctly, its subjects and verbs must fit together. Editing for agreement and consistency errors is one key to writing successfully in college and beyond.

SECTION 5: More Parts of Speech
THEME: INVENTIONS AND DISCOVERIES

One of the world's greatest inventions is the airplane. If a plane were missing a wing, it would not be able to fly. In the same way, if a sentence is missing a vital part, it has trouble transmitting a message.

SECTION 6: Modifiers
THEME: HEALTH CARE

Working out makes your muscles more toned and defined. In the same way, using adjectives and adverbs adds color and definition to the nouns and verbs they describe.

SECTION 7: Word Use and Spelling
THEME: THE LEGAL WORLD

To solve a crime, the people investigating must carefully examine each piece of evidence and make accurate conclusions. Similarly, you should ensure that your choice of words is exact before you submit your written work.

SECTION 8: Punctuation and Mechanics
THEME: THE WORKPLACE

A commuter train has couplers, which are links that hold the individual cars together. In the same way, a sentence has punctuation that links parts together.

SECTION 9: Editing Practice

Editing is as important to a writer as a final rehearsal is to a performer. By taking the time to edit, you ensure that your work is ready to present to an audience.

CHAPTER 16

Simple Sentences

section theme **CULTURE**

CONTENTS

• Identify Subjects
• Identify Prepositional Phrases
• Identify Verbs
• Helping Verbs

In this chapter, you will read about topics related to advertising *and* consumerism.

The Writer's Desk Warm Up

What is your cultural background? How would you identify yourself culturally? Write a paragraph about your cultural identity.

Identify Subjects

A **sentence** contains one or more subjects and verbs, and it expresses a complete thought. Although some sentences can have more than one complete thought, a **simple sentence** expresses one complete thought. The **subject** tells you who or what the sentence is about. The **verb** expresses an action or state. If a sentence is missing a subject or a verb, it is incomplete.

Singular and Plural Subjects

Subjects may be singular or plural. To determine the subject of a sentence, ask yourself who or what the sentence is about.

A **singular subject** is one person, place, or thing.

> **Oprah Winfrey** is known around the world.

> **Chicago** is her hometown.

A **plural subject** is more than one person, place, or thing.

> Contemporary **musicians** try to reach a mass audience.

> Many **countries** import American movies.

Section I
EFFECTIVE SENTENCES

Pronouns

A **subject pronoun** (*he, she, it, you, we, they*) can act as the subject of a sentence, and it replaces the noun.

> Nicole Kidman stars in many films. **She** is known around the world.

> Directors make many action films. **They** hope the films will interest young males.

Gerunds (-*ing* words)

Sometimes a gerund (-*ing* form of the verb) is the subject of a sentence.

> **Relaxing** is important.

> **Kickboxing** was popular in the 1990s.

Compound Subjects

Many sentences have more than one subject. *Compound* means "multiple." Therefore, a **compound subject** contains two or more subjects.

> **Men** and **women** love the singer.

> **Reporters, photographers,** and **visitors** were in the room.

 Recognize Simple and Complete Subjects

In a sentence, the **simple subject** is the noun or pronoun. The complete name of a person, place, or organization is a simple subject.

| he | dancer | Homer Simpson | Sony Music Corporation |

The **complete subject** is the noun, plus the words that describe the noun. In the next examples, the descriptive words are in italics.

| *new electric* piano | *the old, worn-out* shoes | *Anna's green* convertible |

In the following sentences, the simple and complete subjects are identified.

simple subject
The glossy new **magazine** contained interesting articles.
complete subject

PRACTICE 1

Underline the complete subject and circle the simple subject(s).

EXAMPLE:

Academic (institutions) teach popular culture.

1. Popular music, films, books, and fashions are the sources of our common culture.

2. University professors and administrators did not see the value of popular culture in the past.

3. Classical music, art, and literature were standard subjects.

4. Well-known academics made a distinction between "high" and "low" culture.

5. Opinions changed in the 1980s.

6. Some colleges began offering courses on popular culture.

7. Reality television is considered worthy of study today.

8. An old, highly respected college has a course about television game shows.

9. Alison Anthony and James O'Reilly teach popular culture.

10. They and their students enjoy discussing current trends.

Special Subject Problems

Unstated Subjects (Commands)

In a sentence that expresses a command, the subject is unstated, but it is still understood. The unstated subject is *you*.

> Remember to use your coupon.
>
> Pay the cashier.

here/there

Here and *there* are not subjects. In a sentence that begins with *Here* or *There*, the subject follows the verb.

> There are five <u>ways</u> to market a product. (The subject is *ways*.)
>
> Here is an interesting <u>brochure</u> about cosmetics. (The subject is *brochure*.)

PRACTICE 2

Circle the simple subject(s). If the subject is unstated, then write the subject (*you*) before the verb.

EXAMPLE:

To see the announcement, you watch carefully.

1. There are many advertisements on the streets of our cities. 2. Look at any bus shelter, billboard, store window, or newspaper. 3. Certainly, some ads appear in surprising places. 4. There are framed announcements on the doors of hotel bathrooms, for example. 5. Furthermore, there are commercials hidden in the middle of the action in movies and television shows. 6. For instance, soft-drink and car companies advertised during the popular reality show *American Idol.* 7. There were soft drinks on the table in front of the show's judges. 8. The show's singers sang a tribute to an American automobile company. 9. View advertising with a critical eye.

Identify Prepositional Phrases

A **preposition** is a word that links nouns, pronouns, or phrases to other words in a sentence. It expresses a relationship based on movement, motion, or position. Here are some common prepositions.

Common Prepositions

about	before	during	near	through
above	behind	except	of	to
across	below	for	off	toward
after	beside	from	on	under
against	between	in	onto	until
along	beyond	inside	out	up
among	by	into	outside	with
around	despite	like	over	within
at	down			

A **phrase** is a group of words that is missing a subject, a verb, or both and is not a complete sentence. A **prepositional phrase** is made up of a preposition and its object (a noun or a pronoun). In the following phrases, an object follows the preposition.

Preposition	+	**Object**
in		the morning
among		the shadows
over		the rainbow
with		some friends

Be Careful

Because the object of a preposition is a noun, it may look like a subject. However, the object in a prepositional phrase is *never* the subject of the sentence.

Sometimes a prepositional phrase appears before or after the subject. To help you identify the subject, you can put parentheses around prepositional phrases or mark them in some other way. In each of the following sentences, the subject is in boldface type and the prepositional phrase is in parentheses.

(In spite of the costs,) **Ruth Handler** took the assignment.

(On a trip to Germany,) **she** saw an interesting product.

Her **company,** (after 1959,) expanded greatly.

Sometimes a sentence can contain more than one prepositional phrase.

prepositional phrase   prepositional phrase
(In the late 1950s,) (during a period of prosperity,) a new and original **doll** appeared in American stores.

 According to . . .

When a sentence contains *according to,* the noun that immediately follows the words *according to* is *not* the subject of the sentence.

subject
(According to Jack Solomon,) **Americans** are tired of fantasy advertisements.

PRACTICE 3

Place parentheses around the prepositional phrase(s) in each sentence. Then circle the simple subject.

EXAMPLE:

(In 1995,) a successful online (company) began.

1. In Pierre Omidyar's living room, an idea took shape.

2. With friend and co-founder Jeff Skoll, Omidyar decided to create an online flea market.

3. For several years, the company expanded.

4. Then, in 1998, a Harvard business graduate was asked to join the company.

5. Meg Whitman, with a team of top managers, helped turn eBay into a billion-dollar business.

6. Buyers and sellers, with a click of a mouse, can enter a virtual marketplace.

7. For a small fee, sellers can list items on the site.

8. Buyers, with only a picture and description to evaluate, then bid on the item.

9. At the end of the auction, an eBay employee contacts the buyer and seller.

10. In spite of some initial problems, the online flea market has been tremendously successful.

PRACTICE 4

Look at the underlined word in each sentence. If it is the subject, write *C* (for "correct") beside the sentence. If the underlined word is not the subject, then circle the correct subject(s).

EXAMPLES:

In past eras, bustling (markets) sold consumer goods. _____

Enclosed shopping malls are a fairly recent development.   *C*

1. In Edina, Minnesota, the first indoor mall was built. _____

2. The world's largest mall has 800 stores. _____

3. For some consumers, the local dress shop is a dangerous place. _____

4. On her twenty-second birthday, Amber Wyatt divulged a secret. _____

5. During the past four years, she has piled up $60,000 in credit card debts. _____

6. She acknowledges, with a shrug, her shopping addiction. _____

7. Today, with a poor credit rating, Amber is unable to get a lease. _____

8. Her brother, boyfriend, and aunt have lent her money. _____

9. Her parents, with some reluctance, allowed their daughter to move back home. _____

10. Many American men and women, according to a recent survey, have a shopping addiction. _____

Identify Verbs

Every sentence must contain a verb. The **verb** either expresses what the subject does or links the subject to other descriptive words.

Action Verbs

An **action verb** describes an action that a subject performs.

> Halle Berry <u>attended</u> a community college in Cleveland.

> She <u>acted</u> in Spike Lee's film *Jungle Fever*.

Linking Verbs

A **linking verb** connects a subject with words that describe it, and it does not show an action. The most common linking verb is *be*.

> Tom Hanks <u>is</u> a versatile performer.

> American films <u>are</u> popular throughout the world.

Other linking verbs refer to the senses and indicate how something appears, smells, tastes, and so on.

> Tim Burton <u>became</u> a director.

> His latest movie <u>looks</u> terrifying.

Common Linking Verbs

appear	feel	smell
be (am, is, are, was, were, etc.)	look	sound
become	seem	taste

Compound Verbs

When a subject performs more than one action, the verbs are called **compound verbs.**

> In 2003, Mel Gibson <u>produced</u> and <u>directed</u> a controversial film.

> Members of the public either <u>loved</u> or <u>hated</u> the film.

 Infinitives Are Not the Main Verb

Infinitives are verbs preceded by *to* such as *to fly, to speak,* and *to go.* An infinitive is never the main verb in a sentence.

>   V   infinitive   V   infinitive
> Angelica <u>plans</u> **to act** in movies. She <u>hopes</u> **to become** famous.

PRACTICE 5

Underline one or more verbs in these sentences.

EXAMPLE:

Many Americans <u>have</u> mixed cultural roots.

1. Angelica Zoubris has a Greek father and a Russian mother.

2. She respects and admires the music, dance, literature, and food of her parents' countries.

3. Angelica, however, considers herself to be culturally an American.

4. She listens to country music, eats fast food, and reads fashion magazines.

5. She feels very little connection to her Greek or Russian roots.

6. However, American culture is not separate from the cultures of other nations.

7. In past centuries, Native Americans and new immigrants contributed to American culture with their diets, songs, and other traditions.

8. Typical American foods, for example, have roots in Italy (pizza), Germany (hamburger), or Greece (chewing gum).

9. The music of South Africa, Mexico, and Brazil influences popular musicians.

10. In past centuries, other nations introduced sports such as hockey and soccer to American culture.

11. At the same time, the United States exports cultural products to nations around the world.

12. Cultural influences flow into and out of America.

Section 1
EFFECTIVE SENTENCES

Helping Verbs

A verb can have several different forms, depending on the tense that is used. **Verb tense** indicates whether the action occurred in the past, present, or future. In some tenses, there is a **main verb** that expresses what the subject does or links the subject to descriptive words, but there is also a helping verb, or auxiliary verb.

The **helping verb** combines with the main verb to indicate tense, negative structure, or question structure. The most common helping verbs are forms of *be*, *have*, and *do*. **Modal auxiliaries** are another type of helping verb; they indicate ability (*can*), obligation (*must*), possibility (*may*, *might*, *could*), advice (*should*), and so on. For example, here are different forms of the verb *open*. The helping verbs are underlined.

<u>is</u> opening	<u>had</u> opened	<u>will</u> open	<u>should have</u> opened
<u>was</u> opened	<u>had been</u> opening	<u>can</u> open	<u>might be</u> open
<u>has been</u> opening	<u>would</u> open	<u>could be</u> opening	<u>could have been</u> opened

The **complete verb** consists of the helping verb and the main verb. In the following examples, the helping verbs are indicated with *HV* and the main verbs with *V.*

American culture has been spreading across the globe for years.

You must have seen the news articles.

In **question forms,** the first helping verb usually appears before the subject.

Should the coffee chain have expanded so quickly?

Will the coffee and cakes sell in Moscow?

Interrupting words may appear between verbs, but they are *not* part of the verb. Some interrupting words are *easily, actually, not, always, usually, sometimes, frequently, often, never,* and *ever.*

Judith Ortiz Cofer has *often* returned to Puerto Rico.

She has *frequently* written about her cultural identity.

PRACTICE 6

Underline any helping verbs. Then underline each main verb twice. The information in this practice is from Judith Ortiz Cofer's essay "Don't Misread My Signals."

EXAMPLE:

A strong cultural identity has always been important to me.

1. Judith Ortiz Cofer has been a respected novelist and poet since the 1980s.

2. Cofer has always identified with her Puerto Rican heritage.

3. Cultural stereotypes, however, deeply offend her.

4. In her writing, she has fought against depictions of Latinas as domestic workers or "hot tamales."

5. In America, she has had many experiences with the preconceptions of others.

6. For her New Jersey high school's career day, Cofer and her friends wore their mothers' jewelry and colorful clothing to look like career women.

7. Other students in fashionable tailored suits did not respect the style of the Latina girls.

8. The students should not have judged Cofer.

9. Women from tropical islands have always loved to wear bright primary colors, according to Cofer.

10. With her writing, Cofer has tried to educate others to look past skin color, clothing styles, and accents in order to see the real person.

PRACTICE 7

Circle the simple subjects and underline the complete verbs. Remember to underline all parts of the verb.

EXAMPLE:

Japanese (products) <u>have captured</u> the imaginations of children around the world.

1. In 1974, a Japanese greeting card company created a white cat with vacant, staring eyes. The cat was given the name "Hello Kitty." Soon, purses, toasters, cameras, and T-shirts had the image of the little animal. For some reason, the strange cat with a bow on one ear and a missing mouth has become a fashion icon for teenagers worldwide. Thirty years after its debut, Hello Kitty's popularity remains constant.

2. A self-taught illustrator from Japan has created another cute and creepy character. At first glance, you might not notice the details on Mori Chack's bear. The fuzzy pink toy seems to be sweet and cuddly. However, after a closer look, you will see the long, pointed claws and the drop of blood on the bear's mouth. Like Hello Kitty, Gloomy Bear has become trendy. The bear's likeness appears on clothing, key chains, and coffee mugs.

3. Some journalists, including Julia Dault and Kjeld Duits, have written about the trends. They credit Japanese animators with an ability to add a sinister twist to images of saccharine sweetness. Of course, the characters do not simply appeal to children. Gloomy Bear sells briskly to those in their twenties and thirties.

The Writer's Desk Revise and Edit Your Warm Up

Read the sentences that you wrote for the Warm Up on page 254. Circle the subject(s) and underline the verb(s) in each sentence. Remember to underline both the helping verbs and the main verbs. Write *V* over each main verb.

REFLECT ON IT

Think about what you have learned in this chapter. If you do not know an answer, review that concept.

1. What is a sentence? _____

_____

2. What does the subject of a sentence do? _____

_____

3. Write an example of a complete subject and a simple subject.

a. Complete: _____

b. Simple: _____

4. What is a verb? _____

_____

5. Write an example of an action verb and a linking verb.

a. Action: _____

b. Linking: _____

Circle the best answers.

6. Can the object of a preposition be the subject of a sentence?   No   Yes

7. Can a sentence have more than one subject?   No   Yes

8. Can a sentence have more than one verb?   No   Yes

FINAL REVIEW

Circle the simple subjects and underline the complete verbs. Underline *all* parts of the verb. Remember that infinitives such as *to go* or *to run* are not part of the main verb.

EXAMPLE: In the late 1950s, during a period of prosperity, an original new doll appeared on American store shelves.

1. Kristin Riddick, in her book *Barbie: The Image of Us All*, describes the history of a popular toy. 2. The hard plastic doll with an exaggerated figure was a very unusual item. 3. Before Barbie, most dolls in the United States looked like babies or small children. 4. The new toy from the Mattel Toy Company was a grown-up woman.

5. On a Monday morning, in her living room, Mattel founder Ruth Handler observed her daughter, Barbara, playing with paper dolls. 6. Barbara and her friends loved to dress their paper dolls in various pieces of paper clothing. 7. In a moment of inspiration, Handler had a great idea. 8. A three-dimensional adult-looking doll could be a best-seller. 9. Later, during a trip to Germany,

Handler saw a shapely doll. 10. The sexy Lilli doll, with a tiny waist and a large chest, was based on a German comic-strip character. 11. The experience reinforced Handler's determination to create a new doll.

12. After returning home, Handler decided to work on the Barbie doll. 13. She wanted it to look like an innocent American teenager. 14. Ruth and Elliot Handler, with the help of a team of inventors, created the Barbie doll.

Section I
EFFECTIVE SENTENCES

15. In the middle of winter, at a toy fair in New York City, the first Barbies were sold. 16. Then, in 1962, in response to requests from the public, a male companion was created for Barbie. 17. Barbie accessories and clothing in a variety of shapes and colors became an indispensable part of the Barbie empire.

18. Many other companies, in an effort to get part of the lucrative toy market, have tried to replace Barbie. 19. However, until now, no doll has outsold Mattel's toy. 20. In fact, according to a Barbie Internet site, somewhere in the world a Barbie is being sold right now.

 See Chapter 16 of the Visualizing Writing CD for an additional mini-lecture on **Subjects** and **Verbs.**

Compound Sentences

section theme **CULTURE**

CONTENTS

- Compare Simple and Compound Sentences
- Combine Sentences Using Coordinating Conjunctions
- Combine Sentences Using Semicolons
- Combine Sentences Using Transitional Expressions

In this chapter, you will read about topics related to **fads** *and* **fashions.**

The Writer's Desk **Warm Up**

Do you have body art such as tattoos and piercings? In a paragraph, explain why you do or do not have body art.

Compare Simple and Compound Sentences

When you use sentences of varying lengths and types, your writing flows more smoothly and appears more interesting. You can vary sentences and create relationships between ideas by combining sentences.

Review the differences between simple and compound sentences.

A **simple sentence** is an independent clause. It expresses one complete idea, and it stands alone. Simple sentences can have more than one subject and more than one verb.

One subject and verb:	Tattooing is not a new fashion.
Two subjects:	Tattooing and body piercing are not new fashions.
Two verbs:	Della McMahon speaks and writes about current trends.

A **compound sentence** contains two or more simple sentences. The two complete ideas can be joined in several ways.

Section 1
EFFECTIVE SENTENCES

	Trey is a drummer. + He also sings.
Add a coordinator:	Trey is a drummer, **and** he also sings.
Add a semicolon:	Trey is a drummer; he also sings.
Add a semicolon and conjunctive adverb:	Trey is a drummer; **moreover,** he sings.

Combine Sentences Using Coordinating Conjunctions

A **coordinating conjunction** joins two complete ideas and indicates the connection between them. The most common coordinating conjunctions are *for, and, nor, but, or, yet,* and *so.*

Complete idea, **coordinating conjunction** complete idea.

Review the following chart showing coordinating conjunctions and their functions.

Coordinating Conjunction	Function	Example
for	to indicate a reason	Henna tattoos are good options, **for** they are not permanent.
and	to join two ideas	Jay wants a tattoo, **and** he wants to change his hairstyle.
nor	to indicate a negative idea	Cosmetic surgery is not always successful, **nor** is it particularly safe.
but	to contrast two ideas	Tattoos hurt, **but** people get them anyway.
or	to offer an alternative	Jay will dye his hair, **or** he will shave it off.
yet	to introduce a surprising choice	He is good-looking, **yet** he wants to get cosmetic surgery.
so	to indicate a cause and effect relationship	He saved up his money, **so** he will get a large tattoo.

Recognizing Compound Sentences

To be sure that a sentence is compound, place your finger over the coordinating conjunction, and then ask yourself whether the two clauses are complete sentences.

Simple: The fashion model was tall **but** also very thin.

Compound: The fashion model was tall**, but** she was also very thin.

Section I
EFFECTIVE SENTENCES

PRACTICE I

Indicate whether the following sentences are simple (*S*) or compound (*C*). Underline the coordinating conjunction in each compound sentence.

EXAMPLE:

There are many ways to alter your appearance.   *S*

1. Many humans permanently alter their bodies, and they do it for a variety of reasons.   _____

2. Body altering is not unique to North America, for people in every culture and in every historical period have found ways to permanently alter their bodies.   _____

3. In past centuries, some babies in South America had boards tied to their heads, and their soft skulls developed a long, high shape.   _____

4. In Africa, Ubangi women used to extend their lower lips with large, plate-sized pieces of wood.   _____

5. In the 1700s, wealthy European men and women ate tiny amounts of arsenic in order to have very pale complexions.   _____

6. Then, in the next century, European and American women wore extremely tight corsets, and they suffered from respiratory and digestive problems.   _____

7. Today, some people want to improve their physical appearance, so they sculpt their bodies with cosmetic surgery.   _____

8. Others have images tattooed on their skin for decorative, religious, or political reasons.   _____

9. Body altering can be painful, but people do it anyway.   _____

PRACTICE 2

Read the following passages. Insert an appropriate coordinating conjunction in each blank. Choose from the list below, and try to use a variety of coordinating conjunctions.

for	and	nor	but	or	yet	so

EXAMPLE:

Fashions usually take awhile to be accepted, ___*but*___ fads appear and vanish quickly.

1. In the twentieth century, there were some bizarre fashion fads, _____ _____ many people adopted them. For example, in the 1920s, the styles of World War I flyers became popular, _____ young women wore goggles, scarves, and leather aviator helmets and jackets.

2. Men also followed fashion fads, _____ they were generally more conservative than women. In the 1940s, zoot suits were associated with rebellious behavior, _____ they were extremely popular. The name *zoot* came from urban jazz culture, _____ it meant "something extravagant or outrageous." The suit could be in dark, conservative colors, _____ it could be in pastel shades such as light blue. During World War II, the War Production Board restricted the amount of fabric in men's clothing, _____ the zoot suit lost popularity.

3. In the 1950s, boys grew the front part of their hair to at least eight inches in length, _____ then they greased their hair back into a "ducktail." The style took a lot of effort to maintain, _____ many boys carried combs and hair pomade with them. In the late 1970s, punk fashion spread throughout Europe and America. Parents reacted with shock, _____ they hated the spiked, colored hair and the torn clothing. At first, only "punks" dyed their hair blue or green, _____ even some of today's more conservative types now add bright color to their hair.

4. Designers may try to create unique new styles, _____ they may look to past styles for inspiration. Not all old fashions make a comeback, _____ are all of them practical for today's lifestyles.

Section 1
EFFECTIVE SENTENCES

> ⌒Hint⌒ **Place a Comma Before the Coordinating Conjunction**
>
> Add a comma before a coordinating conjunction if you are certain that it joins two complete sentences. If the conjunction joins two nouns, verbs, or adjectives, then you do not need to add a comma before it.
>
> **Comma:** The word *fashion* refers to all popular styles, **and** it does not refer only to clothing.
>
> **No comma:** The word fashion refers to all popular styles **and** not only to clothing.

PRACTICE 3

Create compound sentences by adding a coordinating conjunction and another complete sentence to each simple sentence. Remember to add a comma before the conjunction.

EXAMPLE:

Many people deny it, *but they worry about their personal style.*

1. Everyone has opinions _____

2. You can wear those pants _____

3. Today, hairstyles are varied _____

4. Those shoes are expensive _____

5. You may be surprised _____

Combine Sentences Using Semicolons

Another way to form a compound sentence is to join two complete ideas with a semicolon. The semicolon replaces a coordinating conjunction.

Complete idea	;	complete idea.

Clothing can illustrate a person's personality; an extrovert may wear bright colors.

PRACTICE 4

Insert the missing semicolon in each sentence.

EXAMPLE:

Tattoos are applied with needles; ink is inserted under the skin.

1. Primitive tribes used sharp, thin instruments to introduce color into the skin methods of tattooing have not changed much over the years.

2. In 1990, in the Alps, Austrian hikers found a 5,000-year-old man they photographed the frozen, tattooed body.

3. The body had long straight lines tattooed on the ankles other lines appeared on the stomach region.

4. An Austrian professor, Konrad Spindler, has a theory about the tattoos he published his ideas in a journal.

5. Perhaps the ancient man received tattoos to cure an illness he may have had intestinal problems.

6. In the past, some tattoos celebrated war victories others honored religious figures.

7. The warriors of the Marquesas Islands wanted to intimidate their enemies they tattooed a staring eye on the insides of their arms.

8. A tribesman would raise his arm to attack an opponent his enemy would then see the staring eye and feel frightened.

9. In the early twentieth century, in Western cultures, tattoos were often associated with the lower classes sailors, soldiers, and criminals would get tattoos.

10. Tattoos have had a strong resurgence in our culture people from gang members to Hollywood actors have gotten tattoos.

Section 1
**EFFECTIVE
SENTENCES**

 Use a Semicolon to Join Related Ideas

Do not use a semicolon to join two unrelated sentences.

Incorrect: Some societies have no distinct word for art; I like to dress in bright colors.
(The second idea has no clear relationship with the first idea.)

Correct: Some societies have no distinct word for art; art is an intrinsic part of their cultural fabric.
(The second idea gives further information about the first idea.)

PRACTICE 5

Write compound sentences by adding a semicolon and another complete sentence to each simple sentence. Remember that the two sentences must have related ideas.

EXAMPLE:

Last year my sister had her tongue pierced; *she regretted her decision.*

1. Youths rebel in many ways _____

2. I dislike a recent fashion _____

3. At age thirteen, I dressed like other teens _____

_____

4. Many fashions are recycled _____

Section 1
**EFFECTIVE
SENTENCES**

Combine Sentences Using Transitional Expressions

A third way to combine sentences is to join them with a semicolon and a transitional expression. A **transitional expression** can join two complete ideas together and show how they are related. Most transitional expressions are **conjunctive adverbs** such as *however* or *furthermore*.

Transitional Expressions

Addition	Alternative	Contrast	Time	Example or Emphasis	Result or Consequence
additionally	in fact	however	eventually	for example	consequently
also	instead	nevertheless	finally	for instance	hence
besides	on the contrary	nonetheless	later	namely	therefore
furthermore	on the other hand	still	meanwhile	of course	thus
in addition	otherwise		subsequently	undoubtedly	
moreover					

If the second part of a sentence begins with a transitional expression, put a semicolon before it and a comma after it.

> Complete idea;   **transitional expression** ,   complete idea.

> Miriam was not wealthy; **nevertheless,** she always wore the latest fashions.
> ; **however,**
> ; **nonetheless,**
> ; **still,**

PRACTICE 6

Punctuate the following sentences by adding any necessary semicolons and commas.

EXAMPLE:

A bizarre fashion style can become accepted; however, future generations may find the style ridiculous.

1. Often, a popular personality adopts a fashion later others copy the style.

2. The French king Louis XIV originally disliked wigs however he started to go prematurely bald and changed his mind about the fashion.

3. The king started to wear high, curly wigs subsequently others copied his style.

4. The heavy, elaborate wigs were expensive hence only middle- and upper-class Europeans wore them.

5. The wigs required constant care in fact they needed to be cleaned, powdered, and curled.

6. Later, the king's mustache started to go gray therefore he shaved it off.

7. Others noticed the king's bare face consequently all the fashionable men removed their mustaches too.

8. Not all new fashions are frivolous in fact some fashions signal a change in a group's status.

9. In the 1920s, women gained the right to vote meanwhile pants became associated with women's new freedom.

10. Other fashions have also made political statements for example in the 1970s, the Afro haircut signaled black power.

Section I
EFFECTIVE SENTENCES

PRACTICE 7

Combine sentences using one of the following transitional expressions. Choose an expression from the following list, and try to use a different expression in each sentence.

in fact	for example	~~however~~	of course	for instance
therefore	eventually	nevertheless	thus	in contrast

EXAMPLE:

Today's parents often complain about their children. ~~Kids~~ today are not more violent and rebellious than those of past generations.

; however, kids

1. Youth rebellion is not new. In each era, teenagers have rebelled.

2. Teenagers distinguish themselves in a variety of ways. They listen to new music, create new dance styles, wear odd fashions, and break established social habits.

3. The most visible way to stand out is to wear outrageous fashions. Teenagers try to create original clothing and hairstyles.

4. In the past fifty years, rebellious teens have done almost everything to their hair, including growing it long, buzzing it short, dyeing it, spiking it, shaving it off, and coloring it blue. It is difficult for today's teenagers to create an original hairstyle.

5. Sometimes a certain group popularizes a style. Hip-hop artists wore baggy clothing in the late 1980s.

6. Many parents hated the baggy, oversized pants. Boys wore them anyway.

7. Before the 1990s, most women just pierced their ears. It is now common to see a pierced eyebrow, tongue, or cheek.

8. "Retro" hair and clothing styles will always be popular. People often look to the past for their inspiration.

Section I
EFFECTIVE SENTENCES

  Subordinators vs. Conjunctive Adverbs

A **subordinator** is a term such as *when, because, until,* or *although.* Do not confuse subordinators with conjunctive adverbs. When a subordinator is added to a sentence, the clause becomes incomplete. However, when a conjunctive adverb is added to a sentence, the clause is still complete.

Complete: She wore fur.

Incomplete (with subordinator):   When she wore fur.

Complete (with conjunctive adverb):   Therefore, she wore fur.

When you combine two ideas using a conjunctive adverb, use a semicolon.

No punctuation: She was criticized <u>when she wore fur.</u>

Semicolon: It was very cold<u>; therefore, she wore fur.</u>

PRACTICE 8

Create compound sentences by using the next transitional expressions. Try to use a different expression in each sentence.

   in fact   however   therefore   furthermore   consequently   for example

EXAMPLE:

I have my own style ; *therefore, I refuse to spend money following the latest fad.*

1. Many people like to wear fashionable clothing _____
_____

2. Designer clothing is expensive _____

_____

3. American fashions borrow ideas from different cultures _____

_____

4. Some new fashions are attractive _____

_____

5. Americans spend billions of dollars on clothing _____

_____

The Writer's Desk **Revise and Edit Your Warm Up**

Review the sentences that you wrote for the Warm Up on page 266. Verify that you have punctuated any compound sentences correctly. If you have no compound sentences, then create two for your paragraph.

REFLECT ON IT

Think about what you have learned in this unit. If you do not know an answer, review that concept.

1. a. What is a simple sentence? _____

_____

    b. Write a simple sentence. _____

2. a. What is a compound sentence? _____

_____

    b. Write a compound sentence. _____

3. What are the seven coordinating conjunctions? _____

_____

4. Circle the best answer: When two sentences are joined by a coordinating conjunction such as *but,* should you put a comma before the conjunction?   Yes   No

5. When you join two simple sentences with a transitional expression, how should you punctuate the sentence?

_____

_____

FINAL REVIEW

Read the following comparison and contrast essay. Create at least ten compound sentences by adding semicolons, transitional expressions (*however, therefore,* etc.), or coordinating conjunctions (*for, and, nor, but, or, yet, so*). You may choose to leave some simple sentences.

EXAMPLE: Humans have always killed animals to create clothing. ~~Early~~ humans used animal skins to keep warm.

; for example, early

Section I
**EFFECTIVE
SENTENCES**

1.   In the 1800s and 1900s, humans killed whales. They used whalebone to make corsets. Also, humans hunted millions of birds. They used feathers to adorn fashionable hats. Entire bird species became extinct. The Labrador duck and the passenger pigeon are no longer with us. Today, the use of animal pelts in fashion is controversial. People on both sides of the issue become passionate.

2.   On the one hand, fur producers have many arguments to support their views. First, many people work on fur farms. They want to keep their jobs. According to fur farmers, they raise minks and chinchillas humanely. In some areas, aboriginal people trap animals to make a living. They need an active fur industry to survive. Since the early 1970s, the number of fur manufacturers in the United States has plummeted. Many people have lost their jobs. According to fur traders, their work is a valuable part of human history. Furthermore, people wear leather shoes. They eat meat. Why is it worse to wear fur?

3.   On the other hand, numerous animal rights organizations exist. They do not always work together. Generally, these groups do not want animals to die for luxury fashions. They accuse fur producers of inhumane treatment of animals. Animals are raised in unnatural environments. Minks are kept in tiny cages. According to activists, fur traders have decimated some species of wolves, bears, and tigers. People do not need fur for warmth. They can use synthetic fabrics to make coats. Why should animals suffer to keep wealthy people in the latest fashions?

4.   Clearly, emotions run high for those on both sides of the issue. The fur controversy may never be resolved. Ultimately, consumers will be the ones to decide the value of fur as a commodity.

 See Chapter 17 of the Visualizing Writing CD for an additional mini-lecture on **Combining Sentences.**

Section 1
**EFFECTIVE
SENTENCES**

CHAPTER 18 Complex Sentences

section theme **CULTURE**

CONTENTS

- What Is a Complex Sentence?
- Use Subordinating Conjunctions
- Use Relative Pronouns
- Use Embedded Questions

In this chapter, you will read about topics related to activity fads.

The Writer's Desk **Warm Up**

What types of sports or activities do you like? Choose one type of activity that you enjoy, and write a paragraph explaining why you like it.

What Is a Complex Sentence?

Before you learn about complex sentences, it is important to understand some key terms. A **clause** is a group of words containing a subject and a verb. There are two types of clauses.

An **independent clause** has a subject and a verb and can stand alone because it expresses one complete idea.

> She won the race.

A **dependent clause** has a subject and verb, but it cannot stand alone. It "depends" on another clause to be complete.

>   Although she had injured her leg

A **complex sentence** combines both a dependent and an independent clause.

dependent clause   independent clause

>   **Although** she had injured her leg, <u>she won the race</u>.

> ⭕ **Hint** ▷ **More About Complex Sentences**
>
> Complex sentences can have more than two clauses.
>
> 1
>
> <u>Although women have played organized football for over a century,</u> <u>their</u>
> 2   3
> <u>salaries are not very high</u> <u>because their games are rarely televised</u>.
>
> You can also combine compound and complex sentences. The next example is a
> **compound-complex sentence.**
>
> complex
>
> <u>Although Kyra is tiny,</u> <u>she plays basketball,</u> <u>and she is a decent player</u>.
> compound

Use Subordinating Conjunctions

An effective way to create complex sentences is to join clauses with a subordinating conjunction. When you add a **subordinating conjunction** to a clause, you make the clause dependent. *Subordinate* means "secondary," so subordinating conjunctions are words that introduce secondary ideas. Here are some common subordinating conjunctions followed by examples of how to use these types of conjunctions.

Common Subordinating Conjunctions				
after	because	in order that	unless	whereas
although	before	since	until	wherever
as	even if	so that	when	whether
as if	even though	that	whenever	while
as though	if	though	where	

Crowds cheered **whenever** the team won.

Subordinating conjunction   secondary idea,   main idea.

Whenever <u>the team won</u>, crowds cheered.

PRACTICE 1

Each of the following sentences is complex. In each, circle the subordinating conjunction, and then underline the dependent clause.

EXAMPLE:

(Even if) we cannot know for sure, early humans probably played games and sports.

1. When humans shifted from food gatherers to hunters, sports probably developed in complexity.

2. It would be important to practice cooperative hunting before humans attacked mammoths or other large creatures.

3. Early humans also practiced war games so that they could win battles with other tribes.

4. Spectator sports evolved when societies had more leisure time.

5. In many places, spectators watched while young boys passed through their initiation rituals.

6. Whenever early humans played sports or games, they tested their physical, intellectual, and social skills.

Meanings of Subordinating Conjunctions

Subordinating conjunctions create a relationship between the clauses in a sentence.

Subordinating Conjunction	Indicates	Example
in order that, so that	A purpose	Kevin went to China **so that** he could learn martial arts from a famous master.
as, because, since	A reason or a cause	He learned karate **because** he wanted to be physically fit.
after, before, since, until, when, whenever	A time	**After** he received his black belt, he returned to the United States.
as long as, even if, if, provided that, unless	A condition	He will not fight with a stranger **unless** he feels threatened.
although, even though, though	A contrast	**Although** karate is difficult to learn, millions of people study it every year.
where, wherever	A location	**Wherever** you travel, you will find karate enthusiasts.

PRACTICE 2

In each of the following sentences, underline the dependent clause. Then, indicate the type of relationship between the two parts of the sentence. Choose one of the following relationships.

condition   contrast   location
purpose   reason or cause   time

EXAMPLES:

<u>When someone decided to attach wheels to a plank of wood</u>, a new sport began.   *time*

The name *skateboard* came about <u>because the device was literally a board with roller-skating wheels attached to it</u>.   *reason* or *cause*

Section 1
EFFECTIVE SENTENCES

1. Although kids occasionally rode skateboards and scooters, bicycles were more popular for the next forty years.   _____

2. In the prosperous 1950s, the quality of skateboards improved when modifications were made to the device that holds the wheels.   _____

3. Teenagers bought skateboards so that they could practice an inexpensive and thrilling hobby.   _____

4. Although the sport was quite dangerous, skaters tried doing a variety of tricks.   _____

5. Many surfers took up skateboarding because the sports required similar skills.   _____

6. Wherever surfing was popular, skateboarding was popular too.   _____

7. When the first skateboard movie (*Skater Dance*) was released, over 50 million skateboards had been sold.   _____

8. In 1965, the popularity of skateboarding plummeted because too many people had serious skateboarding accidents.   _____

9. Many cities threatened to ban skateboarding unless manufacturers could develop a safer product. _____

10. According to Michael Brooke, author of *The Concrete Wave*, many accidents happened because the wheels on early skateboards did not grip the road well.   _____

11. After skateboarding died in the 1960s, it had several periods of renewed popularity.   _____

12. Today, skateboarding is once again an important part of popular culture even though it is not exactly a new activity.   _____

Punctuating Complex Sentences

If you use a subordinator at the beginning of a sentence, put a comma after the dependent clause. Generally, if you use a subordinator in the middle of the sentence, you do not need to use a comma.

Comma: **Even though** he is afraid of heights, Malcolm tried skydiving.

No comma: Malcolm tried skydiving **even though** he is afraid of heights.

Section I
**EFFECTIVE
SENTENCES**

PRACTICE 3

Correct eight errors in the following selection by adding the missing commas. If the sentence has a subordinating conjunction, then underline the conjunction.

EXAMPLE:

<u>Although</u> most sports are quite safe, some sports are extremely hazardous.

1. Each year, many people are killed or maimed when they practice a sport. Although skydiving and bungee jumping are hazardous extreme sports like base jumping, free diving, and rodeo events are even more dangerous.

2. Even though they may get arrested many people try base jumping. Wherever there are tall structures there may also be base jumpers. The jumpers wear parachutes and dive off such buildings and bridges so that they can feel an adrenaline rush. Because the parachute may get tangled on the structure base jumping is an extremely dangerous sport.

3. Another extreme sport is free diving. Free divers hold their breath until they are as deep as possible underwater. So that they can break existing records some free divers have dived almost 400 feet. Sometimes when their brains lack oxygen they have to be resuscitated.

4. Although most rodeo sports can be safe bull riding is dangerous. Many bull riders are injured or even killed because the bull throws them off and tramples them.

5. Surprisingly, most sports-related injuries occur when people participate in an innocent-sounding sport. According to the American Academy of Orthopedic Surgeons, almost half a million people are injured each year when they ride bicycles. So, what is the best policy? When playing a sport take precautions to protect yourself.

PRACTICE 4

Add a missing subordinating conjunction to each sentence. Use each subordinating conjunction once.

although	even though	when	whereas
because	unless	whenever	

EXAMPLE:

Whenever you refer to a "football" in Europe, Africa, or Asia, most people assume you are talking about a round black-and-white ball.

Section I
EFFECTIVE SENTENCES

1. British people will assume you are speaking about soccer

   _____ you specifically say "American football."

2. Soccer is the world's most popular sport _____ it is inexpensive to play. _____ someone decides to join a soccer team, he or she does not require expensive padding or equipment.

3. _____ many Americans love to play soccer, there are not many professional teams in the United States. Sports such as basketball, baseball, and football have professional teams and are shown on network television, _____ soccer is not widely viewed.

4. _____ soccer has yet to become as popular as other sports in the United States, it is this country's fastest-growing sport, according to the American Soccer Federation.

 Put a Subject After the Subordinator

When you form complex sentences, always remember to put a subject after the subordinator.

Wrestling is like theater because involves choreographed maneuvers.
(with *it* inserted above "involves")

Boxers do not know who will win the round when enter the ring.
(with *they* inserted above "enter")

Section 1
**EFFECTIVE
SENTENCES**

PRACTICE 5

Add four missing subjects to the next paragraph.

EXAMPLE:

Bullfighting is popular in Mexico and Spain, although $\overset{it}{\wedge}$ is controversial.

Each bullfight is an elaborate ceremony with three parts. In the first part, when the matador enters the arena, is dressed in a fine suit embroidered with gold. Holding a red cape, the matador tries to entice the bull. The spectators cheer when see the bull charging at the cape. In the second part, the banderilleros, or matador's assistants, push short spears into the bull until is tired and angry. In the third part, the matador enters again holding a smaller cape and a sword. After has performed well, the matador kills the bull.

PRACTICE 6

Combine the next sentence pairs with subordinating conjunctions. Write each sentence twice: once with the dependent clause at the beginning of the sentence, and once with the dependent clause at the end. Properly punctuate the sentences.

Use one of the following conjunctions. Use a different conjunction each time.

~~because~~   while   when   even though   although

EXAMPLE:

I try to exercise. It is important.

I try to exercise because it is important.

Because it is important, I try to exercise.

1. I am not very athletic. I will join a team.

   _____

   _____

2. The line is long. I will wait for my turn.

   _____

   _____

3. The game is over. The winners will receive a trophy.

_____

_____

4. I was leaving the field. I heard people cheering.

_____

_____

Use Relative Pronouns

A **relative pronoun** describes a noun or pronoun. You can form complex sentences by using relative pronouns to introduce dependent clauses. Review the most common relative pronouns.

who   whom   whomever   whose   which   that

Use *who* (*whom, whomever, whose*) to add information about a person.

> Jack Roosevelt Robinson, **who** played for the Montreal Royals, broke the color ban in baseball.

Use *that* to add information about a thing.

> In 1947, Robinson joined a team **that** was located in Brooklyn.

Use *which* to add information about a thing.

> Sports such as football, **which** had previously been segregated, included people of different races after the 1940s.

 How to Punctuate Sentences with Relative Pronouns

which Generally, use commas to set off clauses that begin with *which*.

Football, **which** was segregated in 1945, included African-American players the following year.

that Do not use commas to set off clauses that begin with *that*.

The sport **that** is most popular in America is baseball.

who When a clause begins with *who*, you may or may not need a comma. Put commas around the clause if it adds nonessential information. If the clause is essential to the meaning of the sentence, do not add commas.

Essential clause: Most women **who** play sports do not earn as much money as their male counterparts.

Nonessential clause: Tennis player Serena Williams, **who** has won many tournaments, earns millions of dollars in endorsement deals.

GRAMMAR LINK

For more information about punctuating relative clauses, refer to Chapter 33, "Commas."

PRACTICE 7

Using a relative pronoun, combine each pair of sentences to form a complex sentence.

Section I
**EFFECTIVE
SENTENCES**

EXAMPLE:
The Olympic Games celebrate excellence in sports. They occur once every four years.

The Olympic Games, which occur once every four years, celebrate excellence in sports.

1. Steroids can enhance your ability in sports. They are dangerous to your body and mind.

   _____

   _____

2. Some people use steroids. They may experience severe side effects or even death.

   _____

   _____

3. Steroids were first banned at the 1973 Olympic Games. The drugs continue to be used by some athletes.

   _____

   _____

4. Wade Exum is a respected doctor. He ran the U.S. Olympic Committee's doping control program.

   _____

   _____

5. According to Dr. Exum, many U.S. athletes were caught using steroids. Those athletes were not punished.

   _____

   _____

6. In 2000, Dr. Exum quit his Olympic Committee job in disgust. He expressed his concerns in a report.

   _____

   _____

PRACTICE 8

Add a dependent clause to each sentence. Begin each clause with a relative pronoun (*who*, *which*, or *that*). Add any necessary commas.

EXAMPLE:

Teams _that have good leadership_ often win tournaments.

1. The player _____ might be hired to promote running shoes.

2. An athlete _____ should be suspended for at least one game.

3. Bungee jumping is an activity _____

4. I would like to try an extreme sport _____

5. Skydiving _____ is a sport I would like to try.

6. Athletes _____ should be warned about the dangers of steroids.

Section I
**EFFECTIVE
SENTENCES**

Use Embedded Questions

It is possible to combine a question with a statement, or to combine two questions. An **embedded question** is a question that is set within a larger sentence.

Question:	How old are the Olympic Games?
Embedded question:	The sprinter wonders <u>how old the Olympic Games are</u>.

In questions, there is generally a helping verb before the subject. However, when a question is embedded in a larger sentence, you need to remove the helping verb or place it after the subject. As you read the following examples, pay attention to the word order in the embedded questions.

Combine two questions.

Separate:	Do you know the answer? Why **do** they like bullfighting?
	(The second question includes the helping verb *do*.)
Combined:	Do you know <u>why they like bullfighting</u>?
	(The helping verb *do* is removed from the embedded question.)

Combine a question and a statement.

Separate:	I wonder about it. When **should** we go to the arena?
	(In the question, the helping verb *should* appears before the subject.)
Combined:	I wonder <u>when we should go to the arena</u>.
	(In the embedded question, *should* is placed after the subject.)

Section 1
**EFFECTIVE
SENTENCES**

 Use the Correct Word Order

When you edit your writing, ensure that you have formed your embedded questions properly.

> *he thought*
> He wonders why ~~do~~ people like bullfighting. I asked him what ~~did he think~~ about the sport.

PRACTICE 9

Correct six embedded question errors.

EXAMPLE:

people can
The writer explains how ~~can people~~ love dangerous sports.

One activity that generates controversy is bullfighting. Some people wonder why should bulls die for entertainment. They question how can bullfighting be so popular. Many call it a brutal activity because the bull is weakened and then slaughtered. For others, bullfighting is a strong and respected tradition.

Spanish matador Mario Carrión wonders why do some people call bullfighting a sport. In sports, the goal is to win points in a confrontation with an opponent. In Carrión's view, a bullfight is not a sport because a human cannot compete against a thousand-pound beast. He defines bullfighting as "a dramatic dance with death."

Bullfight enthusiasts ask themselves why does bullfighting have a bad reputation. They wonder why is it rejected by so many nations. Do you know what can they do to improve the reputation of bullfighting?

The Writer's Desk **Revise and Edit Your Warm Up**

Review the sentences that you wrote for the Warm Up on page 278. Verify that any complex sentences are correctly punctuated. If you have no complex sentences, then create two for your paragraph.

When you have finished, look at another paragraph that you have written. Try combining sentences into complex sentences.

REFLECT ON IT

Think about what you have learned in this chapter. If you do not know an answer, then review that concept.

1. Write six subordinating conjunctions. _____

_____

2. Write a complex sentence. _____

_____

3. List six relative pronouns. _____

4. Correct the error in the following sentence.

Clayton wonders why should he wear a helmet when he goes skateboarding.

Section 1
**EFFECTIVE
SENTENCES**

FINAL REVIEW

The following paragraphs contain only simple sentences. To give the paragraphs more variety, form at least ten complex sentences by combining pairs of sentences. You will have to add some words and delete others.

EXAMPLE: ~~Some~~ *When* people pierce their tongues~~.~~ *, they* ~~They~~ risk getting an infection.

1.   Many activity fads come and go. Many of these fads are ridiculous. Why do fads become so popular? Nobody knows the answer. There were some unusual fads in the 1950s. College students did phone-booth stuffing. Students entered a phone booth one by one. They tried to stuff as many people as possible into the closed space. Later, hula hoops hit the market. In the 1960s, millions of people bought and used the circular plastic tubes. The hula hoop fad did not last long. It briefly provided people with an innovative way to exercise. People put the hoops around their waists. They would gyrate to keep the hoops spinning.

2.   In the spring of 1974, a streaking fad began. It occurred on college campuses in Florida and California. Young people stripped naked. They may have felt embarrassed. They ran through public places such as football stadiums and malls. They wanted to shock people. The actor David Niven was presenting at the 1974 Academy Awards. A nude streaker dashed behind him. The streaker made a peace sign. Millions of viewers were watching the show. They saw the streaker.

3.   Flash mobbing, a recent trend, is organized on Web sites. Flash mobs first appeared in New York City in the summer of 2003. For no obvious reason, a large group of people gathered on a stone wall in Central Park. They chirped like birds. In Berlin, Germany, about forty people shouted "Yes." They were in a subway car. They shouted into their cell phones at exactly the same moment. In Montréal, Canada, a large group of people began quacking. They threw rubber ducks into a fountain. Do you know the answer to the following question? Why do certain Web sites promote flash mobbing? They do it for a simple reason. They hope to add vibrancy to dull modern life.

Sentence Variety

section theme **CULTURE**

CONTENTS

• What Is Sentence Variety?
• Combine Sentences
• Include a Question, a Quotation, or an Exclamation
• Vary the Opening Words
• Combine Sentences with a Present Participle
• Combine Sentences with a Past Participle
• Combine Sentences with an Appositive

In this chapter, you will read about topics related to cultural icons.

The Writer's Desk **Warm Up**

Would you like to be famous? What are some problems that could be associated with fame? Write a paragraph about fame.

What Is Sentence Variety?

In Chapters 17 and 18, you learned how to write different types of sentences. This chapter focuses on sentence variety. **Sentence variety** means that your sentences have assorted patterns and lengths. In this chapter, you will learn to vary your sentences by consciously considering the length of sentences, by altering the opening words, and by joining sentences using different methods.

Section 1
**EFFECTIVE
SENTENCES**

GRAMMAR LINK

If you forget what compound and complex sentences are, refer to Chapters 17 and 18.

Combine Sentences

A passage filled with simple, short sentences can sound choppy. When you vary the lengths of your sentences, the same passage becomes easier to read and flows more smoothly. For example, read the following two passages about cultural icon Rosa Parks. In the first paragraph, most of the sentences are short, and the style is repetitive and boring. In the second paragraph, there is a mixture of simple, compound, and complex sentences.

Simple Sentences

We know the story. A woman left work. She boarded a bus for home. She was tired. Her feet ached. This was Montgomery, Alabama. It was in December 1955. The bus became crowded. The driver yelled at the black woman to give her seat to a white passenger. She remained seated. Her decision was important. It led to the changes in the South. It ushered in a new era.

Simple, Compound, and Complex Sentences

We know the story. One December evening, a woman left work and boarded a bus for home. She was tired; her feet ached. But this was Montgomery, Alabama, in December 1955, and as the bus became crowded, the woman, a black woman, was ordered to give up her seat to a white passenger. When she remained seated, that simple decision eventually led to the disintegration of institutionalized segregation in the South, ushering in a new era of the civil rights movement.

—Rita Dove, "The Torchbearer"

 Be Careful with Long Sentences

If a sentence is too long, it may be difficult for the reader to understand. If you have any doubts, break up a longer sentence into shorter ones.

Long and complicated: Elvis Presley is a cultural icon who achieved the American dream by using his musical skills and his raw sexual energy to transform himself from a truck driver into a rock-and-roll legend, yet he did not handle his fame very well and at the end of his life he was unhappy and addicted to painkillers.

Better: Elvis Presley is a cultural icon who achieved the American dream. Using his musical skills and his raw sexual energy, he transformed himself from a truck driver into a rock-and-roll legend. However, he did not handle his fame very well. At the end of his life, he was unhappy and addicted to painkillers.

PRACTICE 1

Rewrite the following paragraph using both long and short sentences. Make sure you write some compound and complex sentences.

A cultural icon can be an object, a person, or a place. Cultural icons symbolize a belief or a way of life. Each country has its own icons. They become part of that country's history. For example, Mickey Mouse is a familiar image. The cartoon character symbolizes American optimism. Ellis Island and the Statue of Liberty are cultural icons. People can be icons, too. In Mexico, revolutionary leader Emiliano Zapata is a cultural icon. In America, Elvis Presley is an icon. These icons reflect a shared cultural experience.

Section 1
EFFECTIVE SENTENCES

_____

_____

_____

_____

_____

_____

Include a Question, a Quotation, or an Exclamation

The most common type of sentence is a statement. A simple but effective way to achieve sentence variety is to do the following:

- Ask and answer a **question.** You could also insert a **rhetorical question,** which does not require an answer but is used for effect.

     Did Elvis really do anything shocking?

- Include the occasional **exclamation** to express surprise. However, do not overuse exclamations because they make your writing look less academic.

     Elvis's swinging hips were considered obscene!

- Add a **direct quotation,** which includes the exact words that somebody said.

     Elvis said, "I didn't copy my style from anybody."

In the next passage, a question, an exclamation, and a quotation add variety.

> Norma Jeanne Baker was born to a mentally unstable mother and an absent father. The shy little girl spent her childhood being shuffled between an orphanage and foster parents. From such inauspicious beginnings, a cultural icon was born. Norma, who later changed her name to Marilyn Monroe, bleached her hair, had plastic surgery on her nose, and became one of Hollywood's most recognizable figures. **Why is she remembered?** Perhaps her fame ◄ Question
> is partly due to her untimely death at the age of thirty-six. She is also remembered for her sensuality and her childlike vulnerability. **Even at the height of fame, she exuded unhappiness and once complained, "Everybody is always tugging at you. They'd like a** ◄ Quotation
> **chunk out of you."** Some argue that she was not talented and others suggest that people will forget her. **But the truth is, even half a century after her death, her image is one of the most recognized in** ◄ Exclamation
> **America!**

Section 1
**EFFECTIVE
SENTENCES**

📎 **GRAMMAR LINK**

For more information about
punctuating quotations, refer to
Chapter 34.

  Punctuating Quotations

If you introduce your quotation with a phrase, put a comma after the phrase and before the opening quotation marks. Put the final period inside the closing quotation marks.

> Marilyn Monroe once complained, "Everybody is always tugging at you."

If the end of the quotation is not the end of the sentence, place a comma inside the final quotation mark.

> "They were terribly strict," she once said.

PRACTICE 2

Read the following passage. Change one sentence to a question, one to an exclamation, and one to a quotation.

EXAMPLE:

Why do most   ?
~~Most~~ people want to be famous⁄

    The last one hundred years was a century of celebrities. Many ordinary people achieve almost saintly status. In previous centuries, heroes were those who fought bravely in wars or who rescued others. Today, actors, musicians, politicians, and athletes are routinely deified. Even criminals such as Al Capone and Charles Manson become household names. In the words of Daniel J. Boorstin, celebrity worship and hero worship should not be confused. However, we confuse them every day.

Vary the Opening Words

An effective way to make your sentences more vivid is to vary the opening words. Instead of beginning each sentence with the subject, you could try the following strategies.

Begin with an Adverb

An **adverb** is a word that modifies a verb, and it often (but not always) ends in -*ly*. *Slowly, usually,* and *suddenly* are adverbs. Other adverbs include words such as *sometimes, never, however,* and *often.*

> <u>Generally</u>, a cultural icon arouses strong feelings in members of that culture.

> <u>Often</u>, an extremely gifted and famous person becomes an icon.

Begin with a Prepositional Phrase

A **prepositional phrase** is a group of words made up of a preposition and its object. *Under the chair*, *in the beginning*, and *after the fall* are prepositional phrases.

> <u>In New York's harbor</u>, the Statue of Liberty welcomes visitors.

> <u>At dawn</u>, we photographed the statue.

 Comma Tip

Generally, when a sentence begins with an adverb or a prepositional phrase, place a comma after the opening word or phrase.

> **Cautiously,** the reporter asked another question to the volatile star.

> **Without any warning,** she stood up and left the room.

Section 1
**EFFECTIVE
SENTENCES**

PRACTICE 3

Rewrite the following sentences by placing an adverb or prepositional phrase at the beginning. First, strike out any word or phrase that could be moved. Then, rewrite that word or phrase at the beginning of the sentence. Finally, correctly punctuate your new sentence.

EXAMPLES:

<u>Actually, the</u> ~~The~~ United States' most recognizable symbol was ~~actually~~ made in France.

1. _____ A group of French intellectuals, in 1865, met in a restaurant and discussed the United States.

2. _____ The French artists and thinkers carefully criticized their oppressive emperor, Napoleon III.

3. _____ They then expressed in quiet voices admiration for America's new democratic government.

4. _____ A sculptor gradually developed the idea of creating a gift for the United States.

5. _____ Frederic-Auguste Bartholdi searched for a site to place his sculpture during a visit to the United States.

6. _____ He crafted "Lady Liberty" with the help of many workers.

7. _____ The 305-foot statue was completed in 1884.

8. _____ Bartholdi unfortunately died in 1883 without seeing the completed work.

Section I
**EFFECTIVE
SENTENCES**

PRACTICE 4

Add an opening word or phrase to each sentence. Use the type of opening that is indicated in parentheses. Remember to punctuate the sentence properly.

EXAMPLE:

Adverb

<u>Surprisingly,</u> playwright Naomi Iizuka loves the 50-foot Hollywood sign.

1. (Adverb) _____ the sign is more than just white letters that spell "Hollywood."

2. (Prepositional phrase) _____ the sign is like a beacon to aspiring actors.

3. (Prepositional phrase) _____ thousands of people arrive with dreams of stardom.

4. (Adverb) _____ some people make it, but many do not.

5. (Adverb) _____ the sign is an important American symbol.

Combine Sentences with a Present Participle

You can combine two sentences with a present participle. A **present participle** is a verb that ends in *-ing*, such as *believing, having,* and *using*. Combine sentences using an *-ing* modifier only when the two actions happen at the same time.

Separate sentences:	He looked across the harbor. He saw the Statue of Liberty.
Combined sentences:	<u>Looking</u> across the harbor, he saw the Statue of Liberty.

PRACTICE 5

Combine the next sentences by converting one of the verbs into an *-ing* modifier.

EXAMPLE:

Odessa and Cassius Clay looked at their tiny son. They had no idea of their boy's future fame.

Looking at their tiny son, Odessa and Cassius Clay had no idea of their boy's future fame.

Having no idea of their boy's future fame, Odessa and Cassius Clay looked at their tiny son.

1. Cassius Clay competed in the 1960 Olympics. He won a gold medal.

   _____

   _____

   _____

2. He used a unique boxing method. Clay won many fights.

   _____

   _____

   _____

3. He changed his name to Mohammad Ali. He professed his loyalty to Islam.

   _____

   _____

   _____

4. He spoke with rhymes. Ali became the original rapper.

   _____

   _____

   _____

5. Ali voiced his own opinions. He promoted black power and antiwar beliefs.

   _____

   _____

   _____

6. He proclaimed his opposition to the Vietnam War. He was arrested as a draft dodger.

   _____

   _____

   _____

7. He refused to back down. He lost his boxing license from 1967 to 1970.

   _____

   _____

   _____

8. Ali knocked out George Foreman in 1974. He regained his boxing title.

_____

_____

_____

Section 1
EFFECTIVE SENTENCES

GRAMMAR LINK

For a complete list of irregular past participles, see Appendix 2.

Combine Sentences with a Past Participle

Another way to combine sentences is to use a past participle. A **past participle** is a verb that has an *-ed* ending (although there are many irregular past participles, such as *gone*, *seen*, *broken*, and *known*.)

You can begin a sentence with a past participle. To do this, you must combine two sentences, and one of the sentences must contain a past participle.

Separate sentences:	Jesse Owens was raised in Alabama. He became a famous athlete.
Combined sentences:	<u>Raised in Alabama</u>, Jesse Owens became a famous athlete.

PRACTICE 6

Combine each pair of sentences into one sentence beginning with a past participle.

EXAMPLE:

Jesse Owens was born in 1913. He was the son of sharecroppers and the grandson of slaves.

Born in 1913, Jesse Owens was the son of sharecroppers and the grandson of slaves.

1. Jesse Owens was excluded from team sports in college. The African-American athlete excelled at individual sports such as track and field.

_____

_____

_____

2. He was invited to the 1936 Olympic Games. He competed in twelve events.

_____

_____

_____

3. The 1936 Olympic Games were held in Berlin. They were a showcase for
   the Nazi party.

   _____

   _____

   _____

4. Owens went on to win four gold medals. He was encouraged by his fans.

   _____

   _____

   _____

5. Hitler was surprised at Owens's success. He refused to shake the medal
   winner's hand.

   _____

   _____

   _____

6. The athlete was treated like a hero upon his return. He basked in glory for
   a short while.

   _____

   _____

   _____

7. Owens was forbidden to ride in the front of a bus. He expressed sadness
   about the segregation laws in his state.

   _____

   _____

   _____

8. A Berlin street was renamed Jesse Owens Strasse in 1984. The street leads
   to the Olympic stadium.

   _____

   _____

   _____

PRACTICE 7

A. Fill in each blank with an *-ing* modifier.

EXAMPLE:

<u>Feeling confident,</u> Walt Disney prepared his first film.

1. _____, Disney created his famous mouse.

2. _____, children appreciated the little mouse's feisty attitude.

3. _____, Disney eventually retired.

B. Fill in each blank with a past participle modifier.

EXAMPLE:

<u>Trained in the Peking Opera School,</u> Jackie Chan learned how to do amazing stunts.

1. _____, young movie audiences expect great fight scenes.

2. _____, action movies are a Hollywood staple.

3. _____, film lovers would like to see original, well-written films.

Combine Sentences with an Appositive

An **appositive** is a word or phrase that gives further information about a noun or pronoun. You can combine two sentences by using an appositive. In the example, the italicized phrase could become an appositive because it describes the noun *John Lennon*.

> **Two sentences:** John Lennon was *a founding member of the Beatles.* He went on to have a solo career.

You can place the appositive directly before the word that it refers to or directly after that word. Notice that the appositives are set off with commas.

> appositive
> **Combined:** <u>A founding member of the Beatles,</u> **John Lennon** went on to have a successful solo career.

> appositive
> **Combined:** **John Lennon,** <u>a founding member of the Beatles,</u> went on to have a successful solo career.

Finding an Appositive

To find an appositive, look for a word or phrase that describes or renames a noun. The noun could be anywhere in the sentence.

> John Lennon popularized a new fashion trend. He wore round, wire-rimmed eyeglasses.

In the preceding sentences, "round, wire-rimmed eyeglasses" describe the new fashion trend. You could combine the sentences as follows:

> appositive
> John Lennon popularized **a new fashion trend,** round, wire-rimmed eyeglasses.

Section 1
EFFECTIVE SENTENCES

PRACTICE 8

Combine the following pairs of sentences. In each pair, make one of the sentences an appositive. Try to vary the position of the appositive. In some sentences, you could put the appositive at the beginning of the sentence, and in others, you could put the appositive after the word that it describes. The first one has been done for you.

EXAMPLE:

John Winston Lennon, ~~was~~ a British lad. ~~He~~ grew up in the home of his aunt.

1. John Lennon's father abandoned him. His father was a sailor.

   _____

   _____

2. At the age of five, Lennon witnessed the tragic death of his mother. Her name was Julia.

   _____

   _____

3. An off-duty police officer who was driving home accidentally hit Julia. This was an event that Lennon never got over.

   _____

   _____

4. Later, his aunt Mimi bought Lennon his most valuable gift. She bought him a guitar.

   _____

   _____

5. She never expected her nephew to make a living with music. It was a dream she believed was unattainable.

_____

_____

6. Lennon was a good organizer. He invited some friends to join a band.

_____

_____

7. Their music group was one of the most famous twentieth-century bands. The group was called the Beatles.

_____

_____

8. The group's songs were extremely catchy. The songs were about topics such as love, nonsense, revolution, and lonely people.

_____

_____

9. The band members had distinct personalities. The members were John Lennon, Paul McCartney, George Harrison, and Ringo Starr.

_____

_____

10. In the 1970s, after the band broke up, Lennon created music with his wife, Yoko Ono. She was a Japanese musician and artist.

_____

_____

11. In 1980, Lennon was murdered in front of his home. This was an act that his fans could not forgive.

_____

_____

12. Long after their deaths, Mozart and Beethoven are still remembered. They were famous eighteenth-century composers.

_____

_____

13. Will John Lennon achieve the same level of immortality as Mozart? John Lennon was a rock musician.

_____

_____

The Writer's Desk Revise and Edit Your Paragraph

In the Warm Up on page 291, you wrote a short paragraph about the problems associated with fame. Revise your paragraph for sentence variety, and check it for errors.

REFLECT ON IT

Think about what you have learned in this unit. If you do not know an answer, review that topic.

1. Why is sentence variety important? _____

_____

2. Write a sentence that begins with an adverb. _____

_____

3. Write a sentence that begins with a present participle. _____

_____

4. Write a sentence that begins with a past participle. _____

_____

5. Write a sentence that begins with an appositive. _____

_____

FINAL REVIEW

The next essay lacks sentence variety. Use the strategies that you have learned in this chapter to create at least ten varied sentences.

EXAMPLE: People are obsessed with fame. ~~Perhaps they believe~~ , believing that fame will make them immortal.

1. Andy Warhol was an artist. He made a fortune with silkscreens of famous icons such as Marilyn Monroe and Mick Jagger. He predicted that

Section I
**EFFECTIVE
SENTENCES**

everyone would be famous for fifteen minutes. Today television is filled with ordinary people. They hope to achieve celebrity status. We wonder why this is happening. Our society elevates celebrities above the common human. Certainly celebrities often have great talent. The talent includes exceptional musical ability, great athletic prowess, or a compelling ability to act. However, many celebrities lack moral character. They are models of bad behavior. Celebrities often make poor role models.

2. Some celebrities in the twentieth century were very troubled. There are people such as Marilyn Monroe, Jimi Hendrix, and Kurt Cobain. They turned to drugs in order to cope with their pain. For example, Cobain and Hendrix abused heroin. Monroe abused prescription drugs. Some argue that these celebrities are simply troubled people. They cannot be blamed for their addictions. Others suggest that such celebrities provide children with negative role models. The celebrities make drugs appear glamorous and exciting.

3. Other celebrities have promoted violence. This includes Tupac Shakur and many other rap artists. Shakur certainly had a difficult childhood. He was raised in Baltimore, Maryland. He was accepted to the prestigious Baltimore School for the Arts. He developed his music and writing skills. He also became involved in gangs. He was arrested on several occasions. His rap music often mentioned the thug life. It told stories of gunfights and gang rivalries. He was gunned down during a trip to Las Vegas, Nevada. The rapper died violently.

4. Impressionable youngsters want to emulate their heroes. They do not think about the dangers of drugs or gang life. Some people do not care what celebrities do. Artists are entitled to make mistakes. Others argue that celebrities have a certain responsibility. No matter what your opinion is, people leading public lives will always be under scrutiny.

The Writer's Room **Topics for Writing**

Choose one of the following topics and write a paragraph or an essay. When you write, remember to follow the writing process.

1. Define *hero*. What makes a person a hero?
2. Why do so many people crave fame? How does celebrity status affect people? Write about the causes or effects of fame.
3. Think of a sport or activity that you have tried. Write a paragraph explaining how to play or participate in the activity.
4. Some people argue that humans should not wear animal fur. Others support the fur industry. What is your opinion?

Section 1
EFFECTIVE SENTENCES

 The Writers' Circle

Work with a team of about three students. Using the six words below, create a paragraph. Include simple, compound, and complex sentences in your paragraph.

hero	disappointment	clothing
talent	leader	icon

When you finish, exchange paragraphs with another team. Verify whether the other team has used a variety of sentences. Then, edit the other team's paragraph, looking for any errors in punctuation or sentence form.

READING LINK

Culture
"Fads" by David A. Locher (page 554)
"Growing Up in Cyberspace" by Brent Staples (page 548)
"Bound Feet" by Jung Chang (page 580)
"Old Time Pueblo World" by Leslie Marmon Silko (page 583)
"Nothing But Net" by Scott Bekker (page 552)

See Chapter 19 of the Visualizing Writing CD for an additional mini-lecture on **Varying Sentence Structure.**

CHAPTER 20

Fragments and Run-Ons

section theme **PSYCHOLOGY**

CONTENTS

• Fragments
• Run-Ons

In this chapter, you will read about psychological profiles.

The Writer's Desk **Warm Up**

Do you remember your dreams? Do you think that dreams have a purpose? Write a short paragraph about dreams.

Fragments

A **sentence** must have a subject and verb, and it must express a complete thought. A **fragment** is an incomplete sentence. Either it lacks a subject or verb, or it fails to express a complete thought. You may see fragments in newspaper headlines and advertisements (*Wrinkle-free skin in one month*). However, in college writing, it is unacceptable to write fragments.

> **Sentence:** Sigmund Freud was a famous psychologist.
>
> **Fragment:** Considered to be the founder of psychoanalysis.

Phrase Fragments

A phrase fragment is missing a subject or a verb. In the following examples, the fragments are underlined.

No verb: <u>First, Gestalt theory.</u> It focuses on an individual's perception.

No subject: Wolfgang Kohler was born in 1887. <u>Founded the Gestalt theory of psychology.</u>

How to Correct Phrase Fragments

To correct a phrase fragment, either add the missing subject or verb, or join the fragment to another sentence. The following examples show two ways you can correct the phrase fragments in the previous examples.

Join sentences: First, Gestalt theory focuses on an individual's perceptions.

Add word: Wolfgang Kohler was born in 1887. **He** founded the Gestalt theory of psychology.

Section 2
**COMMON
SENTENCE
ERRORS**

 Incomplete Verbs

A sentence must have a subject and a complete verb. If a sentence has an incomplete verb, it is a phrase fragment. The following example contains a subject and part of a verb. However, it is missing a helping verb; therefore, the sentence is incomplete.

Fragment: Many books about psychology written by Carl Jung.

To make this sentence complete, you must add the helping verb.

Sentence: Many books about psychology <u>were</u> written by Carl Jung.

PRACTICE I

Underline and correct five phrase fragments.

EXAMPLE:

<u>A childhood trauma.</u> ~~It~~ can be the source of an irrational fear.

1.   First, superstitions. People sometimes have irrational beliefs. Many compulsive gamblers, for example, think that they can control the spin of slot machine reels by carrying good luck charms. Some carry a four-leaf clover. Or a rabbit's foot. The illusion of control.

2.   Many athletes have rituals or lucky items of clothing. A lucky number on their jersey. Rams running back Marshall Faulk always wears black to

the stadium. Another football player, Chris Hale. He believes that dressing in a particular sequence is lucky.

Fragments with *-ing* and *to*

A fragment may begin with a **present participle,** which is the form of the verb that ends in *-ing* (*running, talking*). It may also begin with an **infinitive,** which is *to* plus the base form of the verb (*to run, to talk*). These fragments generally appear before or after another sentence that contains the subject. In the examples, the fragments are underlined.

-ing **fragment:**	Thinking about positive outcomes. It helps people cope with stress.
to fragment:	Oprah Winfrey has developed a resilient attitude. To overcome her childhood traumas.

How to Correct *-ing* and *to* Fragments

To correct an *-ing* or *to* fragment, either add the missing words, or join the fragment to another sentence. Here are two ways to correct the previous examples.

Join sentences:	Thinking about positive outcomes helps people cope with stress.
Add words:	Oprah Winfrey has developed a resilient attitude **because she had** to overcome her childhood traumas.

Hint **When the *-ing* Word Is the Subject**

Sometimes a gerund (*-ing* form of the verb) is the subject of a sentence. In the next example, *listening* is the subject of the sentence.

> **Correct:** Listening is an important skill.

A sentence fragment occurs when the *-ing* word is part of an incomplete verb string, or when the subject was mentioned in a previous sentence.

> **Fragment:** Oprah Winfrey has achieved success. Listening to people's problems.

PRACTICE 2

Underline and correct five *-ing* and *to* fragments.

EXAMPLE:

Believing in ghosts. ~~It~~ is very common.

1. Believing they are rational. Many people are actually superstitious.

   Professional athletes follow some strange rituals. To help them succeed.

   For example, Michael Jordan played each game. Wearing blue North

Carolina college shorts under his Bulls uniform. Baseball player Wade

Boggs ate chicken on game days.

2.   Athletes in other sports also have certain strange beliefs. For instance,

rodeo competitors believe that it is bad luck to wear the color yellow.

Carrying coins in their pockets. Golfers hope to have good luck. Clearly,

rational people can have irrational beliefs. To help them cope with

challenges.

Explanatory Fragments

An **explanatory fragment** provides an explanation about a previous sentence
and is missing a subject, a complete verb, or both. These types of fragments
begin with one of the following words.

also	except	for instance	like	such as
as well as	for example	including	particularly	

In each example, the explanatory fragment is underlined.

Fragment: Carl Jung studied with many prominent psychologists.
<u>For instance, Sigmund Freud</u>.

Fragment: Psychologists analyze behavior. <u>Particularly through
methods of observation</u>.

How to Correct Explanatory Fragments

To correct explanatory fragments, add the missing words, or join the explanation
or example to another sentence. Here are two ways to correct the fragments in
the previous examples.

Add words: Carl Jung studied with many prominent
psychologists. For instance, **he worked with**
Sigmund Freud.

Join sentences: Psychologists analyze behavior particularly through
methods of observation.

PRACTICE 3

Underline and correct five explanatory fragments. You may need to add or
remove words.

EXAMPLE:

are considered unlucky.

There are many superstitions. <u>For instance, black cats</u>/

1. Superstitions have their origins in people's psychological behaviors. For example, a desire for rituals. Superstitions have also developed due to other factors. Such as fear and ignorance. Also, early humans found it difficult to explain the causes of natural phenomena. Like thunder or lightning.

2. One common superstition is that the number 13 is unlucky. Some attribute this superstition to stories about devils. As well as witches. Many people believed that witches usually gathered in groups of twelve. When the devil participated in the coven, the number of members became thirteen. Another theory about the unlucky number 13 originated with the early Christians. There were thirteen people at the Last Supper. Including Judas, who betrayed Jesus. Therefore, the number 13 was considered unlucky.

Section 2
**COMMON
SENTENCE
ERRORS**

Dependent-Clause Fragments

A **dependent clause** has a subject and verb, but it cannot stand alone. It *depends* on another clause to be a complete sentence. Dependent clauses may begin with subordinating conjunctions (subordinators) or relative pronouns. The following are some of the most common words that begin dependent clauses.

Common Subordinating Conjunctions				Relative Pronouns
after	before	though	whenever	that
although	even though	unless	where	which
as	if	until	whereas	who(m)
because	since	what	whether	whose

The next two examples contain dependent-clause fragments. In each example, the fragment is underlined.

Fragment: <u>Although I cross my fingers for luck.</u> I know that it is a silly superstition.

Fragment: I will not walk under a ladder. <u>That is leaning against a wall.</u>

How to Correct Dependent-Clause Fragments

To correct dependent-clause fragments, either join the fragment to a complete sentence, or add the necessary words to make it a complete idea. You could also delete the subordinating conjunction. Here are two ways to correct the fragments in the previous examples.

| **Delete the subordinator:** | I cross my fingers for luck. I know that it is a silly superstition. |
| **Join sentences:** | Although I cross my fingers for luck, I know that it is a silly superstition.
I will not walk under a ladder that is leaning against a wall. |

PRACTICE 4

Underline and correct five dependent-clause fragments.

EXAMPLE:

, negative

Whenever they blame themselves. ~~Negative~~ thinkers make their problems larger.

Section 2
COMMON SENTENCE ERRORS

1. Andrew Shatte is a University of Pennsylvania researcher. Who is working on the Resiliency Project. For the project, graduate psychology students taught seventy children. That they can become more resilient. Children learned the difference between productive and self-defeating thinking. After they looked at their own fears. The children had to test their expectations and see if they were realistic.

2. One child in the program who came from a tough inner-city neighborhood had convinced himself that he would probably end up in a gang. Even though he hated violence. The program taught this boy. That there are other possible outcomes. He learned that he did not have to focus on worst-case scenarios.

PRACTICE 5

The next paragraphs contain phrase, explanatory, *-ing*, *to*, and dependent-clause fragments. Correct fifteen fragment errors.

EXAMPLE:

nightmares when

Many people had ~~nightmares. When~~ they were children.

1. In ancient times. People thought that dreams had heavenly origins. The ancient Egyptians thought that dreams had a prophetic function.

The Babylonians and Assyrians also. Some Egyptian pharaohs recorded their strange dreams. For example, Thutmose IV. He dreamed that the Sphinx spoke to him. Using a familiar language. The Sphinx, which was buried in sand, asked Thutmose to remove the sand. If he obeyed. He would then become king. Thutmose cleared the sand off the Sphinx. Soon after, became king.

Section 2
**COMMON
SENTENCE
ERRORS**

2.   Some psychologists believe that dreams are meaningless. Although others disagree. Dreams have a significant purpose. According to Sigmund Freud. Freud believed that dreams could lead to understanding the unconscious mind. He proposed that dreams appeared in symbols or in disguised forms. That dreams had hidden meanings. Freud theorized that dream symbols showed the dreamer's desires. Either sexual or aggressive in nature.

3.   Two modern theories about dreams. In the first theory, some psychologists propose that dreaming is necessary. Because a dream's purpose is to rid the mind of useless data. We forget our dreams because we no longer need the information in them. The second theory. Dreams have no function at all. Some psychologists believe that the brain is responding to high levels of stimuli. Therefore, people have inexplicable dreams. Such as dreams about someone that they have never met. Certainly, there are many psychological theories. To help explain the meanings of dreams.

Run-Ons

A **run-on sentence** occurs when two or more complete sentences are incorrectly joined. In other words, the sentence runs on without stopping. There are two types of run-on sentences.

- A **fused sentence** has no punctuation to mark the break between ideas.

> **Incorrect:**   Psychologists describe human behavior they use observational methods.

▪ A **comma splice** uses a comma incorrectly to connect two complete ideas.

>**Incorrect:**   Wilhelm Wundt was born in 1832, he is often called the founder of modern psychology.

PRACTICE 6

Read the following sentences. Write *C* beside correct sentences and *RO* beside run-ons.

EXAMPLE:

Sigmund Freud and Carl Jung were two famous psychologists they
profoundly influenced the field of psychology.   *RO*

Section 2
**COMMON
SENTENCE
ERRORS**

1. Psychologists study human behavior, researchers have developed many theories on human nature.   _____

2. Instinct theory is one model developed by psychologists it proposes that behavior is based on biology.   _____

3. Learning theory suggests that humans learn through experience. _____

4. Trait theories focus on human characteristics, psychologists describe personality types.   _____

5. Freud developed a theory about personality in which he divided the mind into three parts.   _____

6. Freud named the parts the *id*, *ego*, and *superego* his theory became enormously influential.   _____

7. Psychoanalysis started to lose its popularity by the 1940s, at that time other personality theories were developing.   _____

8. One psychologist, William Sheldon, tried to connect personality to body shapes.   _____

9. Sheldon's types were mesomorphic or lean, endomorphic or fat, and ectomorphic or tall and thin.   _____

10. Human personalities vary greatly it is difficult to categorize them.   _____

How to Correct Run-Ons

You can correct run-on sentences in a variety of ways. Read the following run-on sentence, and then review the four ways to correct it.

>**Run-On:**   Thomas Bouchard Jr. studies twins, he is interested in genetic influences on behavior.

1. Make two separate sentences by adding end punctuation, such as a period.

>Thomas Bouchard Jr. studies twins. **He** is interested in genetic influences on behavior.

2. Add a semicolon.

> Thomas Bouchard Jr. studies twins; he is interested in genetic influences on behavior.

3. Add a coordinator (*for, and, nor, but, or, yet, so*).

> Thomas Bouchard Jr. is interested in genetic influences on behavior, **so** he studies twins.

4. Add a subordinator (*after, although, as, because, before, since, when, while*).

> Thomas Bouchard Jr. studies twins **because** he is interested in genetic influences on behavior.

Section 2
**COMMON
SENTENCE
ERRORS**

PRACTICE 7

A. Correct each run-on to read as two complete sentences.

EXAMPLE:

The twins are identical, ~~they~~ *. They* have brown hair and eyes.

1. Until the 1960s, twins put up for adoption were generally separated they were often adopted by two different families.

2. Psychologists are interested in studying twins raised in different families, they want to determine whether genetics or the environment plays a dominant role in behavior.

3. An amazing case involves Tamara Rabi and Adriana Scott they met each other in 2003.

B. Correct each run-on by joining the two sentences with a semicolon.

EXAMPLE:

The girls are remarkably similar; they both love to dance.

4. Tamara and Adriana were born in Mexico they were separated and raised by different families.

5. The girls were adopted by American families they lived just twenty-five miles apart.

6. Tamara Rabi was raised by a Jewish family in a city Adriana Scott was

     raised by a Catholic family in a suburb.

C. Correct the next run-ons by joining the two sentences with a coordinator (*for, and, nor, but, or, yet, so*).

EXAMPLE:

, but

A boy named Justin dated Adriana there was no mutual attraction.

Section 2
**COMMON
SENTENCE
ERRORS**

7. Justin still wanted to find a girlfriend, his friend set him up with another

     girl.

8. Justin met Tamara he was astounded at her similarity to his previous

     girlfriend, Adriana.

9. Justin convinced the girls to meet each other, they met in a McDonald's

     parking lot.

D. Correct the next run-ons by joining the two sentences with a subordinator such as *although*, *because*, or *when*.

EXAMPLE:

because

The girls were happy to meet ~~they~~ each wanted a sister.

10. The twins did not go to the same type of school their families were not in

     the same income bracket.

11. They received different qualities of education, they were both B students.

12. The girls flew to Mexico they met their birth mother.

PRACTICE 8

Write *F* beside fragments, *RO* beside run-on sentences, and *C* beside correct sentences.

EXAMPLE:

The origins of certain fears.   _F_

1. Maggie Juato, a public relations executive, becomes breathless
   and dizzy whenever she sees one.   _____

2. The red nose, the curly green hair, and the large floppy shoes. _____

3. The fear of clowns is known as coulrophobia. _____

4. The clown's painted face is frightening. _____

5. With a large mocking grin painted over the clown's real mouth. _____

6. Professional clowns are aware of the problem they do not approach the fearful. _____

7. Perhaps the phobia is caused by clown horror movies. _____

8. Stephen King's movie _It_, for example. _____

9. In the film, actor Tim Curry plays the evil clown, Pennywise, he smacks his lips every time he is about to murder a child. _____

10. While such movies are terrifying. _____

11. Real clowns are actors and comedians who need the work, they entertain children in hospitals and the elderly in nursing homes. _____

12. Certain psychologists can help patients overcome their clown phobias. _____

Section 2
**COMMON
SENTENCE
ERRORS**

PRACTICE 9

Correct fifteen fragment and run-on errors.

EXAMPLE:

About 3 percent of births in the United States are twins , but the percentage is increasing.

1. Thomas Bouchard Jr. and some colleagues at the University of Minnesota began studying twins in 1979. Bouchard had read about twins. Who had been raised apart. He contacted them to study their similarities and differences.

2. By 1990, Bouchard's team had studied seventy-seven sets of identical twins. The majority of these separated twins had astounding similarities. For example, two men named Jim. They had been separated at birth. They met in 1979 they found that they were similar in many ways. They smoked the same brand of cigarettes, they drove the same type of car. The men also had the same hobbies. For example, working with wood. Amazingly, the Jims had both built white benches, they placed the benches near a tree.

3.   In the study, one set of twins was unusual. Japanese-born twins were adopted by different families in California. They shared some similarities, researchers were puzzled by their differences. One twin had 20/20 vision, but the other wore glasses. One was afraid to travel by airplane, the other had no such fear. One twin was quite timid, the other was easygoing and friendly.

Section 2
COMMON SENTENCE ERRORS

4.   Researchers suspect that the environment may play a role. In twin differences. For example, one twin could be malnourished, the other could have a healthy diet. The differences in diet could affect the development of the twins' brains. And bodies. Birthing problems may also result in differences. Between twins. One twin may receive less oxygen during delivery.

5.   The separated-twin studies suggest certain possibilities, for example, twins raised separately may be more similar than twins raised together. Twins raised together may emphasize their differences. Twins raised apart would have no need. To search for their individuality. Much more research is needed to know how genes influence behavior.

The Writer's Desk   Revise and Edit Your Warm Up

In the Warm Up on page 306, you wrote several sentences about dreams. Edit your paragraph. Make sure that sentences are complete and that there are no fragments or run-ons.

REFLECT ON IT

Think about what you have learned in this unit. If you do not know an answer, review that concept.

1. What is a sentence fragment? _____

_____

2. What are the types of fragments?

_____   _____

_____   _____

3. What is a run-on? _____

_____

4. Define a comma splice. _____

_____

5. Define a fused sentence. _____

_____

6. Explain the four ways to correct a run-on sentence.

a. _____

b. _____

c. _____

d. _____

Section 2
**COMMON
SENTENCE
ERRORS**

FINAL REVIEW

Correct fifteen fragment and run-on errors.

> First, dreams express our deepest fears.
>
> **EXAMPLE:**   ~~First, dreams and fears.~~

1. "To sleep, perchance to dream," wrote Shakespeare in his play *Hamlet*. Many great writers have written about dreams. Such as Lewis Carroll. His famous work *Alice in Wonderland* is dreamlike, in the story, Alice has an adventure with a white rabbit. Another bizarre character is the Queen of Hearts. Who wants to cut off Alice's head.

2. Dreams sometimes leave the dreamer feeling uncomfortable. In Franz Kafka's novella *Metamorphosis*, the main character, Gregor Samsa, wakes up feeling uneasy. Because he has had bad dreams during the night. When he wakes up, Samsa finds himself transformed into a grotesque insect, he realizes that it is not a dream.

3.   The meaning of dreams. Sigmund Freud and his student Carl Jung proposed a theory, they wrote that dreams have a specific purpose. Jung believed that dreamers could learn from their dreams. In his book *Memories, Dreams, and Reflections.* Jung wrote that dreams forced him to think about important things. Such as life and death.

4.   Dreams have been the source of inspiration to many people. According to the Koran. God revealed many truths to Muhammad through dreams. Muhammad then recorded these revelations. In the Bible. God appeared in dreams to many people. Including Joseph. Others have also drawn inspiration from dreams. For instance, the Japanese filmmaker Akira Kurosawa. He recorded his dreams he stated that man is a genius when he is dreaming.

Section 2
**COMMON
SENTENCE
ERRORS**

5.   Dreams have inspired artists, writers, and religious figures. If you have recurring dreams, you might write them down, dreams can be the source of fascinating stories.

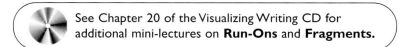

See Chapter 20 of the Visualizing Writing CD for additional mini-lectures on **Run-Ons** and **Fragments.**

Identify Faulty Parallel Structure

It is important to use parallel structure when using a series of words or phrases, paired clauses, comparisons, and two-part constructions.

Series of Words or Phrases

Use parallel structure when words or phrases are joined in a series.

Not parallel:	Students, administrators, and people who teach sometimes volunteer for psychology experiments.
Parallel:	<u>Students</u>, <u>administrators</u>, and <u>teachers</u> sometimes volunteer for psychology experiments.
	(The nouns are parallel.)
Not parallel:	I plan to study for tests, to attend all classes, and listening to the instructor.
Parallel:	I plan <u>to study</u> for tests, <u>to attend</u> all classes, and <u>to listen</u> to the instructor.
	(The verbs are parallel.)

Paired Clauses

Use parallel structure when independent clauses are joined by *and, but,* or *or.*

Not parallel:	The experimenter placed two probes on her head, and her wrist is where he attached a monitor.
Parallel:	The experimenter placed two probes <u>on her head</u>, and he attached a monitor <u>to her wrist</u>.
	(The prepositional phrases are parallel.)
Not parallel:	She felt dizzy, and she also had a feeling of fear.
Parallel:	She felt <u>dizzy</u>, and she also felt <u>afraid</u>.
	(The adjectives are parallel.)

 Use Consistent Voice

When a sentence has two independent clauses and is joined by a coordinating conjunction, use a consistent voice. In other words, if one part of the sentence is active, the other should also be active.

Not parallel:	The researcher conducted the experiment, and then a report was written by him.
Parallel:	The researcher <u>conducted the experiment</u>, and then <u>he wrote a report</u>.
	(Both parts use the active voice.)

Section 2
**COMMON
SENTENCE
ERRORS**

PRACTICE 2

Correct the faulty parallel structure in each sentence.

EXAMPLE:

Some psychology experiments are bold, pioneering, and ~~show their originality.~~ *original.*

1. Ivan Pavlov was a Russian physiologist, a research scientist, and he won a Nobel prize.

2. Pavlov became interested in dog salivation, and digestion also interested him.

3. To get to his lab, Pavlov walked through the door, up the stairs, and the department is where he entered.

4. Pavlov used many sound-making devices to stimulate his dogs, such as metronomes, whistles, and he also used tuning forks.

5. Pavlov noticed that the dogs heard the noise, saw the food dish, and were salivating.

6. Some of the dogs were excited, nervous, and expressed enthusiasm.

7. Western scientists found Pavlov's experiments to be astounding, innovative, and thought they were important.

8. Ivan Pavlov worked quickly and was very efficient.

Section 2
COMMON SENTENCE ERRORS

Comparisons

Use parallel structure in comparisons containing *than* or *as.*

Not parallel:	Creating new experiments is more difficult than to re-create an earlier experiment.
Parallel:	<u>Creating a new experiment</u> is more difficult than <u>re-creating an earlier experiment.</u> (The *-ing* forms are parallel.)
Not parallel:	His home was as messy as the way he kept his laboratory.
Parallel:	His <u>home</u> was as messy as his <u>laboratory.</u> (The nouns are parallel.)

Two-Part Constructions

Use parallel structure for the following paired items.

either . . . or	not . . . but	both . . . and
neither . . . nor	not only . . . but also	rather . . . than

Not parallel: My psychology class was both informative and a challenge.

Parallel: My psychology class was both <u>informative</u> and <u>challenging</u>.
(The adjectives are parallel.)

Not parallel: I would rather finish my experiment than leaving early.

Parallel: I would rather <u>finish</u> my experiment than <u>leave</u> early.
(The verbs are parallel.)

Section 2
**COMMON
SENTENCE
ERRORS**

PRACTICE 3

Correct ten errors in parallel construction.

EXAMPLE:

interesting.

Philip Zimbardo is creative and ~~an interesting person~~.

1. Philip Zimbardo created an experiment that was both unique and startled others. The Stanford Prison Experiment examined how ordinary people would react when placed in positions of power. He chose twenty-four students who were healthy, stable, and they abided the law. Each subject would be either a guard or a prisoner for a two-week period.

2. On the first day of the experiment, each guard was told to wear a uniform, carry a baton, and sunglasses were put on. Ordinary people who had committed no crime, who had broken no laws, and been honest were placed in a cold room. The prisoners were not only arrested but the guards also deloused them.

3. Immediately, the experimenters observed shocking behavior. Some of the guards started to act controlling, sadistic, and they abused the prisoners. On the second day, the prisoners rioted and the guards attacked. Some prisoners decided that they would rather leave than continuing with the experiment.

4.   During the next few days, officials, priests, and teachers observed the experiment. Nobody questioned the morality of the proceedings. Then, on the sixth day, another psychologist arrived. She was appalled and she felt horror when she realized what was happening.

5.   Zimbardo realized that his student actors were taking the experiment too seriously. Both the prisoners and the people playing the guards had to stop the experiment. Zimbardo worried that the student actors would be seriously hurt, distressed, and suffer from depression.

Section 2
**COMMON
SENTENCE
ERRORS**

PRACTICE 4

Correct nine errors in parallel construction.

EXAMPLE:

                                                              interesting.
Information about bystander apathy is surprising and ~~of interest.~~

1.   Bystander apathy is the unwillingness of an individual to help another in an emergency. In the 1960s, psychologists started to collect data, investigate behaviors, and proposing theories about bystander apathy. One celebrated instance of bystander apathy is the Kitty Genovese case.

2.   On March 13, 1964, Kitty Genovese was on her way to her apartment in Queens, New York. She was walking quietly and her steps were quick. Suddenly, she saw a strange man. He attacked her, and she screamed for help. Kitty Genovese died slowly, violently, and in tragic circumstances.

3.   The police investigation was complete, thorough, and done with precision. The results of the investigation were both astounding and were not expected. Apparently, thirty-eight people heard the victim screaming, and the attack was watched by some of them, but no one called the police.

4.   Many psychologists have studied the phenomenon of bystander apathy, and the results have been published by them. There are many reasons a bystander may not help someone in trouble. Bystanders may not want to

risk their own lives, they may not have the skills to help in an emergency, or legal problems could be incurred. In addition, many people do not want to look stupid or be seen as being foolish if there is no real emergency. Psychologists believe that these are only some possible reasons for bystander apathy.

Section 2
**COMMON
SENTENCE
ERRORS**

PRACTICE 5

Write sentences using parallel structure with the following grammatical items.

1. Parallel nouns: _____

   _____

2. Parallel verbs: _____

   _____

3. Parallel adjectives: _____

   _____

4. Parallel *who* phrases: _____

   _____

The Writer's Desk **Revise and Edit Your Warm Up**

In the Warm Up on page 320, you wrote a short paragraph about the personality of a family member or friend. Check for any sentences that contain faulty parallel structure and correct your mistakes.

REFLECT ON IT

Think about what you have learned in this chapter. If you do not know an answer, review that concept.

1. What is parallel structure? _____

   _____

2. Why is parallel structure important? _____

   _____

Fill in the blanks of the following sentences. Make sure the grammatical structures are parallel.

3. The college I attend is both _____ and _____.

4. In my spare time, I _____, _____, and _____.

FINAL REVIEW

Correct twelve errors in parallel construction.

EXAMPLE:

counselors

Psychiatrists, psychologists, and ~~other people who are counselors~~ help patients deal with their mental health problems.

1.   In 1972, psychologist David Rosenhan was young, intelligent, and had enthusiasm. He asked eight of his friends to participate in a psychology experiment. There were some psychologists, a pediatrician, a psychiatrist, a man who was a painter, a homemaker, and a graduate student. Rosenhan told the participants that for five days they had to stop showering, they had to look unclean, and they were wearing old clothes. At the end of the fifth day, the participants traveled to different parts of the country and entered various psychiatric hospital emergency rooms. The psychiatric hospitals were either private and expensive or public and they cost very little. The participants told the admitting psychiatrists that they heard voices. They told the truth about everything else in their lives.

2.   Psychiatrists looked for and were finding serious psychological illnesses in the patients. They diagnosed all eight patients with paranoid schizophrenia. The doctors institutionalized the patients from eight to fifty-eight days. Rosenhan's experiment showed that psychiatric evaluation had to be both stringent and have no bias.

3.   Lauren Slater is a researcher, psychologist, and she writes. In 2003, she decided to reenact Rosenhan's experiment to see if assessment methods in psychiatry had changed. She became the guinea pig in her own experiment. Like Rosenhan's friends, she looked scruffy, she visited different psychiatric institutions, and she was telling the psychiatrists about voices in her head. Psychiatrists asked her neither about her religious beliefs, nor was she asked anything about her cultural background. The examining psychiatrists

Section 2
COMMON SENTENCE ERRORS

asked her some general questions, took her temperature, and she was diagnosed by them with depression.

4.　　Slater knew she did not really suffer from depression because she had asked her real doctor, her family, and her people who were her friends to assess her mental state. Unlike the psychiatrists in Rosenham's experiment, Slater's psychiatrists did not admit her to their hospitals, but they all prescribed antipsychotic and antidepressant drugs for her. She wrote about her experiences in her book *Opening Skinner's Box*. Her book is well written and it is of interest.

Section 2
COMMON SENTENCE ERRORS

 Topics for Writing

Choose one of the following topics and write a paragraph or an essay. When you write, remember to follow the writing process.

1. Explain why people are superstitious, and list some common superstitions.
2. Describe a set of twins. Compare the twins, looking at their similarities and differences.
3. In 2004, some American soldiers in Iraq were photographed abusing prisoners. Many of the accused soldiers argued that they were simply following orders. How valid is the "following orders" defense? You could refer to the Milgram experiment described on page 321.
4. What are some different ways that people deal with their fears? Classify responses to fear into three categories.

 The Writers' Circle

READING LINK

Psychology
"Dealing with People" by Greg McGrew (page 533)
"Religious Faith Versus Spirituality" by Neil Bissoondath (page 589)
"Dancing with Fear" by Bebe Moore Campbell (page 560)
"Interview with Jimmy Baca" by Elizabeth Farnsworth (page 562)
"The Never-Ending Question: Who Am I" by Raúl Reyes (page 557)
"The Diagnosis" by Richard Selzer (page 586)
"Dying to Be Bigger" by H. D. (page 575)

When you apply for a job, the employer often asks you what your strengths and weaknesses are. Work with a team of students to do the following activity.

STEP 1 Think of a successful person. You could choose a person from any of the next categories.

A business tycoon	A politician	A movie star
A rap artist	An athlete	A writer or artist

STEP 2 Brainstorm one list of that person's strengths and another list of that person's weaknesses.

STEP 3   Write a short paragraph about that successful person, discussing the person's strengths and weaknesses.

STEP 4   Exchange paragraphs with another team. Proofread the other team's paragraph, checking especially for fragments, run-ons, and parallel structure.

 See Chapter 21 of the Visualizing Writing CD for an additional mini-lecture on **Parallelism.**

Section 2
**COMMON
SENTENCE
ERRORS**

Present Tense of *Work*

	Singular	Plural
First person:	I work.	We work.
Second person:	You work.	You work.
Third person:	He works.	They work.
	She works.	
	It works.	

Irregular Present Tense Verbs (*be* and *have*)

In the present tense, *be* and *have* do not follow the regular pattern for verb endings. Be particularly careful when writing these verbs.

Present Tense of *Be*

I am	He is	You are
	She is	We are
	It is	They are

Present Tense of *Have*

I have	He has	You have
	She has	We have
		They have

Section 3
**PROBLEMS
WITH VERBS**

GRAMMAR LINK

For more information about subject-verb agreement, see Chapter 25.

 Make Your Subjects and Verbs Agree

In the present tense, the subject and verb must **agree** in number. If the subject is third-person singular (*he, she, it*), the corresponding verb must have the singular form, too.

Although plural nouns usually end in *-s*, plural verbs do not. Instead, singular verbs have the *-s* or *-es* ending. Notice the errors in subject-verb agreement in the next sentences.

works
Edward Rowen ~~work~~ for the Central Intelligence Agency. Why ~~do~~ the *does*
does
agency investigate candidates? It ~~do~~ not want to hire people with criminal records.

PRACTICE I

Circle the correct present tense form of the verbs in parentheses.

EXAMPLE:

Spying (seem, (seems)) like an exciting job.

1. Men and women (betray, betrays) their country for many reasons.

2. According to Christopher Andrew, co-author of *The Sword and the Shield*, the acronym *mice* (sum, sums) up the reasons why a person may become a traitor.

3. *Mice* (stand, stands) for "money, ideology, compromise, and ego."

4. According to Andrew, the most popular reason (is, are) money.

5. Some agents (receive, receives) millions in cash, jewelry, and so on.

6. Another reason (is, are) ideology.

7. Maybe the spy (dislike, dislikes) his or her own political system.

8. Sometimes people (believe, believes) that another country's way of life is better.

9. Some men and women (become, becomes) spies because they are ashamed of something that they have done.

10. For example, if a government bureaucrat (steal, steals) money and another person (find, finds) out, the bureaucrat can be blackmailed to become a spy.

11. Finally, many people (think, thinks) that spies (is, are) celebrities.

12. Andrew (say, says) that "an interesting minority want to be secret celebrities" in their own little world of espionage.

Section 3
**PROBLEMS
WITH VERBS**

Present Tense: Negative and Question Forms

In negative and question forms, you must add a helping verb (*do* or *does*). If the subject is third-person singular, use the helping verb *does*.

Questions:	**Do** you <u>know</u> about the Spy Museum in Washington?
	Does the museum <u>open</u> on weekends?
Negatives:	We **do** not <u>live</u> in Washington. (Contraction: **don't** live)
	The museum **does** not <u>open</u> on holidays. (Contraction: **doesn't** open)

When the main verb is *be* (*is, am, are*), just add *not*.

Questions:	**Is** the spy story suspenseful?
	Are foreign spies in the city?
Negatives:	The story **is not** suspenseful. (Contraction: **isn't**)
	Foreign spies **are not** in the city. (Contraction: **aren't**)

A Note About Contractions

In informal writing, it is acceptable to contract negative verb forms. However, you should avoid using contractions in your academic writing.

does not
The CIA ~~doesn't~~ have enough multilingual interpreters.

Use the Correct Question and Negative Forms

In question and negative forms, always use the base form of the main verb, even when the subject is third-person singular. Put the *-s* or *-es* ending only on the helping verb (*does*).

have
Why does the Spy Museum ~~has~~ so many spy gadgets?

contain
A tube of blood-red lipstick does not ~~contains~~ lipstick at all.

PRACTICE 2

In the spaces provided, write the correct present tense forms of the verbs in parentheses.

EXAMPLES:

Washington's Spy Museum (have) _____*has*_____ a collection of spy cameras.

It (have, not) _*does not have*_ paintings.

Section 3
PROBLEMS WITH VERBS

1. In Washington, D.C., the International Spy Museum (have) _____ hundreds of spy gadgets. For example, on display is a tube of lipstick. The tube (have, not) _____ an obvious function. It (add, not) _____ color to a person's lips. Instead, it (conceal) _____ a tiny pistol.

2. The museum also (display) _____ interesting spy cameras. One camera (be) _____ inside a wristwatch. The best spy camera, the Minox, (be, not) _____ very large. It (have) _____ a high-resolution lens and it (need, not) _____ to be frequently reloaded.

3. Today, spy tools (be) _____ extremely complex and sophisticated. With microtechnology, cameras (be, not) _____ as large as they used to be. New recording devices (be) _____ extremely sensitive. A microphone (have, not) _____ to be in the room to pick up a conversation.

4. Clearly, the Spy Museum (be) _____ an extremely interesting place. Tourists (have, not) _____ to spend the entire day at the museum because it (be, not) _____ a very large place. If you (be) _____ in Washington, D.C., and you (have) _____ some spare time, try to visit the Spy Museum.

The Simple Past Tense

The **simple past tense** indicates that an action occurred at a specific past time. In the past tense, there are regular and irregular verbs. **Regular verbs** end in *-d* or *-ed* (*talked, ended, watched*). **Irregular verbs** do not follow a regular pattern and do not end in any specific letter (*knew, saw, met*).

 The Past Progressive

The **past progressive tense** indicates that an action was in progress at a particular past moment. In this chapter, you will focus on the simple past.

past progressive tense
While the detectives <u>were watching</u> the house, the suspect escaped.

Section 3
PROBLEMS WITH VERBS

Regular Past Tense Verbs

Regular past tense verbs have a standard *-d* or *-ed* ending. Use the same form for both singular and plural past tense verbs.

Singular subject:	One well-known agent **learned** to speak twelve languages.
Plural subject:	During World War II, secret agents **used** codes to communicate.

 Spell Regular Past Tense Verbs Correctly

Most regular past tense verbs are formed by adding *-ed* to the base form of the verb.

walk<u>ed</u>   question<u>ed</u>

However, there are some exceptions.

• When the regular verb ends in -e, just add -d.

realiz<u>ed</u>   appreciat<u>ed</u>

• When the regular verb ends in consonant + -y, change the y to i and add -ed.

reply, repl<u>ied</u>   try, tr<u>ied</u>

When the regular verb ends in the vowel -y, just add -ed.

play<u>ed</u>   employ<u>ed</u>

• When the regular verb ends in a consonant-vowel-consonant combination, double the last consonant and add -ed.

tap, tap<u>ped</u>   plan, plan<u>ned</u>

GRAMMAR LINK

See Chapter 32, "Spelling and Commonly Confused Words," for more information about the spelling of verbs.

PRACTICE 3

Write the simple past form of each verb in parentheses. Make sure you spell the past tense verb correctly.

EXAMPLE:
The U.S. government (form)__*formed*__ the Federal Bureau of Investigation in 1908 to detect enemy spies in the country.

1.   In 1924, the FBI (hire) _____ J. Edgar Hoover to be the director of the Bureau. During the Hoover years, the FBI (improve) _____ training. The agency (plan) _____ to use modern technological investigative methods. During the 1930s, Americans (treat) _____ Hoover as a hero because the FBI (carry) _____ out raids against gangsters such as Al Capone.

2.   However, Hoover also had a dark side. His agents (snoop) _____ on politicians and celebrities. For example, agents (spy) _____ on the Kennedy brothers and on Dr. Martin Luther King Jr. According to King's widow and others, the FBI director (act) _____ unethically.

3.   In 1994, biographer Anthony Summer wrote a book about Hoover. According to Summer, Hoover (study) _____ the private lives of the eight presidents whom he served under. Some presidents (worry) _____ that Hoover would disclose secrets about them. Hoover (retain) _____ his top position at the FBI for forty-eight years, until his death in 1972.

Section 3
PROBLEMS WITH VERBS

GRAMMAR LINK

See Appendix 2 for a complete list of irregular verbs.

Irregular Past Tense Verbs

Irregular verbs change internally. Because their spellings change from the present to the past tense, these verbs can be challenging to remember. For example, the irregular verb *go* becomes *went* when you convert it to the past tense.

The prisoner <u>wrote</u> with invisible ink. (wrote = past tense of *write*)

The guards <u>sent</u> the letter. (sent = past tense of *send*)

The prisoners <u>began</u> a revolt. (began = past tense of *begin*)

Do Not Confuse *Past* and *Passed*

Some people confuse *past* and *passed*. *Past* is a noun that means "in a previous time" or "before now."

> She has many secrets in her <u>past</u>.

> Her mistakes are in the <u>past</u>.

Passed is the past tense of the verb *pass,* which has many meanings. In the first example below, it means "to go by." In the second example, it means "to take something and give it to someone." In the last example, it means "to successfully complete."

> Many days <u>passed</u>, and the nights got shorter.

> Please <u>pass</u> the salt. I <u>passed</u> you the butter a moment ago.

> He <u>passed</u> the entrance test. Did you <u>pass</u> your test?

Section 3
PROBLEMS
WITH VERBS

PRACTICE 4

Write the correct past form of each verb in parentheses. Some verbs are regular, and some are irregular. If you do not know the past form of an irregular verb, consult Appendix 2.

EXAMPLE:

During the American Revolution, armies (write) <u>wrote</u> letters with invisible ink.

1. In 1775, an American soldier named Benjamin Thompson (use) _____ ferrous sulphate and water; when mixed together, the substances (turn) _____ into invisible ink. Later, the reader of the letter (put) _____ it over a candle flame, and the ink (become) _____ brown. The lines with the invisible ink (appear) _____ between the lines of the regular letter.

2. More recently, during World War II, a mysterious person (send) _____ a postcard to Jacob Rosenblum, a resident of Bucharest, Romania. The postcard, dated August 20, 1943, (come) _____ from a death camp and (have) _____ one line. In German, the letter (say) _____, "My darling, I remember you with love" and was signed "Lola." Underneath the black writing, a message (appear) _____ in invisible ink. In that message, the author (speak) _____ of "starvation, degradation, killing by gas," and "an

agonizing hell." The letter writer also (request) _____ signal pistols and invisible ink. The letter (end) _____ with the mysterious words "K is fulfilling his mission. We will do what we have to do."

3. During past wars, people (find) _____ many ways to make invisible ink, and they (pass) _____ secret messages to others. For example, soldiers (make) _____ ink out of acidic liquids such as lemon juice and vinegar. When a soldier (write) _____ with such substances, the ink would later turn brown when heated. In the past, some prisoners of war even (use) _____ their own sweat and saliva to make invisible ink.

Section 3
PROBLEMS WITH VERBS

be (*was* or *were*)

Past tense verbs generally have one form that you can use with all subjects. However, the verb *be* has two past forms: *was* and *were*.

Past Tense of Be

	Singular	Plural
First person:	I was	We were
Second person:	You were	You were
Third person:	He was	They were
	She was	
	It was	

PRACTICE 5

Write *was* or *were* in each space provided.

EXAMPLE:

Robert Barron _was_ not an ordinary artist.

1. During the 1970s, Robert Barron worked for the Pentagon. He _____ not happy with his parking spot because he always had to walk a long way to get to his job. One day, when he _____ alone, he created a perfect fake parking permit. Some other employees _____ aware of what Barron had done, and they told superior officers about it. Barron had to pay a fine. As it happened, some CIA agents _____ impressed with Barron's artistic talents.

2.   Soon, Barron joined the graphic arts department at the CIA. He became

an expert at creating disguises for secret agents, and he _____

happy with his new job. Barron and other artists _____ very

creative, and they made false noses, foreheads, and chins so that agents

could look completely different. Some artists _____ experts

at creating false mustaches, beards, wigs, and teeth. The disguises

_____ important because disguised defectors needed to pass

army checkpoints and borders.

Problems with *be, have,* and *do*

Some writers find it particularly difficult to remember how to use the irregular
verbs *be, have,* and *do* in the past tense. Here are some helpful guidelines.

Avoiding Common Errors with *be*

■ Use *were* in the past tense when the subject is plural. Do not use *was*.

> The spies ~~was~~ arrested in 1965.
> *(were)*

■ Use the standard form of the verb (*is* or *was*), not *be*.

> The camera ~~be~~ small enough to fit in a pen.
> *(was)*

Avoiding Common Errors with *have*

■ Use the past form of the verb (*had*), not the present form (*have* or *has*), when
speaking about a past event.

> The prisoner ~~has~~ to write messages with invisible ink during
> the war.
> *(had)*

Avoiding Common Errors with *do*

■ Use *done* only when it is preceded by a helping verb (*was done, is done,* and so on).

> Barron ~~done~~ an interview with the press yesterday.
> *(did)*

Section 3
**PROBLEMS
WITH VERBS**

PRACTICE 6

Correct ten verb errors. If the verb is incorrectly formed, or if the verb is in the
wrong tense, write the correct form above it.

EXAMPLE:

Some people ~~has~~ very little respect for pigeons.
(have)

1.   Most city dwellers believes that pigeons are nuisances. For example,

at my apartment building, the owner done many things last year to keep pigeons off the balconies. However, people undervalue pigeons. During past wars, the homing pigeon has an important role in international espionage.

2.   During the Napoleonic wars, homing pigeons gived officials a crucial way to communicate. The small birds carried and delivered secret messages because they was able to fly over enemy territories. Those pigeons be able to transmit messages faster than soldiers on horses, and they haved legendary endurance.

3.   According to Richard Platt's book *Spy*, Roman emperor Julius Caesar also used birds to send messages. Pigeons be valued for their speed, size, and reliability. Additionally, over half a million pigeons taked messages to soldiers during World War I, and some soldiers actually hided pigeons in their pockets and cared for them on battlefields. We should appreciate pigeons because they played an important role in previous wars.

Section 3
**PROBLEMS
WITH VERBS**

Hint   Use the Base Form After *Did* and *To*

Remember to use the base form of verbs that follow *did* (question and negative forms) or *to* (infinitive form).

       use
Did he ~~used~~ invisible ink?

             study
Greenstein wanted to ~~studied~~ the postcard.

PRACTICE 7

The next selection contains verb tense, spelling, and *past* vs. *passed* errors. Correct fifteen errors.

EXAMPLE:

         describe
Many books ~~describes~~ the Navaho code talkers of World War II.

1.   Navaho be an incredibly complex language with complicated syntax and tonal qualities. It has no alphabet or written forms, and only Native

Americans in the Southwest speaks it. During World War II, Navaho natives maked an important contribution to the Allied war effort.

2. During the war, Japanese and German troops tapped Allied communication lines and listen to the messages. Japanese code breakers was particularly capable. They managed to figured out every code that the Allies came up with. In 1942, the Marines get hundreds of Navaho volunteers to relayed coded messages about military plans. The Navahos past messages using their language, and they be very efficient code talkers. They call fighter planes "hummingbirds" and submarines "iron fish."

3. The Japanese tought that they could figure out the messages. They work hard, but they did not managed to break the Navaho code. After the war ended, the Navahos did not received recognition for their important work as code talkers until 1969.

Avoid Double Negatives

A double negative occurs when a negative word such as *no nothing, nobody,* or *nowhere* is combined with a negative adverb such as *not, never, rarely,* or *seldom.* The result is a sentence that has a double negative. Such sentences can be confusing because the negative words cancel each other.

The agent <u>does not</u> have <u>no</u> children. (According to this sentence, the agent has children.)

He <u>didn't</u> know <u>nothing</u> about it. (According to this sentence, he knows something about it.)

How to Correct Double Negatives

There are two ways to correct double negatives.

- Completely remove one of the negative forms.

Incorrect: The agent doesn't have no children.
Correct: The agent **doesn't** have children.
The agent has **no** children.

Incorrect: He didn't know nothing about the crime.
Correct: He knew **nothing** about the crime.
He **didn't** know about the crime.

■ Change *no* to *any (anybody, anything, anywhere)*.

Incorrect:	The agent doesn't have no children.
Correct:	The agent doesn't have **any** children.
Incorrect:	He didn't know nothing about the crime.
Correct:	He didn't know **anything** about the crime.

Section 3
**PROBLEMS
WITH VERBS**

PRACTICE 8

Correct the six errors with double negatives. You can correct each error in more than one way.

EXAMPLES:

Mata Hari didn't have ~~no~~ ^{any} close friends.

Mata Hari ~~didn't have~~ ^{had} no close friends.

1. In 1875, Mata Haris Dutch parents named her Margareta Zelle. At the age of eighteen, she married a much older naval officer. Her husband was an alcoholic, and Zelle didn't see no reason to stay with him. Zelle left, and she didn't take none of her furniture or clothing.

2. Zelle didn't have no marketable skills. She decided to become an exotic dancer. She changed her name to Mata Hari and performed authentic Hindu temple dances. She never said nothing to her parents about her new career choice.

3. Due to her beauty, she attracted many influential men, such as the German crown prince and high-ranking German officers. Their wives didn't say nothing nice about Mata Hari. Her career as a dancer lasted for about ten years.

4. According to her biographer, Erika Ostrovsky, Mata Hari became a spy for the Germans in 1914, and her code name was H 21. One day, French officials intercepted a German secret service telegram. They identified Mata Hari's code name and accused her of espionage. Mata Hari said that she didn't do nothing wrong. However, the French courts found her guilty of espionage. In 1918, a firing squad executed her.

The Writer's Desk **Revise and Edit Your Warm Up**

Review the sentences that you wrote in the Warm Up on page 330. Make sure that your regular and irregular verbs are spelled correctly.

REFLECT ON IT

Think about what you have learned in this chapter. If you do not know an answer, review that concept.

1. What are the present and past forms of the verb *be*?

	Present	Past
I	_____	_____
he, she, it	_____	_____
you, we, they	_____	_____

2. Write an example of a regular past tense verb. _____

3. Write an example of an irregular past tense verb. _____

4. What is the simple past form of the following verbs?

   a. think: _____   c. have: _____

   b. mention: _____   d. go: _____

5. Correct one verb tense error in each of the following sentences.

   a. In 1954, a Russian agent surrender to the United States.

   b. Khokhlov defected because he did not wanted to kill another Russian agent.

   c. Khokhlov past many days and nights wondering whether he should give

      himself up.

   d. The agent owned a cigarette case that be a secret weapon.

   e. The cigarette case fired bullets that was poisonous.

Section 3
PROBLEMS WITH VERBS

FINAL REVIEW

Correct fifteen errors in present and past tense verbs.

EXAMPLE:

When people talk about espionage, they generally ~~thinks~~ *think* about secret agents who work for governments.

1. Industrial espionage occurs when companies spy on each other. It be a

    major problem. A nation's economic survival depend on its ability to be

    innovative in the industrial sector. For example, in 1994, a large company

Regular Verbs

The past tense and the past participle of regular verbs are the same.

Base Form	Past Tense	Past Participle
walk	walked	walked
try	tried	tried
use	used	used

Irregular Verbs

The past tense and the past participle of irregular verbs may be different. For a complete list of irregular past participles, see Appendix 2.

Base Form	Past Tense	Past Participle
begin	began	begun
go	went	gone
speak	spoke	spoken

Section 3
PROBLEMS WITH VERBS

PRACTICE 1

Each group of verbs contains one error. Underline the error, and write the correct word in the space provided.

EXAMPLE:

BASE FORM	PAST TENSE	PAST PARTICIPLE	
lose	<u>losed</u>	lost	_lost_
1. cost	cost	costed	_____
2. come	came	came	_____
3. build	builded	built	_____
4. sink	sank	sank	_____
5. bring	brang	brought	_____
6. write	wrote	wrote	_____
7. choose	choosed	chosen	_____
8. fall	felt	fallen	_____
9. feel	felt	fell	_____
10. blow	blew	blowed	_____
11. tear	tore	tore	_____
12. take	taked	taken	_____
13. bite	bited	bitten	_____
14. sit	sat	sitten	_____
15. grow	grew	growed	_____

PRACTICE 2

In the following selection, all irregular past participles are underlined. Correct ten past participle errors.

EXAMPLE:

We have <u>meeted</u> ~~met~~ many times to discuss the problem.

met

1.   Spying on children is not new; in fact, parents have <u>did</u> it for centuries.
Parents have <u>read</u> their children's diaries, and some have <u>gone</u> through
their children's belongings. However, in recent years, the methods used to
spy have <u>became</u> more sophisticated.

2.   According to John Stossel of ABC News, some parents have <u>bought</u> video
cameras and miniature tape recorders to spy on their children. For
example, in 2002, the Roy family bought a small video camera. It was <u>hided</u>
behind a plant in the living room, and their son, Samuel, was not <u>told</u> that
the camera was there. One evening, while his parents were out, Samuel was
<u>catched</u> on the video camera smoking and drinking with friends. When the
boy was <u>shown</u> the tape, he admitted that he had <u>taked</u> the alcohol. The
parents insist that they have <u>tought</u> their child a valuable lesson.

3.   Another spy tool can track the speed of a driver. A Miami father, Ed Jarvis,
has <u>putted</u> the device in his car so that he can monitor his son's driving.
Recently, Ed punished his son, David, when he realized that the boy had
<u>broke</u> the law. The device proved that David had <u>drove</u> over the speed
limit. David's reaction was harsh: "The only thing my father has <u>done</u> is
make me angry. He has no faith in me."

4.   The issue about spying on children is controversial. Some people believe
that parents should snoop. Parents have the right to know if their teenagers
have <u>maked</u> serious mistakes. Others claim that spying can break the bonds
of trust between a parent and a child. If you were a parent, would you spy
on your children?

Section 3
**PROBLEMS
WITH VERBS**

The Present Perfect Tense: *have/has* + Past Participle

A past participle combines with *have* or *has* to form the **present perfect tense.** You can use this tense in two different circumstances.

- Use the present perfect to show that an action began in the past and continues to the present time. You will often use *since* and *for* with this tense.

PAST   NOW

I **have been** a James Bond fan for five years.

Section 3
PROBLEMS WITH VERBS

- Use the present perfect to show that one or more completed actions occurred at unspecified past times.

PAST (unspecified past times)   NOW
?   ?   ?   ?

I **have watched** at least four James Bond movies.

 Use Time Markers

Time markers are words that indicate when an action occurred.

Simple Past Tense
To refer to an incident that occurred at a specific past time, use the following time markers.

yesterday	ago	when I was . . .	last (week, month, year . . .)
in the past	in 2005	during the 1970s	in the early days of . . .

Ian Fleming **wrote** his first novel <u>in 1953</u>.

Present Perfect Tense
- To refer to an action that began in the past and is still continuing, use the following time markers.

since	for (a period of time up to now)	ever
up to now	so far	not . . . yet

Spy films **have been** popular <u>since the 1930s</u>.

- To refer to an action that occurred at unspecified past times, use the following time markers.

once	twice	three times
many	several times	
lately	recently	

I **have seen** *The World is Not Enough* <u>once</u> and *Die Another Day* <u>twice</u>.

Look at the difference between the past and the present perfect tenses.

Simple past: In 1962, Sean Connery <u>appeared</u> in the first James Bond film, *Dr. No.*

(This event occurred at a known past time.)

Present perfect: Many different actors <u>have played</u> James Bond.

(We do not really know when the actors played James Bond.)

James Bond movies <u>have been</u> popular for more than forty years.

(The action began in the past and continues to the present.)

PRACTICE 3

Write the simple past or present perfect form of each verb in parentheses.

EXAMPLE:

For the last six years, my cousin Mike (be) ___*has been*___ a James Bond fanatic.

Section 3
**PROBLEMS
WITH VERBS**

1. Spy fans around the world (watch) _____ James Bond movies

    since the mid-1960s. Although most people (hear) _____ of

    James Bond, few people know about the man behind the movies.

2. Ian Fleming was born in 1906, and his father (be) _____ a

    successful stockbroker. As a result, Ian (spend) _____ his youth

    living a high-class lifestyle. In the 1940s, the British Secret Service (draft)

    _____ Ian Fleming because he could easily mix with

    upper-class officials.

3. In 1953, Fleming (use) _____ his experiences to create his first

    James Bond book. Since then, James Bond (be) _____ extremely

    popular. Over the last forty years, viewers around the world (see)

    _____ the sophisticated spy in action.

4. Since the first film, the James Bond character (age, never) _____.

    For more than forty years, beautiful women (try) _____ to seduce

    him and villains (try) _____ to kill him. Over and over, Bond

    (escape) _____ danger by using his intelligence, his fast cars,

    and his secret weapons. Since its debut, the James Bond character (capture)

    _____ the audience's imagination.

The Past Perfect Tense: *had* + Past Participle

The **past perfect tense** indicates that one or more past actions happened before another past action. It is formed with *had* and the past participle.

```
        PAST PERFECT              PAST            NOW
            ▼                      ▼               ▼
◄───────────────────────────────────────────────────────►
        The robbers **had left** when the police arrived.
```

Notice the differences between the simple past, the present perfect, and the past perfect tenses.

Section 3
**PROBLEMS
WITH VERBS**

Simple past:	Last night I <u>rented</u> *Austin Powers, Goldmember*.
	(The action occurred at a known past time.)
Present perfect:	I <u>have seen</u> all of the *Austin Powers* movies.
	(The actions occurred at unspecified past times.)
Past perfect:	When Myers wrote *Goldmember*, he <u>had</u> already <u>produced</u> two successful *Austin Powers* movies.
	(All of the actions happened in the past, but Myers produced two movies before he wrote *Goldmember*.)

PRACTICE 4

Circle the correct verb forms. You may choose the simple past, the present perfect, or the past perfect tense.

EXAMPLE:

Even though we (saw, ⟨had seen⟩) *Austin Powers*, we watched it again.

1. Mike Myers, a Canadian actor and comedian, was born in 1963. When Myers was a child, his British father (introduced, had introduced) him to James Bond movies and Monty Python comedies. His mother, a trained actress, (read, had read) books to him using various British accents.

2. At the age of eight, Myers (began, has begun, had begun) acting in television commercials. Later, when he became a professional comedian, he was comfortable in front of the camera because he (already did, has already done, had already done) many commercials. In 1989, producer Lorne Michaels (hired, has hired, had hired) Myers as an actor and writer for *Saturday Night Live*. From 1989 to 1995, Myers (created, had created)

characters such as Dieter, the New Age film critic, and Wayne, the heavy-metal enthusiast. The characters were inspired by people whom Myers (knew, had known) in high school.

3.   In 1995, Mike Myers (heard, has heard) a song called "The Look of Love" on the radio. The song reminded him of the British shows he (has seen, had seen) as a child. When he got home, he (started, has started, had started) speaking to his wife in a British accent: "Hey baby, you are one smashing bird. I think you're fabulous." His wife (has heard, had heard) her husband speaking like a British spy for three days when she finally convinced him to write a script. The result (be, was, had been) the successful *Austin Powers* series. Today, millions of people (saw, have seen) the Austin Powers spy comedies.

The Passive Voice: *be* + Past Participle

In sentences with the **passive voice,** the subject receives the action and does not perform the action. Look carefully at the next two sentences.

Active: The diplomat **gave** secret documents to an undercover agent.

(This is active because the subject, *diplomat,* performed the action.)

Passive: Secrets documents **were given** to an undercover agent.

(This is passive because the subject, *documents,* was affected by the action and did not perform the action.)

To form the passive voice, use the appropriate tense of the verb *be* plus the past participle.

Verb Tenses	Active Voice	Passive Voice: *be* + Past Participle
	(The subject performs the action.)	(The subject receives the action.)
Simple present	She writes spy stories.	Spy stories <u>are</u> written (by her).
Present progressive	is writing	<u>are being</u> written
Simple past	wrote	<u>were</u> written
Present perfect	has written	<u>have been</u> written
Future	will write	<u>will be</u> written
Modals	can write	<u>can be</u> written
	could write	<u>could be</u> written
	should write	<u>should be</u> written
	would have written	<u>would have been</u> written

PRACTICE 5

Decide whether each underlined verb is active or passive. Write *A* (for "active")
or *P* (for "passive") above each verb.

EXAMPLE:

P A

Many ordinary citizens <u>have been recruited</u> as spies even though the work <u>is</u>
dangerous.

1. During times of war, armies <u>have used</u> both scouts and spies. Army scouts

    <u>can wear</u> their full uniform. They <u>are sent</u> ahead of advancing forces. Spies,

    on the other hand, <u>wear</u> disguises and <u>try</u> to blend in with the regular

    population.

2. Spying <u>is</u> much more dangerous than scouting because captured scouts

    <u>are treated</u> as prisoners of war. A captured spy, on the other hand,

    <u>may be executed</u> immediately. In spite of the obvious dangers, many

    people <u>are attracted</u> to the field of espionage because they <u>love</u> excitement

    and danger.

Hint **The *by* . . . Phrase**

In many passive sentences, it is not necessary to write the *by* . . . phrase because the
noun performing the action is understood.

    CIA agents are selected according to their abilities.
    (Adding "by CIA recruiters" after "selected" is not necessary.)

PRACTICE 6

A. Complete the following sentences by changing each italicized verb to the
passive form. Do not alter the verb tense. Note: You do not have to include the
by . . . phrase.

EXAMPLE:

The supervisor *spies* on the workers.

The workers <u>are spied on (by the supervisor)</u>.

1. Sometimes employers *place* spy cameras in their factories.

   Sometimes spy cameras _____

   _____

2. Last year, Mr. Roy *installed* three surveillance cameras.

   Last year, three surveillance cameras _____

   _____

3. The video cameras *filmed* some sleeping workers.

   Some sleeping workers _____

   _____

4. As a result, the boss *has fired* three technicians.

   As a result, three technicians _____

   _____

B. The following sentences are in the passive voice. Change them to the active voice, but do not alter the verb tense.

EXAMPLE:

The workers *are spied* on by the bosses.

The bosses <u>spy on the workers.</u>_____

5. For months, Kurt's privacy *has been violated* by the cameras.

   For months, the cameras _____

   _____

6. Last week, a complaint *was made* to the American Civil Liberties Union by Kurt.

   Last week, Kurt _____

   _____

7. The case *will be investigated* by the union.

   The union _____

   _____

8. Complaints about privacy *are often ignored* by companies.

   Companies _____

   _____

Avoid Overusing the Passive Voice

Generally, use the active voice instead of the passive voice. The active voice is more direct and less wordy than the passive voice. For example, read the next two versions of the same message.

Passive voice: The problem has been rectified by us, and a new order is being prepared for you. You will be contacted by our sales department.

Active voice: We have corrected the problem and are preparing a new order for you. Our sales department will contact you.

In rare cases when you do not know who did the action, the passive voice may be more appropriate.

James Bond's miniature camera was made in Italy.

(You do not know who made the camera.)

Section 3
PROBLEMS WITH VERBS

PRACTICE 7

Underline examples of the passive voice in the following letter. Then rewrite the letter using the active voice.

Dear Parents,

Security cameras have been installed in our school for several reasons. First, intruders have been seen by students. Also, if fighting is done by students, the scenes will be recorded and the culprits will be caught. In addition, any vandalism to school property can be viewed by our staff. For further information, we can be contacted at any time during school hours.

Sincerely,
Tony Romano, Principal, Rosedale High School

_____

_____

_____

_____

_____

_____

_____

_____

Be Careful!

In the passive voice, sometimes the verb *be* is suggested but not written. The following sentence contains the passive voice.

                 that were
Many activities done in the 1920s are still common today.

PRACTICE 8

Underline and correct ten errors in past participles.

EXAMPLE:

       enjoyed
I have ~~enjoy~~ some great spy novels.

1. British authors have create some of the best spy novels. Even John Le Carré was really name David Cornwell, and he was borned in Dorset, England, in 1931. Le Carré incorporated his own espionage experiences into his writing. In 2000, in a BBC documentary, Le Carré admitted that he was recruit by the British spy agency, the MI5, in 1959. He spied for many years, and when he studied at Oxford, he even spied on fellow students.

2. Many of Le Carré's novels were influence by his childhood experiences. Le Carré never met his own mother until he was twenty-one. He was raise by his father, Ronnie Cornwell, who was a charismatic con artist. When the senior Cornwell was arrest, he had already swindle millions of British pounds.

3. Although many spy novelists are British, the first complete spy novel was wrote by American author James Fenimore Cooper. *The Spy*, publish in 1852, was about soldiers during the American Revolution.

Section 3
**PROBLEMS
WITH VERBS**

The Writer's Desk **Revise and Edit Your Warm Up**

Review the sentences that you wrote in the Warm Up on page 345. Identify all verbs, and verify that each verb is used and formed correctly. Correct any incorrect or nonstandard verbs.

Section 3
PROBLEMS WITH VERBS

REFLECT ON IT

Think about what you have learned in this chapter. If you do not know an answer, review that concept.

1. What are the simple past and past participle forms of the following verbs?

    EXAMPLE: grow: <u>grew, grown</u>

    a. fly: _____   b. ring: _____

    c. break: _____   d. read: _____

2. Give two circumstances in which you would use the present perfect tense.

    _____

    _____

    _____

    _____

3. When do you use the past perfect tense? _____

    _____

4. How do you form the passive voice? _____

    _____

5. Identify and correct the errors in the following sentences.

    a. Robert Ludlum's first book was publish in 1971.

    b. By 2000, he had wrote twenty-one spy novels.

    c. Millions of people have buyed his novel *The Bourne Identity*.

    d. Have you ever saw a movie that was based on a book by Ludlum?

FINAL REVIEW

Fill in each blank with the appropriate verb tense. The sentence may require active or passive voice.

EXAMPLE:

Cell phone cameras (be) <u>have been</u> on the market since 2003.

1.   Since their debut, cell phone cameras (criticize) _____

_____ by those who are worried about privacy issues. For example, in

2003, cell phone cameras (ban) _____ in many

health clubs. In January 2004, clients in a European spa (film)

_____ by a voyeur in the women's locker room.

Additionally, since 2003, schoolteachers and others who work with the

public (complain) _____ to authorities about the

possible misuse of cell phone cameras in public places. In fact, in 2004, one

government employee's rage (record) _____ by an

astute member of the public.

2.   On the other hand, since their first appearance, cell phone cameras (help)

_____ some people. In August 2003, a fifteen-year-

old boy (approach) _____ by a stranger in a white

car. The boy (ask) _____ by the strange man to get

into the car. The boy refused and walked away after he (take)

_____ a photograph of the man's car with his cell

phone camera. The boy (congratulate) _____ by

the police after the motorist (catch) _____ by a

detective.

Section 3
**PROBLEMS
WITH VERBS**

3.   Clearly, the cell phone camera (cause) _____ a

lot of controversy since its appearance in the marketplace. Last year, many

complaints (register) _____ with authorities about

cell phone camera misuse. However, since 2003, cell phone cameras (help)

_____ people in emergency situations. Since its

debut, the cell phone camera (change) _____ the

way we communicate.

  See Chapter 23 of the Visualizing Writing CD for an
additional mini-lecture on **Verb Tense.**

PRACTICE I

Each sentence has errors with progressive forms. Correct each error.

EXAMPLE:

have been
I <u>been</u> working as a nanny for years.

1. Generally, I am loving my job, but this morning something terrible happened.

2. I was watching TV while the baby be sleeping, and I couldn't believe what was on one of the family's videos.

3. When I pressed the "Play" button, I was shocked because I was recognizing myself on the video.

4. The video had been taken months ago while I be reading to the family's children.

5. There is a hidden video camera in the house, and for months the parents been spying on me.

6. I cannot believe that the parents would use a nanny camera to see what I been doing.

7. I am a good nanny, and every day I am conducting myself professionally.

8. I do not think that families should spy on nannies unless the children been acting upset or the nanny been displaying strange behavior.

Section 3
PROBLEMS WITH VERBS

Nonstandard Forms: *gonna, gotta, wanna*

Some people commonly say *I'm gonna, I gotta,* or *I wanna.* These are nonstandard forms, and you should not use them in written communication.

■ Write *going to* instead of *gonna.*

going to
The nanny is ~~gonna~~ sue her employer.

■ Write *have to* instead of *gotta*.

> have to
> The Smiths ~~gotta~~ go to court to fight the lawsuit.

■ Write *want to* instead of *wanna*.

> want to
> They ~~wanna~~ win their case.

PRACTICE 2

Underline and correct eight incorrect verb tenses or nonstandard verbs.

EXAMPLE:

> have to have
> You and I <u>gotta have</u> a serious discussion.

Section 3
**PROBLEMS
WITH VERBS**

1. On June 24, 1947, Kenneth Arnold was in his plane when he saw what appeared to be a shiny object in the sky. He kept the object in sight for about three minutes. He then decided that he was gonna fly to an FBI office to report what he had seen. The FBI office was not open, so he visit an Oregon-based newspaper office instead.

2. Journalist Bill Bequette listened to Arnold's story. He said that he was gonna produce a report for the Associated Press. After the story was published, more journalists came and asked Arnold to describe, in detail, what he had witnessed. Arnold did not wanna have a lot of publicity, but that week, his description of a "crescent-shaped" object be in over 150 newspapers.

3. Since 1947, UFO sightings have increased dramatically. Today, some people are probably gonna tell you that UFOs are actually spy satellites. Others firmly believe that UFOs contain alien life. I wanna believe in aliens, but I think that I gotta see one first.

Problems with Conditional Forms

In **conditional sentences,** there is a condition and a result. There are three types of conditional sentences, and each type has two parts, or clauses. The main clause depends on the condition set in the *if* clause.

First Form: Possible Present or Future

The condition is true or very possible.

If + present tense,	. . . future tense . . .

condition (*if* clause)　　　　　　　result
If you <u>buy</u> the book, you <u>will learn</u> about satellites.

Section 3
PROBLEMS WITH VERBS

Second Form: Unlikely Present

The condition is not likely and probably will not happen.

If + past tense,	. . . *would* (expresses a condition) . . .
If + past tense,	. . . *could* (expresses a possibility) . . .

condition (*if* clause)　　　　　　result
If I <u>saw</u> a UFO, I <u>would take</u> a picture of it.

Note: In formal writing, when the condition contains the verb *be*, always use *were* in the *if* clause.

If Jenna <u>were</u> a scientist, she would study UFOs.

Third Form: Impossible Past

The condition cannot happen because the event is over.

If + past perfect tense,	. . . *would have* (+ past participle) . . .

condition (*if* clause)　　　　　　　　　　　　result
If aliens <u>had visited</u> the earth in 1947, someone <u>would have photographed</u> them.

> **Hint** **Be Careful with the Past Conditional**
>
> In the third type of conditional sentence, the impossible past, the writer expresses regret about a past event or expresses the wish that a past event had worked out differently. In the *if* part of the sentence, remember to use the past perfect tense.
>
> *If* + past perfect tense,　　　　　 . . . *would have* (past participle) . . .
>
> 　　　　　　　　　　　　　had listened
> If CIA agents ~~would have listened~~ to the tape, they **would have discovered** the agent's identity.

PRACTICE 3

Write the correct conditional form of each verb in parentheses.

EXAMPLE:

If the public (panic, not) _had not panicked_, the news media would have forgotten about the radio show.

1. Many simple actions can have cataclysmic consequences. Back in 1938, a young actor produced a radio play. Orson Welles's drama about an alien invasion caused panic. If Welles (produce, not) _____ that play, he would never have become famous. On the other hand, those who knew Welles claim that even if he (never, do) _____ *War of the Worlds*, he (do) _____ something remarkable.

2. Later in his career, Welles filmed *Citizen Kane*, a thinly veiled biography of the wealthy newspaper magnate William Randolph Hearst. Hearst was furious, and if he (be) _____ able to stop Welles's film, he (do) _____ it. As it was, none of Hearst's newspapers talked about the movie, and it didn't do well at the box office. If Hearst (leave) _____ Welles alone, the movie (make) _____ much more money than it did.

3. In 1942, Welles produced a spy film called *Journey into Fear*. He was fascinated with politics and espionage. In a 1984 BBC interview, Welles said that he would have been more successful if he (go) _____ into politics.

Section 3
**PROBLEMS
WITH VERBS**

Nonstandard Forms: *would of, could of, should of*

Some people commonly say *would of, could of,* or *should of*; they may also say *woulda, coulda,* or *shoulda*. These are nonstandard forms, and you should avoid using them in written communication. When you use the past forms of *should, would,* and *could,* always include *have* + the past participle.

                    would have
If I had been alive in 1963, I ~~woulda~~ tried to meet President Kennedy.
                                should have
Unfortunately, he was assassinated. The president ~~should of~~ traveled in a

bulletproof car.

PRACTICE 4

Correct the ten errors in conditional forms or in the past forms of *could* and *should*.

EXAMPLE:

The assassination should not <del>of</del> ^have^ happened.

Section 3
**PROBLEMS
WITH VERBS**

1.   One of the biggest mysteries of the twentieth century surrounds the death of President John Fitzgerald Kennedy (JFK). On November 22, 1963, at 12:30 p.m., JFK was shot. Some people suggest that Lee Harvey Oswald acted alone and killed the president. Others say that Oswald could not of done the crime by himself. In 1964, Justice Earl Warren headed a commission that investigated the case.

2.   The strongest evidence is home movie footage of the actual assassination taken by a man named Abraham Zapruder. The Warren Commission printed out still images of the Zapruder film in the wrong order. If the investigators would have printed the photos of the assassination in the correct order, they would of known that the bullets came from the front of the car, and not behind it. If Zapruder would not have taken his home movie, we would not of known about the directions of the bullets.

3.   The Warren Commission declared that Lee Harvey Oswald was the sole assassin. However, many witnesses at the scene said that some of the shots could not of come from the library building where Oswald was hiding. Perhaps the investigators shoulda considered eyewitness accounts. On the other hand, maybe the eyewitnesses were unreliable.

4.   Oswald's motive was unclear. Investigators pointed out that Oswald had spent many years living in Russia. If he would have lived in Russia, then he could have been a spy. They argued that Oswald was deeply involved in espionage, and he had secretly passed secrets to the communists. However, others insisted that if Oswald had been a spy, the government woulda arrested him sooner.

5.   Today, the mystery surrounding JFK's assassination is still unsolved.

No accepted truth has emerged, and some say we will never know what

happened on that day. If you would have been alive in 1964, would you

have believed the Warren Commission report?

The Writer's Desk Revise and Edit Your Warm Up

In the Warm Up on page 358, you wrote a short paragraph about
spying on nannies and other caregivers. Check your paragraph
and ensure that you have formed your verbs correctly. Correct
any errors.

Section 3
**PROBLEMS
WITH VERBS**

REFLECT ON IT

Think about what you have learned in this chapter. If you do not know an answer,
review that concept.

1.   When do you use the progressive form of verbs? _____

_____

2.   Circle five nonprogressive verbs in the list below. Nonprogressive verbs cannot
take the *-ing* form.

go	understand	walk	appreciate
believe	carry	know	watch
talk	speak	hear	listen

3.   Write your own examples of the three types of conditional sentences.
First form: _____

_____

Second form: _____

_____

Third form: _____

_____

4.   Correct the following sentences by writing the standard form of each nonstandard
verb.

a. If you wanna succeed, you gotta work hard.

b. J. Rowen been investigating UFOs since 1978.

c. If Kennedy would have taken another route, maybe he woulda lived.

d. Maybe one day somebody is gonna tell the truth about the Kennedy case.

FINAL REVIEW

Correct fifteen errors with verbs.

EXAMPLE:

want to

Many adults ~~wanna~~ go back to school to develop new careers.

Section 3
PROBLEMS
WITH VERBS

Dear Mrs. Adams:

I am an adult student, but I be going back to college because I gotta change my life. I could of gone back last year, but I decided to continue working at a local company. I had a job helping a private detective named Kenneth Rolland. In my job, I had to wait outside motels and take pictures of people who been cheating on their spouses. I also had to write reports, but the job was depressing. Then, one day while I sitting at my desk, I realized that even though I was in my thirties, it was not too late to change my life.

I know that I should of gone to college when I was in my twenties. However, if I would have tried that, I would of wasted a lot of time because I did not know what to do with my life. Now that I am older, I am more settled, and I am thinking that I have a better idea about what I am good at. In fact, I am understanding a lot of things these days. I know that if I wanna reach my goals, I gotta take the steps myself. Nobody else is gonna show me how to succeed.

Thank you for reading this letter. I wanna go to your college. I am motivated now, and I think that I am gonna be a great student.

Yours truly,

D. Mathers

The Writer's Room **Topics for Writing**

Choose one of the following topics and write a paragraph or an essay. When you write, remember to follow the writing process.

1. How would your life have been different if you had lived one hundred years ago? List some ways.

2. What are some types of spies? Think of at least three different categories of spies.

3. Today, many police departments have installed traffic cameras on busy streets. Drivers receive tickets for traffic violations in the mail. Police departments argue that the cameras deter crimes, but others say that such cameras invade our privacy. Should there be cameras on public streets?

4. Define an ideal spy. What qualities should a great spy have?

READING LINK

Espionage
"Nothing But Net" by Scott Bekker
(page 552)

Section 3
PROBLEMS WITH VERBS

 The Writers' Circle

Work with a group of about five students. Your group will have the opportunity to compose a short story. You need one sheet of paper for this activity.

STEP 1 Look at the following present tense verbs. Write the past form of each verb below the verb. Try to do this from memory, and do not look at your verb list.

be	think	drive	break	shake
grow	drink	mutter	go	take

STEP 2 One person in the group must begin by choosing one verb from the list. Cross that verb off the list. Then, on the piece of paper, write a sentence with that verb and be sure to use the past tense. Your sentence can be as serious or as silly as you want.

STEP 3 Pass the piece of paper to the person on your left. That person must choose another past tense verb from the list and add another sentence to the story. Continue going from person to person until all the verbs in the list have been used. When you have finished, one of you can read the story out loud to the group or to the class.

 See Chapter 24 of the Visualizing Writing CD for an additional mini-lecture on **Regular** and **Irregular Verbs.**

PRACTICE I

Write the correct present tense form of each verb in parentheses.

EXAMPLE:

Mila Zahn's family (live) _lives_ near Hamburg, Germany.

1. Mila Zahn is a German exchange student, and she (study) _____ in an American college.

2. Zahn (see) _____ many glaring cultural differences between Americans and Germans.

3. Many American students (juggle) _____ work and school.

4. For example, Mila's friend Amber (do) _____ not have much money.

5. Amber (work) _____ part time so that she can pay for her studies.

6. However, in Germany, the state (sponsor) _____ all levels of education, so students (do) _____ not feel financial pressure.

7. (Do) _____ the average American student pay too much for higher levels of education?

8. (Do) _____ you work and go to college?

Section 4
VERB AGREEMENT AND CONSISTENCY

Troublesome Present Tense Verbs: *be, have, do*

Some present tense verbs are formed in special ways. Review the verbs *be, have,* and *do*.

	Be	**Have**	**Do**
Singular forms			
First person:	I am	I have	I do
Second person:	You are	You have	You do
Third person:	He is	He has	He does
	She is	She has	She does
	It is	It has	It does
Plural forms			
First person:	We are	We have	We do
Second person:	You are	You have	You do
Third person:	They are	They have	They do

> ## Hint · Do Not Use *Ain't*
>
> Although some people say *ain't* in informal conversation, it is a nonstandard form and should not be used in written communication. Instead, write *is not, are not,* or *am not.*
>
>   are not   is not
> They ~~ain't~~ sure about the evidence. It ~~ain't~~ accurate.

PRACTICE 2

In the next selection, each verb is underlined. Correct twelve errors in subject-verb agreement or the incorrect use of *ain't*.

EXAMPLE:

                       study

Many exchange students <u>studies</u> in the United States.

1.   Emi Kawamura <u>is</u> a Japanese exchange student. According to Emi, many

       American students <u>has</u> many misguided ideas about the Japanese. Emi

       <u>remind</u> people that she <u>do</u> not <u>fit</u> any stereotype. For example, her math

       skills <u>is</u> poor and she rarely <u>uses</u> computers.

2.   The educational system in Japan <u>differ</u> from that in the United States.

       Japanese students <u>has</u> a longer school year than American students.

       Japanese college entrance exams <u>is</u> very difficult, and students <u>experience</u>

       high levels of stress. Emi's brother, Jin, <u>attends</u> a private "cramming"

       school called a *juku*. He <u>have</u> to study six days a week because he <u>hopes</u>

       to get into a good university.

3.   Because of complaints from parents and students, Japanese officials

       <u>wants</u> to reform the educational system. One plan <u>is</u> to place less emphasis

       on entrance exams. The current system <u>ain't</u> healthy for students.

4.   Although the average Japanese student <u>have</u> a stressful experience in

       high school, the situation <u>changes</u> in college. American college courses

       <u>is</u> more difficult than those in Japan, in Emi's opinion.

Section 4
**VERB AGREEMENT
AND CONSISTENCY**

Simple Past Tense Agreement

In the past tense, all verbs except *be* have one past form.

Regular:	I worked.	He worked.	You worked.	We worked.	They worked.
Irregular:	I ate.	He ate.	You ate.	We ate.	They ate.

Exception: *Be*

In the past tense, the only verb requiring subject-verb agreement is the verb *be*, which has two past forms: *was* and *were*.

Was	**Were**
I was	We were
He was	You were
She was	They were
It was	

Present Perfect Tense Agreement

When writing in the present perfect tense, which is formed with *have* or *has* and the past participle, use *has* when the subject is third-person singular.

> My college **has** raised tuition fees. Other colleges **have** not raised their fees.

Agreement in Other Tenses

When writing in most other verb tenses, and in modal forms (*can, could, would, may, might,* and so on), use the same form of the verb with every subject.

Future:	I will **work**; she will **work**; they will **work**; you will **work**; we will **work**.
Past perfect:	I had **met**; she had **met**; they had **met**; you had **met**; we had **met**.
Modals:	I can **talk**; she should **talk**; they could **talk**; you might **talk**; we would **talk**.

Section 4
**VERB AGREEMENT
AND CONSISTENCY**

GRAMMAR LINK

For more information about using the present perfect tense, see Chapter 23.

PRACTICE 3

In the next selection, each verb is underlined. Correct ten subject-verb agreement errors.

EXAMPLE:

       exists
A problem <u>exist</u> in many colleges and universities.

1.   Hazing <u>occur</u> on many American campuses. When a new student <u>want</u>

     to gain admittance to a club or organization, the student <u>undergoes</u> an

     initiation ritual.

2.   For example, in 2004, at the University of Central Florida, some fraternity members <u>was wrapped</u> in plastic and tied to a tree. One student <u>was</u> also <u>covered</u> in shaving cream, chocolate syrup, and vegetable oil. Many students <u>was</u> upset when they heard about the incident. Since that time, other fraternity members <u>has denied</u> their involvement in hazing.

3.   Sometimes hazing rituals <u>is</u> dangerous. Hank Newar <u>is</u> a professor and journalist, and he <u>have written</u> a book called *Broken Pledges: The Deadly Rite of Hazing*. Newar states, "Collegiate hazing <u>has resulted</u> in at least 59 fraternity deaths" since the 1970s.

4.   Although hazing <u>has been banned</u> in most states, many clubs <u>continues</u> to perform illegal rituals. When hazing rituals <u>is reported</u>, the offending club <u>can loses</u> its affiliation with the university.

Section 4
**VERB AGREEMENT
AND CONSISTENCY**

More Than One Subject

There are special agreement rules when there is more than one subject in a sentence.

and
When subjects are joined by *and*, use the plural form of the verb.

> <u>Colleges</u>, <u>universities</u>, and <u>trade schools</u> **prepare** students for the job market.

or, nor
When two subjects are joined by *or* or *nor*, the verb agrees with the subject that is closer to it.

> plural
> Neither Amanda Jackson nor her <u>students</u> **use** the computer lab.

> singular
> Either the students or <u>Amanda</u> **uses** the department's portable laptop computer.

PRACTICE 4

Circle the correct verb in each sentence. Make sure the verb agrees with the subject.

EXAMPLE:
Colleges and universities (have, has) various interesting programs.

Collective Nouns

Collective nouns refer to a group of people or things. These are common collective nouns.

army	class	crowd	group	population
association	club	family	jury	public
audience	committee	gang	mob	society
band	company	government	organization	team

Generally, each group acts as a unit, so you must use the singular form of the verb.

> The <u>jury</u> **is** ready to read the verdict.

If the members of the group act individually, use the plural form of the verb. It is a good idea to use a phrase such as *members of.*

Acceptable: The <u>jury</u> **are** not able to come to an agreement.

Better: The <u>members of the jury</u> **are** not able to come to an agreement.

Section 4
VERB AGREEMENT AND CONSISTENCY

 Police **Is Usually Plural**

The word *police* is always thought of as a plural noun because the word *officers* is implied but not stated.

The police **have** arrested a suspect.

The police **are** patrolling the neighborhood.

PRACTICE 6

In each sentence, underline the subject and circle the correct verb.

EXAMPLE:
The <u>National Guard</u> (⟨is⟩, are) a very structured organization.

1. Nantha Kumar's family (is, are) middle class. They (live, lives) in a beautiful community near Austin, Texas. The population (is, are) around 50,000 residents.

2. Although his siblings (have, has) succeeded in various careers, Nantha (have, has) had many problems over the years. The police (have, has) visited his home many times because he (have, has) driven too fast or created a disturbance. Some of Nantha's crimes (has, have) been serious. A local gang (has, have) robbed several stores. Last year, a jury (was, were) asked to decide whether Nantha (was, were) part of that gang. Nantha's friends (was, were) convicted, but he (was, were) released.

3. Nantha's father (want, wants) him to join the National Guard. The National Guard (finance, finances) student educations. The military (force, forces) irresponsible young people to grow up quickly. However, Nantha's extended family (do, does) not think he should join.

4. Nantha's grandparents (plan, plans) to pay for his college education. His family (hope, hopes) that he will become a more responsible citizen.

Verb Before the Subject

Usually the verb comes after the subject, but in some sentences, the verb comes before the subject. In such cases, you must still ensure that the subject and verb agree.

there or here

When a sentence begins with *there* or *here*, the subject always follows the verb. *There* and *here* are not subjects.

      V   S   V   S

Here **is** the college course <u>list</u>.   There **are** many night <u>courses</u>.

Section 4
**VERB AGREEMENT
AND CONSISTENCY**

Questions

In questions, word order is usually reversed, and the main or helping verb is placed before the subject. In the following example, the main verb is *be*.

      V   S   V   S

Where **is** the <u>cafeteria</u>? **Is** the <u>food</u> good?

However, in questions in which the main verb isn't *be*, the subject usually agrees with the helping verb.

    HV   S   HV   S   V

When **does** the <u>library</u> close? **Do** <u>students</u> **work** there?

PRACTICE 7

Correct any subject-verb agreement errors. If the sentence is correct, write *C* in the blank.

EXAMPLE:

~~Has~~ you ever won a competition?   <u>Have</u>

1. There is many athletic scholarships in colleges.   <u>   </u>

2. Has many students benefited from the scholarships?   <u>   </u>

3. Does athletes get preferential treatment?   <u>   </u>

4. Is there a reason to stop giving scholarships to athletes?   <u>   </u>

5. There is many pressures on student athletes.   <u>   </u>

6. Why do Wayne Brydon want to be play basketball professionally? _____

7. Do female athletes have the same opportunities? _____

8. According to Selma Rowen, there have not been enough attention given to academically successful students. _____

9. On the other hand, there is many people who support athletes. _____

10. In addition to doing their course work, do college athletes have to train for several hours each day? _____

Interrupting Words and Phrases

Words that come between the subject and the verb may confuse you. In these cases, look for the subject and make sure that the verb agrees with the subject.

Section 4
VERB AGREEMENT AND CONSISTENCY

            S   interrupting phrase   V
Some <u>rules</u> regarding admission to this college **are** controversial.

        S   prepositional phrase   V
A <u>student</u> in two of my classes **writes** for the college newspaper.

 Identify Interrupting Phrases

When you revise your paragraphs, add parentheses around words that separate the subject and the verb. Then you can check to see whether your subjects and verbs agree.

        S   prepositional phrase   V
A <u>student</u> (in two of my classes) **writes** for the college newspaper

When interrupting phrases contain *of the* or similar words, the subject appears before the phrase.

        S   prepositional phrase   V
<u>One</u> (of my biggest problems) **is** my lack of organization.

PRACTICE 8

Underline the subject in each sentence. Add parentheses around any words that come between each subject and verb. Then circle the correct form of the verb.

EXAMPLE:

<u>One</u> (of the most controversial issues on campus) (**is**, are affirmative action.

1. Some colleges in this country **have/has** more relaxed admission standards for students from ethnic minorities. Such colleges, with good reason, **want/ wants** to have a vibrant and diverse student population. However, arguing that they have been discriminated against, students from across the nation **have/has** sued their colleges. Judges in courtrooms **have/has** had to consider whether affirmative action is unfair.

2. People in favor of affirmative action **have/has** compelling arguments. Historically, some ethnic groups in the United States **has/have** not had access to a higher education. Many factors such as poverty **contribute/contributes** to the problem. University of California professor Norman Matloff, in an article for *Asian Week*, **suggest/suggests** that society suffers when there is a large, poorly educated underclass. Additionally, affirmative action **help/helps** create a diverse student body.

3. Opponents of affirmative action **feel/feels** that admissions should be based purely on test scores. Barbara Grutter, a white student and an applicant to the University of Michigan, **argue/argues** that affirmative action is reverse discrimination. One of her best arguments **is/are** compelling: Grutter, as a forty-year-old single mother, **add/adds** to the university's diversity. On June 23, 2003, a decision about Grutter's affirmative action case **was/were** made. Although justices in the Supreme Court **were/was** divided, they ruled that race can be used as one of the factors in college admissions.

4. For some people, regulations to safeguard affirmative action **help/helps** equalize opportunities in our society. For others, such regulations **is/are** unfair to certain groups. What is your opinion?

Section 4
VERB AGREEMENT AND CONSISTENCY

Interrupting Words: *who, which, that*

If a sentence contains a clause beginning with *who*, *which*, or *that*, then the verb agrees with the subject preceding *who*, *which*, or *that*.

> There is a <u>woman</u> in my neighborhood *who* **counsels** students.

> Here are some old <u>newspapers</u> *that* **discuss** steroid abuse.

> One <u>article</u>, *which* **contains** stories about hazing, is very interesting.

PRACTICE 9

Correct ten subject-verb agreement errors.

EXAMPLE:

The English department has a help center that ~~open~~ *opens* weekdays.

1. Students who needs help with their English can go to the help center. My friend who never speak English at home often goes to the help center. He does exercises that helps him. He says that the woman who work there is friendly.

2. There is some computers in the help center. If a student who have an assignment due need to use a computer, one is available. There is also several tutors available who help the students.

3. Sometimes the administrators who control the budget threatens to close the help center. When that happens, students who uses the center protest. Then the center remains open.

The Writer's Desk Revise and Edit Your Warm Up

In the Warm Up on page 368, you wrote a short paragraph about extracurricular activities on campus. Check for any subject-verb agreement errors.

Section 4
VERB AGREEMENT AND CONSISTENCY

REFLECT ON IT

Think about what you have learned in this unit. If you do not know an answer, review that concept.

1. When should you add –s or –es to verbs? _____
_____

2. Some indefinite pronouns are singular, and the verbs that follow them require the –s or –es ending. List six singular indefinite pronouns.

_____   _____   _____

_____   _____   _____

3. Look at the following nouns. Circle all the collective nouns.

| family | people | army | committee |
| judge | crowd | brothers | audience |

4. When do you use *was* and *were*?
Use *was* _____
Use *were* _____

5. Circle and correct any subject-verb agreement errors in the following sentences.

a. There is many colleges in Florida.
b. Yale is a university that have several secret societies.
c. Either the Edwards sisters or Simon have been initiated.
d. One of our cousins go to Yale.
e. There is no hazing rituals on our campus.

FINAL REVIEW

Correct twenty errors in subject-verb agreement.

EXAMPLE:

looks
This college campus ~~look~~ peaceful.

1. Two years ago, Elmira Reed left home for the first time and went to her state college. Today, Reed, a biology major, has a private dorm room on campus. She admits that she love the feeling of independence. However, last March, Reed's purse and book bag was stolen from her car, and in May, there was robberies in several dorm rooms.

2. College campuses is not always the peaceful and safe places that they appears to be. In fact, according to the *New York Times Magazine*, there is over eight assaults or other violent crimes per year on the average college or university campus. However, if each student take a few simple precautions, he or she can reduce the risk of being a crime victim.

3. First, everyone who live in campus dorms need to act responsibly. Neither Reed nor her roommate take proper precautions. Sometimes, when Reed's roommate go out for the evening, she posts information about her whereabouts on her room door. However, such information provide thieves with an invitation to break in. Students should not leave notes posted on their doors, and they should always lock their room doors even if they plan to be absent for only a short while.

4. Furthermore, students should familiarize themselves with campus security locations. There is usually call boxes in certain buildings, and students should know where to find those emergency phones. Also, if someone want to study in a secluded location at night, he or she should inform campus security. Some campuses has "walk home" services for students who uses the library late at night. New students need to find out what the campus has to offer.

Section 4
**VERB AGREEMENT
AND CONSISTENCY**

5.   Ultimately, anyone who live on campus need to think about security. If nobody take precautions, then more robberies will occur. Remember that colleges are public places, buildings are open late, and there is not always a lot of security guards on campus. Therefore, it is important to be sensible.

  See Chapter 25 of the Visualizing Writing CD for an additional mini-lecture on **Subject-Verb Agreement.**

Section 4
VERB AGREEMENT AND CONSISTENCY

Tense Consistency

section theme **COLLEGE LIFE**

CONTENTS

• Consistent Verb Tense

In this chapter, you will read about college issues.

The Writer's Desk Warm Up

How do images in the media influence the way that people judge their own bodies? Write a short paragraph about the media and body image.

Consistent Verb Tense

When you write, the verb tense you use gives the reader an idea about the time when the event occurred. A **tense shift** occurs when you shift from one tense to another for no logical reason.

Tense shift: College reporter Erica Santiago interviewed a protester and <u>asks</u> about his political philosophy.

Correct: College reporter Erica Santiago interviewed a protester and <u>asked</u> about his political philosophy.

Sometimes the time frame in a text really does change. In those circumstances, you would change the verb tense. The following example accurately shows two different time periods. Notice that certain key words (*during my childhood, today*) indicate what tense the writer should use.

During my childhood, I ^{past} <u>ate</u> a lot of fast food. Today, I ^{present} <u>try</u> to eat a healthy diet.

PRACTICE I

Identify and correct each tense shift. If the sentence is correct, write *C* in the space.

EXAMPLES:

I sent in my college application, but I (do) not hear a response for weeks.   *did*

Last year, Kyle tried out for the basketball team, but he was not chosen.   *C*

1. College is a transitional period; most people discover what they wanted out of life in college.   _____

2. Enrique Morales finished high school in 2002, and he decides to work for a couple of years before going to college.   _____

3. Last summer, he volunteered in a public medical clinic, and there he discovered his true calling.   _____

4. Today, Morales is in his first year of college, and he wants to be a nurse.   _____

5. Enrique's parents are supportive; they hoped that their son succeeds.   _____

6. Some students switch careers several times during their lives, and others find a passion and stayed with it.   _____

7. In 2001, Jaya Oke worked as a sales representative, but after six months she quit because she is not happy with her job.   _____

8. Oke also tried accounting; she takes several courses in 2002.   _____

9. Last year, Oke realized that she likes to work with her hands; today, she is an electrician's apprentice.   _____

10. She enjoys her work and hoped to become an electrician.   _____

Section 4
VERB AGREEMENT AND CONSISTENCY

 Hint   *Would and Could*

When you tell a story about a past event, use *would* instead of *will,* and use *could* instead of *can.*

In 1996, college wrestler Robert Burzak knew that he <u>can</u> ^{could} bulk up if he used steriods, but he promised his coach that he <u>will</u> ^{would} not.

PRACTICE 2

Underline and correct ten tense shifts.

EXAMPLE:

Robert began weight training after he <u>breaks</u> his leg.
broke

1.   In 2003, Robert Burzak joined a health club and tries weightlifting. He
     knew that he can have a sculpted body if he worked out. After a few months
     of weight training, he starts to get impatient. He wanted to get larger
     muscles very quickly, so, after a training partner told him about steroids,
     he decides to try them.

2.   Robert started by taking steroids in pill form. Within weeks he noticed
     a difference. Soon, he graduated to steroid injections. Others noticed his
     large muscles, and Robert feels proud of his "six-pack" stomach and his
     large biceps. He realized that his new look conformed to the images of
     male beauty seen in the media.

3.   Unfortunately, after Robert began to use steroids, side effects kick in.
     Robert developed acne on his back. Most worrisome, he felt wild mood
     swings, and he will alternate between violent outbursts and periods of
     depression. He cannot stop taking the pills because each time he tried to
     stop, his weight will plummet.

4.   Finally, in 2005, Robert gave up steroids. He knew that the risks to his
     health outweighed the benefits of having a sculpted body. Furthermore, his
     girlfriend said that she will leave him if he could not stay off the drugs.
     Today, Robert is drug free.

Section 4
**VERB AGREEMENT
AND CONSISTENCY**

The Writer's Desk **Revise and Edit Your Warm Up**

In the Warm Up on page 383, you wrote a short paragraph about
the media and body image. Check the paragraph for any tense shifts.

REFLECT ON IT

Think about what you have learned in this unit. If you do not know an answer, review that concept.

1. What is tense inconsistency? _____

   _____

2. If you are writing a paragraph about a past event, what word should you use instead of these two?

   a. will: _____   b. can: _____

3. Read the following paragraphs and find five tense inconsistencies. Correct the errors.

   EXAMPLE: Kaitlin diets because she ~~wanted~~ *wants* to look thinner.

   In 2001, college student Amy Heller became severely malnourished. In an attempt to lose weight, Heller ingested diet pills, and she severely restricts her intake of food. When others suggested that she had a problem, Heller will deny it. By July 2004, she weighs only 88 pounds. Heller finally sought treatment, and soon she can eat regular meals.

   In 2001, Wendy Hoyt made a study about body image and college students. She asked over 200 students to rate their level of satisfaction with their own bodies. Her results showed that women are more likely to be dissatisfied with their weight than men were. She attributed the diverse statistics to the influence of the media.

FINAL REVIEW

Correct fifteen tense shifts in the next student essay.

EXAMPLE:

In the 1970s, many college students ~~get~~ *got* involved in politics, and they joined protest marches.

1.   In 2002, Eric Longley wrote an article about draft laws in the *Gale Encyclopedia of Popular Culture*. According to Longley, young people of college age are often forced to participate in wars. For example, during the Civil War, the U.S. government passed a draft law to ensure that there will be enough soldiers to fight.

2.   In the twentieth century, Congress repeatedly passed draft laws. In fact, during both World Wars I and II, young men cannot volunteer for the army. According to Longley, the government "chose to rely solely on the draft for its military needs." After World War II, the ban was lifted, so men can volunteer for the armed services. However, the draft laws were still in effect until 1973.

3.   Draft dodging was common during previous wars. For example, during the Civil War, wealthy young Americans can escape the draft by paying for a "substitute" soldier. During World War II, the government will not draft married men. In 1940, after the draft law passes, five times more men got married than in the previous year. After World War II, young men who were in college can avoid the draft. During the Vietnam War, many men will register in college to avoid going to war. However, when the Vietnam War escalated, the government introduces a lottery system, and college students can be drafted. Finally, a popular way to avoid the draft during previous wars was to flee to another country. In a 2004 interview, V. A. Smith said that he fled to Canada in 1970 when his lottery number is picked because he does not want to fight in Vietnam.

Section 4
VERB AGREEMENT AND CONSISTENCY

4.   In 2001, many young men and women entered the National Guard to get a free college education. Then, many of them had to fight overseas. For example, during the Iraq War, wounded soldier Jessica Lynch said that she just wants to get an education when she enlists.

5.   Do the poorest members of society face a larger risk of fighting overseas? Some argue that a military draft penalizes working-class men and women. Others believed that a military draft is the only fair way to ensure that armies have enough soldiers. As long as conflicts between nations exist, the military will need to find recruits.

READING LINK

College Life

"Dying to Be Bigger" by H. D. (page 575)

"Body Over Mind" by Mitch Albom (page 572)

"It's Class, Stupid" by Richard Rodriquez (page 565)

"The Case for Affirmative Action" by Dave Malcolm (page 568)

Section 4
VERB AGREEMENT AND CONSISTENCY

 The Writer's Room **Topics for Writing**

Choose one of the following topics and write a paragraph or an essay. When you write, remember to follow the writing process.

1. Describe your college campus. You might describe an interesting building or area of the campus.

2. What are some things that new students should know about your college? Explain how to survive the first few semesters in college.

3. Sometimes fraternities, sororities, clubs, and teams make new students undergo initiation rituals. Why do groups do this? How might such rituals affect new students? Explain your view.

4. What is your opinion of the military draft? Should governments force young people to join the armed forces? Should college students and married students be exempt from the draft?

 The Writers' Circle

Work with a team of students and create a short survey. Form at least five interesting questions about college life.

Then one team member should remain seated, and the other team members should split up and sit with other groups in the class. After each member has gathered information, the original group should get together and write a summary of the results.

 See Chapter 26 of the Visualizing Writing CD for additional mini-lectures on **Consistent Verb Tense** and **Active Voice.**

Nouns, Determiners, and Prepositions

section theme **INVENTIONS AND DISCOVERIES**

CONTENTS

- Singular and Plural Nouns
- Count Nouns and Noncount Nouns
- Determiners
- Prepositions

In this chapter, you will read about some interesting inventions *and* discoveries.

The Writer's Desk Warm Up

Write a short paragraph describing the most interesting invention from the last century. Explain why the invention is important.

Singular and Plural Nouns

Nouns are words that refer to people, places, or things. Nouns are divided into common nouns and proper nouns.

- **Common nouns** refer to general people, places, or things and begin with a lowercase letter. For example, *books*, *computer*, and *city* are common nouns.
- **Proper nouns** refer to particular people, places, or things and begin with a capital letter. For example, *Benjamin Franklin*, *Microsoft*, and *Kitty Hawk* are proper nouns.

Nouns are either singular or plural. A **singular noun** refers to one of something, while a **plural noun** refers to more than one of something. Regular plural nouns end in -*s* or -*es*.

	Singular	**Plural**
People:	inventor	inventors
	writer	writers
Places:	town	towns
	village	villages
Things:	computer	computers
	aspirin	aspirins

 Hint **Adding -es**

When a noun ends in *s, x, ch, sh,* or *z*, add -*es* to form the plural.

business/business**es**   tax/tax**es**   church/church**es**

Irregular Plural Nouns

Nouns that do not use -*s* or -*es* in their plural forms are called **irregular nouns.** Here are some common irregular nouns.

Singular	**Plural**
person	people
child	children
man	men
woman	women
tooth	teeth
foot	feet

Section 5
MORE PARTS OF SPEECH

Some nouns use other rules to form the plural. It is a good idea to memorize both the rules and the exceptions.

- For nouns ending in *f* or *fe*, change the *f* to *v* and add -*es*.

Singular	**Plural**	**Singular**	**Plural**
knife	kni**ves**	thief	thie**ves**
wife	wi**ves**	leaf	lea**ves**

Some exceptions: belief, beliefs; roof, roofs; safe, safes.

- For nouns ending in a consonant + *y*, change the *y* to *i* and add -*es*.

Singular	**Plural**	**Singular**	**Plural**
lady	lad**ies**	baby	bab**ies**
berry	berr**ies**	cherry	cherr**ies**

If a vowel comes before the final *y*, then the word retains the regular plural form.

Singular	**Plural**	**Singular**	**Plural**
day	day**s**	key	key**s**

■ Some nouns remain the same in both singular and plural forms.

Singular	Plural	Singular	Plural
fish	fish	deer	deer
moose	moose	sheep	sheep

■ Some nouns are thought of as being only plural and therefore have no singular form.

Plural Form Only

clothes	goods	pants	scissors
eyeglasses	proceeds	savings	series

■ Some nouns are **compound nouns,** which means that they are made up of two or more words. To form the plural of compound nouns, add *-s* or *-es* to the last word of the compound noun.

Singular	Plural	Singular	Plural
bus stop	bus stop**s**	artificial heart	artificial heart**s**
air conditioner	air conditioner**s**	jet airplane	jet airplane**s**

In hyphenated compound nouns, if the first word is a noun, add *-s* to the noun.

Singular	Plural	Singular	Plural
senator-elect	senator**s**-elect	runner-up	runner**s**-up
sister-in-law	sister**s**-in-law	husband-to-be	husband**s**-to-be

■ Some nouns that are borrowed from Latin keep the plural form of the original language.

Singular	Plural	Singular	Plural
millennium	millennia	paparazzo	paparazzi
datum	data	phenomenon	phenomena

Section 5
MORE PARTS
OF SPEECH

 Hint *Persons vs. People*

There are two plural forms of *person*. *People* is the most common plural form.

Some <u>people</u> have great ideas. Many <u>people</u> patent their ideas.

Persons is used in a legal or official context.

The patent was stolen by <u>persons</u> unknown.

PRACTICE I

Correct ten errors in plural noun forms.

EXAMPLE:

The personal computer has changed ~~lifes~~ *lives* in an incredible way.

1. Apple Computer, Inc., marketed the first successful home computer in 1977, and IBM brought out a home machine in 1981.

Although the personal computer was first dismissed as an unnecessary luxury, it is now a necessity. Most persons use computers in the workplace. Childrens learn how to use them at school. At home, familys keep track of personal finances with computers. In my family, everyone has a computer. In fact, I recently gave computers to both of my sister-in-law.

2.   Unfortunately, there is also a negative side to this invention. Computer crime has become a problem. Computer thiefs can hack into computers and steal personal datas. As a result, many unsuspecting peoples lose money. In addition, hackers can steal company records, access customer lists, and cause other problems for both companys and clients. However, even with the problem of computer crime, most mens and womens would not want to have a computer-free environment.

Section 5
MORE PARTS OF SPEECH

PRACTICE 2

Fill in the blanks with either the singular or plural form of the noun. If the noun does not change, put an *X* in the space.

EXAMPLES:

Singular	**Plural**
man	*men*
X	goggles

1. person   _____

2. loaf   _____

3. _____   mice

4. brother-in-law   _____

5. lady   _____

6. _____   pants

7. _____   jeans

8. sheep   _____

9. calf   _____

10. _____ binoculars

11. child _____

12. _____ shelves

13. _____ sunglasses

14. alarm clock _____

15. bathing suit _____

Key Words for Singular and Plural Nouns

Some key words will help you determine whether a noun is singular or plural.

■ Use a singular noun after words such as *a, an, one, each, every,* and *another.*

> As **a** <u>young mother</u>, Dorothy Gerber prepared homemade baby food for her daughter.

> Gerber tried to sell her product to **every** <u>grocery store</u> in her town.

■ Use a plural noun after words such as *two, all, both, many, few, several,* and *some.*

> Very **few** <u>companies</u> produced food targeted to children.

> Today, **many** <u>babies</u> eat Gerber's baby food.

 Hint > **Using Plural Nouns After *of the***

Use a plural noun after the expressions *one (all, two, each, few, lots, many, most, several) of the. . . .*

<u>One of the most</u> useful **items** ever invented is the zipper.

Section 5
MORE PARTS OF SPEECH

PRACTICE 3

Circle the correct noun form in each set of parentheses.

EXAMPLE:

In his speech to the Nobel committee, Dr. Frederick Banting acknowledged Dr. Charles Best and all of the (researcher, (researchers)) whose work was crucial to the discovery.

1. Before the 1920s, there was no (cure, cures) for diabetes.

2. (Person, People) who had diabetes wasted away and eventually died.

3. In a laboratory at the University of Toronto, Dr. Frederick Banting and one of his (assistant, assistants), Dr. Charles Best, discovered insulin.

4. It was one of the most important (discovery, discoveries) in modern science.

5. In the summer of 1921, these two (scientist, scientists) invented an extract of pancreatic insulin.

6. They successfully tested insulin on some diabetic (dog, dogs).

7. Then, in 1922, Banting and Best tested insulin on the first human diabetic, a (man, men) named Leonard Thompson.

8. Every (test, tests) was a great success.

9. Although insulin is not a cure for diabetes, it helps millions of (person, people) with diabetes lead normal (life, lives.)

10. Dr. Banting was awarded a Nobel (prize, prizes) in 1923.

Count Nouns and Noncount Nouns

In English, nouns are grouped into two types: count nouns and noncount nouns. **Count nouns** refer to people or things that you can count, such as *engine, paper,* or *girl.* Count nouns usually can have both a singular and plural form.

> She read a <u>book</u> about inventions. She read five <u>books</u> about inventions.

Noncount nouns refer to people or things that you cannot count because you cannot divide them, such as *electricity* and *music.* Noncount nouns usually have only the singular form.

> The <u>furniture</u> in the inventor's house looked expensive.

> Inventors usually have a lot of specialized <u>equipment</u>.

To express a noncount noun as a count noun, refer to it in terms of types, varieties, or amounts.

> The patent office has **a variety of** <u>furniture</u>.

> My friend works in a patent office where he listens to **many styles of** <u>music</u>.

> The clerk at the patent office likes to drink coffee with **four cubes of** <u>sugar</u>.

Here are some common noncount nouns.

Section 5
MORE PARTS OF SPEECH

Common Noncount Nouns

Categories of Objects		Food	Nature	Substances	
clothing	machinery	bread	air	chalk	hair
equipment	mail	honey	earth	charcoal	fur
furniture	money	meat	electricity	coal	
homework	music	milk	energy	ink	
jewelry	postage	fish	radiation	paint	
luggage	software	rice	water	paper	

Abstract Nouns

advice	evidence	information	progress
attention	effort	knowledge	proof
behavior	health	luck	research
education	help	peace	violence

PRACTICE 4

Change the italicized words to the plural form, if necessary. If you cannot use the plural form, write X in the space. If the word ends in y, you may have to change the y to i for the plural form.

EXAMPLE:

In written communication, there have been many useful *discovery* _____ies_____.

1. Since the beginning of *history* _____, people have used various *method* _____ to compose in written form. Early *human* _____ used *substance* _____ such as *charcoal* _____, *chalk* _____, and *paint* _____ to write on *wall* _____ and *paper* _____. Eventually, a lot of *information* _____ was recorded using ink and a quill.

2. In 1884, Lewis Waterman patented one of the most useful *invention* _____. Although Waterman's fountain *pen* _____ worked reasonably well, they were unreliable, and ink could leak onto *clothing* _____ and *furniture* _____.

3. Since the 1930s, a lot of *progress* _____ has been made in written communication. In 1938, Ladislo Biro was one of the best-known *journalist* _____ in Hungary. He spent a lot of *time* _____ thinking about different *type* _____ of writing *tool* _____. Using quick-drying ink that was common in printing *press* _____, and using a small ball bearing, he created the first ballpoint pen.

4. These days, *company* _____ do a lot of *research* _____ because they want to develop a new, better writing tool. In fact, there are many different *kind* _____ of *pen* _____ on the market.

Section 5
MORE PARTS OF SPEECH

Determiners

Determiners are words that help to determine or figure out whether a noun is specific or general.

> Arthur Scott used **his** imagination and created **a** new invention, **the** paper towel.

You can use many words from different parts of speech as determiners.

Articles:	a, an, the
Demonstratives:	this, that, these, those, such
Indefinite pronouns:	any, all, both, each, every, either, few, little, many, several
Numbers:	one, two, three
Possessive nouns:	Jack's, the teacher's, a man's
Possessive adjectives:	my, your, his, her, its, our, their, whose

 Hint *Each* and *Every*

Always use a singular noun after *each* and *every*.

> Biro personally inspected <u>each</u> ~~items~~ item that he produced. Every ~~pens~~ pen had a high quality.

Section 5
MORE PARTS OF SPEECH

Commonly Confused Determiners

Some determiners can be confusing because you can use them only in specific circumstances. Review this list of some commonly confused determiners.

a, an, the

A and *an* are general determiners, and *the* is a specific determiner.

> I need to find <u>a</u> new car. *(general)* <u>The</u> cars in that showroom are expensive. *(specific)*

- Use *a* and *an* before singular count nouns but not before plural or noncount nouns. Use *a* before nouns that begin with a consonant (*a man*), and use *an* before nouns that begin with a vowel (*an invention*).

  > <u>An</u> ordinary woman created <u>a</u> very useful product.

- Use *the* before nouns that refer to a specific person, place, or thing. Do not use *the* before languages (*he studies Greek*), sports (*we played football*), and most city and country names (*Biro was born in Hungary*).

  > In 1885, Karl Benz invented <u>the</u> first automobile while living in <u>the</u> city of Mannheim, Germany.

many, few, much, little

- Use *many* and *few* with count nouns.

  > <u>Many</u> **people** have tried to develop new products, but <u>few</u> **inventions** are really successful.

■ Use *much* and *little* with noncount nouns.

> Manu Joshi spent too <u>much</u> **money** on very <u>little</u> **research.**

this, that, these, those

■ Use *this* and *these* to refer to things that are physically close to the speaker or at the present time. Use *this* before singular nouns and *these* before plural nouns.

> <u>This</u> **computer** in my purse measures three by five inches. <u>These</u> **days,** computers are very small.

■ Use *that* and *those* to refer to things that are physically distant from the speaker or in the past. Use *that* before singular nouns and *those* before plural nouns.

> In the 1950s, computers were invented. In <u>those</u> **years,** computers were very large. In <u>that</u> **building,** there is a very old computer.

Near the speaker:
this (singular)
these (plural)

Far from the speaker:
that (singular)
those (plural)

PRACTICE 5

Write *a*, *an*, or *the* in the space before each noun. If no determiner is necessary, write *X* in the space.

EXAMPLE:

A modern convenience like ___*a*___ car can make traveling much easier.

1. Most of us admire _____ beautiful, shiny new automobiles, but we do not give _____ same admiration to _____ windshield wipers. Indeed, we take _____ windshield wiper for granted, yet it is _____ extremely necessary tool when we are driving. In fact, before _____ invention of _____ windshield wiper, drivers had to stop to clean the front window of their vehicles.

2. In 1902, when she was on _____ trip to New York City, Mary Anderson observed that streetcar drivers had to look through open windows when they were driving in bad weather. In 1903, she invented _____ gadget that could clean car windows. Her wipers consisted of rubber blades on _____ outside of the windshield and _____ handle on _____ inside of the car. Drivers could turn _____ wipers by turning the handle.

3. Anderson received _____ patent for her invention, and by 1916, all American-made cars had _____ windshield wipers as _____ regular feature.

Section 5
**MORE PARTS
OF SPEECH**

PRACTICE 6

In this paragraph, Ted VanCleave, the creator of the Web site totallyabsurd.com, discusses some odd inventions. Circle the determiner in parentheses that best agrees with the noun before it. If the noun does not require a determiner, circle the *X*.

EXAMPLE:

Most inventions begin with (X, (a), the) great idea.

1.   (Many, much) inventors claim that their inventions help make (X, the) life easier for everybody. (Every, Some, X) inventions are extremely useful while others are totally absurd.

2.   (Few, Little) inventions are as bizarre as (a, X, the) twelve-gauge golf club. It requires very (few, little) equipment. It contains (the, a) barrel, (the, a) muzzle, and (the, a) a trap door to load explosives. (A, The, X) firing pin is in (an, the, X) exact spot where (a, the, X) club is supposed to hit (the, X) ball. (The, An) inventor received (X, a) patent for this item in 1979. There were many odd patents (this, that) year.

3.   There are (much, many) other ridiculous inventions. (The, A, X) motorized ice cream cone was patented in 1999. It helps you eat (the, an, X) ice cream cone (the, X) modern way. When (X, the) switch in (a, the) cone is turned on, (X, the) ice cream turns by itself on your tongue.

4.   These useless devices do not cost (much, many) money, and they have generated very (few, little) interest. Can you think of a (few, little) examples of funny inventions?

Section 5
MORE PARTS OF SPEECH

PRACTICE 7

Correct fifteen errors in singular nouns, plural nouns, and determiners.

EXAMPLE:

One of the most interesting ~~idea~~ *ideas* is a self-cleaning house.

In her autobiography, Agatha Christie wrote that most invention arise from laziness. Peoples invent to save themselves trouble. Christie's comments apply perfectly to Frances Gabe of Newberg, Oregon. Gabe, after a lot of researches, has invented and patented the world's first self-cleaning house. A house will appeal to anyone who hates to clean. On the ceiling of each rooms in Gabe's house, there is a cleaning and drying machines. At the touch of a buttons, each units first sprays soapy water over the room, then rinses and blow-dries the entire area. The rooms' floors are sloped slightly toward the corners so that excess waters runs to a drain. The furnitures is made of waterproof material, and there are no carpets. There are not much decorations in the house. In the kitchen, all dish are cleaned, dried, and stored inside dishwasher cupboards. Every sink, tub, and toilets is self-cleaning. Gabe created the architectural plans and the designs for the specialized equipments. This days, Gabe actually lives in her patented prototype home.

Prepositions

Prepositions are words that show concepts such as time, place, direction, and manner. They show connections or relationships between ideas.

Scientists made many important discoveries **during** World War II.

American scientists raced **to** build the first atomic bomb.

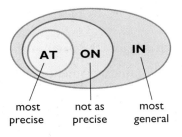

most precise | not as precise | most general

Section 5
MORE PARTS OF SPEECH

Prepositions	Prepositions of Time	Prepositions of Place
at	at a specific time of day (at 8:30 p.m.) at night at breakfast, lunch, dinner	at an address (at 15 Maple Street) at a specific building (at the hospital)
on	on a day of the week (on Monday) on a specific date (on June 16) on a specific holiday (on Martin Luther King Day) on time (meaning "punctual") on my birthday	on a specific street (on 17th Avenue) on technological devices (on TV, on the radio, on the phone, on the computer) on a planet (on Earth) on top
in	in a year (in 2005) in a month (in July) in the morning, afternoon, evening in the spring, fall, summer, winter	in a city (in Boston) in a country (in Spain) in a continent (in Africa)

(continued)

Prepositions	Prepositions of Time	Prepositions of Place
from ... to	from one time to another (from 6 a.m. to 8 p.m.)	from one place to another (from Las Vegas to Miami)
for	for a period of time (for six hours)	for a distance (for ten miles)

Commonly Confused Prepositions

to vs. at

Use *to* after verbs that indicate movement from one place to another.

> Each morning, Albert <u>walks</u> **to** the library, he <u>goes</u> **to** the coffee shop, and he <u>returns</u> **to** his office.

Exception: Do not put *to* directly before *home*.

> Albert returned ~~to~~ home after he won his prize. He didn't go to his friend's home.

Use *at* after verbs that indicate being or remaining in one place (and not moving from one place to another).

> In the afternoon, he <u>stays</u> **at** work. He <u>sits</u> **at** his desk and <u>looks</u> **at** his inventions.

for vs. during

Use *during* to explain when something happens. Use *for* to explain how long it takes to happen.

> **During** <u>the month of August</u>, the patent office closes **for** <u>two weeks</u>.

> The inventors of the bomb experimented **for** <u>many years</u> **during** <u>World War II</u>.

Section 5
MORE PARTS OF SPEECH

PRACTICE 8

Write the correct preposition in each blank. Choose *in, on, at, to, for,* or *from*.

EXAMPLE:

<u>At</u> 5:15 a.m. we heard the news.

1. One of the most influential inventions _____ history was the creation of the atomic bomb.

2. _____ Germany, scientists were trying very hard to develop the atomic bomb _____ the beginning of World War II.

3. _____ August 2, 1939, Albert Einstein wrote a letter to President Franklin Delano Roosevelt about Germany's progress making the bomb.

4. _____ that day, Einstein went _____ his office _____ 1 p.m, and he sat _____ his desk _____ several hours while he composed the letter.

5. Roosevelt was _____ his office speaking _____ the telephone when he heard about Einstein's letter.

6. Roosevelt's advisors were _____ breakfast when the president called them, and they hastily rushed _____ the White House.

7. The president and his advisers stayed _____ Washington and discussed the information _____ two days.

8. _____ 1941, the U.S. government decided to develop the atomic bomb.

9. The U.S. government spent around $2 billion on the Manhattan Project, which lasted _____ 1939 _____ 1945.

PRACTICE 9

Correct five errors with prepositions.

EXAMPLE:

The zipper has been popular ~~during~~ ^{for} many years.

Whitcomb Judson patented a new type of fabric fastener on 1893. Several others contributed to the design of the fastener. Today the zipper is the source of many "fly" jokes. For example, last semester, I went at my math class to make a presentation, and I did not realize that my zipper was down. During twenty minutes, I spoke, and some students giggled. During a month, others teased me. I must have heard "you're flying low" a hundred times. Now, when I go at college, I ensure that my zipper is firmly fastened.

Section 5
MORE PARTS OF SPEECH

Common Prepositional Expressions

Many common expressions contain prepositions. These types of expressions usually express a particular meaning.

EXAMPLE: This morning I <u>listened</u> **to** the radio.

verb   preposition

Here is a list of common prepositional expressions.

accuse (somebody) of	escape from	prevent (someone) from
acquainted with	excited about	protect (someone) from
add to	feel like	proud of
afraid of	familiar with	provide (someone) with
angry with	fond of	qualify for
angry about	forget about	realistic about
agree with	forgive (someone) for	refer to
apologize for	friendly with	related to
apply for	good for	rely on
approve of	grateful for	rescue from
argue with	happy about	responsible for
ask for	hear about	sad about
associate with	hope for	satisfied with
aware of	hopeful about	scared of
believe in	innocent of	search for
belong to	insist on	similar to
capable of	insulted by	specialize in
care about	interested in	stop (something) from
care for	introduce to	succeed in
commit to	jealous of	take advantage of
comply with	keep from	take care of
concern about	located in	thank (someone) for
confronted with	long for	think about
consist of	look forward to	think of
count on	opposed to	tired of
deal with	participate in	upset with
decide to	patient with	upset about
decide on	pay attention to	willing to
depend on	pay for	wish for
be disappointed with	pray for	worry about
be disappointed about	prepared to	
dream of	prepared for	

Section 5
MORE PARTS OF SPEECH

PRACTICE 10

Write the correct preposition in each blank. Use the preceding list of prepositional expressions to help you.

EXAMPLE:

Many American citizens participated _in_ the war effort.

1.   During World War II, many people believed _____ science. Robert Oppenheimer was interested _____ physics. He heard _____ the rise of fascism in Germany. He decided _____ become a scientist with the U.S. government.

2.   Oppenheimer was excited _____ working on atomic bombs for the Manhattan Project. Officials searched _____ a secluded location to develop the bomb and chose a desert area near Los Alamos, New Mexico. Oppenheimer dealt _____ a large team of scientists.

3. When he saw an atomic bomb test, Oppenheimer became afraid
    _____ its power. Later, when a bomb called Little Boy was dropped
    on Hiroshima, he felt partially responsible _____ changing the world
    with his discovery.

4. After the war, Oppenheimer argued _____ some other physicists
    and politicians about atomic weapons. He worried _____ the impact
    of the atomic bomb, and he came to believe that the nuclear arms race was
    not good _____ society. During the 1950s, Oppenheimer was accused
    _____ having communist sympathies. He was disappointed
    _____ the government for taking away his security clearance.

5. At the end of his career, Oppenheimer took advantage _____
    his experience with the Manhattan Project and wrote about ethics and
    morality. In 1967, the world heard _____ Oppenheimer's death from
    throat cancer.

The Writer's Desk Revise and Edit Your Warm Up

In the Warm Up on page 389, you wrote a few sentences about the
most interesting inventions of the last century. Edit your sentences
to check for any errors with nouns, determiners, and prepositions.

Section 5
**MORE PARTS
OF SPEECH**

REFLECT ON IT

Think about what you have learned in this chapter. If you do not know an answer,
review that concept.

1. What is the definition of a noun? _____
    _____

2. Give examples of five noncount nouns.
    _____   _____   _____   _____   _____

3. Make the following nouns plural.
    a. tooth: _____
    b. backseat driver: _____
    c. bride-to-be: _____
    d. kiss: _____
    e. homework: _____
    f. loaf: _____

(continued)

> **4.**   Correct the errors in the following sentences.
>
> $\overset{\textit{many}}{}$
> **EXAMPLE:**   Leonardo da Vinci had ~~much~~ ideas.
>
> a. He invented much things.
>
> b. He developed a idea for a parachute.
>
> c. Da Vinci is one of the most famous artist in the world.
>
> d. Little of his other works are as famous as the *Mona Lisa*.

FINAL REVIEW

Correct fifteen errors in singular nouns, plural nouns, determiners, and prepositions.

EXAMPLE:

$\overset{\textit{a}}{}$
George de Mestral had ~~the~~ splendid idea.

Section 5
MORE PARTS OF SPEECH

One summer day on 1948, George de Mestral decided to go for a hike. As he was walking through some tall weed, burrs stuck to his pants and to his dog's furs. This had happened much times before. However, on that day, de Mestral decided to examine some of the burrs with the microscope, and he discovered some interesting informations. He noticed that each burrs was made up of little hooks that helped it cling to material. He was very interested of this discovery. He thought on a way to use the hook system of the burrs to develop a products for the home. After much attempts, George patented his invention in 1951 and called it Velcro. This days, Velcro is used on different type of products such as shoes, clothings, and toys. Now, many manufacturers depend of Velcro.

 See Chapter 27 of the Visualizing Writing CD for additional mini-lectures on **Parts of Speech, Phrases,** and **Clauses.**

Pronouns

section theme **INVENTIONS AND DISCOVERIES**

CONTENTS

- Pronoun Case
- Relative Pronouns
- Reflexive Pronouns
- Pronoun-Antecedent Agreement
- Indefinite Pronouns
- Vague Pronouns
- Pronoun Shifts

In this chapter, you will read about **discoveries in ancient civilizations.**

The Writer's Desk Warm Up

Write a short paragraph describing a historical figure whom you admire. You could write about a famous politician, actor, writer, artist, scientist, or explorer. Explain what that person did that was admirable.

Pronoun Case

Pronouns are words that replace nouns (people, places, or things), other pronouns, and phrases. Use pronouns to avoid repeating nouns.

Machu Picchu is an ancient city located high in the Andes. ~~Machu Picchu~~ *It* was discovered in 1911.

Pronouns are formed according to the role they play in a sentence. A pronoun can be the subject or object of the sentence, or it can show possession. The next chart shows the three main pronoun cases: subjective, objective, and possessive.

Pronouns

Singular	Subjective	Objective	Possessives	
			Possessive Adjective	**Possessive Pronoun**
First person:	I	me	my	mine
Second person:	you	you	your	yours
Third person:	he, she, it, who, whoever	him, her, it, whom, whomever	his, her, its, whose	his, hers
Plural				
First person:	we	us	our	ours
Second person:	you	you	your	yours
Third person:	they	them	their	theirs

Section 5
MORE PARTS OF SPEECH

Subjective Case

A **subject** performs an action in a sentence. When a pronoun is the subject of the sentence, use the subjective form of the pronoun.

> **She** liked to read mystery novels set in ancient times.

> **We** watched a horror movie about mummies.

Objective Case

An **object** receives an action in a sentence. When a pronoun is the object in the sentence, use the objective form of the pronoun.

> The audience gave **him** an ovation for the lecture on ancient China.

> My sister saw **us** at the lecture.

Possessive Case

A possessive pronoun shows ownership.

- **Possessive adjectives** are always placed before the noun that they modify. In the next sentences, *her* and *their* are possessive adjectives.

> She finished **her** <u>book</u> about the pyramids, but they did not finish **their** <u>books</u>.

■ **Possessive pronouns** replace the possessive adjective and noun. In the next sentence, *her* is a possessive adjective and *theirs* is a possessive pronoun.

> She finished **her** <u>book</u> about the pyramids, but they did not finish **theirs**.

Problems with Possessive Pronouns

When using the possessive pronouns *hers* and *theirs*, be careful that you do not add an apostrophe before the *s*.

GRAMMAR LINK

For more information about apostrophes, see Chapter 34.

>   *hers*   *theirs*
> The archeology book is ~~her's~~. The papyrus map is ~~their's~~.

Some possessive adjectives sound like certain contractions. When using the possessive adjectives *their, your,* and *its,* be careful that you do not confuse them with *they're, you're,* and *it's.*

Their is the possessive adjective.	<u>Their</u> flight to Mexico City was late.
They're is the contraction of *they are.*	<u>They're</u> not going to be on time for the bus tour.
Your is the possessive adjective.	<u>Your</u> tour guide has a map of the Tulum Mayan ruins.
You're is the contraction of *you are.*	<u>You're</u> going to enjoy visiting this ancient site.
Its is the possessive adjective.	The Temple of the Frescoes has a beautiful mural on <u>its</u> wall.
It's is the contraction of *it is.*	<u>It's</u> an important piece of Mayan history.

**Section 5
MORE PARTS
OF SPEECH**

> **Hint**   **Choosing *His* or *Her***
>
> To choose the correct possessive adjective, think about the possessor (not the object that is possessed).
>
> • If something belongs to a female, use *her* + noun.
>
> > Cecilia packed <u>her</u> luggage.
>
> • If something belongs to a male, use *his* + noun.
>
> > Tony booked <u>his</u> flight.

PRACTICE I

Circle the correct possessive adjective or possessive pronoun in each set of parentheses.

Department of World Archeology
University of Concordia
Hivers, France

July 15, 2005

Dr. Imogene McWitter
World Archeological Society
2555 Dig Boulevard
New York, NY 10009

Subject: Request for Funding

Dear Dr. McWitter:

As the World Archeological Society and (its, it's, his) members already realize, the situation in many international museums is extremely grave. Due to a lack of funding, many museums cannot properly house and protect (their, theirs) artifacts. Additionally, some museums have been looted during times of war. As a representative of the Archeological Subcommittee and (its, it's) members, I am requesting additional funding for three specific projects.

The first project would be to find stolen artifacts and restore (they, them) to their proper museums. Not only do citizens of a country lose (their, theirs) heritage, but all of us, as citizens of the world, also lose (our, ours) if the plunder of antiquities continues. We hope that you and (your, you're) colleagues will give due attention to this problem.

The second project would finance the digs at various sites in the ancient Mesopotamian region by leading archeologists and (their, theirs) assistants. Dr. Sonia Richler, because of (her, hers) perseverance, has been able to form a general picture of what the Mesopotamian Empire and (its, it's, his) class structure was like in ancient times.

The third project would be to continue public educational programs on the importance of archeology and (its, it's) contribution to world knowledge. One example of an educational program is the film on Louis and Mary Leakey and (their, they're, theirs) contribution to archeology. As you know, Louis and Mary Leakey and others like (they, them, theirs) excavated in East Africa for many years. Archeologists have often made (their, theirs) discoveries by

Section 5
MORE PARTS OF SPEECH

accident. For example, Mary Leakey made (her, hers) while taking a walk in the valley where she and (her, hers, his) husband had been working. With proper education, perhaps members of the public will force (their, theirs) governments to spend funds protecting national treasures.

I have also attached a proposed budget for these three projects. If you require further information, please do not hesitate to contact (I, me) or (my, mine) assistant, Dale Yamoguchi.

(Yours, Your, Your's) truly,

Mafouz Shah

Mafouz Shah

Pronouns in Comparisons with *than or as*

Avoid making errors in pronoun case when the pronoun follows *than* or *as*. If the pronoun is a subject, use the subjective case, and if the pronoun is an object, use the objective case.

If you use the incorrect case, your sentence may have a meaning that you do not intend it to have. For example, people often follow *than* or *as* with an objective pronoun when they mean to follow it with a subjective pronoun. Look at the differences in the meanings of the next sentences.

> objective case
> I like ancient history as much as **him.**
>
> (I like ancient history <u>as much as I like him.</u>)

> subjective case
> I like ancient history as much as **he.**
>
> (I like ancient history <u>as much as he likes ancient history.</u>)

  Complete the Thought

If you are unsure which pronoun case to use, test by completing the thought. For example:

He likes to visit museums more than **I** (like to visit museums).

He likes to visit museums more than (he likes to visit) **me.**

Pronouns in Prepositional Phrases

In a prepositional phrase, the words that follow the preposition are the objects of the preposition. Therefore, always use the objective case of the pronoun after a preposition.

> <u>To</u> **her,** learning about history is not important.

> <u>Between</u> **you** and **me,** our history class is very interesting.

Pronouns with *and* or *or*

Use the correct case when nouns and pronouns are joined by *and* or *or*. If the pronouns are the subject, use the subjective case. If the pronouns are the object, use the objective case.

Subjective: ~~Him and me~~ had to do a presentation on the Incas.

Objective: The instructor asked ~~he and I~~ to present first.

⟨**Hint**⟩ **Finding the Correct Case**

An easy way to determine whether your case is correct is to say the sentence with just one pronoun.

The librarian asked her and (I, me) to speak quietly.

Choices: The librarian asked I . . . *or* The librarian asked me. . . .

Correct: The librarian asked her and <u>me</u> to speak quietly.

Section 5
MORE PARTS OF SPEECH

PRACTICE 2

Correct any errors with pronoun case. Some sentences may have more than one error. Write *C* in the space if the sentence is correct.

EXAMPLE:

Last summer, my friend and ~~me~~ (I) visited Mexico.

1. My friend, Maria, is older than me. _____

2. Maria gave me a book on the Maya civilization because she is as interested in the subject as me. _____

3. Maria and me took a bus to Chichén Itzá, an ancient site that was built around the middle of the sixth century. _____

4. At the site, we asked a young man to take a picture of we girls. _____

5. Maria's camera was newer than mine, so we used her's. _____

6. The young man, whose name was Karl, climbed with Maria and me to the top of the pyramid. _____

7. Him and his friend Pedro told us that they were afraid of heights. _____

8. Between you and I, I was also getting a bit dizzy, so we decided to climb down. _____

9. Our tour guide told Pedro and me that the Maya abandoned
   Chichén Itzá in the tenth century.   _____

10. Karl said goodbye to us because him and Pedro had to catch the
    bus for Belize.   _____

Relative Pronouns (*who, whom, which, that, whose*)

Relative pronouns can join two short sentences. Here is a list of relative pronouns.

who	whom	which	that	whose
whoever	whomever			

- *Who* (or *whoever*) and *whom* (or *whomever*) always refer to people. *Who* is the subject of the clause, and *whom* is the object of the clause.

  Subject: The <u>archeologist</u> **who** specializes in Mayan culture is speaking today.

  Object: The <u>archeologist</u> **whom** you met is my mother.

- *Which* always refers to things.

  The ancient city of <u>Machu Picchu</u>, **which** I have never seen, is located in the Andes.

- *That* refers to things.

  Hiram Bingham wrote a <u>book</u> **that** is about Machu Picchu.

- *Whose* always shows that something belongs to or is connected with someone or something. It usually replaces possessive pronouns such as *his, her,* or *their.* Do not confuse *whose* with *who's,* which means "who is."

  The archaeologist traced the route. <u>His</u> maps were on the table.

  The archaeologist, **whose** maps were on the table, traced the route.

> **GRAMMAR LINK**
>
> Clauses with *which* are set off with commas. For more information, see Chapter 33, "Commas."

Section 5
MORE PARTS OF SPEECH

 Choosing *Who* or *Whom*

If you are unsure whether to use *who* or *whom,* test yourself in the following way. Replace *who* or *whom* with another pronoun. If the replacement is a subjective pronoun such as *he* or *she,* use *who.* If the replacement is an objective pronoun such as *her* or *him,* use **whom.**

   I know a man **who** works in a museum.

   (<u>He</u> works in a museum.)

   The man to **whom** you gave your portfolio is the director of the museum.

   (You gave your portfolio <u>to him</u>.)

PRACTICE 3

Write the correct relative pronoun in each blank.

EXAMPLE:
The small village of Delphi, _which_ attracts many people during the tourist season, is in Greece.

1. The ancient Greeks _____ worshiped Apollo built a temple to him near Delphi. Pilgrims _____ faith was strong journeyed on foot to worship Apollo.

2. An oracle was a person _____ gave advice to kings and pilgrims on many different matters _____ were considered important, such as where to build monuments, which laws to invoke, and which prayers to repeat. Apollo's oracle was a woman _____ lived at his sanctuary. The sanctuary, _____ was considered holy, was visited by many pilgrims.

3. People believed that Apollo spoke through the oracle _____ used her voice to express his wishes. Many people wished to speak with the oracle _____ advice they sought. She sometimes spoke in riddles _____ caused people to misinterpret the meaning of her advice.

4. One famous example of a misunderstanding involved Croesus, _____ was the king of Lydia. Croesus, _____ had planned to attack the Persians in 550 B.C., went to the oracle for advice. The oracle, _____ he asked about his future chance of victory, told Croesus that if he attacked the Persians, he would demolish "a great empire."

5. Croesus, praising the oracle in _____ he had great faith, decided to wage war against the Persians. After the war, Croesus, _____ was badly defeated by the Persians, was extremely angry, and he wondered why the oracle had lied to him. However, as it turned out, the oracle had seen into the future correctly. By starting a war _____ he eventually lost, Croesus had indeed destroyed a great empire—his own!

Section 5
MORE PARTS
OF SPEECH

Reflexive Pronouns (*-self/-selves*)

Use **reflexive pronouns** when you want to emphasize that the subject does an action to himself or herself.

I asked **myself** many questions.

History often repeats **itself.**

Do not use reflexive pronouns for activities that people do to themselves, such as washing or shaving. However, you can use reflexive pronouns to draw attention to a surprising or an unusual action.

The little <u>boy</u> fed **himself.**

(The boy probably could not feed himself at a previous time.)

The next chart shows subjective pronouns and the reflexive pronouns that relate to them.

Pronouns That End with *-self* or *-selves*

Singular	Antecedent	Reflexive Pronoun
First person:	I	myself
Second person:	you	yourself
Third person:	he, she, it	himself, herself, itself
Plural		
First person:	we	ourselves
Second person:	you	yourselves
Third person:	they	themselves

Hint · **Common Errors with Reflexive Pronouns**

Do not use *hisself* or *theirselves*. These are incorrect ways to say *himself* or *themselves*.

              themselves
The tourists went by ~~theirselves~~ to the museum.

              himself.
Croesus visited the oracle by ~~hisself.~~

Section 5
MORE PARTS OF SPEECH

PRACTICE 4

Fill in the blanks with the correct reflexive pronouns.

EXAMPLE:
He wanted to explore the forest by ___*himself*___.

1. Our guide was upset because she had twisted her ankle while walking by _____ through the jungle. She had forgotten how easily she could hurt _____ by tripping on a tree root.

2. Our guide looked at us and said, "Go to the temple by _____. You are all capable of finding it."

3.   Because our guide could not go with us, we had to climb the steps of the temple by _____. One member of the group, Matt, decided we were too slow for him, so he decided to climb up by _____.

4.   I thought to _____ that he would probably get lost. Sure enough, he did get lost. When we found him, he told us that he had lost his footing and cut _____ on some of the crumbling pieces of rock. We offered him some first aid supplies so he could patch _____ up.

5.   After we found Matt, we got _____ back on track. We reached the top of the temple and felt very pleased with _____.

Pronoun-Antecedent Agreement

A pronoun must agree with its **antecedent,** which is the word to which the pronoun refers. Antecedents are nouns, pronouns, and phrases that the pronouns have replaced, and they always come before the pronoun. Pronouns must agree in person and number with their antecedents.

> The archeologist was frustrated because **she** could not raise enough money for **her** expedition.
> (*The archeologist* is the antecedent of *she* and *her.*)

> My instructor went on a vacation to Peru. **He** took **his** family with **him.**
> (*My instructor* is the antecedent of *he, his,* and *him.*)

> China has many ancient salt mines. **They** date back to the fourth century B.C.
> (*Salt mines* is the antecedent of *they.*)

Section 5
MORE PARTS OF SPEECH

GRAMMAR LINK

For a list of collective nouns, see page 376 in Chapter 25.

Hint   **Using Collective Nouns**

Collective nouns refer to a group of people or things. The group acts as a unit; therefore, it is singular.

> The association had **its** meeting on Monday.
> The government tried to implement **its** policies.

PRACTICE 5

Fill in the blank spaces with the appropriate pronouns or possessive adjectives.

EXAMPLE:

Many people are fascinated with the lost city of Troy, and __*they*__ are curious about the city's history.

1.   The archeologist Heinrich Schliemann believed that finding the lost city of Troy would bring _____ fame and fortune. He was convinced that

_____ idea about the location of Troy was correct. Archeologists at that time thought that the city of Troy was a myth and that they would waste _____ time hunting for _____.

2.   Schliemann was a millionaire who spent _____ time and money pursuing _____ archeological interests. In 1868, Schliemann met Frank Calvert, a businessman who owned land around Hisarlik, Turkey. Both men were convinced that _____ could find the lost city of Troy. Calvert provided the funding, and Schliemann began to excavate on Calvert's land.

3.   Schliemann began digging in 1870. The Turkish government had not yet given Schliemann _____ approval for the excavation. As the work progressed, he made _____ first discovery when he uncovered many stone blocks. In 1873, Schliemann and _____ wife Sophia also discovered gold at the site. Schliemann dismissed the workers because he did not want _____ to know about the gold.

4.   The couple then uncovered a larger hoard of gold, silver, and jewelry. They smuggled _____ treasures out of Turkey. Sophia, Schliemann's wife, wore some of the jewelry around _____ neck. The Turkish authorities were furious because treasures had been removed without _____ permission. Eventually Schliemann got control over the treasures and he presented _____ to the city of Berlin. The treasures somehow disappeared from Berlin after World War II, and _____ were recently rediscovered in Moscow.

Indefinite Pronouns

Use **indefinite pronouns** when you refer to people or things whose identity is not known or is unimportant. The next chart shows some common singular and plural indefinite pronouns.

Section 5
MORE PARTS OF SPEECH

Indefinite Pronouns				
Singular	another	each	nobody	other
	anybody	everybody	no one	somebody
	anyone	everyone	nothing	someone
	anything	everything	one	something
Plural	both, few, many, others, several			
Either singular or plural	all, any, some, none, more, most, half (and other fractions)			

Singular

When you use a singular indefinite antecedent, also use a singular pronoun to refer to it.

> <u>Everybody</u> feels amazed when **he or she** sees China's terracotta army for the first time.

> <u>Nobody</u> should forget to visit China's terracotta army in **his or her** lifetime.

Plural

When you use a plural indefinite antecedent, also use a plural pronoun to refer to it.

> The two objects are ancient, and <u>both</u> have **their** own intrinsic value.

> The world has many illegal excavation sites; there are <u>several</u> operating in China, but **they** cannot be controlled.

Either Singular or Plural

Some indefinite pronouns can be either singular or plural, depending on the noun to which they refer.

> Many archeologists came to the site. <u>All</u> were experts in **their** field.
>
> (*All* refers to archeologists; therefore, the pronoun is plural.)

> We excavated <u>all</u> of the site and **its** artifacts.
>
> (*All* refers to the site; therefore, the pronoun is singular.)

 Hint   *Using of the* **Expressions**

In sentences containing the expression *one of the* . . . or *each of the* . . . , the subject is the indefinite pronoun *one* or *each*. Therefore, any pronoun referring to that phrase must be singular.

> <u>One</u> of the statues is missing **its** weapon.

> <u>Each</u> of the men has **his** own map.

PRACTICE 6

Identify and correct nine errors in pronoun-antecedent agreement. You may change either the antecedent or the pronoun. If you change any antecedents, make sure that your subjects and verbs agree.

EXAMPLE:

                      their
Some of the soldiers had ~~his~~ own swords.

1.   In 1974, in Xi'an, China, some local men were digging a well when they

       made an astounding discovery. One of the men uncovered a clay soldier with their bare hands. Then others, using their shovels, discovered more clay soldiers at the site. Someone rode their bicycle to the local communist party headquarters. The worker described what he and the others had found.

2.　The local communist party sent some archeologists to the site. When they arrived, everyone expressed shock at the sight before their eyes. They realized that the find was significant. The central government sent a message to the local peasants. Each had to leave their land and move to another location. Nobody was allowed to remain in their home.

3.　Over the next years, specialists excavated the site. They uncovered more than 8,000 terracotta soldiers. The soldiers are life-size, and many have his own unique physical features, representing every ethnic group in China. Different male artists sculpted groups of the soldiers. Each engraved their name on the statues.

Section 5
MORE PARTS OF SPEECH

4.　The clay soldiers have been guarding an ancient emperor for over 2,000 years. Everybody in the all-male army, including generals, officers, cavalry, and archers, had their own life-sized weapon. Today the site is a major tourist attraction in China. Anybody who goes to China on their holiday should try to visit the terracotta army.

 Avoid Sexist Language

Terms like *anybody, somebody, nobody,* and *each* are singular antecedents, so the pronouns that follow those words must be singular. At one time, it was acceptable to use *he* as a general term meaning "all people;" however, today it is more acceptable to use *he or she*.

Sexist:	Almost <u>everyone</u> has **his** own opinion about history books.
Solution:	Almost <u>everyone</u> has **his or her** own opinion about history books.
Better solution:	Almost <u>all people</u> have **their** own opinions about history books.

Exception: If you know for certain that the subject is male or female, then use only *he* or only *she*.

PRACTICE 7

Circle the correct pronouns in the following paragraphs.

EXAMPLE:

Some people say that history is not important because (its), it's) information is not relevant to people's everyday lives.

1.   History courses offer information about the past, but many people wonder whether they should spend (his or her, their) time studying the past. In fact, somebody might feel it is more important to think about (his or her, their) future. In other words, some people may not consider history and (it's, its) lessons to be as important as other subjects that are more practical.

2.   In the past, historians and (their, theirs) supporters memorized names and dates. Everybody believed that (his or her, their) knowledge of history indicated a high level of education. Between you and (I, me), I do not think that this reason for studying history is valid. I think that history should be studied for (its, it's) own merits. For example, history tells us about societies and (their, theirs) past behaviors. History also informs us about a critical moment in the past and (its, it's) influence on today's lifestyles. Furthermore, history helps us understand more about (yourselves, ourselves).

3.   I like studying history; however, my brother has always liked it far more than (I, me). He became really interested when we were children. (He, Him) and (I, me) used to read stories about World War I. After school, while the other neighborhood kids were playing outside, my brother preferred to spend hours watching war films (who, that) had great battle scenes.

4.   Now my brother is a historian. He is a man (who, whom) believes that everybody should take (his or her, their) history lessons seriously. In fact, my brother met (his, her) future wife in history class. He was sitting by (hisself, himself, herself) when she sat near him. The rest, of course, is history.

Section 5
**MORE PARTS
OF SPEECH**

Vague Pronouns

Avoid using pronouns that could refer to more than one antecedent.

> **Vague:** Frank asked his friend where <u>his</u> map of ancient Greece was.
>
> (Whose map is it: Frank's or his friend's?)

> **Clearer:** **Frank** wondered where **his** map of ancient Greece was, so he asked his friend about it.

Avoid using confusing pronouns such as *it* and *they* that have no clear antecedent.

> **Vague:** <u>They</u> say that people should get vaccines before traveling to certain countries.
>
> (Who are *they?*)

> **Clearer:** **Health authorities** say that people should get vaccines before traveling to certain countries.

> **Vague:** <u>It</u> stated in the magazine that the tower of Copán in Honduras has more hieroglyphic inscriptions than any other Maya ruin.
>
> (Who or what is *it?*)

> **Clearer:** **The magazine article** stated that the tower of Copán in Honduras has more hieroglyphic inscriptions than any other Maya ruin.

This, *that*, and *which* should refer to a specific antecedent.

> **Vague:** The teacher told us that we should study hard for our history exams because they were going to be difficult. <u>This</u> caused all of us to panic.
>
> (What is *this?*)

> **Clearer:** The teacher told us that we should study hard for our history exams because they were going to be difficult. **This information** caused all of us to panic.

Section 5
MORE PARTS OF SPEECH

 Avoid Repeating the Subject

When you clearly mention a subject, do not repeat the subject in pronoun form.

Egypt's pyramids, ~~they~~ are more than 4,000 years old.

The book ~~it~~ is really interesting.

PRACTICE 8

Each sentence has either a vague pronoun or a repeated subject. Correct the errors. You may need to rewrite some sentences.

EXAMPLE:

The radio reporter announced
~~They said on the radio~~ that archeologists have discovered a new burial ground along the Yangzte River.

1. Professor Schmitt told Mark that a book about the Great Wall of China is on his desk.

2. It states that the Great Wall of China is more than 2,000 years old.

3. They built the wall to protect the Chinese empire from northern invasions.

4. This also helped unify China.

5. The history book it contains information on the emperor Oin Shi Huang.

6. He ordered its construction.

7. They persecuted anyone who disagreed with the emperor.

8. The book it has many other interesting facts about the Great Wall of China.

9. For example, the wall it is over 1,500 miles in length.

10. They say the only man-made object that can be seen from space is the Great Wall.

Section 5
MORE PARTS OF SPEECH

Pronoun Shifts

If your writing contains unnecessary shifts in person or number, you may confuse your readers. Carefully edit your writing to ensure that your pronouns are consistent in number and person.

Making Pronouns Consistent in Number

Pronouns and antecedents must agree in **number**. If the antecedent is singular, then the pronoun must be singular. If the antecedent is plural, then the pronoun must be plural.

singular   *his or her*
The **director** of the museum encouraged ~~their~~ employees to be on time.

When **tourists** visit an excavation site, ~~he~~ *they* should be careful not to touch the artifacts.

[margin note: *plural*]

Making Pronouns Consistent in Person

Person is the writer's perspective. In some writing assignments, you may use first person (*I, we*). For other assignments, especially most college and workplace writing, you may use second person (*you*) or third person (*he, she, it, they*).

When you shift your point of view for no reason, your writing may become unclear, and you may confuse your readers. If you begin writing from one point of view, do not shift unnecessarily to another point of view.

> *we*
> If ~~one~~ considered the expenses involved in visiting another country, **we** would probably never travel.

> *we*
> **We** visited the pyramids at Teotihuacán, but ~~you~~ could not climb one of them because archeologists were working on it.

Hint ▶ **Avoiding Pronoun Shifts in Paragraphs**

Sometimes it is easier to use pronouns consistently in individual sentences than it is in larger paragraphs or essays. When you write paragraphs and essays, always check that your pronouns agree with your antecedents in person and in number. In the next example, the pronouns are consistent in the first two sentences; however, they shift in person in the third sentence.

> **We** went to Mexico City last year. **We** traveled around on the subway to visit
> *we*
> various archeological sites. Sometimes the subway was so crowded that ~~you~~
>
> could barely move.

Section 5
**MORE PARTS
OF SPEECH**

PRACTICE 9

Correct eight pronoun shift errors.

EXAMPLE:

we
We visited the pyramids at Giza, Egypt. The lines were so long that ~~you~~ had to wait for hours.

1. An Egyptian pharaoh built the Great Pyramid as a tomb. All the

    powerful pharaohs believed that material goods must be buried in their

    tombs to help you on their journey in the afterlife.

2. Napoleon invaded Egypt in 1798. Napoleon and his soldiers were amazed when they saw the pyramids. After the army invaded Egypt, they returned to France with many artifacts. Napoleon thought that you had the right to take anything from a country that you had invaded.

3. One of Napoleon's soldiers discovered the Rosetta Stone but did not realize the importance of their discovery. In 1801, British soldiers invaded Egypt and found the Rosetta Stone. They took the stone and brought them back to England.

4. When tourists go to the British Museum in London, one may see many antiquities from Egypt. Every year, people go to see the Rosetta Stone because you know it is impressive.

The Writer's Desk **Revise and Edit Your Warm Up**

In the Warm Up on page 405, you described a historical figure whom you admire. Check for any problems with pronouns.

Section 5
**MORE PARTS
OF SPEECH**

REFLECT ON IT

Think about what you have learned in this chapter. If you do not know an answer, review that concept.

1. What is a pronoun? _____

    _____

2. Write a sentence that includes an objective pronoun. _____

    _____

3. When do you use possessive pronouns (*my, mine, his, hers,* etc.)? _____

    _____

4. Circle the best answer: In a sentence, *whom* replaces
    a. the subject.   b. the object

5. What is an antecedent? _____

    _____

6. Circle the best answer: Pronouns must agree with their antecedents:
    a. only in number.   b. only in person.
    c. both in number and in person.   d. neither in number nor in person.

FINAL REVIEW

Correct fifteen errors with pronouns in the next paragraphs.

EXAMPLE:

A prominent archeologist
~~It~~ says that the dispute between many countries is about cultural property rights.

1.   People learn important things about history by visiting museums filled

     with historical artifacts. For example, Britain and France they have obtained

     antiquities from countries around the world. The British government

     believes in it's right to keep the treasures who are exhibited in museums.

     However, countries such as Greece and Egypt want their treasures back

     because they view antiquities as a part of its cultural heritage. Returning

     antiquities to its native countries is a complicated issue.

2.   The removal of artifacts such as mummies has created an ethical

     problem for the Egyptian government and their archeologists. An

     interesting science article it says that a lot of information can be acquired

     from the scientific study of burial sites. Although some people believe

     it is always unethical to dig up the dead, every archeologist who studies

     Egyptian mummies increases their knowledge of ancient Egypt. For

     example, centuries ago, the pharaohs believed that they could get to

     heaven faster if you were buried with food and treasures for the voyage.

     Each pharoah decided for hisself what he would take on his journey to

     the afterlife. When a pharaoh died, priests mummified the body and buried

     them in the pyramids. Therefore, archeologists whom have excavated

     burial sites not only find mummies, but they find valuable artworks and

     other artifacts.

3.   It says in the newspaper that the dispute between countries such as

     Egypt and Britain will not be resolved. They say that international policy

     should regulate ownership of national treasures. Everybody has their own

     opinion about the issue.

Section 5
**MORE PARTS
OF SPEECH**

The Writer's Room **Topics for Writing**

Choose one of the following topics and write a paragraph or an essay. Remember to follow the writing process.

1. In the past one hundred years, what events have changed the world? List some events.

2. Tell a story about an ideal vacation. Where would you go, and what would you do? Use descriptive language in your writing.

3. Think about a recent invention. Contrast people's lives before and after that invention.

4. How important is history as a school subject? Should history be a compulsory subject?

 The Writers' Circle

Take turns interviewing a partner. Discover three interesting things about each other. Then write a paragraph about your partner. It should have eight to ten sentences.

When you have finished, exchange paragraphs with your partner. Proofread your partner's paragraph. Look carefully at nouns, pronouns, and determiners. Discuss any errors that you find.

Section 5
MORE PARTS OF SPEECH

 See Chapter 28 of the Visualizing Writing CD for an additional mini-lecture on **Prounoun-Antecedent Agreement.**

READING LINK

Great Discoveries
"My Head Rolled in Syria" by Josh Freed (page 541)
"Growing Up in Cyberspace" by Brent Staples (page 548)

Adjectives and Adverbs

CHAPTER 29

section theme **HEALTH CARE**

CONTENTS

- Adjectives
- Adverbs
- Comparative and Superlative Forms

In this chapter, you will read about health care issues.

The Writer's Desk Warm Up

Write a short paragraph describing your opinion about smoking in public places. Should all bars and restaurants be smoke-free? Explain why or why not.

Adjectives

Adjectives describe nouns (people, places, or things) and pronouns (words that replace nouns). They add information explaining how many, what kind, or which one. They also help you appeal to the senses by describing how things look, smell, feel, taste, and sound.

> The **intelligent** <u>woman</u>, Justina Ford, became the first **African American** <u>female</u> in Colorado to be a licensed physician.

Justina Ford delivered more than **seven thousand** <u>babies</u>.

Dr. Ford had to overcome **difficult** <u>obstacles</u> in her career.

Placement of Adjectives

You can place adjectives either before a noun or after a linking verb such as *be*, *look*, *appear*, *smell*, or *become*.

Before the noun: The **young unemployed** <u>man</u> received a
                              scholarship for **medical** school.

After the linking verb: He was **shocked**, but <u>he</u> was **happy**.

PRACTICE I

Underline the adjectives in the next sentences.

EXAMPLE:

<u>About 43 million</u> Americans had no <u>medical</u> insurance in 1999.

1. Self-employed entrepreneurs and small-business owners struggle to get adequate health care.

2. Also, certain groups of elderly Americans cannot afford to get sufficient, reliable medical treatment.

3. For example, Timothy Evans is disappointed and angry because he cannot afford to see a heart specialist.

4. Furthermore, prescription drug costs are higher in the United States than they are in other countries such as England, Switzerland, Canada, and Sweden.

5. Where the average American citizen pays one dollar for a prescription drug, a British citizen pays only sixty-four cents and a Canadian citizen pays only fifty-seven cents.

6. The average annual profit of the top ten drug companies is over three billion dollars.

7. Drug companies argue that they do groundbreaking research on new drugs.

8. Politicians are trying to come up with decent and fair legislation about health-care issues.

Section 6
MODIFIERS

Problems with Adjectives

You can recognize many adjectives by their endings. Be particularly careful when you use the following adjective forms.

Adjectives Ending in *-ful* or *-less*

Some adjectives end in *-ful* or *-less*. Remember that *-ful* ends in one *l* and *-less* ends in double *s*.

> Alexander Fleming, a **skillful** scientist, conducted many **useful** experiments.

> His work appeared in **countless** publications.

Adjectives Ending in *-ed* and *-ing*

Some adjectives look like verbs because they end in *-ing* or *-ed*.

- When the adjective ends in *-ed*, it describes the person or animal's expression or feeling.

> The **overworked** and **tired** scientist presented her findings to the public.

- When the adjective ends in *-ing*, it describes the quality of the person or thing.

> Her **compelling** and **promising** discovery pleased the public.

 Keep Adjectives in the Singular Form

Always make an adjective singular, even if the noun following the adjective is plural. In the next example, "year" acts as an adjective.

Paul was a nine-~~years~~-old boy when he broke his arm while playing with ~~others~~ children.
(year) *(other)*

Section 6
MODIFIERS

PRACTICE 2

Correct seven adjective errors. The adjectives may have the wrong form, or they may be misspelled.

EXAMPLE:

surprising
Many ~~surprised~~ medical findings happen by accident.

1.   One of the world's amazed scientifics discoveries happened by pure

     chance. Born in 1881, Alexander Fleming was a tireles medical doctor.

     He worked in his small London clinic where he treated famous people

     for venereal disease. He also enjoyed doing biologicals experiments.

2.   One day in 1928, he put some *Staphylococcus* bacteria in a culture dish. Two weeks later, Fleming, who was a carefull researcher, discovered that a clear ring encircled the yellow-green mold on the dish. A mold spore had flown into the dish from a laboratory on the floor below. At this point Fleming made an insightfull observation. He had an astounded revelation. He realized that the mold somehow stopped the growth of bacteria in the culture dish.

3.   Fleming named the new product penicillin. In World War II, the drug saved millions of lives, and it continues to be used today to treat differents infections.

Adverbs

Adverbs add information to adjectives, verbs, or other adverbs. They give more specific information about how, when, where, and to what extent an action or event occurred.

verb   adverb

Doctors in ancient Rome <u>performed</u> surgeries **seriously.**

adverb adverb

These surgeons could remove cataracts **quite** <u>quickly</u>.

adverb adjective

The ancient Romans were **highly** <u>innovative</u>.

Forms of Adverbs

Section 6
MODIFIERS

> **Hint**   **Some Adverbs and Adjectives Have the Same Form**
>
> Some adverbs look exactly like adjectives. The only way to distinguish them from adjectives is to see what they are modifying or describing. These next words can be either adjectives or adverbs.
>
> | | | | | |
> |---|---|---|---|---|
> | early | fast | high | often | right |
> | far | hard | late | past | soon |
>
>   adjective   adverb
> Dr. Greenbay has a **hard** job. She works **hard.**

Adverbs often end in *-ly*. In fact, you can change many adjectives into adverbs by adding *-ly* endings.

■ If you add *-ly* to a word that ends in *l*, then your new word will have a double *l*.

scornful + ly

Many ancient Romans viewed surgeons **scornfully.**

■ If you add *-ly* to a word that ends in *e*, keep the *e*. Exceptions to this rule are *truly* and *duly*.

extreme + ly
Doctors were **extremely** careful when they operated on patients.

PRACTICE 3

Circle the correct adjectives or adverbs in each sentence.

EXAMPLE:

Many groups (loud, (loudly)) debate the subject of euthanasia.

1. The average life span for human beings has increased (great, greatly) due to advances in medical technology. Yet (certain, certainly) debilitating diseases decrease the quality of life. Therefore, society has to deal (frequent, frequently) with the issue of a patient's right to choose to die. A debate has (rapid, rapidly) developed among medical professionals on the ethics of prolonging the life of people with debilitating diseases. Many people have (strong, strongly) opinions on the subject of euthanasia.

2. The term *euthanasia* refers to a third party (intentional, intentionally) causing the death of a patient at his or her request. For example, a doctor removing a life support machine is committing euthanasia. *Assisted suicide* refers to a third party (clear, clearly) helping a patient commit the act of dying. For example, a family member who (knowing, knowingly) supplies a patient with drugs is assisting suicide if the patient takes the (powerful, powerfully) drugs in order to die. To date, Oregon is the only state that allows people to participate in assisted suicide (legal, legally).

Section 6
MODIFIERS

Placement of Frequency Adverbs

Frequency adverbs are words that indicate how often someone performs an action or when an event occurs. Common frequency adverbs are *always, ever, never, often, sometimes,* and *usually.* They can appear at the beginning of sentences, or they can appear in the next locations.

■ Place frequency adverbs before regular present tense and past tense verbs.

Medical doctors **always** <u>recite</u> the Hippocratic oath.

Hippocrates **generally** <u>believed</u> in rationality.

- Place frequency adverbs after all forms of the verb *be* (*am, is, are, was, were*).

    My patients <u>are</u> **usually** punctual for appointments.

    Last month, my sister <u>was</u> **occasionally** late for her biology class.

- Place frequency adverbs after helping verbs.

    I <u>have</u> **never** broken any bone in my body.

    I <u>must</u> **always** be careful when I ski.

PRACTICE 4

Correct six errors in the placement of frequency adverbs.

EXAMPLE:

must sometimes take

Medical students ~~must take sometimes~~ a course on the history of medicine.

1. Hippocrates was born around 460 B.C. in Greece. Medical professionals claim generally that Hippocrates is the founder of modern medicine. In ancient Greece, physicians thought that a patient's illness usually was due to evil spirits. Hippocrates rejected often such explanations. He believed that there was a connection between good health and a good diet. He often was criticized for his beliefs.

2. Hippocrates traveled sometimes through Greece teaching medicine. On the island of Cos, Hippocrates founded a school of medicine and also developed his famous oath. To show their respect for Hippocrates, doctors take always the Hippocratic oath before they begin to practice medicine.

Section 6
MODIFIERS

Problems with Adverbs
Use the Correct Form

Many times, people use an adjective instead of an adverb after a verb. Ensure that you always modify your verbs using an adverb.

really quickly

Ancient Greek medicine advanced ~~real quick~~ after the time of Homer.

slowly

However, patients recovered very ~~slow~~.

PRACTICE 5

Correct nine errors in adjective and adverb forms.

EXAMPLE:

Euthanasia is a ~~realy~~ *really* difficult issue.

1. People who oppose the "right-to-die" movement argue that many patients who wish for euthanasia may be extremelly depressed. Patients may also have incomplete information about other options such as long-term care and real effective pain control. Opponents of legal euthanasia also suggest that many desperately people could be coerced into committing euthanasia really quick.

2. People who want to legalize euthanasia feel profound that the quality of a person's life is the most important consideration in this debate. They say that if a patient has become severe disabled due to illness, his or her quality of life is drastically reduced. They believe that a patient should have the right to die with dignity if he or she chooses. Proponents of euthanasia have real firm beliefs. They think that laws can prevent abuse or coercion of the patient.

3. Legislators act slow when it comes to making policy decisions about euthanasia. People on both sides of the issue express their opinions forcefuly. There is no consensus.

Section 6
MODIFIERS

Using *Good* and *Well*, *Bad* and *Badly*

Good is an adjective, and *well* is an adverb.

> **Adjective:** Louis Pasteur had a **good** reputation.
>
> **Adverb:** He explained his theories **well.**

Exception: Use *well* to describe a person's health: I do not feel **well**.

Bad is an adjective, and *badly* is an adverb.

> **Adjective:** My father has a **bad** cold.
>
> **Adverb:** His throat hurts **badly.**

quarter horse in the stable. She was also the (worse, worst) behaved of the bunch. She did not like being saddled.

2. Kelly played (more, most) tricks on her riders than the other horses did. One day, she blew up her stomach when I saddled her. As I mounted her, she blew the air out and the saddle slipped from her back. I fell off and broke my arm. I had the (greater, greatest) pain imaginable. When I went back to riding, I was always (more, most) careful with Kelly than with the other horses.

PRACTICE 8

Complete the sentences in this paragraph by writing either the comparative or superlative form of each adjective in parentheses.

EXAMPLE:
Antonia Novello is one of the (respected) _most respected_ doctors in America.

1. In 1990, Antonia Novello became the first woman as well as the first Hispanic citizen to be appointed surgeon general of the United States. The Office of the Surgeon General is one of the (important) _____ departments in the U.S. government. The surgeon general is the head of the American Public Health Service. Even the (little) _____ known public health issues are important to this department.

Section 6
MODIFIERS

2. Novello was born in Puerto Rico. She was (precocious) _____ _____ than other children her age. She graduated from high school at age fifteen, which was (early) _____ than her peers. As a child, she suffered from one of the (terrible) _____ illnesses, a disease of the colon. During her adolescence, Novello had to spend her time during the summer getting medical treatments. Because of this experience, she found medicine (appealing) _____ to study than other subjects.

3. As a young woman, Novello went to the University of Puerto Rico. She worked (hard) _____ on her studies than on other activities.

She received her medical degree in 1970, excelled in her career, and came to the attention of the government. President George H. W. Bush thought that she was (good) _____ than other candidates, and in 1989, he nominated her to be surgeon general.

4.   During her term, Novello traveled back to Puerto Rico. She was greeted by one of the (large) _____ crowds ever to greet a surgeon general. Her mother's school students were the (young) _____ fans in the crowd. Antonia Novello has become one of the (good) _____ role models for American children.

Problems with Comparative and Superlative Forms

Using *more* and *-er*

In the comparative form, never use *more* and *-er* to modify the same word. In the superlative form, never use *most* and *-est* to modify the same word.

> *better*
> Some people thought that Salk's vaccine was ~~more better~~ than Sabin's
> *best*
> vaccine. But the polio vaccine was one of the ~~most best~~ discoveries of
>
> our times.

Using *fewer* and *less*

In the comparative form, never use *less* to compare two count nouns. Use *less* to compare two noncount nouns. (Noncount nouns are nouns that cannot be divided, such as *information* and *music*.) Use *fewer* to compare two count nouns.

> *fewer*
> Today, ~~less~~ people get vaccinated than in previous decades because
> *Less*
> some question the safety of certain vaccinations. ~~Fewer~~ information
>
> about vaccines was available in the 1950s than is available today.

***Section 6*
MODIFIERS**

GRAMMAR LINK

For a list of noncount nouns, refer to page 394 in Chapter 27.

 Using *the* in the Comparative Form

Although you would usually use *the* in superlative forms, you can use it in some two-part comparatives. In these expressions, the second part is the result of the first part.

action   result
<u>The more</u> you exercise, <u>the better</u> your health will be.

PRACTICE 9

Correct fifteen adjective and adverb errors.

EXAMPLE:

Americans debate ~~continual~~ *continually* on the ethics of organ transplants.

1. One of the most greatest miracles of modern medicine is organ transplants. Organ transplants save most lives than ever before. With donor organs, many recipients can lead more better lives than previously imagined. However, a public debate about organ transplants is growing rapid.

2. The source of donor organs is a controversial issue. Given the scarcity of organs, some individuals who need transplants quick have obtained organs through unscrupulous methods. For instance, some have bought organs from the most poorest segments of the population in developing countries. Destitute people sometimes sell their organs to a rich buyer because they need money real badly.

3. Who should receive an organ transplant? Given the scarcity of supply, should a person who smokes heavy or drinks too much receive a lung or liver transplant? Obviously, the more a person smokes, the worst his or her health will be. Should such people be refused access to organ transplants?

4. In addition, money is an issue in this debate. Hospital administrators are concerned about the high cost of transplants. Less people have adequate medical insurance than ever before. Should those with health insurance be treated more better than those without? According to most experts, the richest a patient is, the best his or her chances are to receive a transplant.

5. Waiting for an organ transplant is one of the worse experiences anyone can go through. Hopefully, in future years, the number of people who sign donor cards will be more higher than it is now.

Section 6
MODIFIERS

The Writer's Desk Revise and Edit Your Warm Up

In the Warm Up on page 425, you wrote a short paragraph about smoking in public places. Check the paragraph for any adjective and adverb errors.

REFLECT ON IT

Think about what you have learned in this unit. If you do not know an answer, review that concept.

1. What is an adjective? _____

_____

2. What is an adverb? _____

_____

3. Write the correct adjective or adverb in each blank.

a. My doctor treats her patients (good, well) _____. She is one of the (better, best) _____ eye surgeons in Berlin.

b. My brother has (less, fewer) _____ work experience than I do, but he also has (less, fewer) _____ responsibilities.

4. The following sentences contain adjective or adverb errors. Correct each mistake.

a. We had a real nice time at the medical conference.

b. Everyone was dressed casual.

c. My sister changes often her mind about her career.

d. The advancing medical textbook is my sister's.

Section 6
MODIFIERS

FINAL REVIEW

Correct fifteen errors in adjectives and adverbs.

EXAMPLE:

                                        amazing

Rosalind Franklin was one of the most ~~amazed~~ scientists of her time.

1.   A dynamic scientist who deserves acknowledgement is Rosalind Franklin. In the 1950s, she worked intense on her research at Cambridge University. At that time, there were less female researchers than there are today. Franklin was hopefull that she would discover the secrets of cell

structure. In 1953, Franklin took a photograph of the structure of a cell and was exciting when it revealed that the structure of DNA had two chains.

2.   Two other scientists, Francis Crick and James Watson, visited sometimes Franklin. One day, they saw her X-ray photograph revealing that DNA molecules had a double spiral structure. Crick and Watson built their DNA model based on Franklin's discovery. In 1962, they both felt real excited when they received a Nobel Prize, and they did not acknowledge Franklin's contribution.

3.   The Nobel Prize can be given only to the living. Unfortunately, Franklin had been ill, and by 1954, her health was worst than before. She died tragic of ovarian cancer in 1958. Of all of the scientists who gained fame for their work on the structure of DNA, Franklin is the less recognized. Both Crick and Watson eventualy admitted that Franklin's photograph had inspired them.

4.   The discovery of DNA's structure is one of the most greatest finds of the last century. Today, many people feel strong that Franklin should receive full credit for her extreme interesting breakthroughs in her work on DNA. Her admirers are very respectfull of her accomplishments. She is a role model because she worked real hard and believed in herself.

Section 6
MODIFIERS

 See Chapter 29 of the Visualizing Writing CD for an additional mini-lecture on **Adjectives** and **Adverbs**.

Mistakes with Modifiers

section theme **HEALTH CARE**

CONTENTS

- Misplaced Modifiers
- Dangling Modifiers

In this chapter, you will read about **alternative medicine.**

The Writer's Desk **Warm Up**

Would you ever consult an acupuncturist, a homeopath, or any other alternative healing practitioner? Why or why not? Write a paragraph about your attitude toward alternative medicine.

Misplaced Modifiers

A **modifier** is a word, phrase, or clause that describes or modifies nouns or verbs in a sentence. For example, *holding the patient's hand* is a modifier. To use a modifier correctly, place it next to the word(s) that you want to modify.

modifier   word that is modified
<u>Holding the patient's hand</u>, **the doctor** explained the procedure.

A **misplaced modifier** is a word, phrase, or clause that is not placed next to the word it modifies. When a modifier is too far from the word that it is describing, then the meaning of the sentence can become confusing or unintentionally funny.

> I saw a pamphlet about acupuncture sitting in the doctor's office.
>
> (How could a pamphlet sit in a doctor's office?)

Commonly Misplaced Modifiers

As you read the sample sentences for each type of modifier, notice how the meaning of the sentence changes depending on where the modifier is placed. In the examples, the modifiers are underlined.

Prepositional Phrase Modifiers

A prepositional phrase is made of a preposition and its object.

> **Confusing:** Cora read an article on acupuncture written by reporter James Reston <u>in a café</u>.
>
> (Who was in the café: James or Cora?)
>
> **Clear:** When Cora was <u>in a café</u>, she read an article on acupuncture written by reporter James Reston.

Present Participle Modifiers

A present participle modifier is a phrase that begins with an *-ing* verb.

> **Confusing:** James Reston learned about acupuncture <u>touring China</u>.
>
> (Can acupuncture tour China?)
>
> **Clear:** While <u>touring China</u>, James Reston learned about acupuncture.

Section 6
MODIFIERS

Past Participle Modifiers

A past participle modifier is a phrase that begins with a past participle (*walked, gone, known*).

> **Confusing:** <u>Called meridians</u>, acupuncturists claim there are two thousand pathways on the body.
>
> (What are called meridians: the acupuncturists or the pathways?)
>
> **Clear:** Acupuncturists claim there are two thousand pathways <u>called meridians</u> on the body.

Limiting Modifiers

Limiting modifiers are words such as *almost, nearly, only, merely, just,* and *even*. In the examples, notice how the placement of *almost* changes the meaning.

> **Almost** all of the doctors went to the lecture that disproved acupuncture.
>
> (Some of the doctors did not attend, but most did.)

> All of the doctors **almost** went to the lecture that disproved acupuncture.
>
> (The doctors did not go.)

All of the doctors went to the lecture that **almost** disproved acupuncture.

(The lecture did not disprove acupuncture.)

 Other Types of Modifiers

There are many other types of modifiers. For example, some modifiers begin with relative clauses and some are appositives.

Relative Clause

Confusing:	The treatments involved acupuncture needles <u>that were expensive</u>.
	(What was expensive: the treatment or the needles?)
Clear:	The treatments <u>that were expensive</u> involved acupuncture needles.

Appositive

Confusing:	<u>A very sick man</u>, Monica helped her uncle find a doctor.
	(How could Monica be a very sick man?)
Clear:	Monica helped her uncle, <u>a very sick man</u>, find a doctor.

PRACTICE I

Circle the letter of the correct sentence in each pair. Underline the misplaced modifier in each incorrect sentence.

EXAMPLE:

   a. Simon Weiss learned about acupuncture <u>with enthusiasm</u>.

   (b.) With enthusiasm, Simon Weiss learned about acupuncture.

1. a. Simon read about acupuncture, which is based on an ancient philosophy.
   b. Based on an ancient philosophy, Simon read about acupuncture.

2. a. By licensed practitioners, many U.S. states allow acupuncture to be performed.
   b. Acupuncture can be performed by licensed practitioners in many U.S. states.

3. a. Only seventeen states allow acupuncturists to practice without medical supervision.
   b. Seventeen states only allow acupuncturists to practice without medical supervision.

4. a. In a hurry, Simon asked for information about acupuncture.
   b. Simon asked for information about acupuncture in a hurry.

5. a. Needing treatment, Mr. Lo examined the patient.
   b. Mr. Lo examined the patient needing treatment.

Section 6
MODIFIERS

6. a. Faced with chronic headaches, Mr. Lo was prepared to treat Simon.

   b. Faced with chronic headaches, Simon was prepared to try Mr. Lo's treatment.

7. a. Carefully guiding the needles, Mr. Lo gently pierced Simon's skin.

   b. Carefully guiding the needles, Simon's skin was gently pierced by Mr. Lo.

8. a. Mr. Lo treated Simon wearing a mask.

   b. Wearing a mask, Mr. Lo treated Simon.

 Hint **Correcting Misplaced Modifiers**

To correct misplaced modifiers, do the following:

• Identify the modifier.

   Manuel saw the accident <u>walking past the hotel</u>.

• Identify the word or words that are being modified.

   Who walked past the hotel? Manuel.

• Move the modifier next to the word(s) being modified.

   <u>Walking past the hotel</u>, Manuel saw the accident.

Section 6
MODIFIERS

PRACTICE 2

Underline the misplaced modifiers in the following sentences. Then, rewrite the sentences. You may have to add or remove words to give the sentence a logical meaning.

EXAMPLE:

<u>Acting recklessly</u>, the motorcycle was driven too quickly by the young man.

Acting recklessly, the young man drove the motorcycle too quickly.

1. In a wheelchair, the nurse sat near the patient.

   _____

   _____

2. The patient took the medication with the red hair.

   _____

   _____

3. Ross was a teenager with a cast on his leg weighing 120 pounds.

   _____

   _____

4. Dr. Zimboro talked to Ross carrying a medical chart.

_____

_____

5. Not wearing a helmet, the accident could have killed the young man.

_____

_____

6. By all motorcyclists, many medical professionals believe that helmets should be worn.

_____

_____

7. Citing freedom of expression, a fight against helmet laws is being proposed by cycling enthusiasts.

_____

_____

8. In some states, there is no helmet law, including Colorado and Iowa.

_____

_____

9. Scared of having another accident, the motorcycle will not be driven again by Ross.

_____

_____

Section 6
MODIFIERS

Dangling Modifiers

A **dangling modifier** opens a sentence but does not modify any words in the sentence. It "dangles" or hangs loosely because it is not connected to any other part of the sentence.

To avoid having a dangling modifier, make sure that the modifier and the first noun that follows it have a logical connection.

Confusing:	<u>While talking on a cell phone</u>, the ambulance drove off the road.
	(Can an ambulance talk on a cell phone?)
Clear:	<u>While talking on a cell phone</u>, the ambulance **technician** drove off the road.
Confusing:	<u>To get into medical school</u>, high grades are necessary.
	(Can high grades get into a school?)
Clear:	<u>To get into medical school</u>, **students** need high grades.

PRACTICE 3

Read each pair of sentences. Circle the letter of each correct sentence.

EXAMPLE:

    a. Having taken <u>a pill</u>, the results were surprising.

    (b.) Having taken a pill, I was surprised by the results.

1. a. With the patient's budget in mind, the least expensive drugs were prescribed.
   b. With the patient's budget in mind, the doctor prescribed the least expensive drugs.

2. a. Believing in their effects, placebos are often given to patients.
   b. Believing in their effects, Doctor Zimboro sometimes gives placebos to patients.

3. a. After taking a sugar pill, patients often feel relieved.
   b. After taking a sugar pill, there is often a feeling of relief.

4. a. Surprised, the word *placebo* means "to please."
   b. Surprised, I read that the word *placebo* means "to please."

5. a. Thinking about the mind-body relationship, scientist Esther Sternberg conducted an experiment.
   b. Thinking about the mind-body relationship, an experiment was conducted.

6. a. Frustrated, Sternberg's temptation was to give up.
   b. Frustrated, Sternberg was tempted to give up.

7. a. Using laboratory rats, Sternberg discovered a link between the mind and body.
   b. Using laboratory rats, a link was discovered between the mind and body.

8. a. Given an antidepressant, the arthritis disappeared.
   b. Given an antidepressant, some rats no longer had arthritis.

9. a. Excited about her discovery, Sternberg wrote an article for a medical journal.
   b. Excited about her discovery, an article was written for a medical journal.

Section 6
MODIFIERS

 Correcting Dangling Modifiers

To correct dangling modifiers, do the following:

• Identify the modifier.

    <u>While dieting</u>, self-control is necessary.

• Decide who or what the writer aims to modify.

    Whose self-control is necessary? People's.

• Add the missing subject (and in some cases, also add or remove words) so that the sentence makes sense.

    While dieting, <u>people</u> need to have self-control.

PRACTICE 4

In each sentence, underline the dangling modifier. Then rewrite each sentence, adding or removing words to provide a logical meaning.

EXAMPLE:

<u>Worried about their weight</u>, a lot of diet books are bought.

Worried about their weight, Americans buy a lot of diet books.

1. When dieting, obsessing about food is common.

   _____

   _____

2. To buy that diet book, $13.95 is required.

   _____

   _____

3. The chicken was roasting while reading my diet book.

   _____

   _____

4. Not eating any bread, rice, or pasta, weight fell off easily.

   _____

   _____

5. Feeling skeptical, the benefits of a meat-based diet are questioned.

   _____

   _____

6. Indulging in fatty foods, heart problems can occur.

   _____

   _____

7. Working with celebrities, diet books are promoted on television.

   _____

   _____

8. When uncertain about which diet to follow, the advice of a nutritionist can be helpful.

   _____

   _____

Section 6
MODIFIERS

PRACTICE 5

Some sentences in this practice have dangling or misplaced modifiers. Write *M* next to misplaced modifiers, *D* next to dangling modifiers, and *C* next to correct sentences. If the modifier is misplaced, move it. If the modifier is dangling, add words to make the sentence complete.

EXAMPLE:

people try different therapies.

Hoping to live a long life, ~~different therapies are tried.~~   *D*

1. Called Ayurveda therapy, ancient Indians developed a school of medicine.   _____

2. Originally written on palm leaves, researchers found 2,000-year-old texts.   _____

3. Possibly causing diseases, Ayurvedic medicine teaches about an imbalance in mental and physical energies.   _____

4. Ayurvedic medicine is widely followed by people in India.   _____

5. Doing meditation and yoga, essential parts of this alternative therapy are learned.   _____

6. Dr. Shah spoke about traditional Indian medicine in a state of excitement.   _____

7. Called homeopathy, India has produced a therapy that uses plants, animals, and minerals to cure a patient's illness.   _____

8. Later, a German doctor organized the rules of homeopathic treatment wearing glasses.   _____

9. In the 1800s, homeopathy became popular in the United States.   _____

10. Feeling skeptical, the merits of homeopathy are questioned.   _____

11. In fact, many conventionally trained doctors do not believe in alternative medical therapies.   _____

12. Having tried many different therapies, the effectiveness of the treatments were discussed.   _____

Section 6
MODIFIERS

The Writer's Desk **Revise and Edit Your Warm Up**

In the Warm Up on page 439, you wrote a short paragraph about your attitude toward alternative health care. Edit the paragraph. Identify any modifiers and ensure that they are not dangling or misplaced. Then correct any modifier errors.

REFLECT ON IT

Think about what you have learned in this unit. If you do not know an answer, review that concept.

1. What is a modifier? _____

   _____

2. What is a misplaced modifier? _____

   _____

3. What is a dangling modifier? _____

   _____

4. What type of modifier error is in each sentence? Write *M* for "misplaced" and *D* for "dangling." Then correct the sentence.

   a. Overeating, a weight problem was developed.

   _____

   b. The doctor examined the X-ray in the lab coat.

   _____

Section 6
MODIFIERS

FINAL REVIEW

Underline ten dangling or misplaced modifier errors in the next selection. Then, correct each error. You may need to add or remove words to ensure that the sentence makes sense.

EXAMPLE:

                                        young girl had a surprising result.
Working on her school project, a <u>surprising result occurred.</u>

1. There are many fraudulent claims in alternative medicine. In fact, feeling desperate, fortunes are spent on suspect therapies. It is difficult for members of the public to determine which therapies are valid and which are pure quackery. At an important medical conference, some doctors discussed healing touch eating lunch together. In recent years, critics have attacked healing touch therapy.

2.   Based on several ancient healing practices, Dolores Krieger developed therapeutic touch therapy. According to touch therapists, a skilled practitioner can pass his or her hands over a patient's body and remove obstacles in the energy field. Using the method all over the United States, therapeutic touch is very popular.

3.   Named Emily Rosa, an experiment at school was conducted by a nine-year-old girl. In 1998, Emily tested twenty-one therapeutic touch practitioners wearing a school uniform. A therapist would place both hands, palms facing up, on the table. A screen prevented the therapist from seeing Emily. Emily then placed her own hand over one of the therapist's hands. Emily asked the therapist which hand was nearest to her own. Unable to see Emily, the guesses were correct only 44 percent of the time.

4.   Emily's results were published in the *Journal of the American Medical Association*. Emily's parents proudly read the article drinking coffee. Dr. George D. Lundberg believes that therapeutic touch practitioners should disclose the results of Emily's experiment to patients. However, those in the therapeutic touch community criticize the experiment feeling angry. They believe that Emily was too healthy for the experiment to work. They also feel that there were too few practitioners in the experiment. Rejecting the results, therapeutic touch continues to be popular.

Section 6
MODIFIERS

 The Writer's Room   **Topics for Writing**

Choose one of the following topics and write a paragraph or an essay. Remember to follow the writing process.

1. Have you ever been to an acupuncturist, a massage therapist, a naturopath, a homeopath, or any other alternative healing practitioner? Describe the treatment that you received.

2. Do you have a scar, or have you ever had an accident? Explain what happened.

3. Right now, millions of Americans are uninsured for medical care. Should the government legislate universal health care? What is the situation in countries where universal health care exists?

4. Should terminally ill patients have the right to die? What are the possible problems if euthanasia is legalized? Write about euthanasia.

READING LINK

Health Care
"The Diagnosis" by Richard Selzer
(page 586)
"Dying to Be Bigger" by H. D.
(page 575)
"How to Get All-Day Energy"
by Maria Noel Mandile
(page 536)
"Bound Feet" by Jung Chang
(page 580)

 The Writers' Circle

Work with a group of students on the following activity.

STEP 1 Write down adjectives, adverbs, and phrases that describe the following people.

  EXAMPLE: A good boss: *honest, listens well, supportive*

  a. A good doctor: _____

  _____

  b. A bad doctor: _____

  _____

STEP 2 Rank the qualities from most important to least important.

STEP 3 As a team, write a paragraph about doctors. Compare the good with the bad.

STEP 4 When you finish writing, edit your paragraph and ensure that you have written all the adjectives and adverbs correctly.

 See Chapter 30 of the Visualizing Writing CD for an additional mini-lecture on **Misplaced** or **Dangling Modifiers.**

Section 6
MODIFIERS

CHAPTER 31

Exact Language

section theme **THE LEGAL WORLD**

CONTENTS

- Use Specific and Detailed Vocabulary
- Avoid Wordiness and Redundancy
- Avoid Clichés
- Standard English vs. Slang

In this chapter, you will read about crimes *and* criminals.

The Writer's Desk **Warm Up**

Write a paragraph that summarizes the events of a well-known crime. Describe what happened.

Use Specific and Detailed Vocabulary

Great writing evokes an emotional response from the reader. Great writers not only have correct grammatical structures, but they also infuse their writing with precise and vivid details that make their work come alive.

When you proofread your work, revise words that are too vague. **Vague words** lack precision and detail. For example, the words *nice* and *bad* are vague. Readers cannot get a clear picture from them.

Compare the following sets of sentences.

Vague: The movie was bad.

Precise: The crime drama contained violent, gory scenes.

Vague: Our instructor told us about the death of Julius Caesar.

Precise: Our history instructor, Dr. London, recounted how Julius
Caesar was murdered on March 15, 44 B.C.

Creating Vivid Language

When you choose the precise word, you convey your meaning exactly.
Moreover, you can make your writing clearer and more impressive by using
specific and detailed vocabulary. To create vivid language, try the next strategies.

- **Modify your nouns.** If your noun is vague, make it more specific by adding
  one or more adjectives. You could also rename the noun with a more specific
  term.

  Vague: the man

  Vivid: the shopkeeper   the thin, nervous soldier

- **Modify your verbs.** Use more vivid, precise verbs. You could also use adverbs.

  Vague: walk

  Vivid: saunter   stroll   march briskly

- **Include more details.** Add more information to make the sentence more
  complete.

  Vague: Several signs foretold of Caesar's murder.

  Precise: Several ominous signs, such as Caesar's horses getting loose
  and a soothsayer's warning, foretold of Caesar's impending
  death.

WRITING LINK

You can find more information
about appealing to the five senses
in Chapter 6, "Description."

  Use Imagery

You can make your writing come alive by using **imagery,** which is description using
the five senses: sight, sound, smell, touch, and taste. In the examples, the underlined
words add details to the sentence and contribute to a more exact description.

The <u>one-eyed</u>, <u>scar-faced</u> pirate <u>jabbed</u> his sword at the <u>frightened</u> crew.

Section 7
**WORD USE
AND SPELLING**

PRACTICE I

Replace the familiar words in parentheses with more vivid words or phrases, and
add more specific details. Use your dictionary or thesaurus if you need help.

EXAMPLE:

Graffiti artists (write) _scrawl words and pictures_ on walls.

1. Many cities spend a lot of money (cleaning) _____

   _____ graffiti.

2. (Youths) _____ spray paint on many (places)

_____

3. They worry about getting caught by (someone) _____

_____

4. Some cities permit graffiti artists to paint on (certain locations) _____

_____

5. Sometimes graffiti artists use (bad words) _____

_____

6. Governments could combat the problem (with many solutions) _____

_____

7. Some people think graffiti artists should be (treated harshly) _____

_____

PRACTICE 2

Underline all the words in the paragraph that add vivid details to the description.

EXAMPLE:

The <u>tappity-tap-tap</u> and the <u>thin bell</u> and <u>muffled whir</u> of Effie Perine's
typewriting came through the <u>closed</u> door.

> Somewhere in a neighboring office a power-driven machine
> vibrated dully. On Spade's desk a limp cigarette smoldered in a brass
> tray filled with the remains of limp cigarettes. Ragged gray flakes of
> cigarette-ash dotted the yellow top of the desk and the green blotter
> and the papers that were there. A buff-curtained window, eight or ten
> inches open, let in from the court a current of air faintly scented with
> ammonia. The ashes on the desk twitched and crawled in the current.
>
> —Dashiell Hammett, *The Maltese Falcon*

Section 7
**WORD USE
AND SPELLING**

 Adding Appositives

An appositive is a word or phrase that gives further information about a noun or
pronoun. You can write sentences that are more exact and detailed by adding
appositives.

appositive   appositive
Sherlock Holmes, <u>the famous detective</u>, was helped by his friend, <u>Dr. Watson</u>.

Avoid Wordiness and Redundancy

Sometimes students fill their writing assignments with extra words to meet length requirements. However, good ideas can get easily lost in work that is too wordy. Also, if the explanations are unnecessarily long, then writing becomes boring.

To improve your writing style, use only as many words or phrases as you need to fully explain your ideas.

> The police department was a distance of two blocks from the municipal library.
>
> (A block is a measure of a distance, so it is unnecessary to repeat that information.)

Correcting Wordiness

You can cut the number of words needed to express an idea by substituting a wordy phrase with a single word. You could also remove the wordy phrase completely.

> *Because*
> ~~By virtue of the fact that~~ we did a survey, we found that most young college students do not study criminology.

Some Common Wordy Expressions and Substitutions

Wordy	Better	Wordy	Better
at that point in time	then, at that time	gave the appearance of	looked like
big, small in size	big, small	great, few in number	great, few
in close proximity	close *or* in proximity	in order to	to
a difficult dilemma	a dilemma	in spite of the fact	in spite of
due to the fact	because	in the final analysis	finally, lastly
equally as good as	as good as	period of time	period
exactly the same	the same	past history	past *or* history
exceptions to the rule	exceptions	return again	return
final completion	end	still remain	remain
for the purpose of	for	a true fact	a fact

PRACTICE 3

In the next sentences, cross out all unnecessary words or phrases, or modify any repeated words.

EXAMPLE:

many
In 1970, ~~a great number of~~ people were interested in Charles Manson's trial.

1. In 1969, Los Angeles citizens were terrified due to the fact that a killer was in their midst.

2. At that point in time, nobody knew why innocent people were being murdered.

Section 7
WORD USE AND SPELLING

Slang is nonstandard language. It is used in informal situations to communicate common cultural knowledge. In any academic or professional context, do not use slang.

Slang:	My friends and I <u>hang</u> together. Last weekend, we watched a movie that was <u>kinda weird but also pretty sweet</u>. It was called *The Untouchables*, and it was about the Mafia during Prohibition.
Standard American English:	My friends and I <u>spend a lot of time</u> together. Last weekend, we watched a movie that was <u>unusual but fascinating</u>. It was called *The Untouchables*, and it was about the Mafia during Prohibition.

 Hint   **Do Not Use Slang in Academic Writing**

Slang changes depending on generational, regional, cultural, and historical influences. For example, rather than saying "I have to *leave*," people in one group might say *scram* or *split* while those in another group might say *bail* or *bounce*. Avoid using slang expressions in your writing because they can change very quickly—so quickly, in fact, that you might remark that this textbook's examples of slang are "lame."

PRACTICE 5

Substitute the underlined slang expressions with the best possible choice in standard American English.

EXAMPLE

Every day, <u>the cops</u> deal with gangs.   _____*police officers*_____

Section 7
WORD USE
AND SPELLING

1. Gang members can be <u>guys or chicks</u>. _____

2. Some young people think that gangs are <u>cool</u>. _____

3. It takes a lot of <u>guts</u> to refuse to join a gang. _____

4. Someone may join a gang because he or she does not want to look like a <u>wimp</u>. _____

5. Others join gangs because they want to earn <u>megabucks</u>. _____

6. Sometimes people <u>hang</u> with gangs because they feel more protected. _____

7. It is <u>dicey</u> to be in a gang. _____

8. Police try to <u>keep their cool</u> when they deal with gangs. _____

9. Gang members are often on the lookout for <u>narcs</u>. _____

10. Many gang members end up in <u>the joint</u>. _____

The Writer's Desk **Revise and Edit Your Warm Up**

In the Warm Up on page 450, you wrote a few sentences about a well-known crime. Revise and edit your sentences. Identify and correct vagueness, wordiness, overused expressions, and slang.

REFLECT ON IT

Think about what you have learned in this unit. If you do not know an answer, review that concept.

1. What is vivid language? _____

    _____

2. Why should you add details to your writing? _____

    _____

3. Edit the following sentences for wordiness and redundancy. Cross out any unnecessary phrases or modify them to make them more concise.

    a. The suspect lived in close proximity to the bank that he had robbed.

    b. Hakim wrote the final completion of his paper on *The Great Train Robbery*.

4. Edit the following sentences for clichés and overused expressions. Replace the clichés with your own words.

    a. Peter will be in for a rude awakening if he does not study for his

       law-enforcement exams.

    b. Peter is feeling under the weather today.

5. Edit the following sentences for slang. Replace the slang words with standard American English.

    a. Replacing the contents of a stolen wallet is such a drag.

    b. I read a cool biography about Al Capone.

Section 7
**WORD USE
AND SPELLING**

FINAL REVIEW

Edit the following paragraphs for slang, clichés, or vague language.

A. Read the paragraph and underline five slang expressions. Then substitute the slang words with standard English words.

EXAMPLE:

An unusual
A freaky film is *Strangers on a Train* by Alfred Hitchcock.

READING LINK

For more information about using a dictionary, see pages 528–529 in Part V, "Reading Strategies" (Chapter 37).

 Using a Dictionary

If you are unsure about the spelling or meaning of a word, consult a dictionary. Try to use a recent edition, and get to know the features of your dictionary.

Writing *ie* or *ei*

Remember the following rule so that you know when to use *ie* or *ei*. Write *i* before *e* except after *c* or when *ei* is pronounced *ay*, as in *neighbor* and *weigh*.

i before e:	ach**ie**ve	bel**ie**ve	fr**ie**nd	
ei after c:	c**ei**ling	conc**ei**ve	perc**ei**ve	
ei pronounced ay:	b**ei**ge	v**ei**n	w**ei**gh	
Exceptions:	effic**ie**nt	**ei**ther	for**ei**gner	h**ei**ght
	l**ei**sure	n**ei**ther	sc**ie**nce	s**ei**ze
	soc**ie**ty	spec**ie**s	th**ei**r	w**ei**rd

PRACTICE I

Circle the correct spelling of each word.

EXAMPLE:

recieve, (receive)

1. decieve, deceive

2. foreigner, foriegner

3. grief, greif

4. hieght, height

5. vien, vein

6. science, sceince

7. efficient, efficeint

8. theif, thief

9. deciet, deceit

10. chief, cheif

11. wieght, weight

12. sufficeint, sufficient

Section 7
WORD USE AND SPELLING

Adding Prefixes and Suffixes

A **prefix** is added to the beginning of a word, and it changes the word's meaning. For example, *con-*, *dis-*, *pre-*, *un-*, and *il-* are prefixes. A **suffix** is added to the ending of a word, and it changes the word's tense or meaning. For example, *-ly*, *-ment*, *-ed*, and *-ing* are suffixes.

When you add a prefix to a word, keep the last letter of the prefix and the first letter of the main word.

un + **n**atural = u**nn**atural   di**s** + **s**atisfaction = di**ss**atisfaction

When you add the suffix *-ly* to words that end in *l*, keep the *l* of the root word. The new word will have two *l*'s.

persona**l** + **l**y = persona**ll**y   actua**l** + **l**y = actua**ll**y

Words Ending in -ful

Although the word *full* ends in two *l*'s, when *-ful* is added to another word as a suffix, it ends in one *l*.

careful   successful   hopeful

Notice the unusual spelling when *full* and *fill* are combined: fulfill.

PRACTICE 2

Read the following words and decide if they are correctly spelled. If the word is correct, write *C* in the space provided. If the word is incorrect, write the correct word in the space.

EXAMPLES:

factualy: _factually_   untrue: _C_

1. naturally: _____   7. beautifull: _____

2. ilogical: _____   8. iresponsible: _____

3. continually: _____   9. unusual: _____

4. imoral: _____   10. carefuly: _____

5. unecessary: _____   11. fataly: _____

6. mispell: _____   12. fulfilled: _____

Adding -s or -es

Add *-s* to nouns and to present tense verbs that are third-person singular. However, add *-es* to words in the following situations.

- When words end in *s*, *sh*, *ss*, *ch*, or *x*, add *-es*.

    Noun: church–church**es**
    Verb: fix–fix**es**

- When words end with the consonant *y*, change the *y* to *i* and add *-es*.

    Noun: berry–berr**ies**
    Verb: marry–marr**ies**

- When words end in *o*, add *-es* in most cases.

    Noun: hero–hero**es**
    Verb: do–do**es**

    Exceptions: piano–piano**s**; radio–radio**s**.

- When words end in *f* or *fe*, change the *f* to *v* and add *-es*.

    leaf–lea**ves**   knife–kni**ves**

    Exception: belief–belief**s**; roof–roof**s**.

Section 7
WORD USE AND SPELLING

PRACTICE 3

Add *-s* or *-es* to each word. Write the new word in the space provided.

EXAMPLE:

reach: *reaches*

1. hero: _____
2. crutch: _____
3. fix: _____
4. echo: _____
5. carry: _____
6. dish: _____

7. potato: _____
8. candy: _____
9. miss: _____
10. fly: _____
11. teach: _____
12. scarf: _____

Adding Suffixes to Words Ending in -e

When you add a suffix to a word ending in *e*, make sure that you follow the next rules.

■ If the suffix begins with a vowel, drop the *e* on the main word. Some common suffixes beginning with vowels are *-ed*, *-er*, *-est*, *-ing*, *-able*, *-ent*, and *-ist*.

　　hope–hop**ing**　　encourage–encourag**ing**

Exceptions: For some words that end in *ge*, keep the *e* and add the suffix.

　　courage–courage**ous**　　change–change**able**

■ If the suffix begins with a consonant, keep the *e*. Some common suffixes beginning with consonants are *-ly*, *-ment*, *-less*, and *-ful*.

　　sure–sure**ly**　　like–like**ness**

Exceptions: Some words lose their final *e* when a suffix is added.

　　acknowledge–acknowledgment　　true–truly
　　argue–argument

PRACTICE 4

Rewrite each word with the suggested ending.

EXAMPLE:

use + ed: *used*

1. achieve + ment: _____
2. strange + est: _____
3. argue + ment: _____
4. love + ing: _____
5. active + ly: _____
6. true + ly: _____

7. large + er: _____
8. endorse + ment: _____
9. argue + ing: _____
10. nine + ty: _____
11. write + ing: _____
12. change + able: _____

Adding Suffixes to Words Ending in -y

When you add a suffix to a word ending in *y*, make sure that you follow the next rules.

- If the word has a consonant before the final *y*, change the *y* to an *i* before adding the suffix.

    beauty–beaut**i**ful   supp**l**y–supp**l**ied

- If the word has a vowel before the final *y*, if it is a proper name, or if the suffix is *-ing*, do not change the *y* to an *i*.

    day–days   try–trying   the Vronsky family–the Vronskys

    Exceptions: Some words do not follow the previous rule.

    day–da**i**ly   lay–la**i**d   say–sa**i**d   pay–pa**i**d

PRACTICE 5

Rewrite each word with the suggested ending.

EXAMPLE:

try + ed: =   *tried* _____

1. happy + est: _____
2. play + er: _____
3. pretty + er: _____
4. Connolly + s: _____
5. lonely + ness: _____
6. envy + able: _____
7. angry + ly: _____
8. day + ly: _____
9. say + ing: _____
10. dirty + est: _____

Doubling the Final Consonant

Sometimes when you add a suffix to a word, you must double the final consonant. Remember the next tips.

One-Syllable Words

- Double the final consonant of one-syllable words ending in a consonant-vowel-consonant pattern.

    bat–ba**tt**er   plan–pla**nn**ed   prod–pro**dd**ed

- Do not double the final consonant if the word ends in a vowel and two consonants or if it ends with two vowels and a consonant.

    cool–coolest   park–parking   clean–cleaner

Words of Two or More Syllables

- Double the final consonant of words ending in a stressed consonant-vowel-consonant pattern.

    pre<u>fer</u>–prefe**rr**ed   oc<u>cur</u>–occu**rr**ed

Section 7
**WORD USE
AND SPELLING**

- If the word ends in a syllable that is not stressed, then do not double the last letter of the word.

    <u>ha</u>ppen–happened   <u>vi</u>sit–visiting

PRACTICE 6

Rewrite each word with the suggested ending.

EXAMPLES:

	Add -ed			**Add -ing**
stop:	<u>stopped</u>		try:	<u>trying</u>

1. slip: _____

2. load: _____

3. mention: _____

4. plan: _____

5. open: _____

6. smile: _____

7. stay: _____

8. enter: _____

9. begin: _____

10. refer: _____

PRACTICE 7

Correct twelve spelling mistakes in the next selection.

EXAMPLE:

The parents reacted ~~angryly~~ ^{angrily} when they were convicted.

Section 7
WORD USE
AND SPELLING

1.   In the United States, every state except New Hampshire has a parental responsibility statute. Such laws make parents legaly responsible for their children's criminal acts. The first parents who were ever tryed and convicted under such laws were from St. Claire Shores, Michigan. In 1995, a sixteen-year-old boy commited a series of crimes after he was released from juvenile detention. The state questionned why the parents could not control their son. The prosecutor was successfull in convicting the parents, and the case brought national attention to the issue. Since then, many parents have been convicted. For example, in one case, a couple's son set the nieghbors' house on fire. The parents had to pay $60,000 to the victims.

2.   Those who are against such laws argue that holding parents responsible definitly does nothing to stop juvenile delinquents from committing crimes. At a certain age, peer groups become more influential than parents. It is unecessary and unfair to force parents to pay for damages. Such laws are ilogical and simply attempt to fix a problem after the fact instead of helping the parents deal with the child before any serious crimes occur.

3.   Some people, argueing for the laws, say parents must be encouraged to take a more active role in their children's lifes. If parents know that they may be charged for their child's actions, they will likly intervene and try to get their child some help before serious crimes can occur. Some supporters also argue that taxpayers should not have to pay for vandalism and other damage caused by juveniles.

Spelling Two-Part Words

Some one-word indefinite pronouns sound as if they should be two separate words, but they are not. Here are some examples of one-word indefinite pronouns.

Words with *any:*	anything, anyone, anybody, anywhere
Words with *some:*	something, someone, somebody, somewhere
Words with *every:*	everything, everyone, everybody, everywhere

 Spelling *another* and *a lot*

Another is always one word: Bonnie committed <u>another</u> crime.
A lot is always two words: She robbed <u>a lot</u> of banks.

PRACTICE 8

Correct ten spelling errors in the next paragraph.

EXAMPLE:

Another
~~An other~~ scandal occurred last year.

Alot of professional athletes have committed criminal acts. Some times the crimes are not serious. For example, Florida State football player Peter Warrick was charged with theft in a designer clothing scheme. Pete Rose is an other athlete who let greed draw him into imoral activities when he bet against his own team. However, some athletes have assaulted, raped, or killed. Ice skater Tonya Harding and her husband hired some body to hit her skating rival in the knee. Boxer Mike Tyson was accused and eventualy convicted of rape, and several professional football players have been charged with murder. Because television and newspapers present professional athletes as icons, many fans refuse to accept that their heroes have done any thing wrong. Basketball fan Trevor Nixon says, "Any body can make accusations. Unfair attacks on successfull athletes can cause their families much greif." Perhaps the public should accept that athletes are not always heroic.

Section 7
WORD USE
AND SPELLING

120 Commonly Misspelled Words

The next list contains some of the most commonly misspelled words in English.

absence	calendar	disappoint	jewelry
absorption	campaign	embarrass	judgment
accommodate	careful	encouragement	laboratory
acquaintance	ceiling	environment	ledge
address	cemetery	especially	leisure
aggressive	clientele	exaggerate	license
already	committee	exercise	loneliness
aluminum	comparison	extraordinarily	maintenance
analyze	competent	familiar	mathematics
appointment	conscience	February	medicine
approximate	conscientious	finally	millennium
argument	convenient	foreign	minuscule
athlete	curriculum	government	mischievous
bargain	definite	grammar	mortgage
beginning	definitely	harassment	necessary
behavior	desperate	height	ninety
believable	developed	immediately	noticeable
business	dilemma	independent	occasion

occurrence	probably	sincerely	until
opposite	professor	spaghetti	usually
outrageous	psychology	strength	vacuum
parallel	questionnaire	success	Wednesday
performance	receive	surprise	weird
perseverance	recommend	technique	woman
personality	reference	thorough	women
physically	responsible	tomato	wreckage
possess	rhythm	tomatoes	writer
precious	schedule	tomorrow	writing
prejudice	scientific	truly	written
privilege	separate	Tuesday	zealous

 Spelling Strategies

Here are some useful strategies to improve your spelling.

• Keep a record of words that you commonly misspell in your spelling log, which could be in a journal or binder. See Appendix 7 for more information about spelling logs.

• Use memory cards or flash cards to help you memorize the spelling of difficult words.

• Write down the spelling of difficult words at least ten times to help you remember how to spell them.

PRACTICE 9

Circle the correctly spelled word in each pair.

EXAMPLE:

(foreigner) foriegner

1. ceiling, cieling

2. ancient, anceint

3. noticable, noticeable

4. echos, echoes

5. writting, writing

6. accommodate, accomodate

7. definitely, definitly

8. sincerly, sincerely

9. running, runing

10. appealled, appealed

11. comittee, committee

12. embarrassed, embarassed

13. recommend, recommand

14. absence, absense

15. wierd, weird

16. niece, neice

17. personallity, personality

18. exaggerate, exagerate

19. butterflys, butterflies

20. responsible, responsable

21. efficeint, efficient

22. fryed, fried

23. independent, independant

24. appointment, apointment

Section 7
**WORD USE
AND SPELLING**

PRACTICE 10

Correct fifteen spelling mistakes in the next selection.

EXAMPLE:

Detectives may never solve some ~~outragous~~ ^{outrageous} crimes.

1. In 1888, in England, a series of sickening and vicious murders horrifyed London society. A serial killer, known only as Jack the Ripper, attacked women in London's East End with a razor blade. He caught the imagineation of the public.

2. Newspaper articles and editorials on the Ripper's crimes appearred every day, but some of the stories were filled with exagerations. London citizens were extremly afraid of the serial killer, and they wanted to know who was responsable for the crimes. Politicians recommanded that the Ripper be executed for his crimes. As time passed, London police felt embarassed because they could not find the killer.

3. Although there was much speculation at that time, the identity of the Ripper was never discovered. A myth has developped about him, and today some people are hopefull that the puzzle can be solved. An American crime writer, Patricia Cornwell, has proposed that the well-known British impressionist painter Walter Sickert was the Ripper. In the early 1900s, Sickert made graphic paintings of murdered women, and he had studioes near the crime scenes. In an interview with *ABC News*, Cornwell said, "Some of his paintings, if you juxtapose them with some of the morgue photos, are extraordinarilly chilling." Cornwell has used her own money to verify DNA evidence from a letter supposedly writen by the Ripper. However, her evidence is inconclusive, so the controversy remains.

4. Not everybody beleives Cornwell's theory, and people have offered other explanations about who Jack the Ripper actualy was. Perhaps the case will remain an unsolved mystery.

Section 7
**WORD USE
AND SPELLING**

Using a Spelling Check

The spelling and grammar tool on a computer will highlight most misspelled words and provide suggested corrections. Be aware that a spelling checker's abilities are limited; it cannot verify that you have used commonly confused words accurately. For example, it cannot determine whether you should use *your* or *you're*.

Because a spelling checker is not 100 percent reliable, remember to proofread for spelling errors before you submit your final work.

Look-Alike and Sound-Alike Words

Sometimes two English words can sound the same but have different spellings and different meanings. For example, two commonly confused words are *defiantly*, which means "to resist or challenge something," and *definitely*, which means "finally" or "decisively." Dictionaries will give you the exact meaning of unfamiliar words. Read the next list to get familiar with many commonly confused words.

Word	Meaning	Example
accept	to receive or to admit	Margaret Hamilton <u>accepted</u> an award for best crime fiction.
except	excluding or other than	Everyone in the audience, <u>except</u> Ian, has read at least one of her novels.
affect	to influence	Writer's block <u>affects</u> a person's ability to write.
effect	the result of something	Writer's block can have bad <u>effects</u> on a person's ability to write.
been	past participle of the verb *to be*	Ms. Cromwell has <u>been</u> a detective for many years.
being	present progressive form (the -*ing* form) of the verb *to be*	She was <u>being</u> very nice when signing autographs.
by	preposition meaning next to, on, or before	The robber sat <u>by</u> the river bank. <u>By</u> nightfall, the police had stopped searching for her. They hoped to find her <u>by</u> the end of the month.
buy	verb meaning to purchase	The robber will <u>buy</u> a mansion with the stolen money.
complement	to add to or to complete	The mansion was a nice <u>complement</u> to her other possessions.
compliment	to say something nice about someone	Detective Smartson <u>compliments</u> the other detectives.
conscience	a personal sense of right or wrong	The robber had no <u>conscience</u>.
conscious	to be aware or to be awake	The robber was <u>conscious</u> of his terrible crime.
disinterested	to be impartial	The trial judge was <u>disinterested</u>, favoring neither side.
uninterested	to lack interest in something	The robber tried to look <u>uninterested</u> when told of his sentence.

(continued)

Section 7
**WORD USE
AND SPELLING**

Word	Meaning	Example
elicit	to get or draw out	The police tried to <u>elicit</u> a confession from the gang member.
illicit	illegal or unlawful	The police found evidence of the gang's <u>illicit</u> activities.
everyday	ordinary or common	Crime is an <u>everyday</u> occurrence.
every day	during a single day or each day	The police have watched the gang members <u>every day</u>.
imply	to suggest	The reporter <u>implied</u> that the police need more time to investigate.
infer	to conclude	The police <u>inferred</u> from the clues the gang's whereabouts.
imminent	soon to happen	The police stated that an arrest was <u>imminent</u>.
eminent	distinguished or superior	Drake Weatherby was an <u>eminent</u> detective.
its	possessive case of the pronoun *it*	Drake Weatherby's car was vandalized, and <u>its</u> windshield was shattered.
it's	contraction for *it is*	<u>It's</u> generally known that he is very good at solving crimes.
knew	past tense of *to know*	Weatherby <u>knew</u> that thieves had stolen the diamonds.
new	recent or unused	He had a <u>new</u> contact in the underworld.
know	to have knowledge of	He <u>knows</u> that I like to read about famous crimes.
no	a negative	The police made <u>no</u> arrests.
lose	to misplace or forfeit something	The police did not want to <u>lose</u> track of the stolen diamonds.
loose	too big or baggy, or not fixed	Detectives sometimes wear <u>loose</u> clothing as part of their disguises.
loss	a decrease in an amount or a serious blow	The bank experienced a serious <u>loss</u> when the diamonds were stolen.
peace	calm, or to stop violence	The two rival gangs finally made <u>peace</u>. They felt a sense of <u>peace</u> when hostilities stopped.
piece	a part of something else	The thieves sold the <u>piece</u> of jewelry.
personal	private	The criminal has a lot of <u>personal</u> problems.
personnel	employees or staff	The police must hire new <u>personnel</u>.
principal	main person, or director of a school	The <u>principal</u> detective talked to the <u>principal</u> of our school.
principle	rule or standard	The police try to follow the <u>principle</u> of law.

Section 7
**WORD USE
AND SPELLING**

Word	Meaning	Example
quiet	silent	The thieves remained <u>quiet</u> when arrested.
quite	very	The public is becoming <u>quite</u> angry at the increase in crime.
quit	stop	The detective sometimes wants to <u>quit</u> the force.
taught	past tense of *teach*	Drake <u>taught</u> a class on criminology.
thought	past tense of *think*	He <u>thought</u> his students were intelligent.
than	word used to compare things	Jack the Ripper is more interesting <u>than</u> other criminals.
then	at a particular time or after a specific time	She investigated the crime, and <u>then</u> she wrote about it.
that	word used to introduce a clause	She wrote <u>that</u> Walter Sickert was the Ripper.
their	possessive form of *they*	The police officers went to <u>their</u> favorite restaurant.
there	a place	They went <u>there</u> by police van.
they're	contraction of *they are*	<u>They're</u> both interesting people.
through	in one side and out the other; finished	The police cruiser passed <u>through</u> a tunnel. They were <u>through</u> for the day.
threw	past tense of *throw*	Somebody <u>threw</u> a rock at the officer's car.
thorough	complete	They did a <u>thorough</u> investigation of the crime scene.
to	indicates direction or movement, or is part of an infinitive	I want <u>to</u> go <u>to</u> the film.
too	also or very	The robber felt <u>too</u> guilty about her life of crime. Her friend felt guilty, <u>too</u>.
two	the number after one	There were <u>two</u> witnesses to the holdup.
where	question word indicating location	The police knew <u>where</u> the diamonds were hidden.
were	past tense of *be*	The diamonds <u>were</u> in a safe place.
we're	contraction of *we are*	<u>We're</u> going to meet the detectives.
write	to draw symbols that represent words	Margaret Hamilton <u>writes</u> about crime.
right	correct, or the opposite of the direction left	The police officer held the diamonds in his <u>right</u> hand. The police knew that they had arrested the <u>right</u> criminal.
who's	contraction of *who is*	The police sergeant, <u>who's</u> a friend, spoke to reporters.
whose	pronoun showing ownership	Criminals, <u>whose</u> crimes hurt society, must be punished.

Section 7
**WORD USE
AND SPELLING**

PRACTICE 11

Circle the correct word in each sentence.

1. Many people (buy, by) mystery novels.

2. Successful writers of detective fiction receive many (complements, compliments) for their ingenious plots.

3. Edgar Allan Poe and Herman Melville are (excepted, accepted) as being the first American mystery writers.

4. Arthur Conan Doyle and Agatha Christie are two (eminent, imminent) British mystery writers.

5. The (principal, principle) characters in their works are Sherlock Holmes and Hercule Poirot, both of whom are detectives.

6. To solve the mystery, both Holmes and Poirot try to (elicit, illicit) clues by talking to various characters.

7. The public has also (thought, taught) highly of other mystery writers such as Earl Stanley Gardner and Dashiell Hammett.

8. Many students were (quite, quiet) when Margaret Hamilton started to give her lecture about detective fiction.

PRACTICE 12

Correct twenty-two errors in the following passages. Commonly confused words are indicated in parentheses.

EXAMPLE:

He is ~~to~~ busy these days.
too

Section 7
**WORD USE
AND SPELLING**

1. (*to, too, two*)

Hollywood has been the center of many famous crimes. In 1995, the O. J. Simpson criminal trial kept Americans glued too their televisions. Simpson was accused of killing to people. Nicole Simpson was killed, and her friend Ronald Goldman was killed, to. Some analysts believe that there was to much media coverage during the trial. The police tried to find clues too solve the murder. On October 3, 1995, Simpson was declared not guilty, although he was later convicted in a civil trial.

2. (*then, than, that*)

Another celebrity accused of murder was Robert Blake. In 2004, prosecutors stated than Blake killed his wife. Apparently, the Blakes were having dinner at a restaurant. Blake claimed than he and his wife walked to their car. He realized that he had forgotten his gun in the restaurant. He said he had a gun because his wife was more afraid then he was of being attacked. Blake than returned to get the gun. When he came back to the car, he saw than his wife had been killed. In 2005, Blake was acquitted of the murder.

3. (*threw, through, thorough*)

Wynona Ryder, another famous Hollywood actor, was accused of shoplifting in 2002. Store detectives claimed that Ryder passed threw the store taking items and then left threw the front doors when she was finished shopping. Store detectives intercepted Ryder as she was leaving and did a through search of her bags. They then charged her with theft of merchandise worth $4,800. In court, the judge threw out some evidence, but he accepted testimony from the store detectives. When the trial was threw, the jury found Ryder guilty, but she did not have to spend time in prison.

4. (*it's, its*)

The preceding three celebrities have received a lot of attention from the media and it's readership. Many people think that its wrong for celebrities to profit from crimes they have been accused of doing. Other people think that its fair if celebrities profit in the long term.

5. (*who's, whose*)

People of all ages idolize celebrities who have committed crimes. However, the public should remember that celebrities who commit crimes are criminals. A person whose famous should not behave criminally. Celebrities who's profession puts them in the public spotlight should be aware of the influence they have, especially on young people.

Section 7
**WORD USE
AND SPELLING**

6. (*their, there, they're*)

However, supporters of celebrities who have committed crimes say that although celebrities lead public lives, there human. They should not be punished for the rest of there lives for making a mistake. Their is much debate about this issue.

The Writer's Desk Revise and Edit Your Warm Up

In the Warm Up on page 459, you wrote about celebrity criminals. Edit your paragraph for errors with spelling or commonly confused words.

REFLECT ON IT

Think about what you have learned in this unit. If you do not know an answer, review that concept.

1. a. In a word containing *ie*, when does *i* come before *e*?

   _____

   b. When does *e* come before *i*?

   _____

2. Circle the correctly spelled words. Correct each misspelled word.

   realy   finally   unatural   illogical   plentifull

3. Write down three pairs of words that you commonly confuse.

   _____   _____

   _____   _____

   _____   _____

4. Correct eight mistakes in the next passage.

   Crimes are quiet a common occurrence in my nieghborhood. The police are planing to increase there surveillance in this area. The public, to, can help. Its important to report any unnusual events. Eventualy, such actions will help lower the crime rate.

Section 7
**WORD USE
AND SPELLING**

FINAL REVIEW

Underline and correct twenty spelling errors and mistakes with commonly confused words in the essay.

EXAMPLE:

Sometimes, laws are unfairly <u>applyed</u>.
applied

1.   Three strikes laws have stired up controversy in the United States. Such laws state that if a person is convicted of two felonys, the felon will recieve a life sentence if convicted of a third crime. The laws aim to make career criminals take responsability for their actions.

2.   The first three strikes law was passed in California in 1994, and it grew out of the public's sense of frustration. The public percieved that there was a steady increase in crime, so the state decided to implement an action plan. Lawmakers excepted the public's viewpoint and designed a law they taught would be tough on criminals. However, the law continus to be debated.

3.   Proponents of this controversial law argue that criminals need a strong deterrent to stop doing ilegal activities. In fact, they claim that the crime rate has definitly droped since the three strikes law was passed. Moreover, supporters say that other states have passed the same law because it has being so successfull in California.

4.   Critics of this law claim that buy harshly punishing criminals who have committed minor crimes, this law ensures that everybody looses. Three strikes laws go against the principal of the punishment fitting the crime. Furthermore, opponents argue that the laws should be applyed only to violent felons. They also say that the cost of enforcing this type of law is great and that the money should not be wasted on jailing those who comit minor offenses such as stealing food or shoplifting.

Section 7
**WORD USE
AND SPELLING**

5. Critics forcefuly condemn three strikes laws, argueing that such laws are inhumane, expensive, and unfair. Supporters do not want the laws to be modified. Both sides have valid points of view; therefore, three strikes laws will continue to generate controversy.

 The Writer's Room **Topics for Writing**

READING LINK

The Legal World
"Enough Is Enough" by Judy Sheindlin, with Josh Getlin (page 545)
"When the Legal Thing Isn't the Right Thing" by Deborah Mead (page 538)
"My Head Rolled in Syria" by Josh Freed (page 541)
"Interview with Jimmy Baca" by Elizabeth Farnsworth (page 562)

Choose one of the following topics and write a paragraph or an essay. Remember to follow the writing process.

1. Compare and contrast graffiti with another type of art.
2. Do you believe that three strikes laws are fair and effective?
3. Should juveniles who commit serious crimes be treated as harshly as adults?
4. What are some steps that parents can take to prevent their children from breaking laws or becoming criminals?

 The Writers' Circle

Work with a partner or a small group of students and compose a paragraph about the qualities of a good comic book hero. Use slang words and clichés in your paragraph. Make sure that your paragraph is double-spaced, and make sure that the writing is clear.

When you have finished your paragraph, exchange sheets with another team of students. Edit the other team's paragraph and imagine that the audience is a college instructor. Change all clichés and slang expressions into standard American English.

Section 7
WORD USE AND SPELLING

 See Chapter 32 of the Visualizing Writing CD for additional mini-lectures on **Spelling** and **Easily Confused Words.**

section theme **THE WORKPLACE**

CONTENTS

- What Is a Comma?
- Commas in a Series
- Commas After Introductory Words or Phrases
- Commas Around Interrupting Words or Phrases
- Commas in Compound Sentences
- Commas in Complex Sentences
- Commas in Business Letters

In this chapter, you will read about work-related topics.

The Writer's Desk **Warm Up**

Have you ever thought about having your own business? What type of business would you like to have? Write a paragraph about owning a business.

What Is a Comma?

A **comma** (,) is a punctuation mark that helps keep distinct ideas separate. There are many ways to use a comma. In this chapter, you will learn some helpful rules about comma usage.

Notice how comma placement changes the meaning of the following sentences.

The dog bites, the cat laughs, and then she has a nap.

The dog bites the cat, laughs, and then she has a nap.

477

Commas in a Series

Use a comma to separate items in a series of three or more items. Remember to put a comma before the final *and* or *or*.

| unit 1 | , | unit 2 | , | and or | unit 3 |

Miami, Los Angeles, and New York have many employment opportunities.

The job search requires courage, perseverance, and energy.

You can network, contact employers directly, or use a placement service.

Hint   **Punctuating a Series**

In a series of three or more items, do not place a comma after the last item in the series (unless the series is part of an interrupting phrase).

Incorrect: Her poise, simplicity, and kindness, impressed us.

Correct: Her poise, simplicity, and kindness impressed us.

Do not use commas to separate items if each item is joined by *and* or *or*.

It is not possible to study <u>and</u> listen to music <u>and</u> have a conversation at the same time.

PRACTICE I

Underline series of items in the next selection. Then add eighteen missing commas where necessary.

EXAMPLE:

Some <u>individuals, small-business owners, and home-based workers design and</u> print their own business cards.

1. Many small companies do not have the money to advertise, so their only means of promoting their product is to hand out cards to friends neighbors and strangers who might be interested in the business. The type of card that people carry depends on the type of business that they have. Photographers pastry chefs artists and musicians often have colors and images on their cards. Doctors lawyers and accountants tend to use a simple black-and-white design printed on good-quality paper.

2. Your business card should transmit more than just your name position telephone number and address. According to consultant Frank Yeoman,

people are attracted to cards that have clear simple and direct messages. At the same time, a business card should stand out in some way, so it is a good idea to think about the color texture and design of the card. The card should be eye-catching. Yeoman says that you should never put your photo on your business cards unless you are a model or an actor. As trends change, you may be embarrassed to have hundreds of business cards depicting you with an unfashionable hairstyle outdated glasses and an unattractive shirt. You get only one chance to make an impression on new customers, so it is important to put some time effort and planning into your business card design.

Commas After Introductory Words or Phrases

Use a comma after an **introductory word.** The introductory word could be an interjection such as *yes*, *no*, or *well*, it could be an adverb such as *usually* or *generally*, or it could be a transitional word such as *however* or *therefore*.

> Introductory word(s)   ,   sentence.

Yes, I will help you complete the order.

Frankly, you should reconsider your customer service promise.

However, the job includes a lot of overtime.

Use a comma to set off **introductory phrases** of two or more words. The phrase could be a transitional expression such as *of course* or *on the contrary*, or it could be a prepositional phrase such as *on a warm summer evening*. The introductory phrase could also be a modifier such as *running out of fuel* or *born in France*.

On the other hand, his career was not going well.

In the middle of the meeting, I received a phone call.

Speaking to the crowd, the manager explained the stock performance.

Section 8
PUNCTUATION AND MECHANICS

PRACTICE 2

Underline each introductory word or phrase. Then add ten missing commas.

EXAMPLE:

In today's job market, people must remain flexible.

1. For the first time in history workers can expect to outlive the organizations that they work for. For example many high-tech companies came and went during the stock market boom of the late 1990s. Additionally many businesses go bankrupt each year.

2. Furthermore those working in successful companies may see their jobs become obsolete. In fact the majority of the nation's bank tellers were laid off in the 1990s. As a result many people in the banking industry have had to retrain or change jobs.

3. According to Myriam Goldman the average person should plan for three different careers. Of course some people love their jobs and have no desire to look elsewhere. However even those in secure jobs may get bored and long for a career change down the road. Working in a volatile job market workers should remain open and flexible.

Commas Around Interrupting Words and Phrases

Interrupting words or phrases appear in the middle of sentences. Such interrupters are often asides that interrupt the sentence's flow but do not affect its overall meaning. Some interrupters are *by the way, as a matter of fact,* and *for example.* Prepositional phrases can also interrupt sentences.

My sister, for example, has never invested in stocks.
The market, by the way, has been down recently.
Mrs. Jayson, frankly, never acknowledges her employees.
My manager, in the middle of a busy day, decided to go to a movie!

Section 8
PUNCTUATION AND MECHANICS

 Using Commas with Appositives

An appositive gives further information about a noun or pronoun. The appositive can appear at the beginning, in the middle, or at the end of the sentence. Set off appositives with commas.

beginning
A large city in Florida, Miami has a variety of public learning centers.

middle
Dr. Anex, a senior surgeon, recommends the transplant.

end
The office is next to Graham's, a local eatery.

PRACTICE 3

The next sentences contain introductory words and phrases, interrupters, and series of items. Add the missing commas. If the sentence is correct, write *C* in the space provided.

EXAMPLE:

E-mail, voice mail, and cell phones are changing the way that people do business. _____

1. Jamaal Khabbaz a marketing manager, complains about high-tech gadgets in the workplace such as pagers, cell phones and personal organizers. _____

2. Many workers in his opinion break rules of basic etiquette. _____

3. He gets annoyed, for example when a lunch meeting is interrupted by a ringing cell phone. _____

4. Unfortunately, many people do not consider it rude to answer a call in the middle of a meal. _____

5. According to Kabbaz the workplace needs new business etiquette rules. _____

6. Electronic mail, a convenient way to send and receive messages is not private. _____

7. Without a doubt, it is offensive to read other people's mail. _____

8. Some people, however have no qualms about standing next to a computer and reading over the shoulder of an e-mail recipient. _____

9. E-mail junkies, those addicted to electronic messages cause the most problems. _____

10. In the middle of a busy day the e-mail addict sends cartoons, videos and messages to co-workers. _____

11. Most shocking of all, they sometimes download offensive films and send them to others. _____

Section 8
**PUNCTUATION
AND MECHANICS**

12. One company, a producer of electronic surveillance equipment

     fired six employees for sending pornographic e-mails to each other. _____

Commas in Compound Sentences

A compound sentence contains two or more complete sentences joined by a coordinating conjunction (*for, and, nor, but, or, yet, so*).

| Sentence | , and | sentence. |

I want a job, **so** I will look in the classified ads.

Some interesting companies are nearby, **and** maybe they are hiring.

I will work in an office, **but** I do not want to work from nine to five.

PRACTICE 4

Add six commas that are missing from this letter.

EXAMPLE:

I am punctual, and I am hardworking.

Dear Ms. Graham:

I saw an ad in the *Miami Herald* stating that you need a junior accountant. I am interested in the job so I have enclosed a résumé highlighting my skills in this field. I have an aptitude for computers and I am able to solve problems in creative ways.

I have taken several courses in accounting at Marshall College but I have not completed the program. I am comfortable with spreadsheets and I have worked with income tax preparation programs.

I am available for an interview at any time so please do not hesitate to contact me. Thank you for your consideration and I look forward to hearing from you.

Yours sincerely,

Marcus Fisher

Marcus Fisher

Section 8
**PUNCTUATION
AND MECHANICS**

Commas in Complex Sentences

A **complex sentence** contains one or more dependent clauses (or incomplete ideas). When you add a **subordinating conjunction**—a word such as *because*, *although*, or *unless*—to a clause, you make the clause dependent.

dependent clause   independent clause
When the stock market opened, he sold his shares.

Use a Comma After a Dependent Clause

If a sentence begins with a dependent clause, place a comma after the clause. Remember that a dependent clause has a subject and a verb, but it cannot stand alone. When the subordinating conjunction comes in the middle of the sentence, it is not necessary to use a comma.

> Dependent clause , main clause.

Comma: After the meeting ends, we will go to lunch.

> Main clause dependent clause.

No comma: We will go to lunch after the meeting ends.

Use Commas to Set Off Nonrestrictive Clauses

Clauses beginning with *who*, *that*, and *which* can be restrictive or nonrestrictive. A **restrictive clause** contains essential information about the subject. Do not place commas around restrictive clauses.

No commas: The only local company that does computer graphics has no job openings.

(The underlined clause is essential to understand the meaning of the sentence.)

A **nonrestrictive clause** gives nonessential information. In such sentences, the clause gives additional information about the noun but does not restrict or define the noun. Place commas around nonrestrictive clauses.

Commas: Her book, which is in bookstores, is about successful entrepreneurs.

(The underlined clause contains extra information, but if you removed that clause, the sentence would still have a clear meaning.)

 Which, That, Who

which
Use commas to set off clauses that begin with *which*.

ImClone, **which** was founded in 1983, creates pharmaceutical products.

that
Do not use commas to set off clauses begining with *that*.

The company **that** Sam Waksal founded creates pharmaceutical products.

(continued)

Section 8
**PUNCTUATION
AND MECHANICS**

> **who**
> When a clause begins with *who,* you may or may not need a comma. If the clause contains nonessential information, put commas around it. If the clause is essential to the meaning of the sentence, it does not require commas.
>
> **Essential:** Many people **who** <u>buy stocks</u> think that they will earn a profit.
>
> **Not essential:** Domestic guru Martha Stewart, **who** <u>became a multimillionaire</u>, was convicted of obstructing justice in 2004.

PRACTICE 5

Edit the following sentences by adding twelve missing commas.

EXAMPLE:

When company executives have insider knowledge ˏ they are not supposed to profit from that knowledge.

1. The title chief executive officer which is abbreviated CEO refers to the leader of a corporation. Often, the CEO of a company knows secrets that can affect the price of a company's stocks. In 2002, the CEO of ImClone who lived in New York State was charged with insider trading.

2. After Sam Waksal learned about a government decision not to approve a cancer drug he knew that the price of the company's shares would drop. Waksal told his daughter who is named Aliza to sell her shares. An employee of ImClone may have told Martha Stewart who was Waksal's friend to sell her shares, too. The next day, the price of ImClone stock which had been selling at a high price plummeted.

3. Waksal was the first CEO who pleaded guilty, and he was sentenced to seven years in prison. Martha Stewart was also found guilty of lying to investigators. After the ImClone scandal exploded there were many other scandals involving corporate executives. Should corporate executives who take advantage of their position be harshly punished?

Section 8
PUNCTUATION AND MECHANICS

Commas in Business Letters

When you write or type a formal letter, ensure that you use commas correctly in the following parts of the letter.

Addresses

In the address at the top of the letter, insert a comma between the following elements.

- The street name and apartment number
- The city and state or country

Do not put a comma before the zip code.

Dr. Brent Patterson

312 Appleby Road, Suite 112

Cleveland, OH 45678

If you include an address inside a complete sentence, use commas to separate the street address from the city and the city from the state or country. If you just write the street address, do not put a comma after it.

Commas: The building at 11 Wall Street, New York, contains the Stock Exchange.

No comma: The building at 11 Wall Street contains the New York Stock Exchange.

Dates

In the date at the top of the letter, add a comma between the full date and the year. If you just write the month and the year, then no comma is necessary.

May 21, 2006   January 2006

If you include a date inside a complete sentence, separate the elements of the date with commas.

On Monday, July 26, 2004, we visited Washington.

 Writing Numbers

In letters, it is not necessary to write ordinal numbers such as *first* (1st), *second* (2nd), *third* (3rd), or *fourth* (4th). Instead, just write the number: 1, 2, 3, 4, and so on.

February 24, 2001   October 11, 1966

Salutations

Salutations are formal letter greetings. The form "To Whom It May Concern" is no longer used regularly by North American businesses. The best way to address someone is to use his or her name followed by a comma or a colon. The colon is preferred in business letters.

Dear Ms. Lewin: Dear Sir or Madam: Dear Mom,

Complimentary Closings

Place a comma after the complimentary closing. Notice that the first word of the closing is capitalized.

Respectfully,   Yours sincerely,   Many thanks,

Section 8
PUNCTUATION AND MECHANICS

Sample Letter of Application

You send a sample letter of application to an employer when you apply for a job. Review the parts of the next letter.

Sender's address
(name, phone, and possibly ➤
an e-mail address)

Date ➤

Recipient's address ➤

Subject line ➤

Salutation ➤

Closing (After the closing,
put your handwritten
signature followed by your
typed name.)   ➤

Section 8
**PUNCTUATION
AND MECHANICS**

Seamus O'Brien
10 Santa Fe Boulevard
Seattle, WA 90001
(661) 234-5678

September 12, 2005

Avant Garde Computers
Adelaide and Sinclair Corporation
6116 Greenway Avenue
Seattle, WA 98711

Subject: Position of junior programmer

Dear Ms. Roebok:

I saw an ad in Saturday's *Seattle Times* stating that you need a junior programmer. I have enclosed a résumé highlighting my skills in this field. I have an aptitude for computers, and, when I was fourteen years old, I created my first game program.

I have just finished a diploma program in computer programming at Marshall College. I took courses in several computer languages. I have also completed a six-week training program, and I have enclosed a letter of reference from the owner of that company.

If you require further information, please contact me. I am available for an interview at any time and could start work immediately. Thank you for your consideration.

Sincerely,

S. O'Brien

Seamus O'Brien

Enclosures: résumé
           letter of reference

PRACTICE 6

The next letter contains ten errors. Add seven missing commas and remove three unnecessary commas.

Red River Publications

1440 Cliff Street

Austin Texas 76780

April 2 2005

Graham Britt

214 Regents Road,

Austin Texas 77787

Dear Mr. Britt:

On Monday March 12 2004 we received your manuscript. We are pleased to inform you that your article will be published in the May, issue of *Phoenix Magazine*.

Could you please meet with me at our branch office? I will be at 44 Hillside Road, during the last week of the month. You can stop by the office at anytime during that week. We are looking forward to meeting with you.

Yours truly

Lydia Halburton

Lydia Halburton

The Writer's Desk Revise and Edit Your Warm Up

Read the paragraph that you wrote for the Warm Up on page 477. Verify that you have used commas correctly. Then add two more sentences to the paragraph. In one sentence, include a restrictive clause. In another sentence, include a nonrestrictive clause.

Section 8
PUNCTUATION AND MECHANICS

REFLECT ON IT

Think about what you have learned in this unit. If you do not know an answer, review that concept.

1. Explain the rules of comma usage in the following situations.

   a. Series of items: _____

   _____

   b. Introductory words or phrases: _____

   _____

   c. Interrupting phrases: _____

   _____

   d. Compound sentences: _____

   _____

2. What is a nonrestrictive clause? _____

   _____

3. Should you place commas around nonrestrictive clauses? ___ Yes ___ No

4. Write a sentence that contains a nonrestrictive clause.

   _____

   _____

5. Write three common closings for a business letter. _____

   _____

Section 8
PUNCTUATION AND MECHANICS

FINAL REVIEW

Edit the next essay by adding seventeen missing commas and removing three unnecessary commas.

EXAMPLE:

Entertainers, including comedians, actors᾽ and musicians, should consult with a financial advisor.
                                          ^

1. Horace Madison co-founder of Madison Smallwood Financial Group, manages the careers of top urban rappers, hip-hop artists and blues musicians. Madison grew up in Harlem and he had a middle-class childhood. He heard about many high-profile artists and musicians M. C. Hammer, for example, who ended up going broke. When he began to work on Wall Street, he decided to focus on entertainers, who were at risk of mismanaging their funds.

2. Madison handles every aspect of his clients' lives. He helps them pay their bills, collect their revenue and plan their investment portfolios. According to Madison, some of his new artists desperately want to buy expensive jewelry or cars. In many cases they have just signed a million-dollar record deal. The artists, explains Madison do not always realize that they owe the record label for some of the money spent on music videos, marketing and travel. In fact, some artists can sell a million records and still end up owing money to the company. Furthermore new artists face pressure from family and friends. When their friends see the artist in a music video they call up the artist asking for a handout or a job.

3. Madison helps artists set up a budget and he carefully monitors what his clients spend. If a client wants to waste an outrageous amount on a frivolous luxury item Madison forces the client to sign a "stupid letter." He wants his clients to understand, that they are making a stupid financial move so the letter states that such spending is against the advice of Madison's firm. In an interview with Mitchell Raphael a journalist with the *National Post* newspaper, Madison told an anecdote. He said that a client wanted to rent a Ferrari for $1,000 a day. Madison without a pause, asked the client to sign the stupid letter. The client, a rapper rethought his plans and decided to rent a different car for $300 a day.

4. Ultimately, excessive spending is not smart. Hip-hop artists must think about their long-term future, because they have a career span of only three or four years. Madison and Smallwood Financial Group have helped a variety of artists manage the minefield of fame. In fact, Eve, a hip-hop artist has thanked Madison for helping her spend her money wisely.

Section 8
**PUNCTUATION
AND MECHANICS**

 See Chapter 33 of the Visualizing Writing CD for an additional mini-lecture on **Commas.**

baseball caps, shoes, shirts, and pants. They called their company Fubu, meaning "For us, by us."

2. They havent always been successful. In the first years, they made some mistakes. For example, John mortgaged his house to finance the business. Today, he says that he shouldnt have done that. He didnt know that he could have asked for a line of credit from a bank.

3. Sometimes the Fubu owners couldnt pay their bills. They werent familiar with common business practices. For example, when they sent orders to stores, theyd get paid four months later. They didnt realize that most businesses operate that way. During the first year of business, Daymond John almost lost his house, but today he is very successful.

PRACTICE 2

Look at each underlined contraction, and then write out the complete word.

EXAMPLE:

They <u>weren't</u> ready to start a business.   *were not*

1. Carol <u>Simon's</u> very happy with her bridal gown company.   _____
2. <u>She's</u> been an entrepreneur for seven years.   _____
3. <u>She's</u> an extremely friendly, ambitious woman.   _____
4. I wish <u>I'd</u> had the same idea as Carol.   _____
5. <u>I'd</u> like to have my own company, too.   _____

Using Apostrophes to Show Ownership

You can also use apostrophes to show ownership. Review the next rules.

Possessive Form of Singular Nouns

Add -'s to a singular noun to indicate ownership, even if the noun ends in s.

> **Daymond's** best friends joined his company.
>
> **Somebody's** house became a factory.
>
> **Ross's** dad has his own business.

Possessive Form of Plural Nouns

When a plural noun ends in s, just add an apostrophe to indicate ownership. Add -'s to irregular plural nouns.

Section 8
PUNCTUATION AND MECHANICS

Many **companies'** Web sites are down.

The four **friends'** business is very successful.

The **children's** clothing company is expanding.

Possessive Form of Compound Nouns

When two people have joint ownership, add -'s to the second name. When two people have separate ownership, add -'s to both names.

Joint ownership: Daymond and **Carl's** company is successful.

Separate ownership: **Daymond's** and **Carl's** offices are in different buildings.

PRACTICE 3

Write the singular and plural possessive forms.

EXAMPLE:

	Singular Possessive	Plural Possessive
Mr. Cohen	*Mr. Cohen's*	*the Cohens'*
1. client		
2. boss		
3. secretary		
4. Mr. Ness		
5. woman		
6. salesperson		

PRACTICE 4

Write the possessive forms of the following phrases.

EXAMPLE:

the sister of the doctor   *the doctor's sister*

1. the locker of the employee

2. the supplies of the employees

3. the profits of the company

4. the directors of the companies

5. the house of Jan and Ted

6. the car of Omar and the car of Roy

Section 8
PUNCTUATION AND MECHANICS

Using Apostrophes in Expressions of Time

When an expression of time (*day*, *week*, *month*, *year*) appears to possess something, use the possessive form of that word.

Singular: The customer won a **year's** supply of paper.

Plural: Mike Roy gave two **weeks'** notice before he left the company.

When writing the numerals of a decade or century, do not put an apostrophe before the final -*s*.

In the **1800s,** many immigrants arrived at Ellis Island.

Many Internet companies failed in the **1990s.**

Hint **Common Apostrophe Errors**

Do not use apostrophes before the final *s* of a verb.

       wants
Simon ~~want's~~ to open a franchise.

Do not confuse contractions with possessive pronouns that have a similar sound. For example, the contraction *you're* sounds like the pronoun *your*. Remember that possessive pronouns never have apostrophes.

          Its
The company is growing. ~~It's~~ slogan is catchy.

           theirs.
That is my idea. It is not ~~their's.~~

PRACTICE 5

Correct fifteen errors with apostrophes and possessive pronouns.

EXAMPLE:

     aren't   *don't*
If you ~~arent~~ willing to work hard, ~~do'nt~~ start your own business.

1. If your thinking of starting a business, you should plan carefully. Spend a few year's learning about the business before you invest your life savings. In an interview with *Smart Money* magazine, Daymond John said that he would'nt have started his Fubu clothing business so soon if hed known how complicated it was. He think's that he should have interned at other fashion companies to learn the business. According to John, "When I started Fubu in 1992, I just thought about the designs. But if you do'nt understand distribution, shipping, financing, and product timing, you can have the greatest designs in the world and still end up losing."

Section 8
**PUNCTUATION
AND MECHANICS**

2.   John say's that he made a lot of mistakes in the 1990's. He and his partner's werent aware of common business practices. They didnt know that they could get salespeople whod work on commission. He advises, "Know how everything works, from the mailroom to the advertising department. If you cant operate every part of your company, then youre dependent on other people. You never know if they are doing their jobs to the fullest or just wasting your money. And if they decide to leave, youll have to teach their replacements, or maybe do the jobs yourself."

Quotation Marks (" ")

Use **quotation marks** to set off the exact words of a speaker or writer. If the quotation is a complete sentence, there are some standard ways that it should be punctuated.

- Capitalize the first word of the quotation.
- Place quotation marks around the complete quotation.
- Place the end punctuation inside the closing quotation marks.

. . . declared	,	"Complete sentence."

Here is an example of a sentence with a quotation.

> Poet William Butler Yeats declared, "Education is not the filling of a pail but the lighting of a fire."

Generally, when using quotations, attach the name of the speaker or writer to the quotation in some way. Review the next rules.

Introductory Phrase

Place a comma after a phrase introducing a quotation.

. . . says	,	"_____."

> Malcolm Forbes jokes, "It is unfortunate we can't buy many business executives for what they are worth and sell them for what they think they are worth."

Interrupting Phrase

When a quotation is interrupted, do the following:

- Place a comma after the first part of the quotation.
- Place a comma after the interrupting phrase.

"_____,"	. . . says,	"_____."

> "I don't know the key to success," Bill Cosby said, "but the key to failure is to try to please everybody."

Section 8
PUNCTUATION AND MECHANICS

Ending Phrase

When you place a phrase at the end of a quotation, end the quotation with a comma instead of a period.

> "_____," says _____.

"You're fired," said Donald Trump.

If your quotation ends with other punctuation, put it before the final quotation mark.

> "_____?" says _____.

"You can't fire me!" she shouted.

"Why can't I fire you?" he asked.

Introductory Sentence

You can introduce a quotation with a complete sentence. Simply place a colon (**:**) after the introductory sentence.

> He explains his views: "_____."

Albert Highfield explains why businesses fail: "They try to grow too quickly."

Inside a Quotation

If one quotation is inside another quotation, use single quotation marks (**' '**) around the inside quotation.

> "Main quotation,   'Inside quotation.' "

According to Shannon Dowell, "Good parents always say, 'Clean up your own mess.' "

Hint) **When the Quotation Is an Incomplete Sentence**

If the quotation is not a complete sentence and you simply integrate it into your sentence, do not capitalize the first word of the quotation.

He says he wants to "learn _____."

Sir Francis Bacon once said that an artist's job is to "deepen the mystery."

**Section 8
PUNCTUATION
AND MECHANICS**

PRACTICE 6

In each sentence, the quotation is in bold. Add quotation marks and commas or colons. Also capitalize the first word of the quotation if necessary.

EXAMPLE:

Comedian Bob Hope made fun of financial institutions **a bank is a place that will lend you money if you can prove that you don't need it.**

1. According to novelist Lisa Alther   **any mother could perform the jobs of several air traffic controllers with ease.**

2. U.S. educator Laurence J. Peter believes that everyone is useful   **a miser, for example, makes a wonderful ancestor.**

3. Fred Delaney proclaimed   **a celebrity is a person who works hard all his life to become well known, and then wears dark glasses to avoid being recognized.**

4. **In the future, a wall could become a computer screen**   according to journalist Kate McNamara.

5. Comedian Mel Brooks believes that humor provides people with a **defense against the universe.**

6. Muhammad Ali describes his profession as a boxer   **grass grows, birds fly, waves pound the sand, and I beat people up.**

7. **Success only breeds a new goal**   observed actress Bette Davis.

8. **Hard work never killed anybody**   declared comedian Edgar Bergen   **but why take a chance?**

9. My mother once said   **remember the words of humorist Erma Bombeck   do not confuse fame with success.**

10. Executive Robert Townsend proclaimed   **a leader needs to have a compass in his head and a bar of steel in his heart.**

11. Author Stephen Beach says that Americans are   **socialized into a strong work ethic.**

12. Actress Mae West expressed her views   **to err is human, but it feels divine.**

Section 8
PUNCTUATION AND MECHANICS

Punctuation of Titles

When using a title within a sentence, place quotation marks around the title of a short work and underline or italicize the title of a longer work. Here are some guidelines for both.

Short Works	Long Works
Short story: "The Lottery"	**Novel:** The Grapes of Wrath
Web article: "Music Artists Lose Out"	**Web site:** CNET News.com
Chapter: Chapter 1, "Exploring"	**Book:** The Writer's World
Newspaper article: "Missing in Action"	**Newspaper:** New York Times
Magazine article: "Young Entrepreneurs"	**Magazine:** Forbes
Essay: "Downsizing"	**Textbook:** Writing Guidelines
TV episode: "The Election"	**TV series:** The West Wing
Song: "Don't Panic"	**CD:** Parachutes
Poem: "Howl"	**Anthology:** Collected Poems of Beat Writers
	Movie: The Matrix

Capitalizing Titles

When you write a title, capitalize the first letter of the first and last words and all the major words.

The Catcher in the Rye   War and Peace   "Stairway to Heaven"

Do not capitalize *.com* in a Web address. Also do not capitalize the following words except as the first or last word in a title.

Articles:	a, an, the
Coordinators:	nor, for, and, but, or, yet, so
Prepositions:	by, in, of, off, out, to, up . . .

 Hint   **Your Own Essay Titles**

When writing the title of your own essay, do not put quotation marks around the title. However, you should capitalize key terms.

A **C**ultural **I**con **I**s **B**orn

Section 8
**PUNCTUATION
AND MECHANICS**

PRACTICE 7

A. Add twenty missing capital letters to the titles in the next paragraph.

EXAMPLE:

        B   W

The magazine *business week* featured successful female entrepreneurs.

1.   In recent years, some ambitious, multitalented women have become

incredibly successful in different fields. Madonna, for example, has released about ten CDs, including one called *american life*. Her popular songs

include "hollywood" and "like a prayer." She has written children's books,

such as *the english roses*. She has also appeared in many movies, including

desperately seeking susan and *swept away*. Critics have not always been kind to

the Michigan native. In his article "no madonna is an island," *new york times*

film critic A. O. Scott called Madonna a poor actress.

B. Underline or add quotation marks to the eight titles in the next paragraph.

EXAMPLE:

In 1999, Hans Beiderman released his book <u>Cultural Icons and the Meanings
Behind Them</u>.

2.   Jennifer Lopez, a successful actress, crossed over into the music and

fashion industries. Lopez, of Puerto Rican descent, grew up in the Bronx.

Her first success was on the television series In Living Color. She went on

to act in films, including Out of Sight and Shall We Dance. Lopez also

decided to become a pop singer. In 2001, her album This Is Me, Then

debuted at number 1. In 2003, the song Jenny from the Block played on

radio stations across the United States. Lopez has generally had much

better movie reviews than Madonna, but she received a lot of criticism for

one role, in particular. As BBC News Online reported in an article titled

Lopez Flop Sweeps Razzie Awards, J. Lo won the Worst Actress Golden

Raspberry award for her role in the 2003 film Gigli.

PRACTICE 8

Correct ten errors with quotation marks, titles, apostrophes, or capital letters.
(An incorrectly capitalized title counts as one error.)

EXAMPLE:

Paul Salopek, in an article titled "Children ~~s~~eeking ~~r~~oyalties," denounced the
treatment of a South African composer.

1.   Every time a song is placed on a CD or album, the writer receives a

royalty. Lee Ann Arbringer, in an article called "How royalties work,"

Section 8
**PUNCTUATION
AND MECHANICS**

says, "currently, the statutory rate is eight cents for each song." To combat illegal file sharing on the Internet, some legal music site's have opened up, but not all artists are happy about it. "I earn almost nothing from the legal file-sharing sites because the users just rent songs", says Jimmy Dee, a guitarist. Roz Hillman, an accountant, agrees, noting that the artist gets "Next to nothing."

2.   Some artists have lost the rights to their own compositions. One of the greatest songs in the last century was written by a nearly unknown South African singer, Solomon Linda. Paul Salopek, of the <u>Chicago tribune</u>, wrote about him. In 1939, Linda wrote a song called "Mbube" and sold the rights to Gallo Records for a mere ten shillings, which is less than $2. Since then, Linda song has been rerecorded almost two hundred times, most famously in the 1961 version "The Lion sleeps tonight." The song is on the soundtrack of fifteen movies, including Disney's The Lion King. He died a pauper, and his family never shared in what would have been millions of dollars in royalties. "We are sad because he died without praise." said his daughter, Elizabeth.

The Writer's Desk **Revise and Edit Your Paragraph**

Read the paragraph that you have written about downloading music. Check that you have used any apostrophes correctly. Also verify that you have punctuated any song titles properly.

Section 8
**PUNCTUATION
AND MECHANICS**

REFLECT ON IT

Think about what you have learned in this unit. If you do not know an answer, review that concept.

1. In contractions, which letter does the apostrophe replace in the word *not*? _____

2. Write the possessive forms of the following phrases.

   Example: the wife of my brother: *my brother's wife* _____

   a. the music of Jennifer Lopez: _____

   b. the books of the professor: _____

   c. the house of Rob and Ann: _____

   d. the cases of the lawyers: _____

3. When a sentence ends with a quotation, the period should be

   a. inside the final quotation marks.

   b. outside the final quotation marks.

4. The titles of short works such as essays, articles, and poems should be

   a. underlined or italicized.

   b. set off with quotation marks.

5. The titles of longer works, such as magazines, newspapers, and movies, should be

   a. underlined or italicized.

   b. set off with quotation marks.

FINAL REVIEW

Edit the following paragraphs for fifteen errors with apostrophes, quotation marks, or underlining. Also, ensure that titles and quotations have the necessary capital letters.

EXAMPLE:

Musician Steve Miller complains, "My royalties have dropped 80 percent since 1999."

1. In recent year's, some recording artists and music companies have complained about the proliferation of music-sharing sites on the Internet. According to a reporter for *Fox News* "An estimated 60 million people participate in file-sharing networks". Opinions about file sharing differ greatly.

Section 8
PUNCTUATION AND MECHANICS

2. File sharing among college students is common. Roz Mingue of Austin Community College says that everybody she knows downloads free music. Roz' friend, Melissa Peng, agrees: "What is the big deal? They can't stop us." Some students think the record companies are simply too greedy. "Music companies say, "Don't do that,' but they still make a lot of money, so they should stop complaining," argues Peng.

3. Recording companies have decided to fight back. Cary Sherman, president of the Recording Industry Association of America (RIAA), compares file swappers to shoplifters. In a press conference, Sherman said, "there comes a time when you have to stand up and take appropriate action". In the 1990s, Napster was successfully sued and shut down. The recording industrys latest tactic is to take individual music file sharers to court.

4. The online magazine Wired News reports that hundreds of downloaders have been sued. Journalist Katie Dean writes "The defendants include a working mom, a college football player, and a 71-year-old grandpa." Joel Selvin and Neva Chonin are reporters for the San Francisco chronicle. Their article, "Artists Blast Record companies," contains quotations from artists who are unhappy with the lawsuits.

5. A prominent rocker points out that artists earn more from touring than from CD sales. "Bruce Springsteen probably earned more in ten nights at Meadowlands last month than in his entire recording career." said rocker Huey Lewis. Certainly music file sharing will not stop anytime soon. David Draiman of the rock band The Disturbed think's that artists should stop fighting because they cant win.

Section 8
PUNCTUATION
AND MECHANICS

See Chapter 34 of the Visualizing Writing CD for additional mini-lectures on **Apostrophes** and **Quotation Marks.**

Capitalization and Other Punctuation Marks

section theme **THE WORKPLACE**

CONTENTS

- Capitalization
- Other Punctuation Marks

In this chapter, you will read about **business innovators.**

The Writer's Desk Warm Up

Have you ever cheated on a test? Why or why not? Write a paragraph about cheating.

Capitalization

There are many instances in which you must use capital letters. Review the following rules for capitalization.

- Always capitalize the pronoun *I* and the first word of every sentence.

    My co-workers and I share an office.

- Always capitalize days of the week, months, and holidays.

    Tuesday   May 22   Labor Day

    Do not capitalize the seasons: summer, fall, winter, spring.

- Always capitalize titles of specific institutions, departments, companies, and schools.

    Apple Computer   Department of Finance   Daleview High School

    Do not capitalize general references.

    the company   the department   the school

- Always capitalize the names of specific places such as buildings, streets, parks, cities, states, and bodies of water.

    Kelvin Street   Times Square   Los Angeles, California
    Sunset Boulevard   Mississippi   Lake Erie

    Exception: Do not capitalize general references.

    the street   the state   the lake

- Always capitalize the names of specific languages, nationalities, tribes, races, and religions.

    Spanish   Mohawk   Buddhist   an Italian restaurant

- Always capitalize titles of specific individuals.

    General Dewitt   President Abraham Lincoln   Dr. Blain
    Professor Cruz   Prime Minister Tony Blair   Mrs. Ellen Ross

    Do not capitalize titles if you are referring to the profession in general, or if the title follows the name.

    my doctor   the professors   Edward M. Kennedy, a senator

- Always capitalize specific course and program titles.

    Economics 201   Topics in Electrical Engineering   Nursing 402

    Do not capitalize if you refer to a course but do not mention the course title.

    an economics course   an engineering program   a nursing class

- Always capitalize major words in titles of literary or artistic works.

    Washington Post   *Men in Black*   *Lord of the Flies*

- Always capitalize historical events, eras, and movements.

    World War II   Cubism   the Middle Ages

Section 8
PUNCTUATION AND MECHANICS

 Capitalizing Computer Terms

Always capitalize software titles, as well as the following computer terms.

    Internet   World Wide Web   Web site

PRACTICE I

Add fifteen missing capital letters.

EXAMPLE:

One of ~~oregon's~~ _{Oregon's} most well-known artists is Matt Groening.

1.   Born on february 15, 1954, Matt Groening grew up with an interest in comic book art. In 1977, he moved to Los angeles with the intention of becoming a writer. He held many different types of jobs, including chauffeur and ghostwriter for an elderly movie producer. He started writing his own comic strip called *Life in hell*. The strip appeared in the *Los Angeles reader* in 1980 and went into syndication in 1983.

2.   In 1987, Groening created a short animated series that served as extra material for the *Tracy Ullman show*. Picked up by Fox in 1990, *The Simpsons* has become the longest-running cartoon show in television history. The fate of the show was at first in doubt because many people, including former First lady Barbara Bush, criticized the show's portrayal of a dysfunctional family.

3.   The show's characters are named after people in Groening's family. Groening's father is named Homer, his mother is Marge, and his two sisters are Lisa and Maggie. The show's central character is a scheming ten-year-old, and the name Bart was created by rearranging the letters in the word *brat*. In the television series, the Simpson family lives in Springfield next to Ned Flanders, a devout christian. Both families live on a street called evergreen terrace.

4.   The show satirizes american society. It contains stereotypical characters such as Wiggum, the corrupt, donut-eating police chief. In addition, at Ainsworth elementary school, principal Skinner takes orders from his mother and punishes students erratically.

Section 8
**PUNCTUATION
AND MECHANICS**

5.   Although the show is a cartoon, both adults and children enjoy it. To appeal to adults, some of the show's stories are based on famous literary works such as Edgar Allan Poe's "The raven." The show has been translated into spanish and other languages, and it has been watched by millions of people around the world.

Other Punctuation Marks

Colon (:)

Use a colon for the following purposes.

- To introduce a quotation with a complete sentence

    The writer Oscar Wilde stated his opinion: "All art is quite useless."

- To introduce a series or a list after a complete sentence

    The United States has produced some great writers: Emily Dickinson, F. Scott Fitzgerald, Ernest Hemingway, John Steinbeck, and William Faulkner.

- After the expression *the following*

    Please do the following: read, review, and respond.

- To separate the hour and minutes in expressions of time

    The meeting will begin at 11:45.

Hyphen (-)

Use a hyphen in the following situations.

- When you write the complete words for numbers between twenty-one and ninety-nine.

    twenty-six men   ninety-nine   seventy-two

- When you use a compound adjective before a noun. The compound adjective must express a single thought.

    | **No hyphen:** | The new employee must work under high pressure. |
    | **Hyphen:** | The new employee has a <u>high-pressure</u> **job.** |

    (You cannot say a "high job" or a "pressure job." *High* and *pressure* must go together.)

    | **No hyphen:** | Our boss is thirty years old. |
    | **Hyphen:** | We have a <u>thirty-year-old</u> **boss.** |

    (The words *thirty, year,* and *old* express a single thought. You cannot remove one of those words.)

    If the adjectives before a noun function independently, do *not* add hyphens.

    | **No hyphen:** | They renovated an old red barn. |

    (The two adjectives function separately.)

Section 8
PUNCTUATION AND MECHANICS

Nonhyphenated Compound Adjectives

Some compound adjectives never take a hyphen, even when they appear before a noun.

  World Wide Web high school senior real estate agent

When you come across these types of adjectives, write them in your spelling log to help you remember them.

PRACTICE 2

Add nine missing colons and hyphens.

EXAMPLE:

        top-notch
The World Wide Web is a ~~top notch~~ communications system.

1. Some revolutionary inventions in human communication are the following paper, the printing press, the personal computer, and the World Wide Web. Tim Berners-Lee, a respected fifty year old man, created the World Wide Web while working as a researcher for the European Laboratory for Particle Physics. His invention has had long term effects in the field of communications.

2. Born in 1955 in London, England, Berners-Lee showed an early interest in mathematics. He had many childhood hobbies designing cardboard computers, doing mental mathematical calculations, and experimenting with electronics. Because his parents were interested in computers, Berners-Lee became a computer savvy child.

3. In 1986, while he was working in Geneva, he had two great ideas designing a software system that linked information on his computer to information on his colleagues' computers, and sharing his program with scientists around the world. The system allowed scientists to communicate with each other by accessing information on each other's computers. Berners-Lee envisioned a web like system of communications links. He named the new system the World Wide Web.

Section 8
**PUNCTUATION
AND MECHANICS**

4. Since 1991, the Internet has become an extremely user friendly research tool. Berners-Lee did not profit monetarily from his creation. In fact, he fights hard to keep it free so that everyone can benefit from it.

Ellipsis Marks (. . .)

You may want to quote key ideas from an author, but you do not always want to quote an entire paragraph. Use ellipsis marks to show that you have omitted information from a quotation.

When you type an ellipsis mark, leave a space before and after each period. If the omitted section includes complete sentences, then add a period before the ellipses. In the next examples, notice how the quote changes when ellipses are used.

Original Selection

You gain strength, courage, and confidence by every experience in which you really stop to look fear in the face. You are able to say to yourself, "I lived through this horror. I can take the next thing that comes along." You must do the thing you think you cannot do.

—Eleanor Roosevelt

GRAMMAR LINK

For more information about quotations, see Chapter 34.

Quotation with Omissions

According to Eleanor Roosevelt, "You gain strength, courage, and confidence by every experience in which you really stop to look fear in the face. . . . You must do the thing you think you cannot do."

—Eleanor Roosevelt

PRACTICE 3

Write quotations incorporating material from each of the next passages. Use ellipses to show where you omit words, and remember to keep important information.

1. Normal thoughts of my future (not pertaining to football), friends, family, reputation, moral status, etc., were entirely beyond me.

—From H.D.'s "Dying to Be Bigger"

According to H. D., _____

_____

_____

Section 8
PUNCTUATION
AND MECHANICS

2. To top it off, our kids are imbued with victimology, which today has become the American way of blame. It is too routine for adults and their kids to explain all their problems as victimization. When a boy in trouble sees himself as a victim, this festers into seething anger. With easy availability of guns, it can explode as murder.

—From Martin Seligman's "The American Way of Blame"

Martin Seligman says, _____

_____

_____

_____

_____

TheWriter's Desk **Revise and Edit Your Warm Up**

In the Warm Up on page 503, you wrote about cheating. Edit your paragraph to ensure that you have punctuated it correctly.

REFLECT ON IT

Think about what you have learned in this unit. If you do not know an answer, review that concept.

1. Give five examples in which capitalization is necessary.

   _____

   _____

   _____

   _____

   _____

2. Write two rules for hyphenating words.

   _____

   _____

   _____

3. Correct the six errors in punctuation and capitalization.

   The famous cuban-american actor Andy Garcia was born in havana on april 12, 1956. He has made many films *The Godfather: Part III, Ocean's eleven,* and *The Untouchables.*

Section 8
PUNCTUATION
AND MECHANICS

FINAL REVIEW

Correct capitalization and punctuation (colon and hyphen) errors in the next selection. Count each hyphen, colon, or capital letter as one error.

EXAMPLE:

Some ~~highly-motivated~~ ^{highly motivated} people risk their careers to do the right thing.

1. The U.S. government passed an act in 1990 to protect whistle-blowers from retaliation in the workplace. However, many people are frightened to come forward for the following reasons their colleagues might think of them as traitors, they might become the target of bad publicity, or they might lose their jobs.

2. In 2002, three women were honored by *Time* Cynthia Cooper, Coleen Rowley, and Sherron Watkins. Cooper worked for WorldCom, Rowley worked for the Federal bureau of investigation, and Watkins worked for Enron. They became the focus of public scrutiny because they revealed their employers' criminal business practices.

3. These risk taking women upheld ethical standards. Cooper revealed WorldCom's illegal accounting practices. The company had inflated its profits, and the multibillion dollar fraud caused many shareholders to lose their investments. In may 2002, Rowley wrote a memo to FBI director Robert Mueller about the agency's failure to investigate a possible terrorist who was later linked to attacks on the United States. Watkins, in a letter to chairman Kenneth Lay, warned of accounting discrepancies at Enron. Later, when the company failed, many employees and investors lost their life savings.

4. Another important whistle-blower is New York Attorney general Eliot Spitzer. In june 2001, forty-three year old Spitzer investigated the illegal actions of Merrill Lynch, a wall street financial firm. Merrill Lynch was accused of illegally downgrading the stock value of a company.

5. Whistle-blowers risk their careers and their reputations to do the right thing. They should be recognized as heroes because they expose corruption and incompetence.

Section 8
**PUNCTUATION
AND MECHANICS**

The Writer's Room **Topics for Writing**

Choose one of the following topics and write a paragraph or an essay. Remember to follow the writing process.

1. What is *success*? In your paragraph or essay, define success. As a supporting example, describe a successful person whom you know.

2. What reasons do people give for downloading music? What are the effects of their actions? Write about the causes or the effects of downloading music.

3. What types of jobs does society place a high value on? Describe at least three different categories or types of workers who get a lot of respect.

4. Describe your work environment.

ESSAY LINK

The Workplace
"Nothing But Net" by Scott Bekker (page 552)
"How to Get All-Day Energy" by Maria Noel Mandile (page 536)
"Aunt Tee" by Maya Angelou (page 530)
"Dealing with People" by Greg McGrew (page 533)

 The Writers' Circle

Work with a partner and think about a job that would interest both of you. Find a job advertisement from a newspaper, a magazine, or an Internet site. You could refer to one of the following sites.

www.monster.com   www.jobs.net   www.jobs.org

With your partner, compose a letter of application. In the first paragraph, explain what job you want, and tell where you heard about the job. In the second paragraph, briefly detail your qualities and experience. Then, in a third paragraph, explain your availability and how you can be contacted.

Remember to be as direct as possible. After you finish writing, proofread your letter and ensure that you have used correct punctuation and capitalization.

 See Chapter 35 of the Visualizing Writing CD for additional mini-lectures on **Capitalization**; **Semicolons, Colons, Dashes, and Parentheses**; and **Final Punctuation**.

Section 8
PUNCTUATION AND MECHANICS

Editing Paragraphs and Essays

EDITING PRACTICE

In this chapter you will read about a variety of topics, including family dynamics, identity theft, and antibiotic use.

After you finish writing the first draft of a paragraph or essay, it is important to edit your work. When you edit, you carefully review your writing to verify that your grammar, punctuation, sentence structure, and capitalization are correct. In this chapter, you can practice editing the types of written pieces that you see every day, including e-mail messages, paragraphs, essays, and business correspondence.

PRACTICE I   EDIT A PARAGRAPH

Correct ten errors in the next student paragraph. An editing symbol appears above each error. To understand the meaning of each symbol, refer to the revising and editing symbols at the end of this book.

Reading <u>teach</u>^agr me a lot of important things. Through books, I

discover that other people have problems just as I do, and I learn

about different ways to solve problems. For <u>exemple</u>^sp, in Jane

Austen's *Emma*, the main character <u>try</u>^agr to control her <u>friend's</u>^p

lives, but she really makes things <u>worst</u>^ad for them. I saw myself in

the story, and now I try to be less controlling. Through reading, I also

learn about different religions and <u>cultures, I</u>^ro realize that people

have the same concerns all over the world. <u>Also, exploring other</u>^frag

<u>places</u>. Reading allows me to visit distant countries. I cannot afford

to fly to India, but when I read Arundhati Roy's *The God of Small*

Things, I learned about the life and culture there. <u>Finaly</u>^sp, in books, I

learn that ordinary people can have extraordinary lives, and it <u>make</u>^agr

me appreciate that I am living my own <u>interresting</u>^sp story.

PRACTICE 2 EDIT AN ESSAY

Correct twenty underlined errors in the next student essay. An editing symbol
appears above each error.

Family Dynamics

One day, my brothers and <u>me</u>^pro were discussing our childhood. We

had very distinct viewpoints about our experiences. We realized that

Section 9
EDITING

our opinions were influence^vt by our birth position in the family.

Certainly, birth order has an impact on a person's personality.

First time^p parents, unsure of what to do, tends^agr to put a lot of pressure on the firstborn child. Although the oldest child benefited^shift from the undivided attention of the parents, he or she also feels more^ad stronger pressure than the younger siblings. Oldest children are most likely to conform to their parents^p expectations and are often compliant high achievers. For example, my brother made my parents proud who became a lawyer.^m

Middle children have certains^ad qualities that sets^agr them apart. Immediately, they must fight for their place in the limelight, especially if they are the same sex than^wc the eldest child. Middle children, therefore, tend to learn how to manipulate others to get what they want, they^ro sometimes act out to get their parents' attention. I 'am a middle child, and I rebelled. Of course, the attention than^wc I received from my parents were^agr not always positive, but attention is attention, and I needed it.

By the time the youngest child is born, the parents are real^ad relaxed and have less^wc financial worries. Therefore, they tend to

Section 9
EDITING

spoil the baby of the family, letting the youngest get away with

mischief. In my family, my youngest brother did things that I would

^{wc} ^{frag}
<u>of</u> been punished for. <u>Including staying out late and taking the car</u>

<u>without permission.</u>

Being a parent is time-consuming, heartbreaking, and ^{//} <u>a reward</u>.

Knowing about birth order can help people become better parents.

Nancy Samalin, in her book *Love and Anger: The Parental Dilemma,*

wrote, "Children will observe one another closely and take

^p
advantage of any edge they can <u>achieve"</u>.

PRACTICE 3 EDIT A PARAGRAPH

There are no editing symbols in the next paragraph. Proofread it as you would
your own writing, and correct twelve errors.

Physicians overprescribe antibiotics and this practice is having a

terrible effect on our health system. First, antibiotics are completely

useless against viruses, yet alot of patients ask for and receive it

when they have a simple cold. When drugs are overprescribed,

some bacterial infections become drugs-resistant. Malaria and

tuberculosis for example, are more difficult to treat than they were

twenty years ago. The problem is especialy serious in hospitals.

According to Dr. Ricki Lewis, antibiotic-resistant infections spread

rapidly in a hospital environment. Furthermore, patients who are

criticaly ill requires large doses of drugs who cause bacteria to

Section 9
EDITING

mutate rapidly. We should remember that the body can fight many illnesses on its own. For instance, some common ear infections. Before accepting a prescription, we should ask whether antibiotics are necessary. We have problems enough in this world, we do not need to create new illnesses by overusing antibiotics.

PRACTICE 4 EDIT A PARAGRAPH

There are no editing symbols in the next paragraph. Proofread it as you would your own writing, and correct fifteen errors.

Identity theft is the ilegal use of someones personal information. It is a serious crime, in fact, last year there was over 10 million cases of identity theft in the United States. To find identities, thieves go threw recycling bins, empty garbage cans, and stealing mail to obtain somebodys personal information. Computer hackers can even steal identities by tapping into personal information that persons keep on their computers. When a criminal has stolen a name, birthplace, address, and social security number, they can take out credit cards in the victim's name. For example, my co-worker, Nick Matsushita. He came home one day and found a large bill from a credit card company. Somebody had use his personal information to apply for credit. Nick and me are good friends, and I know that the identity theft has caused him alot of pain. He says that if he would have known about the way identity thieves work, he would have been more careful with his personal papers. Certainly, victims of identity theft loose time and money trying to fix the problem. To avoid being a victim, be prudent when sharing personal information.

Section 9
EDITING

PRACTICE 5 EDIT A WORKPLACE MEMO

Correct eight errors in the next excerpt from a memo.

Re: Summer vacations

As many of you know, each summers everybody wants to take
their vacation at the same time. For this reason, were asking all
employees to state your vacation preferences before next friday.
Please sign the sheet posted on the bulletin board stating when
you wanna take your time off. If you gotta good reason for needing
a specific time period, please send Judy or I a memo explaining
why.

PRACTICE 6 EDIT AN ESSAY

Correct twenty errors in the next essay.

1. Many courageous explorers has attempted expeditions to the Antarctic.
    Robert Falcon Scott did not want to become an explorer. In fact, he
    once said "I may as well confess that I had no predilection for polar
    exploration". However, he went on to lead two expeditions to the
    South Pole.

2. His first expedition, from 1901 to 1904 was unsuccessful. Scott and his
    crew experienced many problems. Because of the harsh climate and
    terrain. For example many crew members develop scurvy due to a lack
    of vitamin C. They had traveled 960 miles and was only 480 miles short
    of the South Pole when they had to give up. In 1905, Scott wrote a book
    about his journey, *The Voyage of discovery*.

Section 9
EDITING

3.   On June 10 1910, on a ship called the *Terra Nova*, Scott raced to the
     South Pole again. Unfortunately, when Scott reached his destination, he
     found that a norwegian expedition had arrived there first. Every member
     of Scotts team were disappointed.

4.   On the return journey, Scott and his crew faced terrible blizzards. "Great
     God! This is an awful place." Scott wrote in his journal. One man, Captain
     Oates, had severe frostbite on his feet. Knowing that he would never
     make it to the supply camp Oates decided to leave the group and walk
     to certain death. So that he would not have to depend of his friends.
     When they were only eleven miles from the supply camp, Scott and the
     remaining crew members set up their tents. Their frozen bodies were
     discover a few months later. Forty-three-year-old Scott was the last
     to die.

5.   Although Scott was not the first person to reach the South Pole his
     decision to undertake important and dangerous explorations inspired
     many others. In Cambridge, England, the Scott Polar research Institute
     was named after the explorer.

Section 9
EDITING

PRACTICE 7 EDIT A LETTER OF COMPLAINT

Correct fifteen errors in this excerpt from a letter of complaint.

We, the employees of Echo Industries, would like to formaly complain about the presence of cameras in company hallways, and rest areas. We wonder why are there so many cameras in those areas. The cameras they are invading are privacy.

We know the managements point of view. Senior managers argue that the cameras increases security. They also claim that employees take less breaks when the cameras are in leisure areas.

Feeling spied on, there is now an atmosphere of mistrust in our company. We don't have no privacy. We feel insulted, mistreated, and getting no respect. What we do during our breaks should not concern our employers. As long as we obey company rules, we should have the rite to rest and socialize in private. We done nothing to warrant such treatment. Please take our comments serious. We are confident than we can resolve this issue.

Section 9
EDITING

PRACTICE 8 EDIT A FORMAL LETTER

Correct twelve punctuation and capitalization errors in the next formal letter.

Ari Praz
278 First avenue
New York, NY 10009

July 6, 2005

New York Department of Finance
Hearing-by-Mail Unit
P.O. box 29201
Brooklyn, New York 11202

Subject: Parking ticket #4089-01411

Attention: Finance department

I am writing to explain why I am pleading "not guilty" to a parking ticket I received on the morning of friday, june 24, 2005. Please read the following explanation and refer to the enclosed documents.

On the evening of june 23, I parked a rented car on the south side of 18th street. I knew I could park there legally overnight until 8:30 a.m. At approximately 8:15 friday morning, I went to move the car from that parking space. When I arrived, I discovered that the front tire on the passenger side was flat. Unable to move the car, and unable to change the tire myself, I immediately returned to my apartment a few blocks away to phone the rental companys hotline. I estimated that I made the call at about 8:30 a.m. On the photocopies of Continentals service records, you will see they dispatched someone at 8:39 a.m. Unfortunately, while I was away from the car making that call, I received a ticket. The ticket was written at 8:40 a.m.

Section 9
EDITING

I'm sure you can see why I am pleading "not guilty" to this parking offense. I had every intention of moving the car by the specified time but I was not able to do so until roadside assistance arrived to replace the flat tire.

Yours Truly,

Ari Praz

Ari Praz

Enclosures: 2

PRACTICE 9   EDIT AN ESSAY

Correct twenty errors in the next essay.

During world war II, the United States had it's own version of Mata Hari. A debutante by the name of Amy Thorpe became one of the wars most successful secret agents.

At the age of nineteen, Thorpe met and married a much older British diplomat, Arthur Pack. At the beginning of the spanish civil war, the Packs was sent to Spain. During a hot summer day, five desperate Nationalist soldiers approached Amy Pack. With some hesitation, she agreed to smuggle them past enemy lines. The soldier's hid inside the trunk of her car and past through a checkpoint. On that momentous occasion, the young woman discovered her true calling.

Section 9
EDITING

In a revolt against her sheltered upbringing, the diplomats wife desired a life of danger and excitement. In the summer of 1937, Amy Thorpe separated from her husband and becomes a spy for Britain. With the code name of Cynthia, she obtained secret information about Hitlers plan to invade Czechoslovakia.

One of her most dangerous missions occurred in Vichy, France. Posing as an American journalist, "Cynthia" seduced Charles Brousse, an official at the french Embassy, and convinced him to work with her. Thorpes' mission was to photograph secret Nazi codebooks. The couple met in the embassy for several nights and convinced the night watchmen that they were simply an amorous couple. On the third night, they enterred the code room, opened the window, and let a professionnal safecracker into the room. Suddenly, Thorpe had a hunch, and, to the surprise of the men, she decided to remove her clothing. Seconds later, the door opened, and the night watchmans flashlight beamed into the room. When he saw the naked woman, he apologized and retreated. Thorpe quickly dressed. The safecracking expert then opened the safe, Thorpe photographed the codebooks.

Although most Americans have never heard of her, Amy Thorpe's wartime actions were extreme important. Amy Thorpe has been credited with saving over 100,000 Allied lives.

Section 9
EDITING

PRACTICE 10 EDIT AN ESSAY

Correct twenty errors in the next essay.

Sports surround us every day in the papers, on television, and on the radio. Some people criticize our sports-driven culture. Sports critics say that colleges' put young athletes on pedestals and do not emphasize the achievments of students in academic programs. In fact, athletes do not receive enough praise.

First, colleges with good sports teams gets a lot of publicity. For example, during the football season, three national television channels covers the games CBS, NBC, and ABC. During the basketball playoffs, March Madness CBS covers the games during prime-time television. The publicity that colleges receive from sports bring more students to the academic programs. Sports help these programs, they do not harm them.

In addition, colleges and universities make money from their student athletes. For example, the National Collegiate athletic association (NCAA), the organization devoted to the administration of intercollegiate athletics in the United States, showed $422.2 millions in revenue in its 2002–2003 budget. A large part of this money come from television. Most of the money is redistributed to colleges and universities. Educational institutions use the funds not only for their sports programs but also are giving money to academic programs. Clearly, colleges show good long-term planning when they promote star athletes.

Moreover sports are a motivation for athletes to go to college. Last year, there were about 360,000 student athletes in NCAA-affiliated colleges. Over 126,000 of thoses athletes received either a partial or a full scholarship. Therefore, they were real motivated. To attend postsecondary institutions.

Colleges and universities are right to pay special attention to athletes and sports programs. Because of the extra effort that student athletes must give to suceed, and because of the publicity and money that educational institutions receive from sports programs and their athletes colleges and universities have a serious obligation to encourage there athletes.

Section 9
EDITING

■ The concluding sentences of the selection
■ Any photos, graphs, or charts

Finding the Main Idea

After you finish previewing, read the selection carefully. Search for the **main idea,** which is the central point that the writer is trying to make. In an essay, the main idea usually appears somewhere in the first few paragraphs in the form of a thesis statement. However, some professional writers build up to the main idea and state it only in the middle or at the end of the essay. Additionally, some professional writers do not state the main idea directly.

 Making a Statement of Main Idea

If a reading does not contain a clear thesis statement, you can determine the main idea by asking yourself *who, what, when, where, why,* and *how* questions. Then, using the answers to those questions, write a statement that sums up the main point of the reading.

Making Inferences

If a professional writer does not state the main idea directly, you must look for clues that will help you **infer** or figure out what the writer means to say. For example, read the next paragraph and try to infer the writer's meaning.

> The band cost about $4,500 for the night. The hall rented for $900, and we figured we got a good deal. We had to decorate it ourselves. There were flowers on every table ($25 for each bouquet), rented china and silverware ($1,850), and tablecloths, tables, and chairs ($900). The catered food worked out to be $40 per person, multiplied by 300. This is not counting the dresses, the tuxedos, the photographer, or the rented limos. Sure, it was a special night. It is too bad the guests of honor split up three months later.

PRACTICE I

Read the preceding paragraph. Then answer the following questions.

1. What is the subject of the paragraph? _____

2. What is the writer's relationship to the guests of honor? _____

   _____

3. What is the writer's main point? _____

   _____

Finding the Supporting Ideas

Different writers use different types of supporting ideas. They may give steps for a process, use examples to illustrate a point, give reasons for an argument, and so on. Try to identify the author's supporting ideas.

Highlighting and Making Annotations

After you read a long text, you may forget some of the author's ideas. To help you remember and quickly find the important points, you can highlight key ideas and make annotations. An **annotation** is a comment, question, or reaction that you write in the margin of a page.

Each time you read a passage, follow the next steps.

- Look in the introductory and concluding paragraphs. Underline sentences that sum up the main idea. Using your own words, rewrite the main idea in the margin.
- Underline or highlight supporting ideas. You might even number the arguments or ideas. This will allow you to understand the essay's development.
- Circle words that you do not understand.
- Write questions in the margin if you do not understand the author's meaning.
- Write notes beside passages that are interesting or that relate to your own experiences.
- Jot down any ideas that might make interesting writing topics.

Here is a highlighted and annotated passage from an essay titled "The New Addiction" by Josh Freed.

1 Is the cell phone the cigarette of our times? That's what I've been asking myself lately as the (scourge) of smokers slowly disappears from city life and a scourge of cell-phone users takes their place. Everywhere you look, people hold cell phones up to their mouths, instead of cigarettes, and nonusers react as intolerantly as nonsmokers ever did. How does the cell phone resemble the cigarette? Let me count the ways.

2 It's an oral habit. For many users, the cell phone is an obvious substitute for smoking. It's a nervous habit that gives you something to do with your hands—whether you're dialing, checking your messages, or just (fondling) the buttons. Just like cigarettes, the phone sits in your breast pocket or on a restaurant table, ready to bring quickly to your mouth. Often, it's in a fliptop case that pops open as easily as a cigarette pack.

Why?
What is "scourge"?
General background

Main point suggests cell phones are like cigarettes.
Good example. I play with my phone.

"Fondling"?

Understanding Difficult Words

When you read, you will sometimes come across unfamiliar words. You can try to guess the word's meaning, or you can circle it and look it up later.

Using Context Clues

Context clues are hints in the text that help define a word. To find a word's meaning, try the following strategies.

- **Look at the word.** Is it a noun, a verb, or an adjective? Sometimes it is easier to understand a word if you know how that word functions in the sentence.
- **Look at surrounding words.** Look at the sentence in which the word appears and try to find a relation between the difficult word and the words that surround it. Maybe there is a **synonym** (a word that means the same

thing) or an **antonym** (a word that means the opposite). Maybe other words in the sentence help define the word.

- **Look at surrounding sentences.** Sometimes you can guess the meaning of a difficult word by looking at the sentences, paragraphs, and punctuation surrounding the word. When you use your logic, the meaning becomes clear.

PRACTICE 2

1. Can you easily define the word *disseminates?*   No   Yes

2. Can you easily define the word *parity?*   No   Yes

3. If you do not understand the meanings of those two words, then read them in the context of the next paragraph. You will notice that it is much easier to guess their meanings.

> Christina Hoff Sommers, author of *The War Against Boys,* argues that boys are being neglected in order to help girls succeed in school. For years, she argues, feminist groups have spread myths about the disadvantaged girls, yet boys are actually the disadvantaged sex. The Department of Education **disseminates** hundreds of documents about gender equity, Sommers says. While the documents suggest ways to help girls succeed, none of them explain how educators can help boys achieve academic **parity** with girls.

Now write your own definition of the words as they are used in the paragraph.

a. disseminates: _____

b. parity: _____

 Word Twins

Word twins are English words that may look and sound like words in another language. For example, the English word *responsible* is similar to the Spanish word *responsable,* although the words are spelled differently.

If English is not your first language, and you read an English word that looks similar to a word in your language, check how it is being used in context. It may, or may not, mean the same thing in English as it means in your language. For example, in English, *assist* means "to help." In Spanish, *assistar* means "to attend." If you are not sure of a word's meaning, consult a dictionary.

Using a Dictionary

If you do not understand the meaning of an unfamiliar word after using context clues, look up the word in a dictionary. A dictionary is useful if you use it correctly. Review the following tips for dictionary usage.

- **Look at the dictionary's frontmatter.** The preface contains explanations about the various symbols and abbreviations.
- **Read all of the definitions listed for the word.** Look for the meaning that best fits the context of your sentence.
- **Look up root words, if necessary.** If the difficult word has a prefix such as *un-* or *anti-*, you may have to look up the root word.

Here is an example of how dictionaries set up their definitions.

Word Division

Your dictionary may use black dots to indicate places for dividing words.

Stress symbol (') and Pronunciation

Some dictionaries provide the phonetic pronunciation of words. The stress symbol (') lets you know which syllable has the highest or loudest sound.

Parts of Speech

The *n* means that *deception* is a noun. If you don't understand the parts of speech symbol, look in the front or the back of your dictionary for a list of symbols and their meanings.

de•cep'tion / [di-sep'shən] / *n* 1, the act of misleading. 2, a misrepresentation; artiface; fraud.

From *The New American Webster Handy College Dictionary* (New York: Signet, 2000) 606.

From Reading to Writing

After you finish reading a selection, try these strategies to make sure that you have understood it.

- **Summarize the reading.** When you summarize, you use your own words to write a condensed version of the reading. You leave out all information except the main points.
- **Outline the reading.** An outline is a visual plan of the reading. First, write down the main idea of the essay, and then note the most important idea from each paragraph. Under each idea, include a detail or an example.

Make a Written Response

Your instructor may ask you to write about your reaction to a reading. These are some questions you might ask yourself before you make a written response.

- What is the writer's main point?
- What is the writer's purpose? Is the writer trying to entertain me, persuade me, or teach me?
- Who is the audience? Is the writer directing his or her message at someone like me?
- Do I agree or disagree with the writer's main point?
- What aspects of the topic can I relate to?

After you answer the questions, you will have more ideas to use in your written response.

Reading Selections

READING I

Aunt Tee

Maya Angelou

Maya Angelou is a poet, historian, civil rights activist, and writer. In this next essay from her collection *I Wouldn't Take Nothing for My Journey Now*, Angelou writes about an important person in her life. As you read this description essay, also look for elements of narration and comparison and contrast.

1   Aunt Tee was a Los Angeles member of our extended family. She was seventy-nine when I met her, sinewy, strong, and the color of old lemons. She wore her coarse, straight hair, which was slightly streaked with gray, in a long braided rope across the top of her head. With her high cheekbones, old gold skin, and almond eyes, she looked more like an Indian chief than an old black woman. (Aunt Tee described herself and any favored member of her race as Negroes. *Black* was saved for those who had incurred her disapproval.)

2   She had retired and lived alone in a dead, neat ground-floor apartment. Wax flowers and china figurines sat on elaborately embroidered and heavily starched doilies. Sofas and chairs were tautly upholstered. The only thing at ease in Aunt Tee's apartment was Aunt Tee.

3   I used to visit her often and perch on her uncomfortable sofa just to hear her stories. She was proud that after working thirty years as a maid, she spent the next thirty years as a live-in housekeeper, carrying the keys to rich houses and keeping meticulous accounts.

4   "Living in lets the white folks know Negroes are as neat and clean as they are, sometimes more so. And it gives the Negro maid a chance to see white folks ain't no smarter than Negroes. Just luckier. Sometimes."

5   Aunt Tee told me that once she was housekeeper for a couple in Bel Air, California, and lived with them in a fourteen-room ranch house. There was a day maid who cleaned, and a gardener who daily tended the lush gardens. Aunt Tee oversaw the workers. When she began the job, she cooked and served a light breakfast, a good lunch, and a full three- or four-course dinner to her employers and their guests. Aunt Tee said she watched them grow older and leaner. After a few years, they stopped entertaining and ate dinner hardly seeing each other at the table. Finally, they sat in a dry silence as they ate evening meals of soft scrambled eggs, melba toast, and weak tea. Aunt Tee said she saw them growing old but didn't see herself aging at all.

6   She became the social maven. She started "keeping company" (her phrase) with a chauffeur down the street. Her best friend and her friend's husband worked in service only a few blocks away.

7   On Saturdays, Aunt Tee would cook a pot of pigs' feet, a pot of greens, fry chicken, make potato salad, and bake a banana pudding. Then, that evening, her friends—the chauffeur, the other housekeeper, and her husband—would come to Aunt Tee's **commodious** live-in quarters. There the four would eat and drink, play records and dance. As the evening wore on, they would settle down to a serious game of bid whist.

commodious: large; spacious

8   Naturally, during this revelry, jokes were told, fingers were snapped, feet were patted, and there was a great deal of laughter.

9   Aunt Tee said that what occurred during every Saturday party startled her and her friends the first time it happened. They had been playing cards, and Aunt Tee, who had just won the bid, held a handful of trumps. She felt a cool breeze on her back and sat upright and turned around. Her employers had cracked her door open and beckoned to her. Aunt Tee, a little peeved, laid down her cards and went to the door. The couple backed away and asked her to come into the hall, and there they both spoke and won Aunt Tee's sympathy forever.

10   "Theresa, we don't mean to disturb you," the man whispered, "but you all seem to be having such a good time . . ."

11   The woman added, "We hear you and your friends laughing every Saturday night, and we'd just like to watch you. We don't want to bother you. We'll be quiet and just watch."

12   The man said, "If you'll just leave your door ajar, your friends don't need to know. We'll never make a sound." Aunt Tee said she saw no harm in agreeing, and she talked it over with her company. They said it was OK with them, but it was sad that the employers owned the gracious house, the swimming pool, three cars, and numberless palm trees, but had no joy. Aunt Tee told me that laughter and relaxation had left the house; she agreed it was sad.

13   That story has stayed with me for nearly thirty years, and when a tale remains fresh in my mind, it almost always contains a lesson which will benefit me.

14   I draw the picture of the wealthy couple standing in a darkened hallway, peering into a lighted room where black servants were lifting their voices in merriment and comradery, and I realize that living well is an art which can be developed. Of course, you need the basic talents to build upon: they are a love of life and the ability to take great pleasure from small offerings, an assurance that the world owes you nothing, and awareness that every gift is exactly that, a gift. Because of the routines we follow, we often forget that life is an ongoing adventure.

VOCABULARY AND COMPREHENSION

1.   What is a *social maven* (paragraph 6)?

2.   What is the meaning of *revelry* in paragraph 8?

3. Angelou uses descriptive imagery. Descriptive imagery includes active verbs, adjectives, and other words that appeal to the senses (sight, smell, touch, sound, taste). Underline at least six examples of descriptive imagery.

4. Why was it so important for Aunt Tee to be neat and tidy?

_____

_____

_____

CRITICAL THINKING

5. Why does Angelou call her aunt's apartment *dead* (paragraph 2)?

_____

_____

_____

6. In paragraph 4, Angelou quotes Aunt Tee. Why does the author use the slang word *ain't?*

_____

_____

_____

7. What can you infer about the lives of Aunt Tee's wealthy employers? What types of people are they?

_____

_____

_____

_____

8. In paragraph 5, Aunt Tee says that she does not see herself aging. Why does she say this?

_____

_____

_____

WRITING TOPICS

Write a paragraph or an essay about one of the following topics. Remember to explore, develop, and revise and edit your work.

1. Write about a time when you saw an event that changed your perception of someone.
2. Angelou tells a story to make a point about living life to the fullest. Write about a moment in time when you felt that you were living life to its fullest. Use descriptive imagery in your writing.
3. Reflect on the quotation. Do you live in a clean, organized environment or a messy one? Describe a clean or messy room in your home. (You might reread Angelou's depiction of Aunt Tee's home to get some ideas.)

> *I hate housework. You make the beds, you do the dishes, and six months later you have to start all over again.*
> —JOAN RIVERS, ENTERTAINER

READING 2

Dealing with People
Greg McGrew

> Greg McGrew is the president of Hospitality Profit Builders. In the next essay, the author uses the classification writing pattern to describe different types of personalities.

1   It's no secret that most of our problems in life are "people" problems. Whether we are running a coffee cart or a full-service sit-down restaurant, how to solve our people problems seems to be a big secret that most of us struggle with, both in our personal lives as well as on the job. Who of us hasn't reflected on an encounter with another person and asked ourselves if we couldn't have handled the situation better? Yet there are a few people who seem to glide effortlessly through life working with a wide variety of people, achieving success in both their personal and professional lives. How do they do it? Somewhere along their life road, they have learned how to deal effectively with the four basic personality groups: dominants, expressives, analyticals, and amiables.

2   Dominants are naturally highly assertive people, and their behavior is characterized by the way they act. They tend to be active, confident, aggressive, talkative, extroverted, and confrontational. To many people, dominants are a threat to their mental well-being. However, if you know that it is important to look a dominant in the eye when talking to him or her, you can earn this person's respect and cooperation. Working with the other personality styles requires similar techniques.

3   Expressives are also highly assertive. They generally tell rather than ask and do a lot of thinking out loud. Most importantly, work has to be fun, and they will go out of their way to make it so. Expressives love touching, which makes amiables nervous. The expressive is relationship driven and has difficulty saying "no" because doing so may hurt the relationship. To get on the same wavelength with an expressive, be personable. Give the big picture first and then the details. Let the expressive know you are available at any time to talk.

4   Analyticals are thinkers. They take time to weigh everything out in their minds before they answer questions correctly the first time. To make a decision, analyticals need lots of information. They are good at making decisions; they just need a long time to get there. So, when dealing with analyticals, give them three to five seconds to answer you and ask them; do not tell them. If you do that, you will see analyticals as being logical, industrious, orderly, and systematic. Otherwise, you might think they are indecisive, unclear, and confused.

5   Amiables are very task and relationship oriented. They are naturally good listeners, and trust is key to their relationships. They are also perfectionists who like a lot of information before making decisions. To get the information, they will seek consensus from their peers. To work well with amiables, give all the information plus the result. Give them time and space to consult with others on the team. Treat them with respect and talk in a softer tone of voice.

6   Those who know how to deal with people use their knowledge of these personality styles to enhance their communication abilities, resolve conflicts more successfully, improve their working and personal relations, and recognize what motivates others. Look at the people around you and determine who are the dominants, expressives, analyticals, and amiables. Now go look that dominant customer in the eye and start communicating!

Vocabulary and Comprehension

1.   Underline the thesis statement in the essay.
2.   What introduction style does the author use? Circle the best answer.
     a.   General background
     b.   Anecdote
     c.   Definition
3.   Briefly explain the four personality types that the author describes.

_____

_____

_____

_____

_____

_____

_____

4.   Explain the author's suggestions for dealing with each personality type.

_____

_____

_____

_____

5.   According to McGrew, why is it important to know personality types?

_____

_____

CRITICAL THINKING

6.   The author states that it is important to look a dominant in the eye. Why might it be important?

_____

_____

7.   Can you think of certain fields that each personality type might excel in?

_____

_____

_____

_____

8.   Who is the audience for this essay? Identify clues in the essay that tell you about the audience.

_____

_____

_____

_____

_____

_____

_____

WRITING TOPICS

Write a paragraph or an essay about one of the following topics. Remember to explore, develop, and revise and edit your work.

1.   Which personality type do you think you are? Are you a combination of types? Explain your answer.
2.   Do people express different aspects of their personality depending on the role they are in? In other words, could somebody be dominant in one role but amiable in another? Explain your answer.
3.   Read the quotation. Then write about types of personalities, but do not use the same categories as Greg McGrew or Woody Allen.

> *There are two types of people in this world: The good and the bad. The good sleep better, but the bad seem to enjoy their waking hours more.*
> —WOODY ALLEN, COMEDIAN, ACTOR, AND FILMMAKER

READING 3

How to Get All-Day Energy

Maria Noel Mandile

> Maria Noel Mandile is a researcher and journalist at *Natural Health* magazine. In the next essay, she argues that a day at the office does not have to be draining. As you read, notice how the author has used elements of the process writing pattern.

1   Is low energy causing you to drag all day and retire to the couch after 5 p.m.? Feeling peppy takes less effort than you may think. "We don't have to quit our jobs or put our kids up for adoption to get the energy that we need," says Pamela Smith, R.D., a registered dietitian in Orlando, Florida, and author of *The Energy Edge*. Any of the following changes should make you feel more energized in just one day. The more you do, the more you will notice the lift.

2   If you work at a desk all day, make sure you are not sitting improperly or straining to read. Both can drain your energy, says Marvin Dainoff, Ph.D., director of the Center for **Ergonomic** Research at Miami University in Oxford, Ohio. When at the computer, check that your feet are flat on the floor, your back is straight, and you don't have to tilt your head to look at your monitor. If you need to, adjust your chair and the angle of your monitor. Additionally, you should not have to reach down or up to type or use your mouse. Rather, your hands should rest comfortably on the keyboard with your elbows bent at 90 degrees. To prevent eyestrain, increase your computer's font size and prop up books or other reading material so that you can read while looking straight ahead.

3   Feng shui, the ancient Chinese art of placement, holds that living plants have an energy that can invigorate people, says David Kennedy, a feng shui practitioner in Berkeley, California, and author of *Feng Shui for Dummies*. In just one day, office plants helped people working at computers feel 10 percent more attentive than people working in a plant-free office (it also helped them work 12 percent faster on their computers), according to research done at Washington State University in Pullman in 1996. Plants that thrive indoors include Boston ferns, Chinese evergreens, and peace lilies. Vibrant, hardy cut flowers like gerber daisies and tulips also perk up office workers, according to studies.

4   Studies show that whenever your energy flags, inhaling peppermint essential oil (*Mentha piperita*) throughout the day clears thinking and boosts productivity. Other revitalizing essential oils include lemon (*Citrus limon*), lemon balm (*Melissa officinalis*), juniper (*Juniperus communis*), orange (*Citrus sinensis*), and spearmint (*Mentha spicata*), says Kennedy. Keep a bottle by your desk, uncap, and sniff as needed. To sustain your energy after work, plug a car diffuser sprinkled with an essential oil into your car's cigarette lighter, or place a few drops on your defrost vents and turn on the fan.

5   Exercise energizes you, says Smith. And you do not need to do much to reap the benefits. In a 2001 study in *Health Psychology*, people who pedaled a stationary bike for 10 minutes felt more clear-headed,

ergonomic: human engineering; the study of workplace design less fatigued, and in a better mood than those who did nothing. If you are a morning person, waking up an extra 15 minutes early to exercise can help you power through your day. Or, if you prefer, be active when you get home from work: bike, dance like mad to a few songs on the radio, in-line skate, jump rope, or walk around the block.

6   Work can make you forget some of life's joys, and feeling down can drain your energy. To remind yourself that there really is fun to be had, create and keep handy a list of twenty pleasurable activities you could do in less than 15 minutes, recommends Ann McGee-Cooper, Ed.D., a Dallas-based corporate consultant and author of *You Don't Have to Go Home from Work Exhausted*. Whenever you feel run-down, do something from your list. For example, walk through a park, write a letter, or simply step out to feel sunlight on your skin. Ask a friend to dinner or register for a fun class at your gym or local community college. Looking forward to pleasure boosts your energy, says McGee-Cooper, because anticipation can be as much fun as reality.

7   Do not forget to stretch. Sitting in the same position all day tires muscles and saps energy. Every hour, get up and stretch for one minute, recommends Dainoff. It does not matter what you do—just move. Reach to the ceiling, turn your head from side to side, roll your shoulders, arch your back, stand on tiptoe, or touch your toes. If stretching at your desk might raise a few eyebrows, retreat to a bathroom stall. If you cannot remember to stretch regularly, set a timer.

8   On the way home from work, don't tune in to the news. Instead, move that dial to your favorite music station, or pop a CD into your disc or car stereo. Listening to music rebuilds your energy instantly, says McGee-Cooper, because it is pleasurable. It can be any type of music, from classical to jazz to rock-and-roll, as long as you enjoy it, she says.

Vocabulary and Comprehension

1.   In paragraph 1, find a slang word that means "energized."

_____

2.   What does this essay help readers do? Circle the best answer.
     a. Complete a process   b. Understand a process
3.   Look in paragraph 1 and underline the thesis statement of this essay.
4.   List seven steps that the author suggests people can take to feel more energetic.

_____

_____

_____

Critical Thinking

5.   Who is the specific audience for this essay?

_____

6. What kind of supporting details does the author use? You can choose more than one answer.
   a. List of examples   b. Extended examples
   c. Facts and/or statistics   d. Informed opinions
7. What types of experts does Mandile mention in her essay?

   _____

   _____

8. What comment is the author making about our society? Use inference, or reading between the lines, to help you answer this question.

   _____

   _____

WRITING TOPICS

Write a paragraph or an essay about one of the following topics. Remember to explore, develop, and revise and edit your work.

1. Evaluate Mandile's suggestions for getting all-day energy. Are they practical? Are any particular suggestions impractical? Explain your answer.
2. Mandile describes a process for relaxing at work. Describe a process that you follow when you prepare for work, prepare to relax, or prepare for bed.
3. Reflect on this quotation. How is it applicable in your life? You might give examples of things that make you feel stressed.

> *Stress is an ignorant state. It believes that everything is an emergency. Nothing is that important.*
> —NATALIE GOLDBERG, WRITER

READING 4

When the Legal Thing Isn't the Right Thing
Deborah Mead

Deborah Mead is a poet and essayist. In the next article, which appeared in the *Christian Science Monitor*, Mead reflects on a moral dilemma. As you read this illustration essay, also look for elements of narration and comparison and contrast.

1   After spending several hours at the mall, I was stuck. Traffic had slowed to a crawl on my side of the Interstate. I was in the right lane, a mile from my exit, and anxious to get home. Apparently other drivers were anxious too, because they were flying past me in the breakdown lane.

2   On most highways, driving on the shoulder is a clear no-no, but on my particular stretch of road, it's a little murkier. The shoulder functions as a travel lane on weekdays from 6 to 10 a.m. and 3 to 7 p.m. But this was 5 p.m. on a Saturday, and by some Cinderella-style

governmental magic, the special 55-mile-per-hour lane had officially reverted to its lowly breakdown status.

3　　As I watched the smug drivers sail by, my frustration level rising, I tried to reason my way into breaking the law, too. I told myself it's not as if the shoulder is never used as a driving lane. By establishing these windows of travel for the shoulder, the state of Massachusetts is recognizing that periods of high traffic call for breaking the normal rules of the road. This was certainly one of those times.

4　　I told myself the principle of putting the greater good ahead of my own didn't apply here. It is true that if everyone at a concert stood up to get a better view, all would be worse off, with the same mediocre view but sore feet. But, in this case, if everyone regarded the shoulder as a travel lane, we would all travel **incrementally** faster. If anything, my transgression would benefit society.

incrementally: increasingly

5　　I told myself that I was getting off at the next exit, so in fact the shoulder would just be like a one-mile off-ramp. I would not be merging back into traffic later, and I would not be cutting anyone off. No one would be harmed.

6　　I told myself all this—but, still, I couldn't turn onto the shoulder.

7　　Unmoved by common sense, I sat in traffic for ten minutes to go that one mile, while other cars continued to whiz by me on the right. There was a time I would have felt morally superior to those selfish people breaking the law. I would have told myself that they had no regard for other people and congratulated myself on being a model citizen.

8　　I don't feel that way anymore. Instead, I recognize that I am cowed by authority, particularly when that authority is anonymous, mere words on a sign. Somewhere in my civic upbringing, I confused obedience with goodness.

9　　It's too late to reeducate myself now. As much as I reason with myself, and as much as I believe I would be justified in crossing over that solid line, I will bow to rules that make no sense. It is the legal thing to do—it may even be the moral thing to do—but I know it can't be right.

VOCABULARY AND COMPREHENSION

1. In paragraph 4, find a word that means "a broken rule."

   _____

2. Where and when does this story take place?

   _____

3. What moral debate does Mead have with herself?

   _____

   _____

   _____

   _____

4. Write a sentence that sums up the essay's main idea. Use your answers to questions 2 and 3 to form your sentence.

   _____

   _____

   _____

5. Does Mead believe that breaking the law and driving on the shoulder is a good idea? Why or why not?

   _____

   _____

   _____

CRITICAL THINKING

6. How is Mead different from those who drove by her on the shoulder of the road?

   _____

   _____

7. What does Mead mean when she says that she is "cowed by authority" (paragraph 8)?

   _____

   _____

8. Will Mead change her way of thinking in the future when she is confronted with similar dilemmas?

   _____

   _____

9. Mead says that she learned to confuse "obedience" with "goodness." Do you think that these two words mean the same thing? Why or why not?

   _____

   _____

WRITING TOPICS

Write a paragraph or an essay about one of the following topics. Remember to explore, develop, and revise and edit your work.

1. Mead says, "I learned to confuse obedience with goodness" (paragraph 9). Reflect on the author's words. Explain when obedience may not be a sign of goodness. Use specific examples to support your opinion.

2. Do you believe that people should follow all rules and laws, or do you believe that some rules and laws are made to be broken? Explain your opinion using specific examples of rules and laws.

3. Reflect on the quotation. Do you agree with Einstein? Explain why we need or do not need laws.

> *Every kind of peaceful cooperation among men is primarily based on mutual trust and only secondarily on institutions such as courts of justice and police.*
> —ALBERT EINSTEIN, PHYSICIST

READING 5
My Head Rolled in Syria
Josh Freed

Josh Freed is a columnist for the *Montreal Gazette*. Winner of Canada's Stephen Leacock Award for Humor, Freed has published many books, including *Fear of Frying and Other Fax of Life*. In the next essay, Freed uses narration and some description to recount an adventure during his vacation in Syria.

1   It's not every vacation I get involved with grave-robbers and jail threats, so let me tell you a story from my recent Middle East travels: the *Tale of the Supposedly Stolen Syrian Statue*.

2   We had been visiting Syria awhile and had just hired a driver to take us to two famous ruins in the countryside. The first was called Apamea, an ancient Roman-era city of 500,000, which is now deserted. Our driver left us in the middle of nowhere, at a breathtaking mile-long colonnade of giant pillars, and said he'd meet us at the other end. Soon we were wandering alone down a 2,000-year-old street.

3   "Pssst, mister!" said a voice. "You want to buy antiques? Coins? Statues?" Behind some pillars, a man in a headscarf was hawking dusty relics with Roman designs. Or maybe they were fakes he had made at home that morning—who knew? A second man on a motor scooter showed us bigger treasure—a sculpted white marble head almost as big as my fist.

4   It was a haunting Roman-style bust with a gentle face and a mysterious smile—the sort of thing you see in museums. They wanted $250 U.S. but quickly came down to $150, even though I wasn't bargaining. Suddenly one of them hissed "Guard!" and they disappeared.

5   In the distance I saw a guard approaching in a red headscarf, and I went back to ruin watching. He ignored me, but when he was gone the statue salesmen popped up behind another pillar. By then, my wife and I had decided we were not taking artifacts out of Syria. It was wrong—and besides, it could lead to a cold Syrian jail. For the rest of our walk, we tried to ignore the hawkers who literally chased us from pillar to post lowering their price and playing peek-a-boo with the guard.

6   Eventually, we reached the end of the columns, where our driver, Omar, was waiting. A group of British tourists was there, too, with an English-speaking guide from Damascus, and I asked his advice. He

said many Syrian archeological sites were still undiscovered and grave-robbing was common. The old coins were probably real, though the head was more likely a fake. "If you like the head, buy it anyway. It's probably an imitation—and no one will care either way."

7   Unsure of the complications, we decided against it and drove off to our second location. But we had not gone far when three motorcycles appeared behind us, and our salesman-on-a-scooter waved the statue head, shouting, "Mister! For you, special price—only $70!" They raced up beside us, bargaining through our window. Omar put his foot to the gas and left them behind, but two miles on they were waiting around a bend.

8   They drove beside us again, shouting, "$40—very good!" And when the price fell to $30, we impulsively stopped the car and gave in. Why not? At this price, the head was obviously fake and would make a nice memento. I paid them and put the head into my pocket, but just before leaving, the salesman leaned into our car and said, "If anyone sees it at the border, say you got it at the Damascus market. Don't say it's from a grave."

9   And so we drove away, suddenly unsure whether we had bought a cheap fake or a 2,000-year-old treasure. We started to worry about what to do at the Syrian border—declare it, or hope no one noticed? Maybe we should just throw it out? I had barely owned it and the head hung over my soul like an ancient curse.

10   For the next three hours we raced across the country toward our next stop: a 1,500-year-old Christian ruin that is a well-known Syrian attraction. We arrived there in the late afternoon, and a sleepy guard told us the ticket office had just closed. We pleaded, but the guard said, "Sorry—my boss very bad man. If he find you inside, big trouble."

baksheesh: bribe

Omar wouldn't give in. He offered the guard a bit of **baksheesh** and the man opened the gate. "Quick—go inside," the guard said, "but if problem, you leave quickly."

11   We found ourselves alone in a lovely Byzantine complex. We spent ten minutes admiring it all when the guard came racing back. "Car coming—maybe boss!" he shouted. "Must leave—please run!" The next thing we knew, we were racing after him. Ten minutes later, we found ourselves outside the site.

12   I breathed a sigh of relief, but it was premature. As we came around the wall near the parking lot, we saw a tall man dressed in black with a mustache like Saddam Hussein's. He looked as "bad" as our guard had warned, a cinema-style villain, who barked, "Where have you been?"

13   "Walking around the church," I said.

14   "No! You were inside the church. You break law. Now you come to police station. You go to jail."

15   Suddenly I remembered the head—it was still in my pocket—and a chill went down my spine. It was bad enough to be arrested sneaking into ruins after hours, but worse if you had an artifact on you that might be 2,000 years old. And at that moment the head felt all too authentic.

16   Either event could be explained alone, but together they would be enough to send us to the Syrian Political Prison for Grave Robbers. I

could see the headlines back home: "Montreal journalist caught in grave-robbing ring; Canadian embassy refuses to intervene."

17   Ahead in the parking lot, I saw a white police wagon and made a decision. As the "bad man" marched in front of us, I slipped the head from my pocket and threw it quietly onto the ground. If the trouble blew over, maybe I would come back for it later.

18   In the parking lot there was a heated debate in Syrian among Omar, our guard, and the "bad man." The bad man said he was going for the police and ordered us to wait; then he drove away in his white wagon.

19   Omar offered some quick advice: "We must go—before the man comes back." I ran back to find the head, but to my amazement the white stone of the statue was the same color as much of Syria: I saw small white stones everywhere, and when I turned them over, none had a gentle face. The head had vanished.

20   As twilight turned to darkness, we packed into our car and drove away, leaving the head in the land it had come from. Was it genuine or fake? Priceless or worthless? It was best not to know. We had let ourselves be tempted by zany circumstances and a touch of greed, and had made a mistake we were lucky to escape.

21   In the car, Omar was laughing merrily. "Statue no go to Canada," he chuckled, as we drove down the road. "Statue stay home."

22   We joined him in laughter. The head was back where it belonged—in the ruins of Syria.

VOCABULARY AND COMPREHENSION

1.   What is the meaning of "hawking" (paragraph 3)?

    _____

2.   Why does Freed feel anxious about buying the white statue?

    _____

    _____

    _____

3.   Even though Freed feels reluctant, he ends up buying the statue. Why does he change his mind?

    _____

    _____

4.   How is the ending of Freed's adventure appropriate?

    _____

    _____

    _____

    _____

CRITICAL THINKING

5. In your opinion, was the sculpted white marble head an antique, or was it an imitation?

_____

_____

6. What larger issue does this story raise?

_____

_____

_____

7. The author uses dialogue in several paragraphs. How does the dialogue enhance the story?

_____

_____

_____

_____

8. What are some interesting verbs that Freed uses? How do the verbs enhance the text?

_____

_____

_____

_____

WRITING TOPICS

Write a paragraph or an essay about one of the following topics. Remember to explore, develop, and revise and edit your work.

1. If you had been in Josh Freed's position, would you have bought the white marble head? Why or why not?
2. What is the most interesting place that you have traveled to? Describe that place.
3. Respond to the quotation. You might discuss a road you have not taken and explain why you did not take it, or you might write about future choices and how you plan to make your decisions about those choices.

> *Two roads diverged in a wood, and I – I took the one less traveled by, and that has made all the difference.*
> —ROBERT FROST,
> "THE ROAD NOT TAKEN"

READING 6

Enough Is Enough
Judy Sheindlin, with Josh Getlin

Judy Sheindlin is a judge and author who also has her own television show, "Judge Judy." In the next excerpt from her book *Don't Pee on My Leg and Tell Me It's Raining,* the author describes ways to treat young offenders. As you read this example of a process essay, also look for elements of the argument and comparison and contrast writing patterns.

1   As a family court judge, I looked down daily on a pageant of dysfunction that would curl your hair. After twenty-four years on the bench, I came to realize that these are not legal problems. They mirror what is wrong with our society, reflecting just how far we have strayed from personal responsibility and old-fashioned discipline.

2   Most of the kids I prosecuted during my early years in court were involved in petty thefts, but as the 70s passed into the 80s, both the incidence and the **ferocity** of juvenile crime accelerated. A new breed of delinquents was born, and the system did not have a clue how to treat them. We still don't.

ferocity: fierce cruelty

3   To show you the price we pay, let me share some of my experiences in family court. The first case is heard at 9:30 a.m. A boy I'll call Elmo, 15, has been charged for a second time with selling crack cocaine. His lawyer argues that Elmo's troubles started when his grandmother died. In his grief, he had no choice but to deal the hard stuff. "Get a better story," I fire back, startling the boy, who is looking smug. "Nobody goes out and sells drugs because Grandma died."

4   Next is a youth I'll call Tito, a delinquent who confesses to mugging an 80-year-old man in broad daylight. Tito's older brother has just been sent to prison for murder. Tito was very close to his brother, the boy's lawyer insists, and his crime was a result of post-traumatic stress. "You'll have to do better than that," I snap.

5   Then comes a woman who is addicted to crack. She's already given birth to two crack-addicted babies, and she didn't report to her drug-rehab program as promised. Her excuse: She lost the address. "What do you want, a road map?" I exclaim.

6   Welcome to my world.

7   I believe that you deal with these problems the way you would deal with any crisis in a family: by setting strict limits and by showing compassion. As the mother of five children, I know that you have to get tough at the same time that you show love. Family court should be no different. I think we should send a tough message to first-time offenders every chance we get, in the hopes that perhaps there will not be a second offense.

8   The primary obligation of any civilized society is to preserve the peace and protect its citizens. Only after that should you worry about the lawbreakers and their rehabilitation. This might be our last chance to do something about the future of these delinquents—and our own safety. Here are my suggestions for improving our juvenile system.

Spend Public Money on Good Kids

9   The vast majority of the children who suffer from poverty, neglect, and even abuse do not commit crimes. They struggle in their chaotic environments, with little or no support. But for years our concerns have been with those who break the law.

10   A recent set of photographs in my local newspaper illustrated this inversion of priorities. In one picture was a state-of-the-art gymnasium, with Nautilus equipment and gleaming free weights— part of the recreational complex at a state detention facility. The other photo was of an overcrowded, deteriorating inner-city junior high school with peeling paint and broken windows. What kind of insanity is this? We should offer offenders food, clothing, and a bed, plus vocational and academic training. Period. The money we save by not dressing up our detention facilities should be spent on the good kids who struggle just to get by.

No Rules of Confidentiality for Juvenile Offenders

expunged: cleared

11   It is impossible for judges to sentence intelligently if they do not know the offender's criminal history. If a youngster turns his or her life around, those records can be sealed or **expunged** at age 25. If he does not, that record should follow him to the grave.

Make Them Earn Early Release

12   Convicted juveniles, like adult offenders, often gain early and undeserved release from jail. In my opinion, early release should be earned. Juveniles should qualify only if they complete an academic or vocational course of study. The rest should stay behind bars their full term.

Enact a National Curfew

13   Most lawbreaking by youngsters takes place at a time when these kids should be at home. I recommend a national curfew for kids under 18. If parents cannot or will not set limits, then society must do it for them, for their protection and its own.

Make the Parents Pay

14   Too many people treat the juvenile system as a joke. That would change overnight if we required parents to pay for their children's defense attorneys according to their means, even if it is a percentage of their welfare benefits.

15   Furthermore, in too many states, welfare keeps flowing while the kids are in jail, or middle-class parents continue to claim children as tax deductions even as the state pays for their upkeep in detention facilities. We must demand that parents reimburse the state for housing their failures.

No Public Assistance for Parents of Dropouts

16   Kids need an education to have hope for the future. It makes sense to insist that children stay in school or go off welfare. Our message should be clear to everyone: If you want to eat, you have to work. If you stay in school, we'll support you. Otherwise, support yourself. No exceptions. Does it sound like I'm cracking down on the poor? Far from it. If a middle-class kid drops out of school, the $2750 tax break that his parents claim for him should be eliminated. Without proof that a child is attending school, parents should lose the exemption.

17   If I had to boil my message down to one sentence, it would be that people create their own opportunities. As a woman, a mother, and a judge who has seen our criminal system deteriorate for nearly a quarter of a century, I have had it with the victim game. A delinquent is responsible for his crime. Parents are responsible for their children.

18   The prescription so far has been to give them more social programs, and that remedy has failed. Self-discipline, individual accountability, and responsible conduct are the answer. They have always been the answer, but America got lost. It is time to get back on course.

VOCABULARY AND COMPREHENSION

1.   Why does Sheindlin call her courtroom "a pageant of dysfunction" (paragraph 1)?

_____

_____

2.   What is Sheindlin's main point?

_____

3.   Why does the author contrast schools and juvenile detention facilities?

_____

_____

4.   How has crime changed since the author first became a judge?

_____

_____

_____

CRITICAL THINKING

5. Globally, how does she propose that juveniles be treated?

_____

_____

6. Describe the personality of Judy Sheindlin. Use examples from the essay to back up your views.

_____

_____

7. In paragraph 18, the author says, "America got lost." What does she mean?

_____

_____

_____

WRITING TOPICS

Write a paragraph or an essay about one of the following topics. Remember to explore, develop, and revise and edit your work.

1. Sheindlin makes several controversial proposals. Choose one of her suggestions and either agree or disagree with it. Use examples to support your point of view.
2. The author gives a series of steps for improving the juvenile court system. In your opinion, would any of her suggestions help reduce juvenile crime? Explain your answer.
3. Reflect on the quotation. What steps can parents take to help their children become responsible, law-abiding citizens?

> " Tell me and I'll forget. Show me and I may not remember. Involve me and I'll understand. "
> —NATIVE AMERICAN PROVERB

READING 7

Growing Up in Cyberspace
By Brent Staples

Brent Staples, a reporter for the *New York Times*, writes about culture and politics and has written an award-winning memoir called *Parallel Time*. In the next essay, Staples reflects on the effects of new technologies. The selection is mainly an example of cause and effect writing, but it contains elements of the comparison and contrast pattern as well.

1   My tenth-grade heartthrob was the daughter of a fearsome steelworker who struck terror into the hearts of 15-year-old boys. He made it his business to answer the telephone—and so always

knew who was calling—and grumbled in the background when the conversation went on too long. Unable to make time by phone, the boy either gave up or appeared at the front door. This meant submitting to the intense scrutiny that the girl's father soon became known for.

2   He greeted me with a crushing handshake, and then leaned in close in a transparent attempt to find out whether I was one of those bad boys who smoked. He retired to the den during the visit, but cruised by the living room now and then to let me know he was watching. He let up after some weeks, but only after getting across what he expected of a boy who spent time with his daughter and how upset he'd be if I disappointed him.

3   This was my first sustained encounter with an adult outside my family who needed to be convinced of my worth as a person. This, of course, is a crucial part of growing up. Faced with the same challenge today, however, I would probably pass on meeting the girl's father— and **outflank** him on the Internet.

outflank: go beyond the reach of somebody

4   Thanks to e-mail, online chat rooms, and instant messages— which permit private, real-time conversations—adolescents have at last succeeded in shielding their social lives from adult scrutiny. But this comes at a cost: teenagers nowadays are both more connected to the world at large than ever, and more cut off from the social encounters that have historically prepared young people for the move into adulthood.

5   The Internet was billed as a revolutionary way to enrich our social lives and expand our civic connections. This seems to have worked well for elderly people and others who were isolated before they got access to the World Wide Web. But a growing body of research is showing that heavy use of the Net can actually isolate younger socially connected people who unwittingly allow time online to replace face-to-face interactions with their families and friends.

6   Online shopping, checking e-mail, and Web surfing—mainly solitary activities—have turned out to be more isolating than watching television, which friends and family often do in groups. Researchers have found that the time spent in direct contact with family members drops by as much as half for every hour we use the Net at home.

7   This should come as no surprise to the two-career couples who have seen their domestic lives taken over by e-mail and wireless **tethers** that keep people working around the clock. But a startling body of research from the Human-Computer Interaction Institute at Carnegie Mellon has shown that heavy Internet use can have a stunting effect outside the home as well.

tethers: restraining ropes

gregarious: friendly

8   Studies show that **gregarious,** well-connected people actually lost friends, and experienced symptoms of loneliness and depression, after joining discussion groups and other on-line activities. People who communicated with disembodied strangers online found the experience empty and emotionally frustrating but were nonetheless seduced by the novelty of the new medium. As Professor Robert Kraut, a Carnegie Mellon researcher, told me recently, such people allowed low-quality relationships developed in virtual reality to replace higher-quality relationships in the real world.

9   No group has embraced this socially impoverishing trade-off more enthusiastically than adolescents, many of whom spend most of their free hours cruising the Net in sunless rooms. This hermetic existence has left many of these teenagers with nonexistent social skills—a point widely noted in stories about the computer geeks who rose to prominence in the early days of Silicon Valley.

10   Adolescents are drawn to cyberspace for different reasons than adults. As the writer Michael Lewis observed in his book *Next: The Future Just Happened*, children see the Net as a transformational device that lets them discard **quotidian** identities for more glamorous ones. Mr. Lewis illustrated the point with Marcus Arnold, who, as a 15-year-old, adopted a **pseudonym** a few years ago and posed as a 25-year-old legal expert for an Internet information service. Marcus did not feel the least bit guilty and was not **deterred** when real-world lawyers discovered his secret and accused him of being a fraud. When asked whether he had actually read the law, Marcus responded that he found books "boring," leaving us to conclude that he had learned all he needed to know from his family's big-screen TV.

11   Marcus is a child of the Net, where everyone has a pseudonym, telling a story makes it true, and adolescents create older, cooler, more socially powerful selves any time they wish. The ability to slip easily into a new, false self is tailor-made for emotionally fragile adolescents who can consider a bout of acne or a few excess pounds an unbearable tragedy.

12   But teenagers who spend much of their lives hunched over computer screens miss the socializing, which is the real-world experience that would allow them to leave adolescence behind and grow into adulthood. These vital experiences, like much else, are simply not available in a virtual form.

quotidian: daily

pseudonym: false name

deterred: discouraged; stopped

VOCABULARY AND COMPREHENSION

1. Without using a dictionary, define *hermetic* as it is used in paragraph 9. Use clues in the text to help you.

    _____

    _____

2. Underline a sentence in this essay that sums up the author's main point.

3. What are the causes, or reasons, for young people's attraction to Internet technology, according to Staples?

    _____

    _____

    _____

4. Staples gives many examples of the negative effects of Internet technology. List at least three negative effects.

_____

_____

_____

_____

_____

CRITICAL THINKING

5. What does the story about Marcus (paragraphs 10 and 11) tell us about the world of the Internet?

_____

_____

6. Compare Brent Staples's childhood with the childhoods of young people today. How are they different?

_____

_____

_____

7. What positive effect of Internet technology does Staples mention?

_____

_____

8. In your opinion, what are some other ways people benefit from the Internet?

_____

_____

_____

_____

_____

_____

WRITING TOPICS

Write a paragraph or an essay about one of the following topics. Remember to explore, develop, and revise and edit your work.

1. Write about a new technology, and explain how it has affected your life.
2. Compare the effects on society of television and the Internet. How are the effects similar or different?
3. Read the quotation by media commentator Marshall McCluhan, who predicted that electronic media would make printed books obsolete. Reflect on McCluhan's prediction. Will newspapers, magazines, and books disappear one day? Explain why or why not.

“ We shape our tools, and afterwards our tools shape us. ”
— MARSHALL McCLUHAN

READING 8

Nothing But Net
Scott Bekker

> Scott Bekker is a journalist and the editor of *ENT News*. In the next essay, Bekker defends privacy in this era of cyber technology. As you read this argument essay, also look for elements of the cause and effect writing pattern.

1   Once—it seems ages ago—I was asked to surreptitiously examine the content of another employee's computer to look for evidence of wrongdoing. I did it. Even though we found evidence that the employee had broken both work rules and the rules of common decency, I still felt like I had violated someone's privacy. I was glad that it at least took some degree of technical skill to spy on my colleague down the hall. Today, that meager safeguard has disappeared. A whole market of programs has emerged that allows one to secretly record everything a person does with a computer. The emergence of these unethical snooping programs leaves me cold. Doesn't anyone have a conscience anymore?

2   One of the programs, SpectorSoft's eBlaster, promises that it will let the user "find out everything your spouse, children, and employees do online via e-mail." I can imagine some people defending the use of the program—perhaps providing a parent with warnings about drug use, gang participation, thoughts of suicide, or other threats to a child's well-being. It's also possible to imagine an employer using the spying software to ensure compliance with work rules and to detect other wrongdoing. Even so, it's wrong.

3   Defenders of this technology always seem to take the perspective of the person doing the spying and never the children, employees, or spouses he or she is spying upon. Defenders of this technology seldom use the word *trust* either.

4   Spying on children online, for instance, is almost laughable. If parents think their 14-year-old is doing, saying, or seeing things they don't approve of—it is time to move on. If I remember my teenage years correctly, the kids are going to do what they want whether their

parents spy on them or not. If a parent blocks access to the computer in his or her house, the computer at a friend's will do just as well. **Stealthy** technology like eBlaster invites equally stealthy responses by those being spied upon. Today's technology-savvy kids are likely to find a way to disable the software while working online and then start it up again after they are finished—without their parents knowing it.

stealthy: sneaky

5   What about spying on an employee? The truly bad employee is going to be caught anyway—with or without spying technology. Really good employees are going to migrate to companies where there is an atmosphere of trust. The others will forever resent the image of an employer that looks over their shoulders at every possible moment. If I use the corporate e-mail to receive an emergency message from my day care provider, what need does my employer have to discover that my kid has chicken pox?

6   I am well aware that the legal system today says that it is okay for companies to read their employees' e-mail and spy on them as they use their computers. But consider this: just because they can do it, does that make it right?

VOCABULARY AND COMPREHENSION

1.   Find a word in paragraph 1 that means "secretly."

   _____

2.   What introductory style does the author use? Circle the best answer.
     a. Definition   b. Anecdote   c. Historical background

3.   Who is the audience for this essay?

   _____

4.   Underline the thesis statement in paragraph 1.

CRITICAL THINKING

5.   Why does Scott Bekker object to snooping programs?

   _____

   _____

   _____

6.   What two arguments does the author give to acknowledge the opposing point of view?

   _____

   _____

   _____

7.   What two examples does the author give to defend his own position?

   _____

   _____

According to Turner and Killian, in their book *Collective Behavior*, there is nothing wrong with the participants in fads. Most of them are ordinary people. It is the situation that is abnormal. Once confusion and uncertainty set in, people can potentially be led into unusual behavior.

VOCABULARY AND COMPREHENSION

1. How does Locher define a fad?

2. Underline the thesis statement in this essay.
3. Locher divides one of the categories mentioned in the thesis statement into two subcategories. What are they?

4. Give examples of the characteristics of each fad Locher mentions.

CRITICAL THINKING

5. Look at the examples of fads that Locher presents. Which fads, in your opinion, are most ridiculous? Why?

6. Who benefits the most when a product becomes a fad?

7. Why do fads disappear?

WRITING TOPICS

Write a paragraph or an essay about one of the following topics. Remember to explore, develop, and revise and edit your work.

1. What fads have you followed? Have you bought something silly, joined in an activity that was suddenly popular, or worn your hair in a trendy style? Describe one or more fads that you have followed.

2. Write a classification paragraph or an essay about other types of fads. Make sure the fads are linked by a common classification principle. For example, you might write about types of body improvement fads or types of hair fads, or you might break down fashion fads or activity fads into categories.

3. Reflect on the quotation. Why do you think some people are motivated to create or follow fads?

> *A fashion is nothing but an induced epidemic.*
> —GEORGE BERNARD SHAW,
> IRISH AUTHOR

READING 10

The Never-Ending Question: Who Am I?
Raúl A. Reyes

> Raúl A. Reyes, a graduate of Harvard University and Columbia Law School, has worked as an actor, a TV reporter, and an attorney. In the next essay, Reyes writes about ethnic labels. As you read this definition essay, also look for elements of the narration and illustration writing patterns.

1 Black is black. White is white. But what about everything in between?

2 When I was a little boy in Texas, I was so happy. My world was small, and I knew my place in it. I grew up in the center of *mi familia*, surrounded by my cousins, aunts, uncles, and my grandpa. I felt secure. I belonged. In those days, if anyone asked me what I was, the answer was easy: Mexican. Like all my relatives, I was proud of my heritage, and I never felt like a "minority." In fact, everywhere I looked, I saw faces just like mine, so I felt like a "majority."

3 Yet when my family moved to Los Angeles, one of the first things I learned was that I wasn't Mexican anymore, I was "Mexican-American." But that was okay; in Southern California, everyone seemed to have a hyphenated ethnicity. There were Asian-Americans, African-Americans, and the occasional exotic hyphen hybrid, like Filipino-Hawaiian.

4 Whoa! The multicultural-all-inclusive-pan-ethnic attitude of my new state was, like, totally cool! Then in high school one of my friends told me, "Wake up, *idiota!* You're not Mexican-American, you're Chicano!" Although this was a new word to me, I adjusted. In truth I liked being Chicano. It sounded a little macho. When I was alone, I looked in the mirror from different angles and wondered if I looked like Erik Estrada from *CHiPs*.

5 Around this same time, the movie *La Bamba* was a big hit, so I felt very "in." I even tried to put a "Chicano Power" sticker on our station wagon, but my father said that was too militant.

6   However, by the time I got to college, Chicano was *pa'fuera*—out! I was turning in my scholarship applications when it dawned on me that I was now "Hispanic." Fine, I thought, I can deal with that too. Hey, it's hip to be Hispanic! I rushed out and bought Linda Ronstadt's new *Canciones de Mi Padre* CD.

7   But "Hispanic" didn't last long either. A few years ago my own mother corrected me when I used the term in passing.

8   "Raúl," she said, "You know, we're not Hispanic anymore. We're Latino."

9   "Why aren't we Hispanic?"

10   "I'm not sure. It has something to do with the colonization of the New World . . ."

11   "What?"

12   "On Oprah, I saw this guy who said that the term Hispanic represented the oppression of our ancestors by Europeans. I think. Or maybe it was on Cristina . . ."

13   I spent the rest of the 90s ostentatiously self-identifying as "Latino." I watched *novelas* on TV, took *salsa* lessons, and got all sentimental about **Selena.**

14   More recently, with Ricky Martin and Jennifer López on every magazine cover in sight, I started noticing headlines about the "Latin Explosion." Did this mean I wasn't Latino anymore? Had I morphed into "Latin?" Wondering if I had missed some type of demographic referendum, I perused a few of these articles. Although sexy words like *intoxicating* and *sultry* were being tossed around with wild abandon in reference to my people, for once I resisted the impulse to conform.

15   Who decides these terms anyway? And how come I'm always the last to know? While I'm not sure where all these names and labels are leading, I do know that this Latin right here is pretty close to exploding!

16   So what exactly am I going to be called next? I think I'll make that decision on my own, gracias. In the future, I plan to write my own ethnic nametag. I'm not sure what it's going to say, but I'm working on it. In the meantime, if anyone asks what I am, I am just going to say, "BROWN."

Selena: A late pop star, born in Texas, of Mexican heritage

VOCABULARY AND COMPREHENSION

1.   What is a hybrid? Look for context clues in paragraph 3.

2.   What are the various names that Reyes uses to describe himself?

3.   Why does the author say that he feels "pretty close to exploding" (paragraph 15)?

4. What does the author learn?

_____

_____

5. Using your own words, state the main idea of this essay.

_____

_____

_____

CRITICAL THINKING

6. In paragraph 2, Reyes says, "When I was a little boy in Texas, I was so happy. The world was small, and I knew my place in it." How does his world change?

_____

7. In your opinion, why have there been so many different names for Mexican-Americans?

_____

_____

_____

8. On the surface, Reyes's purpose for writing is to entertain. What is his deeper purpose?

_____

_____

_____

_____

WRITING TOPICS

Write a paragraph or an essay about one of the following topics. Remember to explore, develop, and revise and edit your work.

1. What is your ethnicity? Do you identify with a particular ethnic group? Give examples of traditions or customs that link you to that group. If you do not identify with a particular group, explain why.
2. Should new immigrants adapt their lifestyles to the general lifestyle in the new country, or should they attempt to retain some of their cultural differences? Argue for one side of this issue.
3. Read the quotation. Then write about labels that are placed on groups of people. What are the causes or effects of such labels?

> *I came to live in a country I love; some people label me a defector. I have loved men and women in my life; I've been labeled 'the bisexual defector.' Want to know another secret? I'm even ambidextrous. I don't like labels. Just call me Martina.*
> —MARTINA NAVRATILOVA, PROFESSIONAL TENNIS PLAYER

6. Why does the author compare her first panic attack with the fear caused by the terrorist attacks of September 11, 2001?

_____

_____

7. In the last paragraph, the author says that she has learned how to "dance with fear." What does she mean?

_____

_____

WRITING TOPICS

Write a paragraph or an essay about one of the following topics. Remember to explore, develop, and revise and edit your work.

1. Compare your childhood fears with your adult fears. How are they similar or different?
2. The author says that September 11, 2001, has changed the collective American psyche. Do you agree or disagree? Explain your answer and give examples.
3. Read the quotation. Then define *courage*. Give examples to support your definition.

" *Courage is one step ahead of fear.* "
—COLEMAN YOUNG, POLITICIAN

READING 12

Interview with Jimmy Baca
Elizabeth Farnsworth

Elizabeth Farnsworth, a senior correspondent for the *The NewsHour with Jim Lehrer*, interviewed author and poet Jimmy Santiago Baca. Baca, of Chicano and Apache ancestry, was born in New Mexico. He taught himself to read and write while serving a six-year prison sentence. He has since written a memoir of his childhood called *A Place To Stand*, as well as many award-winning volumes of poetry. In the interview, Baca discusses some pivotal moments in his life.

1   ELIZABETH FARNSWORTH: You tell the story of your childhood. You were deserted by your parents, and your grandparents took care of you for a while. Then you ended up in a orphanage and finally in prison. Tell the specific story of how words and language entered your life and helped save you.

2   JIMMY SANTIAGO BACA: . . . In dark times, it seemed that words were really special to me. We didn't really have a lot of books around the house when I was growing up except the bible. Then, of course, I never had any books until I was in county jail when I took that one book.

3   ELIZABETH FARNSWORTH: Tell us what happened.

4   JIMMY SANTIAGO BACA: Well, I stole the book from the clerk, the desk clerk, and I took it up to my cell. Late at night, I was tearing pages out of it so I could cook up some coffee. The other prisoners were yelling for their coffee. They were wondering why I wasn't coming because I was on time most of the time. As the fire beneath the coffee can was flaring, I caught a couple of words that I recognized phonetically. As I read more and more, I quit tearing the pages out of the book and I began to read. It was about a man who was walking his dog around a lake. That triggered phenomenal memories in me of my grandfather and the love I had for him and how we went around the pond with our sheep and dog. Incidentally, the man's name that I was reading later on that night, which I fell asleep enunciating, was words—words—**Wordsworth.**

5   ELIZABETH FARNSWORTH: Eventually you had poetry published in *Mother Jones Magazine* even while you were in prison. How did you go from being almost illiterate to that?

6   JIMMY SANTIAGO BACA: It was really funny because I didn't know how to address a letter, and I didn't know people paid for poetry. I was charging people cigarettes and coffees to write letters to their mothers and write letters to their girlfriends and poems and so forth for Mother's Day. A friend of mine came by with a *Mother Jones Magazine* and said, hey, they're buying poems here. I asked how to address a letter. I took my shoebox and grabbed a bunch of poems that I had written on **baby paper.** I sent them to a place called San Francisco— never expecting to hear back from them. When $300 came in, I bought the whole cellblock ice cream that day. Everyone ate ice cream.

7   ELIZABETH FARNSWORTH: Tell us how you love language and why. You've called it almost a physical thing for you.

8   JIMMY SANTIAGO BACA: Oh, I love language. Language, to me, is what sunrise is to the birds. Language, to me, is what water is to a man that just crossed the desert. I remember, as a boy, when grown-ups looked like huge redwood trees in a storm. And the grown-ups in my life were always caught up in dramas. The one thing that they all had in common was they couldn't express that storm inside of themselves. And I was so caught up in that drama that I vowed, one day, I would grasp hold of the power that could evoke their emotions. For me, at least, I wanted to know how to say what was happening to them and I wanted to name things.

Wordsworth: William Wordsworth (1770–1850), renowned English Romantic poet

baby paper: scrap paper

VOCABULARY AND COMPREHENSION

1. In paragraph 4, what is the meaning of *enunciating?* Try to guess without using a dictionary.

   _____

2. What was Baca's life like as a child?

   _____

   _____

3. How did Baca become interested in reading?

_____

_____

_____

4. In paragraph 8, Baca describes language metaphorically. A metaphor is a comparison without the word *like* or *as*. Underline two metaphors.

CRITICAL THINKING

5. Baca compares adults to "huge redwood trees . . . in a storm" (paragraph 8). What does he mean?

_____

_____

_____

6. How does control over language give Baca a sense of empowerment?

_____

_____

_____

_____

_____

7. What lessons can be learned from Baca's life experiences?

_____

_____

_____

_____

WRITING TOPICS

Write a paragraph or an essay about one of the following topics. Remember to explore, develop, and revise and edit your work.

1. What experiences have you had that helped make you the person that you are today?
2. Conduct a short interview with someone who you think is very interesting. You might choose someone who is much older than you are. Ask questions to discover what major lessons the person has learned in life. Then write about that person.
3. Write about the quotation. You might describe ways you have invested in yourself.

" If you want to be truly successful, invest in yourself. "
—SIDNEY MADWED, POET AND MOTIVATIONAL SPEAKER

READING 13

It's Class, Stupid!

Richard Rodriguez

Richard Rodriguez is a writer and an essayist who published the novel *Days of Obligation*. He also writes for the *Los Angeles Times* and *Harper's*. The next selection is an argument essay about affirmative action that originally appeared in the webzine Salon.com. As you read, also look for elements of the comparison and contrast writing pattern.

1   Some weeks ago, a law professor at the University of Texas got in trouble for saying that African Americans and Mexicans are at a disadvantage in higher education because they come from cultures that tolerate failure. Jesse Jackson flew to Austin to deliver a fiery speech; students demanded the professor's **ouster.**

ouster: dismissal

2   It was all typical of the way we have debated affirmative action for years. Both sides ended up arguing about race and ethnicity; both sides ignored the deeper issue of social inequality. Even now, as affirmative action is finished in California and is being challenged in many other states, nobody is really saying what is wrong with affirmative action: It is unfair to poor whites.

3   Americans find it hard to talk about what Europeans more easily call the lower class. We find it easier to sneer at the white poor—the "rednecks," the trailer-park trash. The rural white male is Hollywood's politically correct villain **du jour.**

du jour: French term meaning "of the day" or "at the present time"

4   We seem much more comfortable worrying about race; it's our most important metaphor for social distinction. We talk about the difference between black and white, not the difference between rich and poor. American writers—Richard Wright, James Baldwin, Toni Morrison—are brilliant at describing what it is like to be a racial minority. But America has few writers who describe as well what it is like to be poor. We don't have a writer of the stature of D.H. Lawrence—the son of an English coal miner—who grew up embarrassed by his soft hands. At the University of Texas, it was easier for the Sicilian-born professor Lino Graglia to notice that the students who dropped out of school were Mexican-American or black than to wonder if they might be poor.

5   At the same time, the angry students who accused the law professor of racism never bothered to acknowledge the obvious: Poor students *do* often come from neighborhoods and from families that tolerate failure or at least have learned the wisdom of slight expectations. Education is fine, if it works. I meet young people all the time who want to go to college, but Mama needs her oldest son to start working. It is better to have a dollar-and-cents job working at Safeway or McDonald's than a college diploma that might not guarantee a job.

6   Anyone who has taught poor children knows how hard it is to persuade students not to be afraid of success. There is the boy who is mocked by male classmates for speaking good English. There is the girl who comes from a family where women are not assumed to need, or want, education.

7   We also don't like to admit, though we have argued its merits for 20 years, that the chief beneficiaries of affirmative action—black, brown, female—are primarily middle class. It still doesn't occur to many progressives that affirmative action might be unfair to poor whites. That is because poor whites do not constitute an officially recognized minority group. We don't even notice the presence or, more likely, the absence of the poor white on college campuses. Our only acknowledgment of working-class existence is to wear fashionable working-class denim.

8   A man I know, when he went to Harvard, had only a pair of running shoes to wear and had never owned a tie. He dropped out of Harvard after two years. I suppose some of his teachers imagined it was because he was Hispanic, not that he was dirt poor. The advantage I had, besides my parents, were my Irish nuns—who themselves had grown up working class. They were free of that middle-class fear (typical today in middle-class teachers) of changing students too much. The nuns understood that education is not an exercise in self-esteem. They understood how much education costs, the price the heart pays.

9   Every once in a while, I meet middle-class Americans who were once lower class. They come from inner cities and from West Texas trailer parks. They are successful now beyond their dreams, but bewildered by loss, becoming so different from their parents. If only America would hear their stories, we might, at last, acknowledge social class. And we might know how to proceed, now that affirmative action is dead and so many poor kids remain to be educated.

VOCABULARY AND COMPREHENSION

1.   Find a word in paragraph 6 that means "made fun of."

_____

2.   Circle the best answer: The word *constitute* in paragraph 7 means
      a. govern.   b. appoint.   c. represent.
3.   According to the author, in addition to financial hardship, what prevents many poor people from attending college?

_____

_____

_____

_____

4.   Who benefits the most from affirmative action, according to the author?

_____

_____

_____

5.   Look in the first two paragraphs and underline the thesis statement.

CRITICAL THINKING

6. Explain why Rodriquez disagrees with affirmative action.

_____

_____

_____

7. The author compares the English writer D.H. Lawrence with American writers such as Toni Morrison. How is this comparison relevant for this essay?

_____

_____

_____

_____

8. In paragraph 1, Rodriquez includes an anecdote about a University of Texas law professor. Explain why you think the author agrees or disagrees with the professor.

_____

_____

_____

9. The author writes that his teachers, Irish nuns with working-class backgrounds, "understood how much education costs, the price the heart pays." What does he mean? (Look in paragraphs 8 and 9 for clues.)

_____

_____

_____

_____

WRITING TOPICS

Write a paragraph or an essay about one of the following topics. Remember to explore, develop, and revise and edit your work.

1. In your employment or education, have you had any positive or negative experiences because of your gender, ethnic, or racial background?
2. Do you agree or disagree with the author's argument? Back up your point of view with specific examples.

3. Respond to Baldwin's quotation. What is his deeper meaning? Do you agree with him? Give examples or anecdotes to support your views.

READING 14

The Case for Affirmative Action
An Open Letter to Five Justices
Dave Malcolm

> Dave Malcolm is a professor in San Diego. In 1995, the following letter was entered into the *Congressional Record* by U.S. Representative Esteban Torres in response to anti–affirmative action decisions by the Supreme Court. In this letter, the author has used the illustration writing pattern along with the definition, comparison and contrast, and argument patterns.

1 On Monday, June 12, 1995, at 10:50 a.m., I left the office of my cardiologist having just been informed that my aortic valve implant was "leaking" and that replacement surgery would be required within the next three to six months. At 10:55 a.m., on the same date, I heard on my car radio about two new Supreme Court 5-4 decisions, each apparently placing serious additional limitations on programs of affirmative action. I drove homeward, feeling sick at heart—not from feelings of anxiety about my imminent open-heart surgery but from feelings of dismay at the direction in which the country seems to be moving, especially in regard to affirmative action.

2 You see, I know a lot about affirmative action. I count myself an expert on the subject. After all, I have benefited from it all my life. That is because I am white, I am male, I am Anglo, and I am Protestant. We male WASPs have had a great informal affirmative action program going for decades, maybe centuries. I am not speaking only of the way our "old boy networks" help people like me get into the right colleges or get jobs or get promotions. That is only the surface. Underneath, our real affirmative action is much more than just a few direct interventions at key moments in life. The real affirmative action is also indirect and at work twenty-four hours a day, seven days a week, year in and year out. Because it is informal and indirect, we tend to forget or deny just how all-important and pervasive it really is.

3 However, far be it from me to put the direct "old boy" surface stuff down. I was admitted without difficulty to the Ivy League college my father had attended. This was back in the days when the only quotas were quotas to keep certain people out, not to help them get in. There were no limits on reasonably bright kids like me—the admissions people spoke of the children of alumni as "legacies," but whether this was because the college was inheriting us as students or because the college hoped to inherit money from our families, I was never quite sure. I got a teaching job right out of college in the heart of the Depression—my father was a school superintendent well liked among his colleagues.

4 After World War II, when I became a university professor, I received promotion and tenure in minimum time, more quickly than

many of my female colleagues. Of course, the decision makers knew me better; I was part of the monthly poker group and played golf every Friday afternoon. Yes, direct affirmative action—direct preferential treatment because of my gender and my color and good connections—have been good to me.

5   But, like other white males, I have benefited less obviously but far more significantly from indirect preferential treatment. Indirect affirmative action is at work to greater or lesser degree on behalf of virtually all white males, whether one is aware of it or not. It is what did not happen to me. There were destructive, painful experiences that I did not have to endure. Early in life, I knew that boys were more important than girls and so did the girls. I have never had to worry about whether my skin color was light enough or dark enough.

6   For two of my long-time colleagues and closest personal friends, it has been a very different story. Raymond was the lightest skinned member of his family. He recalls that he was the only one who could get his hair cut downtown—but the family had to drop him off a block away from the barber shop. He once told me that he had probably spent more time worrying about his light skin than any other one thing in life. Would his fellow African Americans think he was black enough? When whites thought he was East Indian or South American, should he let them think so?

7   Maria had the opposite problem. As a child, she was called *la prieta* ("the little dark one"). Even though she knew the **diminutive** was a mark of affection, she still was aware that the label was no compliment. When she became a young woman, well-meaning whites told her, "You don't look Mexican," meaning that she looked more Spanish and hence almost white. The message always hurt deeply not simply because the speakers personally so clearly believed that there was something inferior about being Mexican but also because they had unhesitatingly assumed that she did, too, and hence would consider such a statement to be a compliment.

diminutive: affectionate nickname

8   I have never had to endure "what-is-he-doing-here?" looks any time I walked along a residential street in a suburban area. I have not had to notice white women clutching their purses more tightly when they meet me walking along the street. I have never seen the "For Rent" or "For Sale" signs **figuratively** snatched out of the window as I walked up to the front door. I cannot even begin to imagine the insults, large and small, that send a five- or six-year-old running tearfully home to ask Mommy or Daddy, "Why can't I be white?"

figuratively: symbolically; not literally

9   Out of the dozens of times I have crossed the border from Tijuana to San Diego, the one time I was pulled over to have my car inspected was when returning with my friend, Raymond, and another African American male as passengers. I was furious, but my friends restrained me, assuring me it was no big deal and that it happened to them all the time. That day I got some small sense of the rage and fury and helplessness and frustration that some people experience daily and are forced to smother.

10   I have never been so bombarded by negative messages that I began to internalize them and to suspect they might in part be true. As a professional person, I have never had to carry the burden of

knowing that the slightest mispronunciation or grammatical error on my part will be seized upon by some people as validation of their negative stereotypes, not only about me but also about my people. But entire populations of my potential competitors have labored and still are laboring under disadvantages of this very sort as they compete with me. This is white male "affirmative action" at its most effective—the flip side of destructive life-long bombardment by negative messages.

11   Yes, affirmative action for some folks remains alive and well and unthreatened by court decisions. I ought to know. All my life I have been an indirect beneficiary because indirect affirmative action has been so effective at crippling or eliminating so many of those who might have been my competitors. As a white male, I have never had to compete with them on a level playing field.

12   The promise of the American dream is a society which is color-fair, not color-blind. Formal affirmative action programs play a dual role. They make the playing fields a bit more level and they remind us that we still have far to go. It is no solution for society to trash its current formal efforts to make opportunity a little more equal as long as so many powerful informal barriers to equality of opportunity still persist. Think about it.

VOCABULARY AND COMPREHENSION

1.   What introduction style does the author use? Circle the best answer.
     a. General background   b. Definition
     c. Opposing position   d. Anecdote
2.   Using your own words, describe the main idea of this essay.

     _____

     _____

3.   How has the author benefited from indirect affirmative action? List some examples.

     _____

     _____

     _____

     _____

4.   What examples does the author give to illustrate that members of less-favored groups have to live with destructive, painful experiences?

     _____

     _____

     _____

_____

_____

CRITICAL THINKING

5. Why was Malcolm promoted more quickly than his female colleagues?

_____

_____

6. Explain how a "For Rent" sign could be "figuratively snatched from a window" (paragraph 9).

_____

7. What are Malcolm's main arguments for supporting affirmative action?

_____

_____

_____

_____

_____

8. Who is Dave Malcolm? What have you learned about him after reading this text? List characteristics that describe him, and make some educated guesses about his personality.

_____

_____

_____

_____

_____

_____

WRITING TOPICS

Write a paragraph or an essay about one of the following topics. Remember to explore, develop, and revise and edit your work.

" All humans are born equal, but they cannot continue in this equality. Society makes them lose it, and they recover it only by the protection of the law. "
—CHARLES DE MONTESQUIEU, PHILOSOPHER

1.   Compare Malcolm's view of affirmative action with the view expressed by Richard Rodriguez in the essay titled "It's Class, Stupid." With whom do you agree, and why?

2.   How can parents teach their children to be open-minded and to avoid stereotyping other groups of people? What steps can they take?

3.   Read and reflect on the quotation. What is your view about equality? Should laws protect some members of society to ensure equal access to work, education, and housing? Why or why not?

READING 15

Body Over Mind
Mitch Albom

Award-winning sports columnist Mitch Albom writes for the *Detroit Free Press*. He is also the author of eight books, including *Five People You Meet in Heaven* and *Tuesdays with Morrie*. In this comparison and contrast essay, Albom discusses the culture of college sports. As you read, also look for elements of narration, cause and effect, and argument writing.

1   The little chocolate doughnuts were in a box next to the coffee urn. Normally, high schools don't provide food for their assemblies, but today was special with all of these TV crews, radio people, and sports writers. A table was arranged near the front of the room, and a reporter set down a microphone alongside a dozen others. "Testing 1-2 testing 1-2," he said.

2   Suddenly, the whole room seemed to shift. The guest of honor had arrived. He didn't enter first. He was preceded by an entourage of friends, coaches, his grandmother, his aunt, his baby brother, more friends, more coaches, and his girlfriend. She wore a black dress and jewelry and had her hair pinned up, as if going to the prom, even though it was mid-afternoon and math classes were in progress upstairs.

3   Her boyfriend took his seat. He wore a stud earring and a colorful jacket. Only 18 years old, he was the largest person in the room at 6-feet-9, 300 pounds. It was for his body—and what he could do with it—that these people had come.

4   "Good afternoon," Robert Traylor began, reading from a sheet of paper. His voice was deep as a businessman's, but his words were those of a nervous teen. "I'd like to welcome everyone. My dream is to play in the NBA one day. I've chosen the college that can best help me achieve my dream."

5   The crowd held its breath. For three years, a parade of grown men, employed by major universities, had been coming to Detroit to watch Robert Traylor play. They called him at home, they called his friends, and they called his relatives. They showed him videos and promised him stardom. They wooed him like a golden child.

6   "The school I will be attending," Traylor said, "will be the University of Michigan."

7   The room erupted in applause.

8   Down the hall, sitting alone by a computer, was another high school senior named Kevin Jones. Like Traylor, Jones is black, lives in Detroit, and is being raised with no father in the house. His mother supports the family by working as a janitor. Like Traylor, Jones will also be attending Michigan next fall—on a full scholarship.

9   But unlike Traylor, Jones, a thin kid with a disarming smile, got his scholarship for studying three hours a day, getting the highest grades, keeping his attendance over 95 percent, and never violating school conduct rules.

10   Kevin Jones is the most important currency in the city of Detroit, a kid with a brain. He did not announce his college decision at a press conference; he had to wait for Michigan to accept him. A letter finally arrived at the house his family shares with another family in northwest Detroit. He peeked through the envelope and saw the word "Congratulations." He smiled. His grandmother hugged him and said, "I'm so proud of you! I'm so proud of you."

11   Back at the press conference, reporters were yelling questions: "Robert, when did you decide on Michigan?"

12   "Robert, do you think you'll start?"

13   "Robert, what did the Michigan coaches say?"

14   Traylor smiled at the last one. "I don't know. I haven't told them yet." Not that it mattered. At that moment, it was being announced all over the radio.

15   This is crazy. A press conference for a high school ballplayer? What message are we sending the other students at Murray-Wright High School who were peeking through the doors wondering what the fuss was about?

16   Don't misunderstand. Robert Traylor is a bright young man with a special talent, but why have a press conference about where he will dribble and shoot? Isn't there enough spotlight on these kids already? Besides, encouraging inner-city teens to shoot for the NBA is like encouraging them to win the lottery. Most will be disappointed.

17   Several years ago, a high school star named Chris Webber had one of these press conferences—and two years later, he held another to say he was leaving school for the pros. Someone asked Traylor about that Monday.

18   "I hope (I can) leave college in two years," he said excitedly. Later he tried to correct this, but everyone knew what he meant. In his dreams of swimming in NBA waters, college is the diving board.

19   It is more than a diving board to Kevin Jones. He has no plans of leaving early. "I want to study business and open my own one day," he said. He showed a résumé he had done himself. It noted his awards in the Navy ROTC, and his computer literacy in IBM and Macintosh systems.

20   This is no nerd. This is a good-looking kid who hears bullets in his neighborhood and remembers what his grandmother said: "When there's trouble, just keep walking." He works hard, because he was taught to work hard, and he doesn't read off a sheet when he says, "One day, after I get my business going, I'm going to come back to this

school and teach math." That is more important than coming back to sign autographs.

21   The doughnuts were mostly gone now. Traylor's aunt was being interviewed; so were his friends, who mugged for the cameras. Traylor himself posed, wearing a maize and blue Michigan cap. Down the hall, the computer flipped on, and a young man began a new application for room and board money. He started with his name, "Kevin Jones."

22   No offense, but if there had to be a press conference Monday, it should have been Kevin's.

VOCABULARY AND COMPREHENSION

1.   Why does Robert Traylor receive so much attention from the media?

   _____

   _____

2.   Why does Kevin Jones want to attend college?

   _____

   _____

3.   What steps has Kevin Jones taken to ensure that he can go to college?

   _____

   _____

   _____

4.   Using your own words, describe the main idea of this essay.

   _____

   _____

   _____

   _____

CRITICAL THINKING

5.   How are the personalities and physical characteristics of Robert Traylor and Kevin Jones similar? How are they different?

   _____

   _____

   _____

   _____

   _____

6. The University of Michigan shows a different attitude toward Traylor and Jones as future students. How does the author suggest this difference in attitude?

7. Albom writes that "encouraging inner-city teens to shoot for the NBA is like encouraging them to win the lottery" (paragraph 16). Why does he make such a comparison?

WRITING TOPICS

Write a paragraph or an essay about one of the following topics. Remember to explore, develop, and revise and edit your work.

1. Argue against Albom's main point. Argue that high school athletes deserve the attention and praise that others give to them.
2. Many people tend to idolize great athletes. Think of an athlete who is deserving of public praise and adulation, and think of another who is not worthy. Compare and contrast the two sports heroes. (If you are not familiar with sports, then compare two other types of people, such as actors, writers, musicians, or politicians.)
3. Write about the quotation. You might mention how it relates to the events in "Body Over Mind."

" I pay no attention whatsoever to anybody's praise or blame. I simply follow my own path. "
—WOLFGANG AMADEUS MOZART, MUSICIAN AND COMPOSER

READING 16

Dying to Be Bigger
H.D.

> This cause and effect essay first appeared in *Seventeen* magazine and was written by a young steroid user. As you read, notice how the author also uses elements of narration and description writing.

1   I was only fifteen years old when I first started maiming my body with the abuse of anabolic steroids. I was always trying to fit in with the "cool" crowd in junior high and high school. Willingly smoking or buying pot when offered, socially drinking in excess, displaying a macho image—and, of course, the infamous "kiss and tell"—were essentials in completing my insecure mentality.

2   Being an immature, cocky kid from a somewhat wealthy family, I was not very well liked in general. In light of this, I got beat up a lot, especially in my first year of public high school.

3   I was one of only three sophomores to get a varsity letter in football. At five-foot-nine and 174 pounds, I was muscularly inferior to the guys at the same athletic level and quite conscious of the fact. So when I heard about this wonderful drug called steroids from a teammate, I didn't think twice about asking to buy some. I could hardly wait to take them and get bigger.

4   I bought three months' worth of Dianobol (an oral form of steroids and one of the most harmful). I paid 55 dollars. I was told to take maybe two or three per day. I totally ignored the directions and warnings and immediately started taking five per day. This is how eager I was to be bigger and possibly "cooler." Within only a week, everything about me started to change. I was transforming mentally and physically. My attention span became almost nonexistent. Along with becoming extremely aggressive, I began to abandon nearly all academic and family responsibilities. In almost no time, I became flustered and agitated with simple everyday activities. My **narcissistic** ways brought me to engage in verbal as well as physical fights with family, friends, teachers, but mostly strangers.

narcissistic: self-involved

5   My bodily transformations were clearly visible. In less than a month, I took the entire three-month supply. I gained nearly thirty pounds. Most of my weight was from water retention, although at the time I believed it to be muscle. Instead of having pimples like the average teenager, my acne took the form of grotesque, cyst-like blood clots that would occasionally burst while I was lifting weights. My nipples became the size of grapes and hurt severely, which is common among male steroid users. My hormonal level was completely out of whack.

6   At first, I had such an overload of testosterone that I would have to masturbate daily, at minimum, in order to prevent having "wet dreams." Obviously, these factors enhanced my lust, which eventually led to acute perversion. My then almost-horrifying physique prevented me from having sexual encounters.

7   All of these factors led to my classification as a wretched menace. My parents grew sick and tired of all the trouble I began to get in. They were scared of me, it seemed. They cared so much about my welfare, education, and state of mind that they sent me to a boarding school that summer.

8   I could not obtain any more steroids there, and for a couple of months, it seemed I had subtle withdrawal symptoms and severe side effects. Most of the time that summer I was either depressed or filled with intense anger, both of which were uncontrollable unless I was in a state of intoxication from any mind-altering drug.

9   After a year of being steroid-free, things started to look promising for me, and I eventually gained control over myself. Just when I started getting letters from big-name colleges to play football for them, I suffered a herniated disc. I was unable to participate in any form of physical activity the entire school year.

10   In the fall, I attended a university in the Northeast, where I was on the football team but did not play due to my injury. I lifted weights with the team every day. I wasn't very big at the time, even after many weeks of working out. Once again I found myself to be physically inferior and insecure about my physique. And again, I came into contact with many teammates using steroids.

11   My roommate was a six-foot-three, 250-pound linebacker who played on the varsity squad as a freshman. As the weeks passed, I learned of my roommate's heavy steroid use. I was exposed to dozens of different steroids I had never even heard of. Living in the same room with him, I watched his almost daily injections. After months of enduring his drug offerings, I gave in.

12   By the spring of my freshman year, I had become drastically far from normal in every way. My body had stopped producing hormones due to the amount of synthetic testosterone I injected into my system. At five-foot-eleven, 225 pounds, disproportionately huge, acne-infested, outrageously aggressive, and nearing complete sterility, I was in a terrible state of body and mind. Normal thoughts of my future (not pertaining to football), friends, family, reputation, moral status, etc., were entirely beyond me. My whole entire essence had become one of a primitive barbarian.

13   This was when I was taking something called Sustunon (prepackaged in a syringe labeled "For equine use only") containing four types of testosterone. I was "stacking" (a term used by steroid users which means mixing different types) to get well-cut definition along with mass.

14   It was around this time when I was arrested for threatening a security guard. When the campus police came to arrest me, they saw how aggressive and large my roommate and I were, so they searched our room and found dozens of bottles and hundreds of dollars' worth of steroids and syringes. We had a trial, and the outcome was that I could only return the next year if I got drug-tested on a monthly basis. I certainly had no willpower or desire to quit my steroid abuse, so I transferred schools.

15   After a summer of even more heavy-duty abuse, I decided to attend a school that would cater to my instinctively backward ways. That fall I entered a large university in the South. Once again I simply lifted weights without being involved in competition or football. It was there that I finally realized how out of hand I had become with my steroid problem.

16   Gradually I started to taper down my dosages. Accompanying my reduction, I began to drink more and more. My grades plummeted again. I began going to bars and keg parties on a nightly basis.

17   My celibacy, mental state, aggressiveness, lack of athletic competition, and alcohol problem brought me to enjoy passing my pain onto others by means of physical aggression. I got into a fight almost every time I drank. In the midst of my insane state, I was arrested for assault. I was in really deep this time. Finally I realized how different from everybody else I had become, and I decided not to taper off but to quit completely.

18   The average person seems to think that steroids just make you bigger. But they are a drug, and an addictive one at that. This drug does not put you in a stupor or in a hallucinogenic state but rather gives you an up, all-around "bad-ass" mentality that far exceeds that of either normal life or any other narcotic I have tried. Only lately are scientists and researchers discovering how addictive steroids are—only now, after hundreds of thousands may have done such extreme damage to their lives, bodies, and minds.

19   One of the main components of steroid addiction is how unsatisfied the user is with his overall appearance. Although I was massive and had dramatic muscular definition, I was never content with my body, despite frequent compliments. I was always changing types of steroids, places of injection, workouts, diet, etc. I always found myself saying, "This one ought to do it," or "I'll quit when I hit 230 pounds."

20   When someone is using steroids, he has psychological disorders that increase when usage stops. One disorder is anxiety from the loss of the superior feeling you get from the drug. Losing the muscle mass, high energy level, and superhuman sensation that you are so accustomed to is terrifying.

21   Another ramification of taking artificial testosterone over time is the effect on the natural testosterone level (thus the male sex drive). As a result of my steroid use, my natural testosterone level was ultimately depleted to the point where my sex drive was drastically reduced in comparison to the average 21-year-old male. My testicles shriveled up, causing physical pain as well as extreme mental anguish. Thus, I desired girls less. This, however, did lead me to treat them as people, not as objects of my desires. It was a beginning step on the way to a more sane and civil mentality.

22   The worst symptoms of my withdrawal after many months of drug abuse were emotional. My emotions fluctuated dramatically, and I rapidly became more sensitive. My hope is that this feeling of being trailed by isolation and aloneness will diminish and leave me free of its constant haunting.

VOCABULARY AND COMPREHENSION

1. Find a word in paragraph 1 that means "harming."

   _____

2. Circle the best answer: The word *ramification* in paragraph 21 means
   a. consequence.   b. understanding.   c. origin.

3. Why did the author use steroids?

   _____

   _____

   _____

   _____

4. How did the author change with continued steroid use? List physical and psychological changes that occurred.

_____

_____

_____

_____

_____

_____

5. The essay lists both short- and long-term effects of steroid use. What are some long-term effects?

_____

_____

_____

CRITICAL THINKING

6. What is the significance of the title of this essay?

_____

_____

7. The author stopped using steroids for one year. Why did he start up again in college even though he knew the risks?

_____

_____

_____

8. In paragraph 18, the author refers to steroids as "a drug." List five similarities between steroids and other illegal narcotics.

_____

_____

_____

_____

9. Basically, the author narrates what happened to him. What can you infer from the author's story? In other words, what is the deeper message?

_____

_____

_____

WRITING TOPICS

Write a paragraph or an essay about one of the following topics. Remember to explore, develop, and revise and edit your work.

1. What can cause a person to have a poor body image? List some examples.
2. Since 1973, performance-enhancing drugs have been banned at the Olympic Games. However, at each Olympics, athletes from nations around the world are disqualified because they have used banned substances. Should officials simply allow performance-enhancing drugs rather than trying to police the use of such drugs? Explain your answer.
3. How does the quotation relate to the essay? What do both Morissette and the essay writer seem to be saying about body image?

> *I think of my body as an*
> *instrument rather than an*
> *ornament.*
> —ALANIS MORISSETTE,
> SINGER AND COMPOSER

READING 17

Bound Feet
Jung Chang

> Jung Chang was born in Yibin, China, and teaches Oriental and African studies at London University. In the next excerpt from her novel, *Wild Swans, Three Daughters of China,* Chang writes about her grandmother. As you read this descriptive essay, also look for elements of the narration and process writing patterns.

1 My grandmother was a beauty. She had an oval face with rosy cheeks and lustrous skin. Her long, shiny black hair was woven into a thick plait reaching down to her waist. She could be demure when the occasion demanded, which was most of the time, but underneath her composed exterior she was bursting with suppressed energy. She was petite, about five feet three inches, with a slender figure and sloping shoulders, which were considered the ideal.

2 But her greatest assets were her bound feet, called in Chinese "three-inch golden lilies" (*san-tsun-gin-lian*). This meant she walked "like a tender young **willow shoot** in a spring breeze," as Chinese connoisseurs of women traditionally put it. The sight of a woman **teetering** on bound feet was supposed to have an erotic effect on men, partly because her vulnerability induced a feeling of protectiveness in the onlooker.

3 My grandmother's feet had been bound when she was two years old. Her mother, who herself had bound feet, first wound a piece of

willow shoot: the new growth of a willow tree

teetering: walking unsteadily

white cloth about twenty feet long round her feet, bending all the toes except the big toe inward and under the sole. Then she placed a large stone on top to crush the arch. My grandmother screamed in agony and begged her to stop. Her mother had to stick a cloth into her mouth to gag her. My grandmother passed out repeatedly from the pain.

4   The process lasted several years. Even after the bones had been broken, the feet had to be bound day and night in thick cloth because the moment they were released they would try to recover. For years my grandmother lived in relentless, **excruciating** pain. When she pleaded with her mother to untie the bindings, her mother would weep and tell her that unbound feet would ruin her entire life, and that she was doing it for her own future happiness.

excruciating: extremely painful

5   In those days, when a woman was married, the first thing the bridegroom's family did was to examine her feet. Large feet, meaning normal feet, were considered to bring shame on the husband's household. The mother-in-law would lift the hem of the bride's long skirt, and if the feet were more than about four inches long, she would throw down the skirt in a demonstrative gesture of **contempt** and stalk off, leaving the bride to the critical gaze of the wedding guests, who would stare at her feet and insultingly mutter their **disdain.** Sometimes a mother would take pity on her daughter and remove the binding cloth; but when the child grew up and had to endure the contempt of her husband's family and the disapproval of society, she would blame her mother for having been too weak.

contempt: disapproval

disdain: disapproval

6   The practice of binding feet was originally introduced about a thousand years ago, allegedly by a concubine of the emperor. Not only was the sight of women hobbling on tiny feet considered erotic, men would also get excited playing with bound feet, which were always hidden in embroidered silk shoes. Women could not remove the binding cloths even when they were adults, as their feet would start growing again. The binding could only be loosened temporarily at night in bed, when they would put on soft-soled shoes. Men rarely saw naked bound feet, which were usually covered in rotting flesh and stank when the bindings were removed. As a child, I can remember my grandmother being in constant pain. When we came home from shopping, the first thing she would do was soak her feet in a bowl of hot water, sighing with relief as she did so. Then she would set about cutting off pieces of dead skin. The pain came not only from the broken bones, but also from her toenails, which grew into the balls of her feet.

7   In fact, my grandmother's feet were bound just at the moment when foot-binding was disappearing for good. By the time her sister was born in 1917, the practice had virtually been abandoned, so she escaped the torment. However, when my grandmother was growing up, the prevailing attitude in a small town like Yixian was still that bound feet were essential for a good marriage.

VOCABULARY AND COMPREHENSION

1.   Find a word in paragraph 1 that means "modest, quiet, and reserved."

2. In the past, why were Chinese women's feet bound?

    _____

    _____

    _____

3. Did the author's grandmother choose to have bound feet? Support your answer with evidence from the reading.

    _____

    _____

    _____

4. The author describes the process of binding feet. List the steps in the process.

    _____

    _____

    _____

    _____

CRITICAL THINKING

5. Why would women who had been through the pain of foot-binding subject their daughters to the same torture? Think of some reasons.

    _____

    _____

    _____

    _____

6. What are some of the most effective images in Chang's narrative?

    _____

    _____

    _____

7. What is the narrator's point of view about her grandmother's bound feet? Look for clues in the text.

    _____

    _____

    _____

DISCUSSION AND WRITING

1. This reading describes a painful process that Chinese women went through in the past. Although foot binding seems shocking and distasteful, there are parallels in contemporary society. Explain how people alter their bodies today. Try to use descriptive imagery.
2. How is your life different from that of your grandparents or people of their generation? Explain your answer.
3. Reflect on the quotation. Compare and contrast some old fashions that people laugh at and new fashions that they follow.

> *Every generation laughs at the old fashions, but follows religiously the new.*
> —HENRY DAVID THOREAU, AUTHOR

READING 18

The Old-Time Pueblo World
Leslie Marmon Silko

Born in 1948 on a Laguna Pueblo reservation near Albuquerque, New Mexico, Leslie Marmon Silko has mixed heritage—white, Native American, and Mexican. An award-winning author, Silko has written novels, short stories, poems, articles, and film scripts. In the following example of an illustration essay, the author discusses some characteristics of Pueblo communities. As you read, also look for elements of narration and description writing.

1   In the view of the old-time people, we are all sisters and brothers because the Mother Creator made all of us—all colors and all sizes. In everyday Pueblo life, not much attention was paid to one's physical appearance or clothing. Ceremonial clothing was quite elaborate but was used only for the sacred dances. The traditional Pueblo societies were communal and strictly **egalitarian,** which means that no matter how well or how poorly one might have dressed, there was no social ladder to fall from. All food and other resources were strictly shared so that no one person or group had more than another. I mention social status because it seems to me that most of the definitions of beauty in contemporary Western culture are really codes for determining social status. People no longer hide their face-lifts, and they discuss their liposuctions because the point of the procedures isn't just cosmetic, it is social. It says to the world, "I have enough spare cash that I can afford surgery for cosmetic purposes."

egalitarian: supporting equal rights for all

2   In the old-time Pueblo world, beauty was manifested in behavior and in one's relationships with other living beings. Beauty was as much a feeling of harmony as it was a visual, aural, or sensual effect. The whole person had to be beautiful, not just the face or the body; faces and bodies could not be separated from hearts and souls. Health was foremost in achieving this sense of well-being and harmony; in the old-time Pueblo world, a person who did not look healthy inspired feelings of worry and anxiety. A healthy person, of course, is in harmony with the world around her; she is at peace with herself too. Thus, an unhappy or spiteful person would not be considered beautiful.

READING 19

The Diagnosis
Richard Selzer

Richard Selzer is a celebrated surgeon, and he is the author of best-selling collections of stories and essays. In the next excerpt from his book *Mortal Lessons: Notes on the Art of Surgery*, Selzer describes a profound encounter. As you read this narrative, notice how the author has used other writing patterns, including description, process, and comparison and contrast.

Dalai Lama: the spiritual leader of Tibetan Buddhists

sangfroid: indifference

inimical: hostile

dubiety: doubtfulness

desultory of ablutions: the most quick, basic cleansing

furtively: secretly

supine: lying on the back

1 On the bulletin board in the front hall of the hospital where I work, there appeared an announcement. "Yeshi Dhonden," it read, "will make rounds at six o'clock on the morning of June 10." The particulars were then given, followed by a notation "Yeshi Dhonden is Personal Physician to the **Dalai Lama.**"

2 I am not so leathery a skeptic that I would knowingly ignore an emissary from the gods. Not only might such **sangfroid** be **inimical** to one's earthly well-being, it could take care of eternity as well. Thus, on the morning of June 10, I join the clutch of whitecoats in the small conference room adjacent to the ward selected for the rounds. The air in the room is heavy with ill-concealed **dubiety** and suspicion of bamboozlement. At precisely six o'clock, he materializes, short, barely dressed in a sleeveless robe of saffron and maroon. His scalp is shaven, and the only visible hair is a scanty black line above each hooded eye.

3 He bows in greeting while his young interpreter makes the introduction. Yeshi Dhonden, we are told, will examine a patient selected by a member of the staff. The diagnosis is as unknown to Yeshi Dhonden as it is to us. The examination of the patient will take place in our presence, after which we will convene in the conference room where Yeshi Dhonden will discuss the case. We are further informed that for the past two hours Yeshi Dhonden has purified himself by bathing, fasting, and praying. I, having breakfasted well, performed only the most **desultory of ablutions,** and given no thought at all to my soul, glance **furtively** at my fellows. Suddenly, we seem a soiled, uncouth lot.

4 The patient has been awakened early and told that she is to be examined by a foreign doctor, and has been asked to produce a fresh specimen of urine, so when we enter her room, the woman shows no surprise. She has long ago taken on that mixture of compliance and resignation that is the face of chronic illness. This was to be but another in an endless series of tests and examinations. Yeshi Dhonden steps to the bedside while the rest stand apart, watching. For a long time he gazes at the woman, favoring no part of her body with his eyes, but seeming to fix his glance at a place just above her **supine** form. I, too, study her. No physical sign nor obvious symptom gives a clue to the nature of her disease.

5 At last he takes her hand, raising it in both of his own. Now he bends over the bed in a kind of crouching stance, his head drawn down into the collar of his robe. His eyes are closed as he feels for her pulse. In a moment he has found the spot, and for the next half hour he

remains thus, suspended above the patient like some exotic golden bird with folded wings, holding the pulse of the woman beneath his fingers, cradling her hand in his. All the power of the man seems to have been drawn down into this one purpose. It is palpation of the pulse raised to the state of ritual. From the foot of the bed, where I stand, it is as though he and the patient have entered a special place of isolation, of apartness, about which a vacancy hovers, and across which no violation is possible. After a moment, the woman rests back upon her pillow. From time to time, she raises her head to look at the strange figure above her, then sinks back once more. I cannot see their hands joined in a correspondence that is exclusive, intimate, his fingertips receiving the voice of her sick body through the rhythm and throb she offers at her wrist. All at once I am envious—not of him, not of Yeshi Dhonden for his gift of beauty and holiness, but of her. I want to be held like that, touched so, received. And I know that I, who have palpated a hundred thousand pulses, have not felt a single one.

6   At last Yeshi Dhonden straightens, gently places the woman's hand upon the bed, and steps back. The interpreter produces a small wooden bowl and two sticks. Yeshi Dhonden pours a portion of the urine specimen into the bowl, and proceeds to whip the liquid with the two sticks. This he does for several minutes until a foam is raised. Then, bowing above the bowl, he inhales the odors three times. He sets the bowl down and turns to leave. All this while, he has not uttered a single word. As he nears the door, the woman raises her head and calls out to him in a voice at once urgent and serene. "Thank you, Doctor," she says and touches with her other hand the place he has held on her wrist, as though to recapture something that has visited there. Yeshi Dhonden turns back for a moment to gaze at her, then steps into the corridor. Rounds are at an end.

7   We are seated once more in the conference room. Yeshi Dhonden speaks now for the first time, in soft Tibetan sounds that I have never heard before. He has barely begun when the young interpreter begins to translate, the two voices continuing in tandem: a bilingual **fugue,** the one chasing the other. It is like the chanting of monks. He speaks of winds coursing through the body of the woman, currents that break against barriers, **eddying.** These **vortices** are in her blood, he says, and are the last spendings of an imperfect heart. Between the chambers of her heart, long, long before she was born, a wind had come and blown open a deep gate that must never be opened. Through it charge the full waters of her river, as the mountain stream cascades in springtime, battering, knocking loose the land, and flooding her breath. Thus he speaks, and is silent.

fugue: a repeated musical form

eddying: going back and forth

vortices: whirling mass of fluid

8   "May we now have the diagnosis?" a professor asks.

9   The host of these rounds, the man who knows, answers.

10   "Congenital heart disease," he says. "Interventricular septal defect, with resultant heart failure."

11   A gateway in the heart, I think. That must not be opened. Through it charge the full waters that flood her breath. So! Here then is the doctor listening to the sounds of the body to which the rest of us are deaf. He is more than doctor. He is a priest.

12   I know . . . I know . . . The doctor to the gods is pure knowledge, pure healing. The doctor to man stumbles, must often wound; his patient must die, as must he.

13   Now and then it happens, as I make my own rounds, that I hear the sounds of his voice, like an ancient Buddhist prayer, its meaning long since forgotten, only the music remaining. Then jubilation possesses me, and I feel myself touched by something divine.

VOCABULARY AND COMPREHENSION

1. Circle the best answer: In paragraph 2, the word *bamboozlement* means
    a. alcoholism.   b. avoidance.   c. trickery.

2. What is the meaning of *palpate?* Look at the end of paragraph 5 for context clues. Circle the best answer.
    a. To meet   b. To examine by touching   c. To throw off

3. Who is Yeshi Dhonden?

    _____

4. Why has Dhonden come to the hospital?

    _____

5. What steps does Dhonden take to diagnose the patient?

    _____

    _____

    _____

    _____

    _____

CRITICAL THINKING

6. What is the author's initial attitude toward Yeshi Dhonden?

    _____

7. How does the patient feel after Dhonden examines her?

    _____

    _____

    _____

8. In paragraph 5, Selzer writes that he is envious of the patient. Why does he feel that way?

    _____

    _____

    _____

9.   Does Selzer's attitude toward Dhonden change? If so, how?

_____

_____

10.   In this essay, the author makes some comparisons. What are some of them?

_____

_____

_____

_____

WRITING TOPICS

Write a paragraph or an essay about one of the following topics. Remember to explore, develop, and revise and edit your work.

1.   What could regular doctors learn from a physician like Yeshi Dhonden?
2.   In your opinion, is our current medical system too dependent on science? Explain your answer.
3.   The quotation links science and religion, as does Selzer in his essay. In a paragraph or essay, compare and contrast medicine and religion.

> *Formerly, when religion was strong and science was weak, men mistook magic for medicine. Now, when science is strong and religion weak, men mistake medicine for magic.*
> —THOMAS SZASZ, PSYCHIATRIST AND AUTHOR

READING 20
Religious Faith Versus Spirituality
Neil Bissoondath

Neil Bissoondath, a journalist and writer, was born in Trinidad and immigrated to Canada. His works include *A Casual Brutality* and *Digging Up the Mountains*. In the next selection, the author contrasts religion and spirituality. As you read this comparison and contrast essay, also look for elements of argument writing.

1   *Wait till someone you love dies. You'll see. You'll know God exists. You'll want Him to.* The prediction, repeated with minimal variation through the years by believers challenged by my non-belief, was never offered as a promise but as a vague threat, and always with a sense of satisfied superiority, as if the speakers relished the thought that one day I would get my comeuppance.

2   They were, without exception, enthusiastic practitioners of their respective faiths—Roman Catholics, Presbyterians, Hindus, Muslims, God-fearing people all. Which was, to me, precisely the problem: Why all this fear?

3   And then one day, without warning, my mother died. Hers was the first death to touch me to the quick. Her cremation was done in the

pundit: Hindu priest

pyre: a pile of burning wood used to cremate a dead body

lassitude: weariness, fatigue

traditional Hindu manner. Under the direction of a **pundit,** my brother and I performed the ceremony, preparing the body with our bare hands, a contact more intimate than we'd ever had when she was alive.

4   As I walked away from her flaming **pyre,** I felt myself soaring with a lightness I'd never known before. I was suddenly freed from days of physical and emotional **lassitude,** and felt my first inkling of the healing power of ritual, the solace that ceremony can bring.

5   Still, despite the pain and the unspeakable sense of loss, the oft-predicted discovery of faith eluded me. I remained, as I do today, a nonbeliever, but I have no doubt that I underwent a deeply spiritual experience. This was when I began to understand that religious faith and spirituality do not necessarily have anything to do with each other—not that they are incompatible but that they are often mutually exclusive.

6   Western civilization has spent two thousand years blurring the distinction between the two, and as we enter the third millennium we are hardly more at peace with ourselves than people were a thousand years ago. Appreciating the distinction could help soothe our anxieties about the days to come.

7   Spirituality is the individual's ability to wonder at, and delight in, the indecipherable, like a baby marveling at the wiggling of its own toes. It is to be at ease with speculation, asking the unanswerable question and accepting that any answer would necessarily be incomplete, even false. It is recognizing that if scientific inquiry has inevitable limits, so too do religious explanations, which base themselves on unquestioning acceptance of the unprovable: neither can ever fully satisfy.

8   A sense of the spiritual comes from staring deep into the formation of a rose or a hibiscus and being astonished at the intricate delicacy of its symmetry without needing to see behind its perfection of form the fashioning hand of deity.

9   It comes from watching your child being born and gazing for the first time into those newly opened eyes, from holding that child against your chest and feeling his or her heartbeat melding with yours.

10   It comes from gazing up into the sparkling solitude of a clear midnight sky, secure in the knowledge that, no matter how alone you may feel at moments, the message of the stars appears to be that you most indisputably are not.

dogma: principle, tenant

11   At such moments, you need no **dogma** to tell you that the world seen or unseen, near or distant, is a wonderful and mysterious place. Spirituality, then, requires neither science nor religion, both of which hunger after answers and reassurance—while the essence of spirituality lies in the opening up of the individual to dazzlement. Spirituality entails no worship.

12   At the very moment of my mother's cremation, her brother, trapped thousands of miles away in England by airline schedules, got out his photographs of her and spread them on his coffee table. He reread her old letters and spent some time meditating on the life that had been lived—his way, at the very moment flames consumed her body, of celebrating the life and saying farewell, his way of engaging with the spiritual.

Vocabulary and Comprehension

1. Circle the best answer: In paragraph 1, *comeuppance* means
   a. rising up. b. punishment. c. reward.

2. Write a synonym for the word *solace* in paragraph 4.

3. How does Bissoondath define spirituality? Give examples from the essay.

4. Why does the author object to believers who try to challenge his nonbelief?

Critical Thinking

5. How does the death of the author's mother change him?

6. Why does the author give a lesser value to science and religion than to spirituality?

7. To support his belief in spirituality, why does Bissoondath give the example of his uncle in paragraph 12?

8. Bissoondath "soared with lightness" during the traditional Hindu ceremony and mentions the "healing power of ritual." Do you believe that such words contradict his strong opinions about religion? Explain your answer.

WRITING TOPICS

Write a paragraph or an essay about one of the following topics. Remember to explore, develop, and revise and edit your work.

1. Present a point of view opposed to the one presented in this essay. Defend a belief in religion. You can use yourself and others as examples.
2. Bissoondath went to a traditional Hindu ceremony. Why do all human cultures have special ceremonies, festivals, and holidays? For example, Americans may celebrate Martin Luther King Day, Valentine's Day, April Fool's Day, birthdays, anniversaries, and marriages. Explain why people celebrate such events.
3. Reflect on this proverb. What are some reasons that people have for believing in a god or a higher power?

66 *The believer is happy; the doubter is wise.* 99
—HUNGARIAN PROVERB

Appendix 1
Grammar Glossary

The Basic Parts of a Sentence

Parts of Speech	Definition	Some Examples
Noun	is a person, place, or thing.	singular: man, dog, person plural: men, dogs, people
Verb	expresses an action or state of being.	action: run, eat, walk, think linking: is, become, seem
Adjective	adds information about the noun.	tall, beautiful, blue, cold
Adverb	adds information about the verb, adjective, or other adverb; expresses time, place, and frequency.	friendly, quickly, sweetly sometimes, usually, never
Pronoun	replaces the noun.	he, she, it, us, ours, themselves
Preposition	shows a relationship between words (source, direction, location, etc.).	at, to, for, from, behind, above
Determiner	identifies or determines if a noun is specific or general.	a, an, the this, that, these, those any, all, each, every, many, some
Coordinating conjunction	connects two ideas of equal importance.	but, or, yet, so, for, and, nor
Subordinating conjunction	connects two ideas when one idea is subordinate (or inferior) to the other idea.	after, although, because, unless, until
Conjunctive adverb	shows a relationship between two ideas. It may appear at the beginning of a sentence, or it may join two sentences.	also, consequently, finally, however, furthermore, moreover, therefore, thus

Types of Clauses and Sentences

Other Key Terms	Definition	Example
phrase	a group of words that is missing a subject, a verb, or both, and is not a complete sentence.	in the morning after the storm
clause	An **independent clause** has a subject and verb and expresses a complete idea.	The movie is funny
	A **dependent clause** has a subject and verb but cannot stand alone. It "depends" on another clause in order to be complete.	Although it is violent
simple sentence	one independent clause that expresses one complete idea.	The movie is funny.
compound sentence	two or more independent clauses that are joined together.	Some movies are funny, and others are deeply moving.
complex sentence	at least one dependent clause joined with one independent clause.	Although the movie is violent, it conveys an important message.
compound-complex sentence	at least two independent clauses joined with at least one dependent clause.	Although the movie is violent, it is very entertaining, and it conveys an important message.

Appendix 2
Irregular Verbs

Irregular Verbs

Base Form	Simple Past	Past Participle	Base Form	Simple Past	Past Participle
arise	arose	arisen	feel	felt	felt
be	was, were	been	fight	fought	fought
beat	beat	beat, beaten	find	found	found
become	became	become	flee	fled	fled
begin	began	begun	fly	flew	flown
bend	bent	bent	forbid	forbade	forbidden
bet	bet	bet	forget	forgot	forgotten
bind	bound	bound	forgive	forgave	forgiven
bite	bit	bitten	forsake	forsook	forsaken
bleed	bled	bled	freeze	froze	frozen
blow	blew	blown	get	got	got, gotten
break	broke	broken	give	gave	given
breed	bred	bred	go	went	gone
bring	brought	brought	grind	ground	ground
build	built	built	grow	grew	grown
burst	burst	burst	hang	hung	hung
buy	bought	bought	have	had	had
catch	caught	caught	hear	heard	heard
choose	chose	chosen	hide	hid	hidden
cling	clung	clung	hit	hit	hit
come	came	come	hold	held	held
cost	cost	cost	hurt	hurt	hurt
creep	crept	crept	keep	kept	kept
cut	cut	cut	kneel	knelt	knelt
deal	dealt	dealt	know	knew	known
dig	dug	dug	lay	laid	laid
do	did	done	lead	led	led
draw	drew	drawn	leave	left	left
drink	drank	drunk	lend	lent	lent
drive	drove	driven	let	let	let
eat	ate	eaten	lie*	lay	lain
fall	fell	fallen	light	lit	lit
feed	fed	fed	lose	lost	lost

*When *lie* means "tell a false statement," then it is a regular verb: *lie, lied, lied*.   (continued)

Irregular Verbs (continued)

Base Form	Simple Past	Past Participle	Base Form	Simple Past	Past Participle
make	made	made	speed	sped	sped
mean	meant	meant	spend	spent	spent
meet	met	met	spin	spun	spun
mistake	mistook	mistaken	split	split	split
pay	paid	paid	spread	spread	spread
prove	proved	proved, proven	spring	sprang	sprung
put	put	put	stand	stood	stood
quit	quit	quit	steal	stole	stolen
read	read	read	stick	stuck	stuck
rid	rid	rid	sting	stung	stung
ride	rode	ridden	stink	stank	stunk
ring	rang	rung	strike	struck	struck
rise	rose	risen	swear	swore	sworn
run	ran	run	sweep	swept	swept
say	said	said	swim	swam	swum
see	saw	seen	swing	swung	swung
sell	sold	sold	take	took	taken
send	sent	sent	teach	taught	taught
set	set	set	tear	tore	torn
shake	shook	shaken	tell	told	told
shine	shone	shone	think	thought	thought
shoot	shot	shot	throw	threw	thrown
show	showed	shown	thrust	thrust	thrust
shrink	shrank	shrunk	understand	understood	understood
shut	shut	shut	wake	woke	woken
sing	sang	sung	wear	wore	worn
sink	sank	sunk	weep	wept	wept
sit	sat	sat	win	won	won
sleep	slept	slept	wind	wound	wound
slide	slid	slid	withdraw	withdrew	withdrawn
slit	slit	slit	write	wrote	written
speak	spoke	spoken			

Appendix 3
A Quick Guide to Verb Tenses

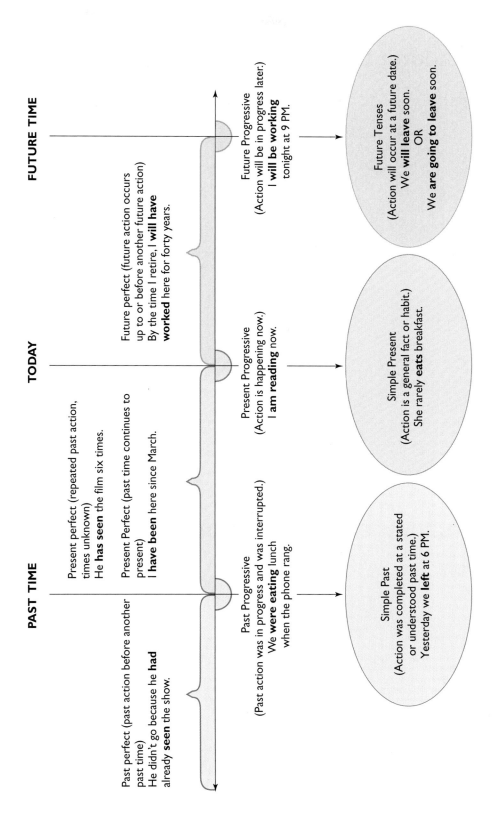

PAST TIME

Past perfect (past action before another past time)
He didn't go because he **had** already **seen** the show.

Present perfect (repeated past action, times unknown)
He **has seen** the film six times.

Present Perfect (past time continues to present)
I **have been** here since March.

Past Progressive
(Past action was in progress and was interrupted.)
We **were eating** lunch when the phone rang.

Simple Past
(Action was completed at a stated or understood past time.)
Yesterday we **left** at 6 PM.

TODAY

Future perfect (future action occurs up to or before another future action)
By the time I retire, I **will have worked** here for forty years.

Present Progressive
(Action is happening now.)
I **am reading** now.

Simple Present
(Action is a general fact or habit.)
She rarely **eats** breakfast.

FUTURE TIME

Future Progressive
(Action will be in progress later.)
I **will be working** tonight at 9 PM.

Future Tenses
(Action will occur at a future date.)
We **will leave** soon.
OR
We **are going to leave** soon.

Appendix 4

Combining Ideas in Sentences

Making Compound Sentences

A.

Complete idea

, coordinator
, but
, or
, yet
, so
, for
, and
, nor

complete idea.

B.

Complete idea

;

complete idea.

C.

Complete idea

; transitional expression,
; however,
; in fact,
; moreover,
; therefore,
; furthermore,

complete idea.

Making Complex Sentences

D.

Complete idea

subordinator
although
because
before
even though
unless
when

incomplete idea.

E.

Subordinator
Although
Because
Before
Even though
Unless
When

incomplete idea

,

complete idea.

Apostrophe (')

Use an apostrophe

- to join a subject and verb together.

    We're late.

- to join an auxiliary with *not*.

    I **can't** come.

- to indicate possession.

    Ross's computer is new.

Comma (,)

Use a comma

- to separate words in a series (more than two things). Place a comma before the final *and*.

    The doctor is kind, considerate, and gentle.

- after an introductory word or phrase.

    In the evenings, Carson volunteered at a hospital.

- around interrupting phrases that give additional information about the subject.

    Alan, an electrician, earns a good salary.

- in compound sentences before the coordinator.

    We worked for hours, and then we rested.

- around relative clauses containing *which*.

    The documents, which are very valuable, are up for auction.

- in quotations, after an introductory phrase or before an ending phrase.

    Picasso said, "Find your passion."

    "Find your passion," Picasso said.

Note: Do not join two complete sentences with a comma!

Colon (:)

Use a colon

- after a complete sentence that introduces a list, or after *the following*.

    The course has the following sections: pregnancy, labor, and lactation.

- after a complete sentence that introduces a quotation.

    Picasso's advice was clear: "Find your passion."

Semicolon (;)

Use a semicolon to join two independent but related clauses.

> Mahatma Gandhi was a pacifist; he believed in nonviolence.

Quotation Marks (" ")

Use quotation marks around direct speech. When a quotation is a complete sentence, capitalize the first word in the quotation. Place the end punctuation inside the closing quotation marks.

> In his essay, Levi said, "We were interchangeable."

If the end of the quotation is not the end of your sentence, end the quotation with a comma. If your quotation ends with other punctuation, put it inside the closing quotation marks.

> "We were interchangeable," according to Levi.
> "You can't be serious!" she shouted.
> "What did you call me?" he replied.

Integrated Quotations

If you integrate a quotation in a sentence, add quotation marks around the words the speaker quoted.

> Dorothy Nixon calls herself a "terrible mother."

"Inside" Quotations

If one quotation is inside another quotation, add single quotation marks (' ') around the inside quotation.

> Bernice was forced to act: "She turned to Charlie Paulson and plunged. 'Do you think I ought to bob my hair?'"

Citing Page or Paragraph Numbers

If you are using MLA style, write the page or paragraph number in parentheses and place it after the quotation. Place the final period *after* the parentheses if the quotation ends the sentence.

> In his essay, Levi says, "We were interchangeable" **(4)**.

Capitalization

Always capitalize

- the pronoun *I* and the first word of every sentence.
- the days of the week, the months, and holidays.

> **T**uesday   **M**ay 22   **L**abor **D**ay

- the names of specific places, such as buildings, streets, parks, public squares, lakes, rivers, cities, states, and countries.

> **K**elvin **S**treet   **L**ake **E**rie   **W**hite **P**lains, **N**ew **Y**ork

- the names of languages, nationalities, tribes, races, and religions.

> **S**panish   **M**ohawk   **B**uddhist

- the titles of specific individuals.

General **D**ewitt   **D**r. **F**ranklin   **M**r. **B**lain

- the major words in titles of literary or artistic works.

The Great Gatsby   *The Diviners*   *Crime and Punishment*

Punctuating Titles

Place the title of short works in quotation marks. Capitalize the major words. Short works include songs, short stories, newspaper and magazine articles, essays, and poems.

The Beatles' worst song was "Help."

Underline (or italicize, if you are using a computer) the title of a longer document. Long works include television series, films, works of art, magazines, books, plays, and newspapers.

We watched the classic movie <u>West Side Story</u>.

We watched the classic movie *West Side Story*.

Appendix 6
Writing Paragraphs and Essays in Exams

In many of your courses, you will have to answer exam questions with a paragraph or an essay. These types of questions often allow you to reveal your understanding of the topic. Although taking any exam can be stressful, you can reduce exam anxiety and increase your chances of doing well by following some preparation and exam-writing strategies.

Preparing for Exams

Here are some steps you can take to help prepare for exams.

- Before you take an exam, make sure that you know exactly what material you should study. Do not be afraid to ask the instructor for clarification. Also ask what materials you should bring to the exam.
- Review the assigned information, class notes, and the textbook, if any.
- Read and repeat information out loud.
- Take notes about important points.
- Study with a friend.

 Predict Exam Questions

An effective study strategy is to predict possible exam questions. Here are some tips:

- Look for important themes in your course outline.
- Study your notes and try to analyze what information is of particular importance.
- Look at your previous exams for the course. Determine whether any questions or subjects are repeated in more than one exam.

After you have looked through the course outline, your notes, and previous exams, write out possible exam questions based on the information that you have collected. Then practice writing the answers to your questions.

Writing Exams

Knowing your material inside and out is a large part of exam writing; however, budgeting your time and knowing how to read exam questions are important, too. When you receive the exam paper, look it over carefully and try these test-taking strategies.

Schedule Your Time

One of the most stressful things about taking an exam is running out of time. Before you write, find out exactly how much time you have. Then, plan how much time you will need to answer the questions. For example, if you have a one-hour exam and you have three questions worth the same point value, try to make sure that you spend no more than twenty minutes on any one question.

Determine Point Values

As soon as you get an exam, scan the questions and determine which questions have a larger point value. For example, you might respond to the questions with the largest point value first, or you might begin with those that you understand well. Then go to the more difficult questions. If you find yourself blocked on a certain answer, do not waste a lot of time on it. Go to another question, and then go back to the first question later.

Carefully Read the Exam Questions

You have probably heard the following anecdote.

> A teacher gave students a test sheet with twenty questions on it. In the instructions at the top of the page, the students were asked to skip to the last question and then hand the test in. Most students did not read the instructions, and they spent a lot of time carefully answering the twenty exam questions.

As this anecdote illustrates, it is important to read the exam instructions thoroughly.

Identify Key Words and Phrases

When you read an exam question, underline or circle key words and phrases in order to understand exactly what you are supposed to do. In the next example, the underlined words highlight three different tasks.

1. Discuss how each time period differs from the other.

<u>Distinguish</u> between Paleolithic, Mesolithic, and Neolithic. <u>Place these periods in chronological order</u> and <u>describe</u> how the people lived during those times.

2. Organize the essay according to each period's date.

3. Discuss what people did for shelter, food, and leisure activities.

Examine Common Question Words

Exam questions direct you using verbs (action words). This chart gives the most common words that are used in both paragraph- and essay-style questions.

Verb	Meaning
describe discuss review	Examine a subject as thoroughly as possible. Focus on the main points.
narrate trace	Describe the development or progress of something using time order.
evaluate explain your point of view interpret justify take a stand	State your opinion and give reasons to support your opinion. In other words, write an argument paragraph or essay.

(continued)

Verb	Meaning
analyze criticize classify	Explain something carefully by breaking it down into smaller parts.
enumerate list outline	Go through important facts one by one.
compare contrast distinguish	Discuss important similarities and/or differences.
define explain what is meant by . . .	Give a complete and accurate definition that demonstrates your understanding of the concept.
explain causes explain effects explain a process summarize illustrate	Analyze the reasons for an event. Analyze the consequences or results of an event. Explain the steps needed to perform a task. Write down the main points from a larger work. Demonstrate your understanding by giving examples.

PRACTICE I

Determine the main type of response that you would use to answer each essay question.

narrate	explain a process	explain causes/effects	define
argue	classify	compare and contrast	give examples

EXAMPLE:

Discuss the term *affirmative action*.

define

1. Distinguish between the interest rate and the rate of return.

2. Explain what is meant by *democracy*.

3. Describe what happened during the Tet Offensive.

4. List and describe five types of housing.

5. What steps are required to improve your city's transportation system?

6. List the causes of global warming.

_____

7. Give a short but thorough description of narcissism.

_____

8. Briefly explain the differences between a terrorist and a freedom fighter.

_____

9. Discuss whether religious symbols should be banned from schools.

_____

10. Give three instances of how advertising has influenced consumer trends.

_____

Follow the Writing Process

When you answer paragraph or essay exam questions, remember to follow the writing process.

Explore	▪ Jot down any ideas that you think can help you answer the question.
Develop	▪ Use the exam question to guide your topic sentence or thesis statement.
	▪ List supporting ideas. Then organize your ideas and create a paragraph or essay plan.
	▪ Write the paragraph or essay. Use transitions to link your ideas.
Revise and edit	▪ Read over your writing to make sure it makes sense and that your spelling, punctuation, and mechanics are correct.

PRACTICE 2

Choose three topics from Practice 1 and write topic sentences or thesis statements.

EXAMPLE:

Discuss the term *affirmative action*.

Topic sentence or thesis statement: *Affirmative action policies give certain groups in society preferential treatment in order to correct a history of injustice.*

1. _____

    _____

2. _____

_____

3. _____

_____

PRACTICE 3

Read the following test material and answer the questions that follow.

Essay Exam

You will have ninety minutes to complete the following test. Write your answers in the answer booklet.

A. Define the following terms (2 points each).

1. Region
2. Economic geography
3. Territoriality
4. Spatial distribution
5. Gross national product

B. Write an essay response to one of the following questions. Your essay should contain relevant supporting details. (20 points)

6. Define and contrast an open city with a closed city.
7. Discuss industrial location theories in geography, and divide the theories into groups.
8. Explain the steps needed to complete a geographical survey. List the steps in order of importance.

Schedule Your Time and Determine Point Values

1. What is the total point value of the exam? _____

2. How many questions do you have to answer? _____

3. Which part of the exam would you do first? Explain why. _____

_____

4. Schedule your time. How much time would you spend on each part of the exam?

Part A: _____ Part B: _____

Explain your reasoning. _____

_____

Carefully Read the Exam Questions

5. Identify key words in Part B. What important information is in the instructions?

_____

6. What two things must you do in question 6?

   a. _____   b. _____

7. What type of essay is required to answer question 7?
   a. Comparison and contrast   b. Classification   c. Process

8. What type of essay is required to answer question 8?
   a. Comparison and contrast   b. Classification   c. Process

Appendix 7
Spelling, Grammar, and Vocabulary Logs

In the first few pages of your writing portfolio, you can keep spelling, grammar, and vocabulary logs (see pages 609–611 for examples). The goal of keeping spelling and grammar logs is to help you stop repeating the same errors. When you write new assignments, you can consult the lists and hopefully break some ingrained bad habits. The vocabulary log can provide you with interesting new terms that you can incorporate into your writing.

Spelling Log

Every time you misspell a word, record both the mistake and the correction in your spelling log. Then, before you hand in a writing assignment, consult your spelling log. The goal is to stop repeating the same spelling errors.

EXAMPLE:

Incorrect	Correct
realy	rea*ll*y
exagerated	exa*gg*erated

Grammar Log

Each time a writing assignment is returned to you, identify one or two repeated errors and add them to your grammar log. Then, before you hand in writing assignments, consult the grammar log in order to avoid making the same errors. For each type of grammar error, you could do the following:

- Identify the assignment and write down the type of error.
- In your own words, write a rule about the error.
- Include an example from your writing assignment.

EXAMPLE: <u>Illustration Paragraph</u>   (Feb. 12)   Run–On

Do not connect two complete sentences with a comma.

Bad drivers cause <u>accidents, other</u> drivers do not expect sudden lane changes.

(accidents. Other)

Vocabulary Log

As you use this book, you will learn new vocabulary words. Keep a record of the most interesting and useful vocabulary words and expressions. Write a synonym or definition next to each new word.

EXAMPLE: <u>Exasperating</u> means "annoying."

Spelling Log

Grammar Log

Vocabulary Log

_____
_____
_____
_____
_____
_____
_____
_____
_____
_____
_____
_____
_____
_____
_____
_____
_____
_____
_____
_____
_____
_____
_____
_____
_____
_____
_____
_____
_____
_____
_____
_____
_____
_____

Index

A

a, an
  determiners before, 396
  in titles, 190
abstract nouns, 395
academic writing
  avoiding slang in, 456
  research for, 237–38
accept/except, 469
according to, 258
action verb, 260
active voice, 351, 354
addresses, 485
  Web, 498
adjective(s), 425–28, 593
  comparative form, 432
  compound, 506–7
  -ed and *-ing* ending, 427
  -ful or *-less* ending, 427
  good/bad, 431–32
  parallel, 321
  placement of, 426
  possessive, 396, 406, 407, 408–9
  with same form as adverbs, 428
  singular form, 427
  superlative form, 432
adverb(s), 428–32, 593
  adjectives with same form as, 428
  beginning sentence with, 294
  comparative form, 432
  conjunctive, 272, 274, 593
  forms of, 428–29
  frequency, 429–30
  negative, 341
  problems with, 430–32
  superlative form, 433
  well and *badly*, 431–32
affect/effect, 145, 469
agreement
  pronoun-antecedent, 414–21
  subject-verb, 332, 368–82
ain't, 371
almost, 440–41
a lot, 465
American Psychological Association (APA)
    format, 246
and, pronouns joined by, 410
anecdote, 159
  in argument essay, 231
  in introduction, 182
annotations, making, 527
another, 465
antecedent, 414
  pronoun-antecedent agreement, 414–21
  to reflexive pronouns, 413
  vague pronouns referring to, 419–20
antonym, 528
any, spelling two-part words with, 465
apostrophe, 490–95, 500
  common errors, 494

  in contractions, 490–92
  defined, 490
  in expressions of time, 493–95
  possessive pronouns and, 407
  to show ownership, 492–93
appealing to readers' senses, 78, 81, 198, 451
application, letter of, 486
appositive, 300
  adding, 452
  combining sentences with, 300–303
  commas with, 300, 480
  finding, 301
  modifiers, 441
argument, 154–55, 194
  emotional, 162
  titles related to, 190
argument essay, 231–36
  plan/outline, 232–33
  research for, 160
  supporting ideas, 231–32
  thesis statement, 231
  topics, 235
argument paragraph, 155–67
  audience, 155
  both sides of issue, 161
  circular reasoning, avoiding, 159
  direct manner, 158
  first draft, 163–64
  passion in, 156
  pitfalls, 162
  plan/outline, 162–63
  purpose, 155
  revising and editing, 164–66
  supporting ideas, 155, 158–60
  topic sentences, 157
articles
  as determiners, 396
  in titles, 190, 498
artificial breaks in paragraph, 187
as, comparisons with, 409
assignment, understanding, 5
attitude, 78
at vs. *to*, 400
audience, 5–7, 169
  argument paragraph, 155
  definition paragraph, 102
  instructor as, 6
  paraphrasing vs. summarizing and, 241
autobiography, 65–66, 67

B

background information in introduction,
    182
bad/good, 431–32
badly/well, 431–32
base form of verb
  after *did*, 340
  after *to* (infinitive form), 340

coordinating conjunctions (*cont.*)
    comma before, 270
    in compound sentence, 267–70, 482
    in titles, 498
could, 384
could of, 363–65
count nouns, 394–95
    comparing two, 435
    determiners before, 396

D

dangling modifiers, 443–46
    correcting, 444
dates
    in letters, 485
    numerals of decade or century, writing, 494
definition, 101, 102, 193
    by category, 103–4, 213
    enhancing, 214
    in introduction, 182
    by negation, 104, 213
    by synonym, 103, 213
    titles related to, 190
definition essay, 213–17
    plan/outline, 214–15
    supporting ideas, 213–14
    thesis statement, 213
definition paragraph, 101–12
    audience for, 102
    first draft, 108–9
    plan/outline, 107–8
    precise language in, 105–6
    revising and editing, 109–10
    supporting ideas, 106–7
    topic sentences, 103–6
    transitional words and expressions, 108
demonstratives, as determiners, 396
dependent-clause fragments, 310–12
dependent clauses, 279, 285–87, 310, 483, 594
description, 77, 193
    titles related to, 190
descriptive essay, 203–8
    figurative devices in, 203–4
    plan/outline, 204–5
    supporting ideas, 203–4
    thesis statement, 203
    topics, 207–8
descriptive language, 198
descriptive paragraph, 77–87
    attitude toward subject in, 78
    concrete details, 78–79
    dominant impression created in, 77
    first draft, 83–84
    plan/outline, 82–83
    revising and editing, 84–85
    supporting details, 78–79, 81–82
    topics, 86
    topic sentence, 80
descriptive titles, 190

details. *See* supporting details
determiners, 396–99, 593
developing stage of writing process, 16–37
    answering exam questions, 606
    first draft of paragraph, 35–36
    narrowing topic, 18–19
    plan/outline of paragraph ideas, 31–35
    supporting details, 24–31
    topic sentence, 17, 19–24
dialogue, 199
dictionary, using, 460, 528–29
differences
    focus on contrasting, 130–31
    transitional words and expressions showing, 135
direct quotation, 199, 244, 293–94
disinterested/uninterested, 469–70
documentation style, 246
dominant impression, creating, 77, 80, 81, 203
double negatives, 341–42
do verb
    base form of verb after *did*, 340
    common errors with, 339
    present tense forms, 370
drafts. *See* final draft; first draft
during vs. *for*, 400

E

each, single noun after, 396
editing, 38, 51
    argument paragraph, 164–66
    cause and effect paragraph, 149–50
    classification paragraph, 121–23
    comparison and contrast paragraph, 136–37
    definition paragraph, 109–10
    descriptive paragraph, 84–85
    for errors, 39, 47–49
    essay, 187, 189
    exam question answers, 606
    illustration paragraph, 60–62
    narrative paragraph, 72–74
    process paragraph, 96–97
    tips, 47
editing practice
    essay, 513–15, 517, 521–22, 523
    formal letter, 520–21
    letter of complaint, 519
    paragraph, 512–13, 515–16
    workplace memo, 517
effect/affect, 145, 469
effects, thinking about, 227. *See also* cause and effect essay;
    cause and effect paragraph
elicit/illicit, 470
ellipsis marks, 508–9
embedded questions, 287–89
eminent/imminent, 470
emotional arguments, 162
emphatic order, 28–29, 146, 177
    descriptive essay in, 203
    series of examples in, 58

ending phrase after quotation, 496
English, nonstandard vs. standard American, 331,
    455–56
entertaining writing, 8
errors
    with apostrophes, 494
    in argument paragraph, 162
    with *be* verb, 339
    with *do* verb, 339
    editing for, 39, 47–49
    with *have* verb, 339
    with progressive tense, 359
ESL teaching tips (AIE), 291, 328, 330, 389, 449, 511
    activities, 367, 388, 424, 476
    adjectives, 426, 427
    apostrophes, 491, 494
    argument paragraph, 158, 159
    brainstorming, 424
    business letters, 484, 485
    capitalization rules, 504
    causes or effects, 151
    circular reasoning, 41
    clichés, 454
    comparative forms, 435
    comparison and contrast, 127
    coordinating conjunctions chart, 267
    culture-specific examples, 58
    culture-specific topics, 77, 89
    definitions, 111
    determiners, 396, 397
    double subjects, 419
    explaining Helen Keller, 27
    freewriting, 9
    group work, 43, 272
    his and *her*, 407
    infinitives, 260
    -ing form, 255
    language style, 67
    negative verbs, 333, 334
    noncount nouns, 394–95
    nonprogressive verbs, 359
    paragraph form, 17
    past conditional, 544
    past progressive tense, 335
    past tense, 340
    plural nouns, 391, 393
    prepositional phrases, 257
    prepositions, 399, 400, 401
    present perfect tense, 348, 349
    question and negative forms, 369
    reading selections, 544, 545, 554, 592
    reflexive pronouns, 413
    relative pronouns, 411
    simple and progressive verb forms, 331
    spelling, 459, 461, 463
    subject after subordinator, 283
    subject-verb agreement, 372, 377
    subordinating conjunctions, 280
    tense shifts, 384
    time markers, 348
    topic sentences, 22

topics for writing, 305
    vivid vocabulary, 81
    word twins, 528
essay(s), 168–92
    argument, 231–36
    body, 3
    cause and effect, 227–31
    characteristics, 3–4
    classification, 217–22
    comparison and contrast, 222–26
    conclusion, 4, 185–86
    defined, 168
    definition, 213–17
    descriptive, 203–8
    editing, 187, 189
    editing, practice at, 513–15, 518, 520–21, 523
    exam, writing, 602–7
    final draft, 191
    first draft, 186–87
    illustration, 194–98
    introduction, 3, 181–84
    narrative, 198–202
    narrowing topic of, 169–71
    plan/outline, 178–81
    process, 208–13
    pronoun shifts in, avoiding, 421
    revising, 187–89
    supporting ideas, 174–78
    thesis statement, 3, 4, 171–74
    title, 189–91, 498
essay links, 16, 104
    argument essay, 155, 158
    cause and effect essay, 144, 147
    classification essay, 114, 119, 120
    coherence, 43
    comparison and contrast essay, 128, 132, 134
    concluding paragraph, 33
    controlling idea, 19
    definition essay, 103, 107
    descriptive essay, 77, 80, 81, 82
    editing, 189
    exploring steps, 4
    illustration essay, 54, 57, 58
    narrative essay, 66, 68, 71
    organizational methods, 27
    plan/outline, 31
    process essays, 89, 92, 93, 94
    revising and editing, 39, 40
    style, 45
    supporting ideas, 24
    thesis statements, 19, 103
    topics, 18, 22
    workplace, 511
even, 440
every
    single noun after, 396
    spelling two-part words with, 465
everyday/every day, 470
evidence. *See* supporting details
exact language, 450–58
exaggerated claims, 162

exam, 602–7
   point values on, 603
   practice, 604–7
   preparing for, 602
   questions and question words, 603–4
   time management on, 602
   writing, 602–3
examples, 158–59
   categories vs., 115
   extended, 54, 56, 58, 194
   in illustration paragraph, 54–56
   series of, 54–55, 58, 194
except/accept, 469
exclamation, 293
explanatory fragments, 309–10
exploring stage of writing process, 4–13, 605
exploring strategies (prewriting strategies), 9–13
   to generate ideas, 25
   to narrow topic, 18

F

facts, 159
   in argument essay, 232
feedback, peer, 48–49
few, 396
fewer/less, 435
figurative devices, 203–4
final draft
   of essay, 191
   of paragraph, 49–50
first draft
   of argument paragraph, 163–64
   of cause and effect paragraph, 148–49
   of classification paragraph, 121
   of comparison and contrast paragraph, 135–36
   of definition paragraph, 108–9
   of descriptive paragraph, 83–84
   of essay, 186–87
   illustration paragraph, 59–60
   of narrative paragraph, 72
   of paragraph, 35–36
   of process paragraph, 95–96
first-person narration, 65–66, 67, 198
Florida Exit Test competencies
   capitalization, 496, 498, 503–6
   effectively using coordination, 267–70, 322, 482, 498, 593, 598
   effectively using irregular verbs, 332, 335, 336–41, 346
   effectively using semicolons, 104, 267, 270–73
   effectively using subordination, 274, 279–85, 310, 483, 593, 598
   effectively using transitions, 27, 28, 29, 43–45, 60, 72, 84, 95–96, 121, 135, 148–49, 188, 267, 272–75, 479
   effectively using verb tense, 261, 321, 330–44, 348–51, 358–60, 362–63, 369–71, 372, 429
   effectively using verb tense/consistency, 383–88
   look-alike words, 469–74
   parallel structure, 320–29

prefixes and suffixes, 460–65
pronoun case, 405–11
pronoun consistency, 420–21
pronoun reference, 414–21
recognizing comma splices, 61, 313
recognizing fused sentences, 312
recognizing misplaced modifiers, 439–43
recognizing sentence fragments, 306–12, 318–19
recognizing unclear pronoun reference, 419–21
sound-alike words, 469–74
spelling, 459–76
subject-verb agreement, 332, 368–82
understanding adjectives/adverbs, 294, 321, 341, 396, 406, 407, 408–9, 425–38, 506–7
understanding apostrophes/possessives, 407, 490–95
understanding comparatives/superlatives, 432–36
understanding topic sentences, 3, 4, 17, 19–24, 57, 68–70, 80, 92–93, 103–6, 119, 132–33, 141, 144–46, 157, 174–75, 188
understanding word choice/vocabulary, 450–52, 527–29
formal essay plan, 179
formal letter, 522
for vs. *during*, 400
fragments, sentence, 306–12, 318–19
   dependent-clause fragments, 310–12
   explanatory fragments, 309–10
   with *-ing* and *to*, 308–9
   phrase fragments, 307–8
freewriting, 9–10
   to generate ideas, 25
   to narrow topic, 18
frequency adverbs, 429–30
fused sentence, 312
future conditional, 362
future perfect tense, 597
future progressive tense, 359, 597
future tense, 597
   subject-verb agreement and, 372

G

gender of possessive adjective, 407
generalizations, 162
general purpose, 8
gerunds, 255, 308
gonna, gotta, 360–61
good/bad, 431–32
grammar glossary, 593–94
grammar links
   apostrophes, 407
   collective nouns, 413
   commonly confused words, 433
   editing, 47
   irregular verbs, 336
   noncount nouns, 435
   past participles, 298, 345
   present perfect, 372
   present tense, 369
   progressive forms, 331

punctuating quotations, 294
punctuating relative clauses, 285
quotations, 199, 244, 294, 508
sentence variety, 292
spelling, 335
subject-verb agreement, 332
titles, 247
which clause set off with commas, 411
grammar log, 50, 608, 610

H

have verb
common errors with, 339
present tense forms, 332, 339, 348–49, 370
helping verb(s), 261–63, 307
with *done*, 339
embedded questions and, 287
fragment beginning with, 308–9
frequency adverbs after, 430
in negative forms, 333
past participle with, 345
in progressive form, 358–60
in questions, 262, 333, 377
here, sentence beginning with, 377
here/there, 256
highlighting your reading, 527
his or *her*, choosing, 407
hisself, 413
hyphen, 506–8
hyphenated compound nouns, 391

I

I, capitalizing, 503, 600
if clause, 362–63
illicit/elicit, 470
illustration, 54, 193
titles related to, 190
illustration essay, 194–98
plan/outline, 195
supporting ideas, 194
thesis statement, 194
topics, 197
illustration paragraph(s), 54–63
first draft, 59–60
plan/outline, 58–59
revising and editing, 60–62
supporting ideas in, 57–58
topic sentence of, 57
topics for, 62
transitional expressions in, 60
ways to write, 54–56
imagery, 78–79, 81, 198, 451
imminent/eminent, 470
imply/infer, 470
incomplete verbs, 307

indefinite pronouns, 374–75, 415–18
as determiners, 396
one-word, spelling, 465
plural, 374, 375
singular, 374
independent clause, 267, 278, 594
parallel structure of joined, 322
indirect quotation, 199, 244–45
inferences, making, 526
infinitives, 260, 340
fragment beginning with, 308–9
informational writing, 8
informed opinion, 159, 232
-ing verbs, 358–60
integrated quotation, 245–46, 600
Internet, research using, 160
evaluating sources, 239
Internet sites, 239, 240, 251
citing, 247, 249
recording information about, 239
useful, 248
interrupting words and phrases
commas around, 480–82
in quotation, commas around, 495
subject-verb agreement and, 378–80
between verbs, 262
introduction to essay, 3, 181–84
introductory paragraph, 181–84
lead-in, 181
styles, 182–84
thesis statement placement in, 182
introductory phrase, 479
comma to set off, 295, 479–80, 495
introducing quotation, comma after, 495
introductory sentence, 496
introductory word, 479
comma after, 295, 479–80, 495
irregular comparative and superlative forms, 433
irregular plural nouns, 390–91
irregular verbs, 335, 595–96
base forms, 595–96
be (*was* or *were*), 338–39
past participles of, 298, 346, 595–96
past tense, 336–41, 595–96
present tense, 332
italicizing title, 498, 601
its/it's, 470

J

journal, 13
just, 440

K

knew/new, 470
know/no, 470

L

language
    clichés, 454–55
    descriptive, 198
    exact, 450–58
    precise, 105–6
    redundancy and wordiness, 453–54
    sexist, 417, 547
    slang vs. standard English, 455–56
    vivid, 81, 182, 451–52
language clues, 7
lead-in, 181
less/fewer, 435
letter(s)
    addresses, 485
    of application, 486
    business, 484–87
    of complaint, editing, 519
    complimentary closings, 485
    dates, 485
    formal, editing, 522
    salutations, 485
limiting modifiers, 440
linking verb, 260
list, colon to introduce, 506
little, 396
logical consequences of argument, 159, 232
look-alike words, 469–74
lose/loose/loss, 470

M

magazine sources, 239
main idea
    finding in reading, 526
    making statement of, 526
main verb, 261
many, 396
memo, workplace, 517
merely, 440
metaphor, 203
misplaced modifiers, 439–43
misspelled words, commonly, 466–67
modal auxiliaries, 261
modals, subject-verb agreement and, 372
Modern Language Association (MLA), 240
    citing page or paragraph numbers in style of, 600
    format, 246
modifiers, 439
    creating vivid language with, 451
    dangling, 443–46
    introductory phrase, 479
    limiting, 440
    misplaced, 439–43
    modifying clichés, 454
more, 433, 435
most, 433, 435
much, 396

N

names
    capitalizing, 504, 600
    historical events, eras, and movements, 504
    languages, nationalities, tribes, races, and religions, 504, 600
    places, 504, 600
narration, 65, 193
    first-person, 65–66, 67, 198
    third-person, 66, 68, 198
    titles related to, 190
narrative essay, 198–202
    first-person, 198
    plan/outline, 199–200
    supporting ideas, 198–99
    thesis statement, 198
    third-person, 198
    topics for, 202
narrative paragraph, 65–75
    first draft, 72
    first-person narration, 65–66, 67
    plan/outline, 71–72
    revising and editing, 72–74
    sequence of events, 70
    supporting details, 70–71
    third-person narration, 66, 68
    topics, 66, 74
    topic sentence, 68–70
    transitional words and expressions in, 72
narrowing topic, 18–19, 169–71
nearly, 440
negation, definition by, 104, 213
negatives, double, 341–42
negative verb forms, 369
    contractions, 333, 491
    present tense, 333–34
new/knew, 470
newspaper sources, 239
no/know, 470
noncount nouns, 394–95
    comparing two, 435
    determiners before, 397
nonprogressive verbs, 359–60
nonrestrictive clause, comma to set off, 484
nonstandard English, 331
    ain't, 371
    gonna, gotta, wanna, 360–61
    verb forms, 360–61, 363–65, 371
    would of, could of, should of, 363–65
not, contractions with, 333, 491
nouns, 389–95, 593. *See also* pronouns
    appositive and, 300
    collective, 376–77, 413
    common, 389
    compound, 391, 493
    count, 394–95, 396, 435
    determiners and, 396–99, 593
    irregular, 390–91
    noncount, 394–95, 435

parallel, 320
plural, 390–94, 492–93
possessive, 396, 492–93
proper, 389
singular, 390, 393, 492
-*s* or -*es* endings, 390
number(s)
    as determiners, 396
    hyphens in, 506
    numerals of decade or century, writing, 494
    pronouns consistent in, 420–21
    writing, 485

O

object in prepositional phrase, 258
objective case, 406, 409, 410
of the expressions, 416
only, 440
opinion, informed, 159, 232
opposing position in introduction, 182
opposition, refuting argument of, 159
    in argument essay, 232
    transitional words and expressions for, 163–64
or, pronouns joined by, 410
order
    emphatic, 28–29, 58, 146, 177, 203
    space, 29, 177, 203
    time, 27–28, 58, 70, 89, 94, 96, 177, 198, 203
    word, 287, 288, 377
organization of supporting details, 27–31, 128, 129, 177–78, 222
outline
    of argument essay, 232–33
    of argument paragraph, 162–63
    of cause and effect essay, 228
    of cause and effect paragraph, 147–48
    of classification essay, 218–19
    of classification paragraph, 120
    of comparison and contrast essay, 223
    of comparison and contrast paragraph, 134–35
    of definition essay, 214–15
    of definition paragraph, 107–8
    of descriptive essay, 204–5
    of descriptive paragraph, 82–83
    essay, 178–81
    of illustration essay, 195
    of illustration paragraph, 58–59
    of narrative essay, 199–200
    of narrative paragraph, 71–72
    paragraph, 31–35
    of process essay, 209–10
    of process paragraph, 94–95
    as reading strategy, 529
oversimplification, avoiding, 146

P

paired clauses, 322
paired items, parallel structure for, 324
paragraph(s), 3–15, 17. *See also specific types of paragraphs*
    body, 3
    characteristics, 3–4, 17
    coherence of, 39, 43–45, 51
    concluding, 185–86
    concluding sentence, 3, 4, 17, 33–35
    editing, practice at, 512–13, 516–17
    emphatic-order, 28–29
    exam, writing, 602–7
    final draft, 49–50
    first draft, 35–36
    form, 17
    introductory, 181–84
    patterns, 52. *See also specific types of paragraphs*
    peer feedback on, 48–49
    plan/outline, 31–35
    pronoun shifts in, avoiding, 421
    rambling, 187
    revising, 38–47
    space-order, 29
    supporting details, 24–31, 38, 40–42, 51
    time-order, 27–28
    topic, 18–19, 170
    topic sentence, 3, 4, 17, 19–24
    unity, 25, 38, 39–40, 51
paragraph links, 187–88
    argument writing, 231
    cause and effect, 227
    classification writing, 217
    comparison and contrast, 222
    definition writing, 213
    descriptive writing, 203
    illustration, 194, 197
    narrative writing, 198
    process writing, 208
    supporting ideas, 231
    topics, 202, 207, 212, 216, 221, 225, 230, 235
paragraph plan, 31–35
parallel structure, 320–29
    in comparisons, 323
    faulty, 322–26
    in paired clauses, 322
    in series of words or phrases, 322
    in two-part construction, 324
paraphrasing, 240, 241–44
    summarizing vs., 241
parentheses, cited sources inside, 247
parts of speech, 593. *See also specific parts of speech*
passive voice, 351–55
    by . . . phrase understood in, 352
    overuse of, 354
    verb *be* suggested but not written, 355
past conditional, 362
past participle(s), 345–57, 363
    combining sentences with, 298–300
    of irregular verbs, 298, 346, 595–96

past participle(s) (*cont.*)
    modifiers, 440
    passive voice and, 351–55
    past perfect tense, 350–51, 372, 597
    present perfect tense, 348–49, 372, 597
    of regular verbs, 346
past/passed, 337
past perfect progressive, 359
past perfect tense, 350–51, 597
    subject-verb agreement and, 372
past progressive tense, 335, 359, 597
past tense
    agreement, 372
    be verb, 338–39
    frequency adverbs before, 429
    irregular verbs, 336–41, 595–96
    regular, 335
    simple, 335–41, 348–49, 350–51, 372, 595–96, 597
peace/piece, 470
peer feedback, 48–49
perception verbs, 359
perfect tense
    past, 350–51, 372, 597
    present, 348–49, 372, 597
    present perfect progressive, 359
periodicals, citing, 248
periods, in quotations, 294
person, pronouns consistent in, 421
personal/personnel, 470
personification, 203
persons vs. *people*, 391
persuasive writing, 8. *See also* argument; argument essay;
    argument paragraph
phrase, 257, 594. *See also* prepositional phrase(s); transitional
    words and expressions
    interrupting, 262, 378–80, 480–82, 495
    introductory, 295, 479–80, 495
phrase fragments, 307–8
phrase introduction of quotation, 245
piece/peace, 470
plagiarism, 240
plan. *See* outline
plural nouns, 390–94
    irregular, 390–91
    key words for, 393
    possessive forms of, 492–93
plural subject, 255
plural verbs. *See* subject-verb agreement
point-by-point organization, 128, 222
police, as plural noun, 376
portfolio, writing, 13–14
possession verbs, 359
possessive case, 406–9
    adjectives, 396, 406, 407, 408–9
    pronouns, 407, 408–9
possessive nouns, 396, 492–93
    -'s to show ownership, 492–93
prediction, ending conclusion with, 185
preference verbs, 359
prefixes, 460–61

preposition(s), 399–402, 593
    common, 257
    commonly confused, 400
    common prepositional expressions, 401–2
    of place, 399–400
    of time, 399–400
    in titles, 190, 498
prepositional phrase(s), 257–59
    as interrupting phrase, 378, 480
    as introductory phrase, 479
    modifiers, 440
    object in, 258
    parallel, 321
    pronouns in, 409
    sentence beginning with, 295
present conditional, 362
present participle
    combining sentences with, 296–98
    modifiers, 440
present perfect progressive, 359
present perfect tense, 348–49, 597
    agreement, 372
present progressive tense, 331, 359, 597
present tense
    agreement, 369–71
    be verb, 332, 370
    frequency adverbs before, 429
    have verb, 332, 339, 348–49, 370
    negative, 333–34
    simple, 331–34, 369–71, 597
previewing, 525–26
prewriting strategies (exploring strategies), 9–13, 18, 25
principal/principle, 470
process, 89, 193, 208
    steps vs. examples of, 93
    titles related to, 190
process essay, 208–13
    plan/outline, 209–10
    supporting ideas, 209
    thesis statement, 208–9
    types of, 208
process paragraph, 89–99
    complete a process type of, 89, 90–91
    first draft, 95–96
    plan/outline, 94–95
    revising and editing, 96–97
    supporting details, 93–94
    tools or supplies in, 94
    topics, 98
    topic sentence, 92–93
    understand a process type of, 89, 91–92
progressive tense, 358–60
    common errors with, 359
    future, 359
    past, 335, 359
    present, 331, 359, 597
pronoun-antecedent agreement, 414–21
    consistency in number, 420–21
    consistency in person, 421
    vague pronouns, 419–20

pronouns, 405–24, 593
  with *and* or *or*, 410
  appositive and, 300
  case, 405–11
  in comparisons with *than* or *as*, 409
  I, capitalizing, 503, 600
  indefinite, 374–75, 396, 415–18, 465
  objective case, 406, 409, 410
  possessive, 407, 408–9
  in prepositional phrases, 409
  pronoun-antecedent agreement, 414–17,
    420–21
  pronoun shifts, 420–22
  reflexive, 412–14
  relative, 285–87, 310, 411–12
  subject, 255
  subjective case, 406, 409, 410
  vague, 419–20
pronoun shifts, 420–22
proofreading, 47, 49. *See also* editing
proper nouns, 389
punctuation, 477–511, 599–601. *See also*
    capitalization
  apostrophe, 407, 490–95, 599
  with appositives, 300
  colon, 496, 506, 599
  commas, 270, 272–73, 282, 285, 294, 295,
    300, 411, 412, 477–89, 495, 496, 599
  of complex sentences, 282–83
  of compound sentences, 267, 270–73
  ellipsis marks, 508–9
  hyphen, 391, 506–8
  periods, 294
  quotation marks, 495–97, 601, 602
  of quotations, 294, 496, 506, 601
  with relative pronouns, 285
  in run-on sentences, 312–14
  semicolons, 104, 267, 270–73, 601
  of series, 478–79, 506
  in titles, 498–500, 602
  before and after transitional expressions, 272–73
purpose for writing, 7–9, 169

Q

questioning (strategy), 11–12
questions
  embedded, 287–89
  exam, 602–4
  helping verbs in, 262, 333, 377
  to narrow topic, 18
  rhetorical, 293
  for sentence variety, 293–94
  word order in, 377
question verb forms, 333–34, 369
quiet/quite/quit, 470–71
quotation(s), 240, 244–46
  inside another quotation, 496, 600
  colon to introduce, 506

  commas in or ending, 294, 496
  direct, 199, 244, 293–94
  ending conclusion with, 185
  incomplete sentence, 496
  indirect, 199, 244–45
  introducing or integrating, 245–46, 600
  in narrative essay, 199
  with omissions, ellipsis marks in, 508
  punctuating, 294, 496, 506, 600
  quoting sources, 240, 244–46
  from respected source, 232
  for sentence variety, 293–94
quotation marks, 495–97, 600
  around title of short works, 601
  in sentence with ending phrase, 496
  in sentence with interrupting phrase, 495
  in sentence with introductory phrase, 495
  in sentence with introductory sentence, 496
  single, 496

R

rambling paragraph, 187
reading links
  argument readings, 166
  cause and effect readings, 151
  classification readings, 124
  college life, 388
  comparison and contrast readings, 138
  culture, 305
  definition readings, 111
  descriptive readings, 87
  dictionary use, 460
  espionage, 367
  great discoveries, 424
  health care, 449
  illustration readings, 62
  legal world, 476
  narrative readings, 75
  process readings, 98
  psychology, 328
reading selections, 524, 530–92
  "Aunt Tee" (Angelou), 530–33
  "Body Over Mind" (Albom), 572–75
  "Bound Feet" (Chang), 580–83
  "Case for Affirmative Action, The" (Malcolm), 568–72
  "Dancing with Fear" (Campbell), 560–62
  "Dealing with People" (McGrew), 533–35
  "Diagnosis, The" (Selzer), 586–89
  "Dying to Be Bigger" (H.D.), 575–80
  "Enough Is Enough" (Sheindlin, with Getlin), 545–48
  "Fads" (Locher), 554–57
  "Growing Up in Cyberspace" (Staples), 548–52
  "How to Get All-Day Energy" (Mandile), 536–38
  "Interview with Jimmy Baca" (Farnsworth), 562–64
  "It's Class, Stupid!" (Rodriguez), 565–68
  "My Head Rolled in Syria" (Freed), 541–44
  "Never-Ending Question: Who Am I?, The" (Reyes),
    557–59

reading selections (*cont.*)
"Nothing But Net" (Bekker), 552–54
"Old-Time Pueblo World, The" (Silko), 583–85
"Religious Faith Versus Spirituality" (Bissoondath), 589–92
"When the Legal Thing Isn't the Right Thing" (Mead), 538–41
reading strategies, 525–29
difficult words, understanding, 527–29
finding main idea, 526
finding supporting ideas, 526
highlighting and making annotations, 527
making written response, 529
outlining, 529
previewing, 525–26
summarizing, 529
redundancy, avoiding, 453–54
references list. *See* Works Cited page
reflexive pronouns, 412–14
regular verbs
past participles of, 346
past tense, 335–36
relative clause, modifiers beginning with, 441
relative pronouns, 285–87, 411–12
dependent clauses beginning with, 310
punctuation with, 285
repeated subject, 419
research, 160, 237–51
for academic writing, 237–38
citing sources, 8, 246–49
evaluating sources, 238–40
Internet sites, 239, 240, 247, 248, 249, 251
paraphrasing, 240, 241–44
plagiarism, 240
quoting sources, 240, 244–46
summarizing, 240, 241–44
tools, 239
research links, 232
evaluating and documenting sources, 160
MLA and its guidelines, 240
research paper, 237
restrictive clause, 483
revising, 38–47. *See also* editing
for adequate support, 38, 40–42, 51, 187, 188–89
argument paragraph, 164–66
cause and effect paragraph, 149–50
classification paragraph, 121–23
for coherence, 39, 43–45, 51, 187–89
comparison and contrast paragraph, 136–37
definition paragraph, 109–10
descriptive paragraph, 84–85
essay, 187–89
exam question answers, 605
illustration paragraph, 60–62
narrative paragraph, 72–74
process paragraph, 96–97
for style, 39, 45–47, 51, 189
for unity, 38, 39–40, 51, 187
rhetorical question, 293
right/write, 471

root words, looking up, 529
run-on sentences, 312–19
comma splice, 61
correcting, 313–17
punctuation in, 312–14

S
salutations, 485
-self/-selves, 412–14
semicolons, 600
in compound sentences, 267, 270–72
joining related ideas, 271–72
joining two independent ideas, 104
before transitional expression, 272–73
senses, imagery using, 78–79, 81, 198, 451
sensory details, listing, 81–82
sentence(s), 254–305. *See also* topic sentence
basic parts of, 593
capitalizing first word of, 503, 600
combining, 292, 296–303, 598
complex, 278–90, 292, 483–84, 594, 598
compound, 266–77, 292, 482, 594, 598
compound-complex, 279, 594
concluding, 3, 4, 17, 33–35
conditional, 362–63
fragments, 306–12, 318–19
fused, 312
as introduction of quotation, 245
introductory, 496
long, 292
opening words of, 294–96
parallel structure in, 320–29
run-on, 61, 312–19
simple, 254–67, 292, 594
style, 45–47
subject of, 254–57
variety, 291–305
verb in, 259–63
series
colon to introduce, 506
comma in, 478–79
of examples, 54–55, 58, 194
of words or phrases, parallel structure in, 322
sexist language, 417, 547
should of, 363–65
similarities
focus on comparing, 130–31
transitional words and expressions showing, 135
simile, 203
simple past tense, 335–41, 597
agreement, 372
irregular, 336–41
past perfect tense compared to, 350–51
past progressive, 335, 359, 597
present perfect tense compared to, 348–49, 350
regular, 335–36
simple present tense, 331–34, 597
agreement, 369–71

forms of, 331–32
  irregular verbs, 332
  negative and question forms, 333–34
simple sentence(s), 254–65, 594
  combining, 292
  comparing compound and, 266–67
simple subject, 255–56
singular nouns, 390
  key words for, 393
  possessive forms of, 492
singular subject, 255
slang vs. standard English, 455–56
some, spelling two-part words with, 465
sound-alike words, 469–74
sources
  citing, 8, 246–49
  evaluating, 238–40
  finding complete source information, 240
  Internet, 239, 240, 247, 248, 249, 251
  keeping track of, 239–40
  mentioning, 243
  quotation from respected, 232
  quoting, 240, 244–46
space order, 29, 177, 203
Spanish speakers, words misused by, 528
specific purpose, 8
spelling, 459–76
  adding prefixes, 460–61
  adding -s or -es, 461–62
  adding suffixes, 460–65
  changing *y* to *i*, 463
  commonly misspelled words, 466–67
  doubling final consonant, 463–65
  dropping final *e*, 462
  -*ful*, words ending in, 461
  ie or *ei*, 460
  look-alike and sound-alike words, 469–74
  regular past tense verbs, 335
  rules, 459–66
  strategies, 467
  two-part words, 565
spelling checker, computer, 469
spelling log, 50, 608, 609
standard American English, 331, 455–56
state verbs, 359
statistics, 159
style, revising for
  essay, 189
  paragraph, 39, 45–47, 51
subjective case, 406, 409, 410
subject(s) of sentence, 254–57
  complete, 255–56
  compound, 255
  contraction joining verb and, 491
  multiple, 373–74
  plural, 255
  repeated, 419
  in sentence fragment, 306, 307, 309
  simple sentence, 267
  simple subject, 255–56

singular, 255
  special problems, 256–57
  after subordinator, 283–84
  unstated, 256
  verb before, 377–78
subject pronoun, 255
subject-verb agreement, 332, 368–82
  basic rules, 368–73
  collective nouns, 376–77
  future tense, 372
  indefinite pronouns, 374–75
  interrupting words and phrases, 378–80
  modals, 372
  more than one subject, 373–74
  past perfect tense, 372
  present perfect tense agreement, 372
  simple past tense agreement, 372
  simple present tense agreement, 369–71
  verb before subject, 377–78
subordinating conjunctions, 279–85, 593, 598
  comma usage with, 282
  common, 279
  in complex sentences, 279–85, 483
  conjunctive adverbs vs., 274
  dependent clauses beginning with, 310
  meanings of, 280–81
  subject after, 283–84
suffixes, 460–65
suggestion, ending conclusion with, 185
summarizing, 240, 241–44
  paraphrasing vs., 241
  as reading strategy, 529
superlative forms, 432–36
  -*est* ending, 433, 435
  irregular forms, 433
  most, 433, 435
  problems with, 435–36
supporting details, 24–31
  adding specific, 32
  in argument essay, 231–32
  in argument paragraph, 155, 158–60
  to avoid circular reasoning, 41–42
  in cause and effect essay, 228
  in cause and effect paragraph, 146–47
  choosing best, 25–27
  in classification essay, 218
  in classification paragraph, 120
  in comparison and contrast essay, 222
  in comparison and contrast paragraph, 134
  concrete, 78–79
  in definition essay, 213–14
  in definition paragraph, 106–7
  in descriptive essay, 203–4
  in descriptive paragraph, 78–79, 81–82
  dominant impression, 203
  for essay, 174–78
  finding in reading, 526
  generating, 25
  identifying best, 26
  in illustration essay, 194

supporting details (*cont.*)
  in illustration paragraph, 57–58
  in narrative essay, 198–99
  in narrative paragraph, 70–71
  organizing, 27–31, 128, 129, 177–78, 222
  point-by-point organization, 128, 222
  in process essay, 209
  in process paragraph, 93–94
  revising for adequate, 38, 40–42, 51, 187, 188–89
  sensory details, 81–82
  strength of, 46
  topic-by-topic organization, 128, 222
  types of, 158–59, 231–32
synonyms, 527–28
  definition by, 103, 213

T

taught/thought, 471
teaching tips (AIE), 64, 423, 449. *See also* ESL teaching tips
  activities, 88, 100, 126, 140
  activities verifying students' understanding, 14, 36, 50, 62, 74, 85–86, 98, 110, 123, 137, 150, 165–66, 191, 264, 275, 289, 303, 318, 326, 343, 356, 365, 380, 386, 403, 422, 437, 447, 457, 474, 488, 501, 509
  ain't, 371
  annotating paragraph, 68
  appeal to readers' senses, 78
  argument essay, 233
  argument paragraph, 154, 155, 157, 161, 162, 163, 164, 165
  attitude about topic, 78
  audience and language style, 6
  brainstorming, 99, 195, 389, 405, 450, 535
  categories, 115, 118, 124
  cause and effect essay, 228
  cause and effect paragraph, 141, 142, 143, 145, 149, 150, 151
  classification, 113, 114
  classification essay, 219
  classification paragraph, 114, 115, 117, 118, 120, 122, 123, 124
  class work, 20
  clustering, 13
  collective nouns, 422
  commas, 477, 478
  comma splices, 313
  comparison and contrast, 127, 129
  comparison and contrast essay, 224
  comparison and contrast paragraph, 127, 129, 135, 136, 137, 138
  complex sentence, 278
  compound sentences, 268, 270, 271, 274, 275, 280, 281, 287, 288, 289
  concluding sentence, 33
  constructive criticism, 48
  definition, 102
  definition essay, 213, 215
  definition paragraph, 102, 106, 109, 110, 111

descriptive essay, 204
descriptive paragraph, 77, 78, 82, 84, 85–87
double negatives, 341
ellipsis, 508
embedded questions, 287
essay plans, 179, 180, 195, 200, 210, 215, 219, 224, 228, 233
essay practices, 186
essays, 170, 172, 175, 177, 179, 180, 181, 184, 186, 191
essay topics, 170
essential vs. nonessential clauses, 483
evaluating sources, 239
examples, 55
exploring strategies, 14
fewer or *less*, 435
first- and third-person narration, 67
first draft, 35
freewriting, 170
grammar, 254
group work, 6, 8, 184, 204, 263, 326, 388, 451
helping verbs, 359
if clause, 362
illustration essay, 53, 195
illustration paragraph, 53, 55, 59, 60, 62
indefinite pronouns, 415
introductory paragraph, 181
job, thinking about, 511
letter of application, 486
misplaced modifiers, 440
modifiers, 441, 445, 447
narrative essay, 200
narrative paragraph, 67, 68, 71, 72, 73, 74
narrowed topics, 18
nonstandard verb forms, 360, 363
nouns, 403
outlining reading, 529
pair work, 22, 30, 111, 117, 124, 138, 143, 145, 151, 157, 172, 180, 243, 251, 274, 281, 289, 292, 300, 354, 441, 445, 447, 455, 456, 471, 475
paragraph plan, 120, 135
parallel structure, 320, 323, 326, 327, 328
paraphrasing, summarizing, or quoting sources, 240
passive verbs, 356
past participles, 350
Peer Feedback Form, 49
pen-pal activity, 13
portfolio, 13
prepositional phrases, 263, 264
process essay, 209, 210
process paragraph, 90, 93, 95, 96, 98, 99
pronoun case, 409
pronouns, 255
proofreading, 422
quotation marks, 496
quotations, 238
for reading selections, 530, 533, 535, 540, 541, 547, 552, 564, 565, 567, 568, 575, 586, 589
research, 238, 239, 240, 243, 251
researching topics, 448
revising activities, 96, 109, 122, 136, 149, 164

revising and editing, 39, 45, 47, 48, 50, 60, 72, 84
rewriting, 343
run-on sentences, 97, 312, 318
sentence fragments, 318
sentence variety, 292, 297, 300, 303
sexist language, 417, 547
slang or nonstandard English, 82, 456, 530, 541
spelling, 465, 466, 469, 471
subordinating conjunctions, 280
supporting ideas, 17, 32, 59, 71, 78, 83, 108, 163, 177
test materials, 264, 276, 289, 303, 318, 327, 343, 356, 366, 381, 386, 404, 423, 437, 447, 458, 475, 488, 501
topics, 5, 53, 76, 124, 328
topic sentences, 21, 22, 39
transitional words, 45
types of errors, 47
understanding difficult words, 586
use of "I," 216
using research, 224
verbs, 260
verb tense, 330
vocabulary, 457
voice, 351
warm up activities, 153
which clause, 412
whose vs. *who's*, 411
word order, 288
writing plans vs. final drafts, 25
technology links, 10
    cutting and pasting, 26
    spelling and grammar checkers, 47
    topic sentences, 21
tense, verb, 261, 330–44, 597
    active vs. passive voice, 351
    conditional forms, 362–63
    consistency, 383–88
    future, 372, 597
    future perfect, 597
    future progressive, 359, 597
    parallel, 321
    past. *See* past tense
    past perfect, 350–51, 372, 597
    past perfect progressive, 359
    past progressive, 335, 359, 597
    present. *See* present tense
    present perfect, 348–49, 372, 597
    present perfect progressive, 359
    present progressive, 331, 359, 597
    progressive forms, 358–60
    simple past, 335–41, 348–49, 350–51, 372, 595–96, 597
    simple present, 331–34, 369–71, 597
tense shift, 383–87
Texas Higher Education Assessment
    adjectives and adverbs, 272, 274, 294, 321, 341, 396, 406, 407, 408–9, 425–32, 433, 506–7
    comparatives/superlatives, 432–36
    concrete examples, 54–56, 58, 115, 158–59, 194
    coordinators, 267–70, 322, 482, 498, 593, 598

development, 16–37
enhancing writing with research, 160, 237–51
introductions and conclusions, 3, 4, 181–86
look-alike words, 469–74
organization, 27–31, 128, 129, 177–78, 222
parallel structure, 320–29
prefixes and suffixes, 460–65
prewriting skills, 9–13, 18, 25
pronoun-antecedent agreement, 414–21
recognizing dangling modifiers, 443–46
recognizing effective organization, 27–31, 128, 129
recognizing effective sentences, 254–305
recognizing fragments, 306–12, 318–19
recognizing ineffective word choice, 450–52, 527–29
recognizing purpose and audience, 5–9, 102, 155, 169, 241
recognizing run-on sentences, 61, 312–19
recognizing standard American English, 331, 455–56
recognizing unity, focus and development, 16–37, 38, 39–40, 51, 176, 187
rough outline of essay, 178–81. *See also* outline
sound-alike words, 469–74
subordinators, 274, 279–85, 310, 483, 593, 598
subject-verb agreement, 332, 368–82
thesis statements, 3, 4, 171–74, 182, 185–86, 188–89, 194, 198, 203, 208–9, 213, 217–18, 222, 227, 231
unity and focus, 25, 38, 39–40, 51, 176, 187
verb forms, 331–36, 338–39, 345–67, 369–74
than, comparisons with, 409
than/then/that, 471
that, *those*, 397
that clause, 285–87, 411, 483
    subject-verb agreement and, 379
the
    in comparative forms, 435
    determiners before, 396
    in titles, 190
the following, colon after, 506
theirselves, 413
their/they're, 471
there, sentence beginning with, 377
there/here, 256
thesis statement, 3, 4, 171–74
    of argument essay, 231
    of cause and effect essay, 227
    characteristics of good, 171
    of classification essay, 217–18
    of comparison and contrast essay, 222
    of definition essay, 213
    of descriptive essay, 203
    of illustration essay, 194
    of narrative essay, 198
    placement of, 182
    of process essay, 208–9
    repeating words or phrases from, 188
    rephrased in conclusion, 185–86
    specific details in, 172
    support for, 187, 188–89
    writing effective, 171–74
third-person narration, 66, 68, 198

third-person singular form, 369
  negative and question forms, 333, 334
  of simple present tense, 331
this, these, 397
thought/taught, 471
through/threw, 471
time
  apostrophes in expressions of, 493–95
  colon separating hour and minutes, 506
  scheduling, for writing exam, 603
time/chronological order, 27–28, 177
  descriptive essay in, 203
  extended example in, 58
  narrative essay, 198
  narrative paragraph, 70
  process in, 89
  process paragraph, 94, 96
time markers, 348
titles
  articles in, 190, 498
  capitalizing, 498, 504, 601
  for cited material, writing, 247
  of courses and programs, 504
  descriptive, 190
  essay, 189–91, 498
  of individuals, 504, 601
  of institutions, departments, companies, and schools, 504
  of literary or artistic works, 504, 601
  pitfalls, 190
  prepositions in, 190, 498
  punctuation of, 498–500, 601
  related to writing pattern, 190
  underlining or italicizing, 498, 601
to, sentence fragments with, 308–9
to be. See be verb
to do. See do verb
to have. See have verb
tone, 5
topic-by-topic organization, 128, 222
topics, 5
  argument essay, 235
  cause and effect essay, 230
  classification essay, 221
  comparison and contrast essay, 225–26
  descriptive essay, 207–8
  descriptive paragraph, 86
  essay, 169–71
  exploring/prewriting strategies, 9–13
  generating, 53–54, 64–65, 76–77, 88–89
  illustration essay, 197
  illustration paragraphs, 62
  journal writing, 13
  narrative essay, 202
  narrative paragraph, 66, 74
  narrowing, 18–19, 169–71
  paragraph, 18–19, 170
  process paragraph, 98
  tone and, 5
topic sentence, 3, 4, 17, 19–24
  in argument paragraph, 157

  in cause and effect paragraph, 141, 144–46
  characteristics, 19
  in classification paragraph, 119
  in comparison and contrast paragraph, 132–33
  in definition paragraph, 103–6
  in descriptive paragraph, 80
  identifying, 20–21
  in illustration paragraph, 57
  making a point in, 92
  in narrative paragraph, 68–70
  paragraph links using, 188
  in process paragraph, 92–93
  thesis statement and, 174–75
  writing effective, 21–23
to/too/two, 471
transitional words and expressions, 27, 135
  in cause and effect paragraph, 148–49
  in classification paragraph, 121
  for coherence, 43–45
  common, 43–44
  in comparison and contrast paragraph, 135
  with complete sentences, 44
  in compound sentences, 267, 272–75, 598
  in definition paragraph, 108
  in descriptive paragraphs, 84
  in emphatic-order paragraphs, 28
  in illustration paragraphs, 60
  introductory phrase, 479
  in narrative paragraphs, 72
  as paragraph link, 188
  in process paragraph, 96
  punctuation before and after, 272–73
  in space-order paragraphs, 29
  in time-order paragraph, 27
two-part constructions, parallel structure for, 324

U

underlining title, 498, 601
understand a process type of paragraph, 89, 91–92
Uniform Resource Locator (URL) address, 239
uninterested/disinterested, 469–70
unity
  in essay, 176, 187
  in paragraph, 25, 38, 39–40, 51
  problems, 187
  revising for, 38, 39–40, 51, 187

V

vague words, 450–51
  pronouns, 419–20
verb(s), 254, 593. *See also* helping verb(s); subject-verb agreement; tense, verb
  action, 260
  adjectives looking like, 427
  complete, 261–63
  compound, 260

conditional forms, 362–63
contraction joining subject and, 491
-*d* or -*ed* ending, 335–36
in exam questions, 603–4
gerunds, 255, 308
incomplete, 307
infinitives, 260, 308–9, 340
irregular, 298, 332, 335, 336–41, 346, 595–96
linking, 260
main, 261
negative forms, 333–34, 369, 491
nonprogressive, 359–60
nonstandard forms, 360–61, 363–65, 371
past participles, 345–57, 363
progressive forms, 358–60
question form, 333–34, 369
regular, 335–36, 346
in sentence fragment, 306, 307, 309
simple past tense, 335–41
simple present tense, 331–34
in simple sentence, 267
in simple sentences, 259–63
-*s* or -*es* ending, 331, 332, 369
spelling, 335
standard English forms, 331
before subject, 377–78
vivid language, 81, 182, 451–52
vocabulary. *See also* word(s)
difficult words, understanding, 527–29
specific and detailed, 450–52
vocabulary log, 50, 608, 611
voice
active, 351, 354
consistent, 322
passive, 351–55

W

wanna, 360–61
Web addresses, 239, 498
Web sites. *See* Internet sites
well/badly, 431–32
were/we're/where, 471
which clause, 285–87, 411
comma to set off, 411, 412, 483
subject-verb agreement and, 379
who clause(s)
comma to set off, 483
parallel, 321
subject-verb agreement and, 379
who or *whom*, choosing, 411
who's/whose, 411, 471
who (*whom, whoever, whomever, whose*) clauses, 285–87, 411
word(s)
commonly misspelled, 466–67
introductory, 295, 479–80, 495
look-alike and sound-alike, 469–74
question words, on exams, 603–4
two-part, spelling, 565

understanding difficult, 527–29
vague, 419–20, 450–51
wordiness, avoiding, 453–54
word order
embedded questions and, 287, 288
in questions, 377
word twins, 528
workplace memo, 517
Works Cited page, 247–49
would, 384
would of, 363–65
write/right, 471
Writers' Circle activities, 305, 328–29, 367, 388, 424, 449, 476, 511
Writer's Desk exercises
for and against arguments, 161
classification chart, 120
clustering, 13
conclusion, 186
distinct categories, finding, 118
essay plan, 181
final drafts, 49, 191
first drafts, 35, 60, 72, 84, 96, 109, 121, 136, 149, 164, 187
freewriting, 10
identifying causes and effects, 143–44
introductions, 184
main steps in process, 94
narrowing topics, 18–19, 170–71
paragraph plans, 32, 59, 71, 83, 95, 108, 134–35, 148, 163
questioning, 12
revising and editing essay, 189
revising and editing paragraph, 48, 61, 74, 85–86, 97, 110, 123, 137, 150, 165–66, 303, 500
revising and editing warm ups, 263–64, 275, 288, 317, 326, 343, 356, 365, 380, 385, 403–4, 422, 437, 447, 457, 474, 487, 509
sensory details, 82
supporting ideas, 25, 27, 58, 70–71, 107, 147, 177, 178
thesis statements, 174
topic sentences, 24, 57, 69–70, 80, 106, 119, 133, 145–46
warm ups, 53–54, 64–65, 76–77, 88–89, 100–101, 113–14, 126–27, 140–41, 153–54, 254, 266, 278, 291, 306, 320, 330, 345, 358, 365, 383, 389, 405, 425, 439, 450, 459, 477, 490, 503
Writer's Room activities
essay topics, 192
paragraph topics, 50–51
research, 251
topics, 14–15, 36–37, 62–63, 74–75
topics for argument essays, 235
topics for argument paragraphs, 166
topics for cause and effect essays, 230
topics for cause and effect paragraphs, 151
topics for classification essays, 221
topics for classification paragraphs, 124
topics for comparison and contrast essays, 225–26
topics for comparison and contrast paragraphs, 138
topics for definition essays, 216–17
topics for definition paragraphs, 111

Writer's Room activities (*cont.*)
  topics for descriptive essays, 207–8
  topics for descriptive paragraphs, 86
  topics for illustration essays, 197
  topics for narrative essays, 202
  topics for process essays, 212
  topics for process paragraphs, 98–99
  topics for writing, 305, 328, 367, 388, 424, 448–49, 476, 511
writing from reading. *See also* reading selections
  outlining reading, 529
  summarizing reading, 529
  written response, 529
writing links, 169, 177
  appealing to five senses, 451
  argument writing topics, 166
  cause and effect writing topics, 151
  classificative writing topics, 124
  comparison and contrast writing topics, 138
  definition writing topics, 111

descriptive writing topics, 86
  illustrative writing topics, 62
  narrative writing topics, 74
  process writing topics, 98
  revising for unity and support, 187
  transitions, 188
writing patterns, 193–94
  titles related to, 190
writing portfolio, 13–14
writing process, 2–15
  answering exam questions and, 605
  audience, 5–7
  developing stage in, 16–37, 605
  exploring stage of, 4–13, 605
  exploring strategies, 9–13
  journal, 13
  portfolio, 13–14
  purpose, 7–9, 169
  revising and editing, 38–47, 605
  topic, 5